PATERNOSTER BIBLICAL MONOGRAPHS

Ritual Water, Ritual Spirit

An Analysis of the Timing, Mechanism, and Manifestation of Spirit-Reception in Luke-Acts

PATERNOSTER BIBLICAL MONOGRAPHS

Ritual Water, Ritual Spirit

An Analysis of the Timing, Mechanism, and Manifestation of Spirit-Reception in Luke-Acts

David J. McCollough

Copyright © David J. McCollough 2017

First published 2017 by Paternoster

Paternoster is an imprint of Authentic Media
PO Box 6326, Bletchley, Milton Keynes MK1 9GG

www.authenticmedia.co.uk

The right of David J. McCollough to be identified as the Author of this Work has been asserted by him in accordance with the Copyright, Designs and Patents Act 1988.

All rights reserved. No part of this publication may be reproduced, stored in a retrieval system, or transmitted, in any form or by any means, electronic, mechanical, photocopying, recording or otherwise, without the prior permission of the publisher or a license permitting restricted copying. In the UK such licenses are issued by the Copyright Licensing Agency, Barnard's Inn, 86 Fetter Lane, London EC4A 1EN

British Library Cataloguing in Publication Data A catalogue record for this book is available from the British Library

ISBN 978-1-78078-179-2
978-1-78078-180-8 (e-book)

Printed and bound by Lightning Source

PATERNOSTER BIBLICAL MONOGRAPHS

Series Preface

One of the major objectives of Paternoster is to serve biblical scholarship by providing a channel for the publication of theses and other monographs of high quality at affordable prices. Paternoster stands within the broad evangelical tradition of Christianity. Our authors would describe themselves as Christians who recognise the authority of the Bible, maintain the centrality of the gospel message and assent to the classical creedal statements of the Christian belief. There is diversity within this constituency; advances in scholarship are possible only if there is freedom for frank debate on controversial issues and for the publication of new and sometimes provocative proposals. What is offered in this series is the best of writing by committed Christians who are concerned to develop well-founded biblical scholarship in a spirit of loyalty to the historic faith.

Series editors

I. Howard Marshall, Honorary Research professor of New Testament, University of Aberdeen, Scotland, UK

Robert P. Gordon, Regius Professor of Hebrew, University of Cambridge, UK

Tremper Longmann III, Robert H. Gundry Professor and Chair of the Department of Biblical Studies, Westmont College, Santa Barbara, California, USA

Stanley E. Porter, President and Professor of New Testament, McMaster Divinity College, Hamilton, Ontario, Canada

Acknowledgements

This work is a revision of my PhD thesis at The London School of Theology. I am very grateful to my supervisor, William Atkinson, for both his rigorous standards and his support. I also wish to acknowledge my examiners, Professor Max Turner and Dr Glenn Balfour. I owe a special debt of gratitude to The London School of Theology for making it possible to continue studies during the period when my US loans were unavailable.

Table of Contents

Abbreviations
Introduction   1

Chapter 1
The Spirit in Christian Initiation in Luke-Acts:
    A Literature Review   5
Principles of Arrangement   5
Authors and Works   5
    Hermann Gunkel, *Die Wirkungen des Heiligen Geistes* (1888)   5
    Arthur James Mason, *The Relation of Confirmation to Baptism* (1891)   6
    Hans Leisegang, *Pneuma Hagion: Der Ursprung des Geistbegriffs der synoptischen Evangelien aus der griechischen Mystik* (1922)   6
    Heinrich von Baer, *Der Heilige Geist in den Lukasschriften* (1926)   8
    Friedrich Büchsel, *Der Geist Gottes im Neuen Testament* (1926)   10
    Nikolaus Adler, *Taufe und Handauflegung: Eine Exegetisch-Theologische Untersuchung von Apg 8, 14-17* (1951)   11
    G.W.H. Lampe, *The Seal of the Spirit: A Study in the Doctrine Of Baptism and Confirmation in the New Testament and the Fathers*, and other writings (1951)   13
    Hans Conzelmann, *Die Mitte der Zeit: Studien zur Theologie des Lukas* (1954)   15
    Eduard Schweizer, 'πνεῦμα' (1959)   15
    Frederick Dale Bruner, *A Theology of the Holy Spirit: The Pentecostal Experience and the New Testament Witness* (1970)   16
    James Dunn, *Baptism in the Holy Spirit: A Re-examination of the New Testament Teaching on the Gift of the Spirit in Relation to Pentecostalism Today* (1970)   19
    Gonzalo Haya-Prats, *Empowered Believers: The Holy Spirit in the Book of Acts* (French edition, 1975)   21
    David Petts, *The Baptism in the Holy Spirit in Relation to Christian Initiation* (1987)   22
    Robert P. Menzies *Empowered for Witness: The Spirit in Luke-Acts* (1991)   23

Max Turner, *Power from on High: The Spirit in Israel's Restoration and Witness in Luke-Acts* (1996)   26
Ju Hur, *A Dynamic Reading of the Holy Spirit in Luke-Acts* (2001)   30
Friedrich Avemarie, *Die Tauferzählungen der Apostelgeschichte: Theologie und Geschichte* (2002)   32
Youngmo Cho, *Spirit and Kingdom in the Writings of Luke and Paul: An Attempt to Reconcile these Concepts* (2005)   35
Randall A. Harrison, *L'Esprit dans le Récit de Luc: Une Recherche de Cohérence dans la Pneumatologie de L'Auteur Implicite de Luc-Actes* (2007)   36
Clayton David Robinson, *The Laying on of Hands: With Special Reference to the Reception of the Holy Spirit in the New Testament* (2008)   37
Randal J. Hedlun, *The Social Function of Glossolalia in Acts with Special Attention to the Ephesian Disciples Pericope (Acts 18:24-19:7)* (2009)   38
William P. Atkinson, *Baptism in the Spirit: Luke-Acts and the Dunn Debate* (2011)   39
Heidrun Gunkel, *Der Heilige Geist bei Lukas: Theologisches Profil, Grund und Intention der lukanischen Pneumatologie* (2015)   41
Summary of Key Issues   41

Chapter 2
Methodology   43
Introduction   43
    A Brief Background Sketch of the Narrative Critical Method   43
    Specific Methodological Tools of the Book   44
Narrative Progression/Sequential Reading – The Fruit of Literary and Discourse Analysis   45
    Progressive/Sequential Reading   45
    Aurality and Sequential Reading   46
    Sequential Reading, the Second Reading, and Luke's Implied Reader   46
        Rereading   46
        The Implied Reader of Luke-Acts   47
        Rereading, Again   50
    Sequential Reading and the Unity of Luke and Acts   53
    Sequential Reading and Accumulation   55
    Sequential Reading and Discourse Analysis   57
Entity Representations   62
Focalization   63

Other Literary Devices	64
Metalepsis and Narrative Asides	64
Functional Redundancy	65
Action Peaks and Didactic Peaks	66
Type-Scenes	67
Rhetorical Criticism and Amplification	71
Identifying Didactic Intent	73
Conclusion	79

Chapter 3
Jesus' Baptismal Praying and Spirit Experience in Luke's Gospel — 81

Introduction	81
Jesus' Jordan Experience	82
Jordan and Pentecost	82
Standard Views	82
Jordan as Influencing the Reader's View of Pentecost:	
Objections and Responses	84
Objections	84
Responses	85
The Possibility of a Vision	87
Differentiation between Immersion and Prayer within the	
One Baptismal Ceremony	88
Praying for the Spirit and Preventing Repossession: Jesus on	
Initiatory Prayer	92
Conclusion	96

Chapter 4
Xenolalic Experience: An Evaluation of its Prominence and Potential in the Pentecost Story — 97

Introduction	97
Narrative Focus Forward on Spirit-Reception	99
Anticipation and Suspense	99
Expectations	100
Expectations of Isaianic New Exodus Restoration	
for Israel	100
Expectations of the Promise of the Father	101
Expectations Intensified	102
Expectations Resolved	107
Narrative Focus Backward on the Xenolalia Experience	109
The Initial Redundant Focalization of the	
Xenolalia Experience	109

The Triple Identification	113
First Identification	113
Second Identification	117
Third Identification	120
The Timing of Forgiveness and Water Baptism	127
The Timing of Spirit-Reception in Relation to Water Baptism	131
Conclusion	135

Chapter 5
Prayer and Handlaying:
What to do When the Spirit Does not Come — 137

Introduction	137
Summary of Acts 8:4-25	138
Focalization of Handlaying	139
Further Examination of Handlaying	145
A Noticeable Failure	148
An Individual Experience	149
A Mediated Experience	150
Luke's Conception of the Giving of the Spirit	152
Correcting the Failure	154
The Relationship Between Prayer and Handlaying	160
The 'Delay' of the Spirit	161
The Alternate Western Reading of the Ethiopian Eunuch Story	164
Menzies' View of Handlaying as Commissioning for Service	166
Samaria: Simply Possible	168
Conclusion	171

Chapter 6
Saul's Conversion and Cornelius' House:
Continuing the ER for Initiation — 172

Section 1: Saul's Initiation by a Local Initiator	172
Introduction	172
Narrative Analysis	172
First Story (Acts 9:1-18)	172
Second Story (Acts 22:3-16)	174
Third Story (Acts 26:9-20)	174
Theological Analysis	175
Conclusion	177
Section 2: Cornelius' Initiation (Acts 10, 11 & 15)	178
Introduction	178
Analysis of the Story	179

Exposition and Rising Action	179
The Story's Climax	180
The Mechanism of Spirit Impartation/Facilitation	182
Dissociative Xenolalia *Plus* a Praise Element as the Apostolic Standard	184
Cornelius' House as Programmatic	188
The 'Spirit Baptism' Metaphor	189
Conclusion	191

Chapter 7
The Culmination of the ER for Initiation - Paul, Apollos, and the Ephesians (Acts 18:24-28; 19:1-7)

	193
Introduction	193
The Linguistic Argument for Christian 'Disciples'	193
The Argument for Christian 'Disciples' from the Relationship to Apollos	196
Robert P. Menzies and Friedrich Avemarie – Apollos and the Ephesians Were Christian	196
Conrad Gempf – Apollos Alone Was Christian	198
Response to the Argument from Apollos – John's Baptism as a Demarcation Line	199
Spirit Experience Belongs to the People of God	199
The Demarcating Function of John's Baptism	199
The Argument from Authorial Intent for the Ephesians as Christians	202
Response to the Argument from Authorial Intent – Luke's 'People of God' Concept	203
The Ephesian Disciples and Luke's Initiation Ritual	204
Paul's Questions About the Spirit and Luke's Focalization of Baptism	204
Timing of Belief and Spirit-Reception	207
Baptism and Laying on of Hands	207
The Ephesian Story and the ER for Initiation	209
Conclusion	211

Conclusion	**214**
Bibliography	**217**
Author Index	**243**
Scripture Index	**249**
Subject Index	**254**

Abbreviations[1]

ABib	Academia Biblica
AF	The Apostolic Fathers: A New Translation and Commentary
AJPS	*Asian Journal of Pentecostal Studies*
AJT	*The American Journal of Theology*
AncB	The Anchor Bible
ANCL	Ante-Nicene Christian Library
AThANT	Abhandlungen zur Theologie des Alten und Neuen Testaments
AThR	*Anglican Theological Review*
AThR.SS	*Anglican Theological Review Supplement Series*
BDAG	*A Greek-English Lexicon of the New Testament and Other Early Christian Literature, 3rd Edition*
BECNT	Baker Exegetical Commentary on the New Testament
BHTh	Beiträge zur Historischen Theologie
Bib.	*Biblica*
BibIS	Biblical Interpretation Series
BS	*Bibliotheca Sacra*
BTB	*Biblical Theology Bulletin*
BTCL	Biblical and Theological Classics Library
BWANT	Beiträge zur Wisssenschaft vom Alten und Neuen Testament
BZ	*Biblische Zeitschrift*
BZNW	Beihefte zur Zeitschrift für die Neutestamentliche Wissenschaft und die Kunde der Älteren Kirche
CBET	Contributions to Biblical Exegesis and Theology
CBibW	*Conversations with the Biblical World*
CBQ	*Catholic Biblical Quarterly*
CI	*Critical Inquiry*
CistSS	Cistercian Studies Series
CNTDS	Commentaire du Nouveau Testament Deuxième Série
ConJ	*Concordia Journal*
CrThR	*Criswell Theological Review*
CWE	Collected Works of Erasmus
DBSJ	*Detroit Baptist Seminary Journal*
DGL	De Gruyter Lehrbuch
EBC	The Expositor's Bible Commentary
EHS.T	Europäische Hochschulschriften, Reihe XXIII Theologie

---

[1] These follow Siegfried M. Schwertner, *Internationales Abkürzungsverzeichnis für Theologie und Grenzgebiete*, 2. Auflage (Berlin: Walter de Gruyter, 1992).

EKK	Evangelisch-Katholischer Kommentar zum Neuen Testament
ET	*Expository Times*
ETBKNT	Evangelisch-Theologische Bibliothek Kommentar zum Neuen Testament
EvQ	*Evangelical Quarterly*
EzNT	Erläuterungen zum Neuen Testament
FCBS	Fortress Classics in Biblical Studies
FRLANT	Forschungen zur Religion und Literatur des Alten und Neuen Testaments
Glotta	*Glotta: Zeitschrift für griechische und lateinische Sprache*
GOTR	Greek Orthodox Theological Review
GTL	Göttinger Theologische Lehrbücher
Hermeneia	Hermeneia: A Critical and Historical Commentary on the Bible
HNT	Handbuch zum Neuen Testament
HP	Héritage et Projet
HThR	*Harvard Theological Review*
HThK	Herders Theologischer Kommentar zum Neuen Testament
HThS	Harvard Theological Studies
IKaZ	*Internationale katholische Zeitschrift*
Interp.	*Interpretation*
ISBL	Indiana Studies in Biblical Literature
JAAC	*Journal of Aesthetics & Art Criticism*
JAAR	*Journal of the American Academy of Religion*
JAC	*JAC: A Journal of Rhetoric, Culture, & Politics* [formerly *Journal of Advanced Composition*]
JBL	*Journal of Biblical Literature*
JECS	*Journal of Early Christian Studies*
JEH	*Journal of Ecclesiastical History*
JEPTA	*The Journal of the European Pentecostal Theological Association*
JETS	*Journal of the Evangelical Theological Society*
JMT	*The Journal of Ministry and Theology*
JPT	*Journal of Pentecostal Theology*
JPT.S	Journal of Pentecostal Theology Supplement Series
JSNT	*Journal for the Study of the New Testament*
JSNT.S	Journal for the Study of the New Testament Supplement Series
JSOT	*Journal for the Study of the Old Testament*
KTI	Kommunikative Theologie – interdisziplinär
LeDiv	Lectio Divina
LNTS	Library of New Testament Studies
LoF	A Library of Fathers of the Holy Catholic Church

MarT	*Marketing Theory*
MFSt	*Modern Fiction Studies*
NACS	New American Commentary Studies in Bible and Theology
Nar.	Narratologia
NDIEC	New Documents Illustrating Early Christianity
NIC	The New International Commentary on the New Testament
NIGTC	New International Greek Testament Commentary
NSBT	New Studies in Biblical Theology
NT	*Novum Testamentum*
NTA	Neutestamentliche Abhandlungen
NTesC	The New Testament in Context
NTOA	Novum Testamentum et Orbis Antiquus
NTS	*New Testament Studies*
NTSR	New Testament for Spiritual Reading
OiC	*One in Christ*
OT	*Oral Tradition*
PaThSt	Paderborner Theologische Studien
PBM	Paternoster Biblical Monographs
PCNT	Paideia Commentaries on the New Testament
PeSt	*PentecoStudies*
PFKP	Problemata: Forschungen zur Klassischen Philologie
PiNTC	The Pillar New Testament Commentary
Pn.	*Pneuma*
PoeT	*Poetics Today*
PRN	*Psychiatry Research: Neuroimaging*
PTX	*Prooftexts*
RestQ	*Restoration Quarterly*
RBB	*Religion, Brain and Behavior*
RNT	Das Regensburger Neue Testament
StBL	Studies in Biblical Literature
SBL.DS	Society of Biblical Literature Dissertation Series
SBL.MS	Society of Biblical Literature Monograph Series
SBS	Stuttgarter Bibelstudien
Se.	*Semeia*
SEP	*Stanford Encyclopedia of Philosophy*
SHS	Scripture and Hermeneutics Series
SJTh	*Scottish Journal of Theology*
SLJT	*Saint Luke's Journal of Theology*
SN	*Studia Neotestamentica*
SNTS.MS	Society for New Testament Studies Monograph Series
SOTBT	Studies in Old Testament Biblical Theology

StLi	*Studia Liturgica*
Sty.	*Style*
StUNT	Studien zur Umwelt des Neuen Testaments
TANZ	Texte und Arbeiten zum neutestamentlichen Zeitalter
ThHK	Theologischer Handkommentar zum Neuen Testament
ThLZ	*Theologische Literaturzeitung*
THNTC	The Two Horizons New Testament Commentary
ThPh	*Theologie und Philosophie*
ThSLG	Theologische Studien der Österreichischen Leo-Gesellschaft
ThStKr	*Theologische Studien und Kritiken*
ThWNT	*Theologisches Wörterbuch zum Neuen Testament*
TJ	*Trinity Journal*
TNTC	Tyndale New Testament Commentaries
TPNTC	The Pillar New Testament Commentary
TRE	*Theologische Realenzykopädie*
TynB	*Tyndale Bulletin*
TZ	*Theologische Zeitschrift*
TZTh	*Tübinger Zeitschrift für Theologie*
VFVRG	Veröffentlichungen des Forschungsinstituts für Vergleichende Religionsgeschichte an der Universität Leipzig
VMStA	Veröffentlichungen des Missionspriesterseminars St. Augustin bei Bonn
VoxEv	*Vox Evangelica*
VT	*Vetus Testamentum*
WBC	Word Biblical Commentary
WMANT	Wissenschaftliche Monographien zum Alten und Neuen Testament
WTJ	*Wesleyan Theological Journal*
WUNT	*Wissenschaftliche Untersuchungen zum Neuen Testament*
WUNT2	*Wissenschaftliche Untersuchungen zum Neuen Testament 2. Reihe*
WuW	*Wort und Wahrheit*
ZLThK	*Zeitschrift für die gesammte lutherische Theologie und Kirche*
ZNW	*Zeitschrift für die neutestamentliche Wissenschaft und die Kunde der älteren Kirche*
ZThK	*Zeitschrift für Theologie und Kirche*

Introduction

Most interpreters suppose Luke has either not clearly explained himself regarding Christian initiation details or that he has no normal model.[1] Charles H. Talbert writes, 'There is in Acts no set procedure for receiving the Holy Spirit.'[2] Craig S. Keener states, 'Luke provides variety rather than a single normative pattern of initiation-conversion.'[3] William H. Shepherd, Jr., states, 'It is difficult to attribute to Luke's narrative a coherent and normative doctrine of Baptism, laying-on-of-hands, and the reception of the Spirit.'[4] Many others make similar observations.[5] Presenting a dissenting view, G.W.H. Lampe initially said that

---

[1] Josef Kürzinger attributed the apparent confusion to a spiritual mystery, *The Acts of the Apostles* (London: Sheed and Ward, 1969), 147. Regarding tense, the present will be used for living commentators, the past for those deceased, including biblical authors.

[2] Charles H. Talbert, *Reading Acts: A Literary and Theological Commentary on the Acts of the Apostles* (Macon: Smyth & Helwyn, 2005), 72.

[3] Craig S. Keener, *Acts, An Exegetical Commentary* (Grand Rapids: Baker Academic, 2013), 2.1524.

[4] William H. Shepherd, Jr., *The Narrative Function of the Holy Spirit as a Character in Luke-Acts* (Atlanta: Scholars, 1994), 22; Similarly, Gerard Austin, *The Rite of Confirmation: Anointing with the Spirit* (Collegeville: Liturgical, 2004), 6; Kirsopp Lake, 'The Theology of the Acts of the Apostles,' *AJT* 19.4 (October, 1915), 489-508; 500. Cf. Maurice Goguel, trans. H.C. Snape, *The Primitive Church* (London: George Allen & Unwin, 1964 [French, 1947]), 302.

[5] I. Howard Marshall, *Luke – Historian and Theologian* (Carlisle: Paternoster, 1988), 379. Eduard Schweizer, trans. Reginald H. and Ilse Fuller, *The Holy Spirit* (Philadelphia: Fortress, 1980 [German, 1978]), 62. D.A. Carson, *Showing the Spirit: A Theological Exposition of 1 Corinthians 12-14* (Carlisle: Paternoster, 1995; Grand Rapids: Baker, 1987), 143. Aaron J. Kuecker, 'The Spirit and the 'Other': Social Identity, Ethnicity and Intergroup Reconciliation in Luke-Acts' (Ph.D. dissertation, University of St. Andrews, 2008), 159. M.J. Moreton, 'A Reconsideration of the Origins of a Christian Initiation Rite in the Age of the New Testament,' *Studia Biblica 1978: III. Papers on Paul and Other New Testament Authors* (Sheffield: JSOT, 1980), 265-75; 271. Kilian McDonnell and George T. Montague, *Christian Initiation and Baptism in the Holy Spirit, Evidence from the First Eight Centuries*, Second, Revised Edition (Collegeville: Liturgical, Michael Glazier, 1994), 24. Ju Hur, *A Dynamic Reading of the Holy Spirit in Luke-Acts* (London: T&T Clark, 2004; Sheffield: Sheffield Academic, 2001), 270. Silva New, 'Note XI. The Name, Baptism, and the Laying on of Hands,' F.J. Foakes Jackson and Kirsopp Lake (eds), *The Beginnings of Christianity, Part I: The Acts of the Apostles*, Kirsopp Lake and Henry J. Cadbury (eds), *Volume V, Additional Notes to the Commentary* (London: Macmillan, 1933), 121-40; 134. Petr

Ritual Water, Ritual Spirit

Luke's picture of initiation in Acts is seemingly 'contradictory' and 'inconsistent', but then concluded that Luke is not really self-contradictory because, 'he shapes his material with far too great care to allow discrepancies to remain in his narrative'.[6] Also in the minority, Randall Harrison has argued for Lukan narrative coherence.[7]

Summaries of the problem of 'inconsistency' by Silva New and Hans-Josef Klauck suggest a way forward by recognizing that diversity springs from a more fundamental unity. New wrote:

> Belief in Jesus (or in his name), baptism, the remission of sins, the laying on of Apostolic hands, and the reception of the Spirit seem to have formed a single complex of associated ideas, any one of which might in any single narrative be either omitted or emphasized.[8]

Klauck writes similarly, 'Luke deconstructs the unified process into its individual elements and varies their arrangement according to context.'[9] A literary analysis could address the issues of *why* a particular element is fronted at a particular narrative moment and *how* the various emphases work together over the course of the narrative to present a unified picture.

Though the book follows the familiar narrative-critical tradition, it utilizes current narratological/literary techniques, as well as principles from discourse analysis and rhetorical criticism to analyse Luke's understanding of Spirit-reception. In doing so, the book makes *no* claim to uniqueness. Narratological/literary/discourse approaches to Luke-Acts are not new, and they have already been applied to specific questions such as the Holy Spirit and suffering, and 'wealth

---

Pokorný, *Theologie der lukanischen Schriften* (Göttingen: Vandenhoeck & Ruprecht, 1998), 71. Friedrich Avemarie, *Die Tauferzählungen der Apostelgeschichte: Theologie und Geschichte* (Tübingen: Mohr Siebeck, 2002), 17. John R.W. Stott, *Baptism and Fullness: The Work of the Holy Spirit Today* (Leicester: IVP, 1975), 30. Graham A. Cole, *He Who Gives Life: The Doctrine of the Holy Spirit* (Wheaton: Crossway, 2007), 205. Ben Witherington, *The Problem with Evangelical Theology: Testing the Exegetical Foundations of Calvinism, Dispensationalism and Wesleyanism* (Waco: Baylor University Press, 2005), 221. Mikeal C. Parsons, *Acts* (Grand Rapids: Baker Academic, 2008), 50. Mark Darrel Caldwell, *Interpreting Spirit-Baptism in Acts: 2:37-39 as a Paradigm* (Ph.D. dissertation, Southwestern Baptist Theological Seminary, 2007), 171.

[6] G.W.H. Lampe, *The Seal of the Spirit, A Study in the Doctrine of Baptism and Confirmation in the New Testament and the Fathers* (Eugene: Wipf and Stock, 2004 [SPCK, 1951]), 64, 79.

[7] Randall Harrison, *L'Esprit dans le Récit de Luc: Une Recherche de Cohérence dans la Pneumatologie de L'Auteur Implicite de Luc-Actes* (self-published Ph.D. dissertation, La Faculté Libre de Théologie Évangélique Vaux-sur-Seine, 2007).

[8] New, 'Note XI', 134.

[9] Hans-Josef Klauck, trans. Brian McNeil, *Magic and Paganism in Early Christianity: The World of the Acts of the Apostles* (Edinburgh: T&T Clark, 2000), 20.

and possessions'.[10] They are methods in current use, which the works of Max Turner, Ute Eisen, and Anja Cornils, Randal Harrison, as well as Joel B. Green's application of discourse analysis to baptism, demonstrate.[11]

The book employs three primary tools: narrative progression/sequential reading from discourse analysis and literary theory, the principle of presupposition pools/entity representations (ERs) from discourse analysis, and the concept of focalization from narratology. Type-scene studies also come into play. The ancient rhetorical technique of amplification reinforces the first two methods. Sequential/progressive reading seeks to understand a story as it unfolds. How did Luke arrange his material to be encountered by a reader moving linearly through the narrative? ERs are the mental constructs developed sequentially through the text as the reader (audience is understood in the term 'reader') accumulates data about characters, places, circumstances, etc.[12] When new information appears in the narrative, a reader will fit it into the network of associations s/he already has in mind. The concept is similar to Theo Vennemann's presupposition pools,[13] only more topic specific and primarily intra-textual. Finally, when narrators tell a story from the perspective, point of view, or 'orientation',[14] of a character, they 'focalize' through that character. The narrative camera draws attention to the thing 'focalized'. These three tools complement each other; as one reads a story, one accumulates information, noting what has been focused upon in the text.

The book will focus on the Spirit-reception scenes. Not every reference to baptism or belief in Luke-Acts will be discussed. This is unnecessary because mention of belief, such as at Acts 4:4, references an earlier established principle, that belief and repentance are to be followed by water baptism (Acts 2:38). After making programmatic statements about initiation, Luke did not need to repeat

---

[10] Martin William Mittelstadt, *The Spirit and Suffering in Luke-Acts: Implications for a Pentecostal Pneumatology* (London: T&T Clark, 2004); James A. Metzger, *Consumption and Wealth in Luke's Travel Narrative* (Leiden: Brill, 2007), 1.

[11] Max Turner, *Power from on High: The Spirit in Israel's Restoration and Witness in Luke-Acts* (Sheffield: Sheffield Academic Press, 2000 [1996]); Peter Cotterell and Max Turner, *Linguistics and Biblical Interpretation* (Downers Grove: IVP, 1989); Ute E. Eisen, *Die Poetik der Apostelgeschichte: Eine Narratologische Studie* (Fribourg: Academic Press, 2006; Göttingen: Vandenhoeck & Ruprecht, 2006); Anja Cornils, *Vom Geist Gottes erzählen, Analyzen zur Apostelgeschichte* (Tübingen: Francke Verlag, 2006); Joel B. Green, 'From 'John's Baptism' to 'Baptism in the Name of the Lord Jesus': The Significance of Baptism in Luke-Acts', in *Baptism, the New Testament and the Church: Historical and Contemporary Studies in Honour of R.E.O. White* (Sheffield: Sheffield Academic Press, 1999), 157-72.

[12] Catherine Emmott, *Narrative Comprehension, A Discourse Perspective* (Oxford: OUP, 1999), 81-84.

[13] Theo Vennemann, 'Topics, sentence accent, and ellipsis: a proposal for their formal treatment,' in Edward L. Keenan, ed., *Formal Semantics of Natural Language: Papers from a colloquium sponsored by the King's College Research Centre, Cambridge* (Cambridge: CUP, 1975), 313-28; 314.

[14] Michael Toolan, *Narrative, A Critical Linguistic Introduction* (London: Routledge, 2001), 60.

those statements at every mention of initiation. For example, having linked belief to baptism in Acts 2:38, simply stating that five thousand men believed (Acts 4:4) is sufficient to alert the reader that five thousand were also baptised. Furthermore, the book will not address systematic theology concerns, nor will it seek to understand how Luke's theology applies today. Luke's theology of conversion will not be discussed.[15] The book aims simply to grasp Luke's understanding of timing, mechanism, and manifestation with regard to Spirit-reception. Finally, the book will focus strictly upon Luke-Acts. This study is intra-textual for the following reasons: 1) We do not have certain knowledge that Luke drew upon intertestamental literature for his work, 2) Luke could have presented a theological perspective of initiation different from that found in other NT writings. That perspective needs to be understood before attempting to integrate it with the rest of the NT.

---

[15] Cf. Fernando Mendez-Moratalla, *The Paradigm of Conversion in Luke* (London: T&T Clark, 2004).

CHAPTER 1

The Spirit in Christian Initiation in Luke-Acts: A Literature Review

Principles of Arrangement

This chapter reviews modern theorists of the Spirit in Luke-Acts arranged chronologically. Positions are outlined, but marginally interacted with. Critical engagement comes in the book's body. It will not primarily address the authors' views on the nature of the gift of the Spirit,[1] or other theological concerns, or their discussions outside of Luke-Acts, but will focus upon how authors understand the Spirit in terms of the ritual dynamics of Christian initiation within Lukan writings.

Authors and Works

Hermann Gunkel, *Die Wirkungen des Heiligen Geistes* (1888)

In emphasizing the reality of the early church's experience, Gunkel denied the early community had any doctrinal position on the Spirit, Paul excepted.[2] He saw reception of the Spirit as separate from faith, noting that faith is associated with preaching, whereas the Spirit is associated with handlaying before, after or during (Acts 2:38) baptism.[3] Allowing for the case of Cornelius' house, Gunkel said, 'if then according to early Christian view the Spirit is granted to the individual only under a certain mediation of the church, so is nevertheless every outpouring of the Spirit a new independent act of God'.[4] For Gunkel, the Spirit is tangible and tied to the charismata.[5]

---

[1] Cf. surveys by Turner, *Power*, 20-79; Robert P. Menzies, *Empowered for Witness: The Spirit in Luke-Acts* (London: T&T Clark, 2004 [1991]), 17-45; Matthias Wenk, *Community Forming Power: The Socio-Ethical Role of the Spirit in Luke-Acts* (Sheffield: Sheffield Academic Press, 2000), 13-44.

[2] Hermann Gunkel, *Die Wirkungen des Heiligen Geistes: Nach der Populären Anschauung der Apostolischen Zeit und nach der Lehre des Apostels Paulus* (Göttingen: Vandenhoeck & Ruprecht, 1899 [1888]), 4.

[3] *Ibid.*, 6-7.

[4] 'wenn also nach urchristlicher Anschauung der Geist nur unter einer gewissen Vermittelung der Gemeinde den Einzelnen verliehen wird, so ist doch jede Geistesausgiessung eine neue selbständige Tat Gottes', *Ibid.*, 28.

[5] *Ibid.*, 20-23.

Arthur James Mason, *The Relation of Confirmation to Baptism* (1891)

In the 1970s, J.K. Parratt could regard Mason's argument about Jesus' baptism as ignored but still 'cogent' and without 'any clear counter-arguments'.[6] Consequently, Mason's perspective is worthy of review. He presented a clear thesis: 'The Holy Ghost is given in baptism by the laying on of hands.'[7] Jesus' baptism is not directly parallel with Christian baptism. The gift of the Spirit was not associated with the water, but with a 'distinct, though connected, movement'.[8] By observing the episodes of Samaria and Ephesus, he saw that the gift of the Spirit is definitively linked to the ritual of handlaying which forms an integral part of the baptismal procedure. At Samaria, Luke clearly related an unfulfilled expectation, indicating that Christian initiation was incomplete without the gift of the Spirit which came through handlaying. At Ephesus, we see an ordinary baptismal procedure, with no hint of the extraordinary circumstances at Samaria. Thus, the leading apostles, Peter, John, and Paul, were united in initiatory practice.[9] Acts 2:38 indicates that baptism is a 'condition' but not a 'means', and the gift of the Spirit was given to converts through the handlaying aspect of baptism.[10] Cornelius' house indicates that baptism's spiritual effect is of a different 'kind' than that of confirmation.[11] Mason struggled, however, to understand how someone without baptism's spiritual grace could experience the grace of the gift of the Spirit. Yet, he would not declare baptism to be a 'mere form'.[12] He had no resolution to the problem.

Hans Leisegang, *Pneuma Hagion: Der Ursprung des Geistbegriffs der synoptischen Evangelien aus der griechischen Mystik* (1922)

Leisegang set out to challenge the commonly accepted idea that the Synoptic Gospels' concept of Holy Spirit, except for Luke's redactional activity, was strictly Jewish and uninfluenced by Hellenism.[13] Rather, all places where the Synoptics refer to the Spirit are later additions and do not stem from the actual teachings of Jesus but from paganism.[14] His arguments for Hellenistic origins are

---

[6] J.K. Parratt, 'The Holy Spirit and Baptism, Part I: The Gospels and the Acts of the Apostles', *ET* 82 (1970-1971), 231-35; 233.

[7] Latin quote from Primasius on title-page. Arthur James Mason, *The Relation of Confirmation to Baptism as Taught in Holy Scripture and the Fathers* (London: Longmans, Green, 1891), 50.

[8] *Ibid.*, 17.

[9] *Ibid.*, 25-28.

[10] *Ibid.*, 37.

[11] *Ibid.*, 39.

[12] *Ibid.*, 38.

[13] Hans Leisegang, *Pneuma Hagion: Der Ursprung des Geistbegriffs der synoptischen Evangelien aus der griechischen Mystik* (Leipzig: J.C. Hinrichs'sche Buchhandlung, 1922), 4-5.

[14] *Ibid.*, 5.

tangential to the book and will be illustrated but not pursued in depth. Rather, the focus will be upon his views with regard to Luke's understanding of the Spirit.

He first addressed the conception of Jesus by the Holy Spirit. Two examples of his arguments will suffice. He found parallels in the Pythia of Delphi, the Sibylline Oracles, gnostic prophetesses, and participants in the mystery religions. It was not that they gave supernatural birth, but that a spirit entered them and they, like Mary, prophesied.[15] He also found similarities with the conception of Dionysius, whose mother, again supposedly like Mary, experienced an ecstatic condition. The child became a prophet who could impart the divine spirit.[16]

He next analysed the 'fire baptism' of John the Baptist. By noting that in Acts 19, the Ephesian disciples of John were unaware of the Spirit, Leisegang concluded that the original message of John did not include anything about one who would baptise in the Spirit. Luke, as composer of both the Gospel and Acts, drew upon the 'spirit and fire' saying in his Pentecost narrative.[17] He argued that Luke's thinking about fire had similarities with apocryphal depictions of Jesus' baptism. Pagan parallels include Dionysius, with whose arrival a fire manifestation was associated, and the Maenads, who had non-consuming fire in their hair.[18]

Jesus' baptism again shows links to paganism in that his prayer was the means of obtaining the Spirit. 'That the gift of the Spirit before all through prayer is secured, is an essential theme of Hellenistic spirituality.'[19] Leisegang listed the following examples: the Mithras liturgy, magical papyri, Philo, and Plutarch's story of Timarchus' vision in the Trophonius Oracle, where a prayer is followed by a spiritual experience (*De Genio Socratis* 22). The 'bodily' descent of the Spirit seems to Leisegang to indicate what the Greeks conceived of as a daemon (dämonisches Wesen) that enters Jesus and governs him.[20] He also argues that Luke's presentation of Jesus as 'full' of the Spirit after his baptism is a Hellenistic concept of enthusiastic spirit experience (Leisegang cites Luke 4:1, emphasizing both his being full and his being led by the Spirit; he also cites 4:14 and the Isaiah quote).[21]

The Lukan reference to the sin against the Holy Spirit, unlike Matthew's, is placed separate from Jesus' statement about driving out demons. Luke's Jesus does not exorcise by the Spirit, but by the 'finger of God', which is not the same thing.[22] The sin of blasphemy against the Holy Spirit (Luke 10) is in the context of the Spirit-inspired witness under persecution known to the early church. It is

---

[15] *Ibid.*, 35.
[16] *Ibid.*, 41.
[17] *Ibid.*, 74.
[18] *Ibid.*, 75.
[19] 'Daß die Gabe des Geistes vor allem durch Gebet erlangt wird, ist ein der hellenistischen Frömmigkeit wesentlicher Zug', *Ibid.*, 94.
[20] *Ibid.*
[21] *Ibid.*, 93-94.
[22] *Ibid.*, 100.

resisting, even criticising this Spirit-uttered testimony that Luke saw as unforgivable blasphemy.[23]

The Synoptics' reference to the Spirit being given to the disciples (Matthew 10:20; Mark 13:11; Luke 12:12) Leisegang understood in terms of the speaking in tongues that occurred within the Christian community. This becomes a springboard for Leisegang to explore the giving of the Spirit in Acts. In pursuing the background to the Pentecost story, he asserted that Philo speaks of fire, but not of a language miracle. The rabbis speak of a language miracle, but not of a fire manifestation. Therefore, originally, speaking in tongues was not associated with a fire manifestation.[24] Luke understood the fire and tongues speaking as σημεῖα ἐπὶ τῆς γῆς κάτω. The τέρατα ἐν τῷ οὐρανῷ ἄνω are likely the rushing mighty wind.[25] Again, Leisegang found similarities with Timarchus, who, in association with the coming of a spirit, heard a blowing sound from which a voice came (*De Genio Socratis* 22).[26]

Heinrich von Baer, *Der Heilige Geist in den Lukasschriften* (1926)

Von Baer viewed Pentecost as 'analogue' to Jesus' baptism.[27] For von Baer, Jesus' Spirit-reception is a Spirit baptism.[28] Though von Baer recognized that Jesus grew in spirit, the baptism was a new equipping of the Spirit.[29] Jesus' baptism functions as a Spirit imparting, 'new procreation' (Neuzeugung) experience.[30] Jesus' Spirit-reception is linked to prayer, and, von Baer noted, prior prayer is linked to significant events in Jesus' life and in Acts.[31] For von Baer, the Spirit is power and the baptismal prayer is a request for power: 'Also Jesus, who is nevertheless conceived from the Holy Spirit, prays for power, petitions the Father for the Holy Spirit.'[32] Jesus' ministry was one of the Spirit's abiding presence punctuated by moments of increased experience of the Spirit as power for ministry. The same holds true for the disciples in Acts.[33]

---

[23] *Ibid.*, 108-109.
[24] *Ibid.*, 127-28.
[25] *Ibid.*, 129-30.
[26] *Ibid.*, 130.
[27] Heinrich von Baer, *Der Heilige Geist in den Lukasschriften* (Stuttgart: Verlag W. Kohlhammer, 1926), 19.
[28] *Ibid.*, 57.
[29] *Ibid.*, 61.
[30] *Ibid.*, 59.
[31] *Ibid.*, 61-62; cf. 168.
[32] 'Auch Jesus, der doch von dem Heiligen Geiste empfangen ist, betet um Kraft, bittet den Vater um den Heiligen Geist', *Ibid.*, 61.
[33] *Ibid.*, 61.

Jesus' Nazareth sermon reflects possession of the 'Messiah Spirit' (Messiasgeist) received at the Jordan.³⁴ This 'Messiah Spirit' establishes Jesus' equipping and his calling: 'The Spirit-reception established the capability, as well as the calling, to the Messiah.'³⁵ Von Baer gave the idea that Jesus is almost 'controlled' or 'governed' by the Spirit.³⁶ Throughout the rest of Luke, all that Jesus does is seen as done by the Spirit as well. Von Baer argued with a narratological sensitivity to the reader and to the impact initial statements have on subsequent narrative: 'Jesus' own statement, 'πνεῦμα κυρίου ἐπ' ἐμέ' should accompany the reader through the entire gospel and should, at the same time, serve as key to the correct evaluation of the following narrative.'³⁷ In contrast to the view that Menzies will later take, von Baer understood Luke's references to δύναμις and ἐξουσία as references to the Spirit, not to a power separate from the Spirit.³⁸

Contrary to what Frederick Bruner will later argue,³⁹ the disciples pray in preparation for the Spirit. With sound narrative awareness, von Baer credited the use of lots to the lack of the Spirit's presence.⁴⁰ He saw Acts 1:8 as programmatic for Acts as the Isaiah citation was programmatic for Luke. He noted that in both cases, the Spirit is placed in the initial position and has a similar function. The Pentecostal wind and fire parallel Jesus' Jordan experience in that the Spirit's coming is tangibly marked.⁴¹ The Pentecostal tongues are not presented as ecstatic glossolalia, but as xenolalia, though this is not evidence that Luke was unfamiliar with glossolalia.⁴²

From Acts 2:38, von Baer concluded that Spirit-reception is the certain result of water baptism.⁴³ He rejected Stromberg's claim that originally Spirit impartation in Samaria took place through Peter's handlaying apart from any baptism as being a 'too mechanically on the handlaying bound form of Spirit transmission'⁴⁴

---

³⁴ *Ibid.*, 65. Cf. Otto Pfleiderer's reference to, 'messianischen πνεῦμα', *Der Paulinismus: Ein Beitrag zur Geschichte der Urchristlichen Theologie* (Leipzig: Fues's Verlag, R. Reisland, 1873), 199.
³⁵ 'Die Geistesempfängnis begründet sowohl die Befähigung wie die Berufung zum Messias'. Von Baer, *Geist*, 65.
³⁶ *Ibid.*, 65.
³⁷ 'Die Selbstaussage Jesu 'πνεῦμα κυρίου ἐπ' ἐμέ' soll den Leser durch das ganze Evangelium begleiten und soll ihm gleichsam als Schlüssel zur richtigen Bewertung der folgenden Erzählungen dienen', *Ibid.*, 69.
³⁸ *Ibid.*, 72.
³⁹ Frederick Dale Bruner, *Theology of the Holy Spirit: The Pentecostal Experience and the New Testament Witness* (London: Hodder and Stoughton; n.p.: Eerdmans, 1970), 162.
⁴⁰ Von Baer, *Geist*, 83.
⁴¹ *Ibid.*, 88.
⁴² *Ibid.*, 91.
⁴³ *Ibid.*, 171.
⁴⁴ 'zu mechanisch an die Handauflegung gebundenen Form der Geistesübermittlung'. *Ibid.*, 174. A. von Stromberg, *Studien zur Theorie und Praxis der Taufe in der christlichen Kirche der ersten zwei Jahrhunderte* (Aalen: Scientia Verlag Aalen, 1973 [1913]), 157.

and as being contradicted by the accounts where the Spirit comes apart from handlaying, namely, Pentecost, Act 4:31, and Cornelius' house. Despite Luke's multiple accounts of Spirit-reception, von Baer believed that there is not enough material to resolve this issue.

However, von Baer did not see charismatic experience as the evidence of possessing the Spirit because, though tongues, prophecy and healing were widespread phenomena, all Christians did not possess these gifts. Moreover, such gifts were viewed by Luke as extraordinary and not normal. Therefore, Paul's question in Acts 19 about whether the Ephesians had received the Spirit could not have been prompted by a lack of charismata. There must have been some other behavioural indicator that the Spirit was missing.[45] Moreover, all Christians possessed the Spirit (Acts 2:14-16). Therefore, since the charismata were not possessed by all, but the Spirit was possessed by all, the charismata cannot be seen as the only marks of Spirit possession. He objected to Gunkel's link between possession of the Spirit and charismata.[46] For von Baer, the Spirit is the universally possessed source of empowerment both for service and for basic Christian life.

Friedrich Büchsel, *Der Geist Gottes im Neuen Testament* (1926)

Büchsel was at pains to distinguish the *pneumatischen* character of the early church from *Enthusiasmus*, the spirit of *schwärmen*, or 'raving'.[47] All the baptised received the Spirit: 'There is no pneuma aristocracy.'[48] Yet, there were prophets among the people, and Spirit experience varied from times of fullness to times when individuals were not 'full'.[49] '*Sprachenreden*', or speaking in languages, is a better translation than '*Zungenreden*', speaking in tongues, because Luke intended meaningful speech.[50] Language speaking occurs strictly in connection with Spirit-reception and is related closely to prophecy. Büchsel emphasized that it is not unintelligible, nor are analogies of ecstatic speech from the history of religions appropriate. The thing which distinguishes language speech is its origin in God's Spirit and the fact that not everyone understood it. He raised the question of whether it is a miracle of hearing or a miracle of speaking and concluded the latter, because a hearing miracle would mean God worked a miracle in people who had not received the Spirit and worked no miracle in those who had.[51] However, one should not think that a language speaking miracle actually occurred. This is only Luke's 'stylization'[52] of an original tongues speech

---

[45] Von Baer, *Geist*, 190.
[46] *Ibid.*, 191.
[47] Friedrich Büchsel, *Der Geist Gottes im Neuen Testament* (Gütersloh: T. Bertelsmann, 1926), 233.
[48] 'Eine Pneumatikeraristokratie gibt es nicht', *Ibid.*, 240.
[49] *Ibid.*
[50] *Ibid.*, 242-43.
[51] *Ibid.*, 243.
[52] *Ibid.*, 244.

similar to what, in Büchsel's time, occurred among cults and sectarian religious groups. He likely meant the nascent Pentecostal movement.[53] He wrote, 'Originally, it only had to do with tongues speaking.'[54]

Regarding a question central to this book, Büchsel asked, 'How does the human person receive the Spirit?'[55] His answer was from Jesus through the apostles. But he qualified this statement in that the apostles do not do any work of their own, but are the means by which the exalted Lord transfers the Spirit to his church.[56] Preaching the gospel always comes before Spirit-reception: 'The connection between Word and Spirit is inseparable.'[57] Büchsel located the reception of the Spirit, however, not in the preaching of the word, which plays a significant preparatory role, but in baptism. Büchsel recognized exceptions to the rule. Baptism can follow Spirit-reception. Baptism may also fail to impart the Spirit. In such cases, handlaying rectifies the situation.[58] Büchsel raised the question of how the Spirit could be tied to a cultic act. Is it not reading into the early church a later Catholicism? Is it not by nature contradictory? 'Does it not contradict too strongly the spirituality of the Spirit?'[59] Neither the early church's spirituality nor the spirituality of Jesus was without cultic acts. Both contained water baptism. Jesus commanded the Lord's Supper as well.[60] Baptism is first a cleansing, and only secondly the means of imparting the Spirit, but it is the means.[61] The distinction between water baptism and handlaying is a difficult matter. Originally, the baptiser was the one who laid hands upon the one baptised, and that someone other than the baptiser did the handlaying ritual was an exception.[62] One should not identify water with forgiveness of sins and handlaying with impartation of the Spirit. The entire process was always named 'baptism' and not 'baptism and handlaying'.[63]

Nikolaus Adler, *Taufe und Handauflegung: Eine Exegetisch-Theologische Untersuchung von Apg 8, 14-17* (1951)

Adler's work defends the confirmationist position. Early on, he addressed the issue of the apparent discrepancy between Acts 2:38 and the Samaritan story. Luke could have written 2:38 to read, 'you will receive forgiveness and the gift of the Spirit', thus linking both to the prior action of water baptism. However, Luke did not do this, but instead used two different phrases, εἰς ἄφεσιν, with

---

[53] *Ibid.*
[54] 'Ursprünglich wird es sich nur um ein Zungenreden handeln', *Ibid.*, 245.
[55] 'wie erhält der Mensch den Geist?' *Ibid.*, 256.
[56] *Ibid.*, 256.
[57] 'Die verbindung von Wort und Geist ist untrennbar', *Ibid.*, 256-57.
[58] *Ibid.*, 257.
[59] 'Widerspricht sie nicht zu stark der Geistigkeit des Geistes?' *Ibid.*
[60] *Ibid.*, 258.
[61] *Ibid.*, 260.
[62] *Ibid.*, 262-63.
[63] *Ibid.*, 263.

which he linked baptism to forgiveness, and καὶ λήμψεσθε, with which he connected baptism to Spirit-reception. The two phrases indicate two different relationships to water baptism. The καί is consecutive because it comes between an imperative and a future. Adler concluded, 'according to the wording from Acts 2:38, baptism is the effective cause for forgiveness of sins, but only the prerequisite for Spirit-reception'.[64]

The individuals who heard Peter promise the Spirit were either 'direct' or 'indirect' witnesses to the Spirit's coming, and therefore knew that the Spirit was not given in baptism, but came from heaven. They would not, therefore, expect the Spirit to be given in baptism, but would understand that to be a prerequisite for receiving the Spirit. Thus, the stories of Pentecost and Samaria do not conflict.[65] The case of Cornelius' house also does not present a contradiction, but rather an exception, for the disciples of Jesus, as well as the Ephesian disciples, received the Spirit after baptism, and this was the 'regular' order.[66]

The Samaritans believed the genuine gospel and were properly baptised.[67] However, Luke's statement that they were 'only' baptised indicates, 'that the reception merely of baptism was the deeper reason for the absence of Spirit-reception'.[68] After prayer, the apostles laid hands upon the Samaritans. All the Samaritans received handlaying, not just the leaders.[69] In the case of healings or blessings, the act of stretching out the hand and laying it upon another indicates, 'that the inherent power in handlaying transfers to a second person'.[70] In this case, the Spirit that dwells in the first individual is transferred to the second, and the physical contact of handlaying symbolizes this actual transfer. Yet, it is even more than symbol, it is also 'means of Spirit-granting', as 8:17 and Simon's observation in verse 18 and request in verse 19 show. Through the 'ceremony' of handlaying, the Spirit is actually communicated.[71] This is not merely Simon's mistaken idea, for Luke used ὅτι to show reality, as in Luke 2:49; 8:53 and Acts 2:30; 3:17.[72] God alone gives the Spirit, but, 'The question here is only, how and in what way God sends the human person the Holy Spirit.'[73]

---

[64] 'nach dem Wortlaut von Apg 2, 38 ist die Taufe für die Sündenvergebung die Wirkursach, für den Geistempfang aber nur die Voraussetzung', Nikolaus Adler, *Taufe und Handauflegung: Eine Exegetisch-Theologische Untersuchung von Apg 8, 14-17* (Münster: Aschendorffsche Verlagsbuchhandlung, 1951), 27-28.
[65] *Ibid.*, 28.
[66] *Ibid.*, 29.
[67] *Ibid.*, 44-47, 58-59.
[68] 'daß der Empfang bloß der Taufe der tiefere Grund für das Ausbleiben des Geistempfanges war', *Ibid.*, 58.
[69] *Ibid.*, 68-69.
[70] 'daß die dem handauflegenden innewohnende Kraft auf eine zweite Person übergeht', *Ibid.*, 72.
[71] 'Mittel der Geistspendung', *Ibid.*, 72-73.
[72] *Ibid.*, 74.
[73] 'Die Frage ist hier nur, wie und auf welche Weise Gott den Hl. Geist den Menschen sendet', *Ibid.*, 75.

Adler denied that handlaying communicates only the outward gifts of the Spirit. He affirmed, however, seemingly in contradiction to all his foregoing exegesis of Acts 2 and 8, that there is a sense in which the Spirit is received in baptism.[74] Baptism gives 'grace of the Holy Spirit', yet, 'laying on of hands perfects this gift of the Spirit, in that it bestows the fullness of the Holy Spirit'.[75] The relationship between handlaying and baptism he described as follows: 'handlaying builds a complement, or rather a supplement, of baptism, nevertheless not in the sense, as though handlaying were an integral component of baptism'.[76] As to the normativity of Samaria, Adler pointed to Acts 19, 'where it has to do with a complete parallel'. Samaria is highly significant for doctrine. This is not because Luke deliberately intended to teach on confirmation, however.[77] Adler drew one more conclusion from the Samaria story – the exclusive apostolic right to Spirit impartation via handlaying. He defended himself against the objection that Ananias, a non-apostle, gave Paul the Spirit, by denying that Ananias gave the Spirit. The text does not depict Ananias giving the Spirit and, therefore, someone else did it.[78]

G.W.H. Lampe, *The Seal of the Spirit: A Study in the Doctrine of Baptism and Confirmation in the New Testament and the Fathers*, and other writings (1951)

Luke's presentation of Jesus receiving the Spirit while praying parallels the Acts church's reception of the Spirit after prayer (Acts 1:14; 4:31). For both Jesus and his followers, 'the grand object of prayer is the reception of the Holy Spirit'.[79] Lampe emphasized, however, the association between the water and the reception of the Spirit and did not suggest that Luke viewed Jesus' prayer as interrupting that link.[80] The Spirit was power for Jesus' ministry and so was also power for the Church post-Pentecost. Because of this, for Luke, 'it is therefore primarily thought of as the Spirit of prophecy and of "tongues", making its presence obvious to all and sundry'.[81] Ultimately, because, 'Christian baptism is a re-presentation of the Baptism of Jesus', it is through baptism that the believer receives the Spirit, not through an additional rite.[82] However, Lampe did not argue this

---

[74] *Ibid.*, 82-93, 95.
[75] 'Gnaden des Hl. Geistes', yet, 'die Handauflegung vervollkommnet diese Geistesgaben, indem sie die Fülle des Hl. Geistes schenkt', *Ibid.*, 106.
[76] 'bildet die Handauflegung ein Komplement bzw. Supplement der Taufe, jedoch nicht in dem Sinn, als ob die Handauflegung ein integrierender Bestandteil der Taufe wäre', *Ibid.*, 107.
[77] 'wo es sich um einen vollständig parallelen Vorgang handelt', *Ibid.*, 110-11.
[78] *Ibid.*, 115-17.
[79] Lampe, *Seal*, 43-44. Similarly, G.W.H. Lampe, 'The Holy Spirit in the Writings of St. Luke', D.E. Nineham (ed.), *Studies in the Gospels* (Oxford: Basil Blackwell, 1957), 169-70.
[80] Lampe, *Seal*, 42.
[81] *Ibid.*, 53. Cf. Lampe, 'Spirit', 159-200; 162.
[82] Lampe, *Seal*, 45.

specifically from Luke's theology, but by drawing generally upon the gospel writers.

When Lampe did focus upon Luke's theology, he altered his position slightly. Observing that Apollos apparently had the Spirit without any Christian baptism, Lampe wrote, 'possibly the Spirit is regarded by Luke as normally, but not universally, imparted through Baptism'.[83] Regarding the Acts accounts of handlaying, Lampe turned to Pentecost, where no handlaying is recorded, and to the Ethiopian eunuch story, upon whom hands were not laid; yet he must have received the Spirit because he was rejoicing, because he received Christian baptism, and because this was his only chance to receive.[84] The term βάπτισμα did not reference any larger initiation ceremony that included handlaying. At Samaria, the Spirit was 'withheld' to show unity of the Church with Philip.[85] Handlaying at Samaria and Ephesus was, 'more akin to Ordination than to Confirmation'.[86] New Christians were brought into 'association with the missionary, apostolic, ministry' so they also could participate in that task. Luke highlighted this happening at 'two important turning-points in the Gentile mission'.[87] Lampe suggested that at Samaria, Damascus, and Ephesus, 'a special transference of the missionary power is given to converts of special importance in the development of the missionary enterprise'.[88] The ordinary believer's Spirit-reception at baptism is not related to these three exceptional 'turning-points in the history of the mission'.[89]

Lampe's comments upon Luke's theology must be taken with his 1976 Bampton Lectures in which he flatly denied that any rite transmits the Spirit. After observing, from a pastoral perspective, that conversion can occur in a variety of ways not all of which coincide with ritual, he stated, 'the Spirit cannot be actually mediated *by* a rite, though a rite may well be an occasion for receiving the Spirit'.[90] Moreover, the Spirit, being omnipresent, is already in, 'all [God's] personal creatures', and therefore receiving the Spirit is simply a matter of new openness and awareness to what was always present.[91] Lampe recognized that Luke, 'gives the impression, when the story of Pentecost is read in conjunction with the promise, which follows it', that all baptised believers will speak in tongues.[92] However, this initial impression is not to be taken at face value, for Pentecost 'is a theological construction' in which the various phenomena play

---

[83] *Ibid.*, 66.
[84] *Ibid.*, 67.
[85] *Ibid.*, 70.
[86] *Ibid.*, 75.
[87] *Ibid.*
[88] Lampe, 'Spirit', 199.
[89] *Ibid.*, 200.
[90] G.W.H. Lampe, *God as Spirit: The Bampton Lectures 1976* (London: SCM, 1983 [Oxford: OUP, 1977]), 196, original italics.
[91] *Ibid.*, 196.
[92] *Ibid.*, 68.

upon the Sinai story, 'dramatically portraying the truth that the law has been superseded by the Spirit'.[93] All Acts references to glossolalia are similarly atypical of ordinary Christian experience.[94]

Hans Conzelmann, *Die Mitte der Zeit: Studien zur Theologie des Lukas* (1954)

Luke 'has not presented his concept coherently',[95] and Acts does not present a model for today.[96] Baptism gives forgiveness and the Spirit, but is itself given upon condition of repentance and conversion.[97] Uniquely in Luke's story of Jesus' baptism, 'the Spirit comes as response to *prayer*'.[98] How is the Spirit communicated? Conzelmann stated, 'the Spirit is in the church; it is transferred through her official acts and office holders'.[99]

The Acts church is not a model for today. Witness the early church's keeping the law while the Gentiles are not required to,[100] the presence of 'the eyewitness', the early church's positive relationship to the Temple, and the motif of peace that the early church at first experienced (in contrast to later persecution).[101] Thus, the early presentation of the church in Acts is unique from the present and 'unrepeatable'.[102] How then do we apply Acts to the present day? 'Not imitatio, rather succession.' We are not to imitate, but be successors according to 'the times'.[103] For this reason, 'there is also no ideal of the imitatio of the *apostle*'.[104] The message and the sacraments are the common elements between the Acts church and today. Baptism 'transmits' the Spirit and forgiveness.[105]

Eduard Schweizer, 'πνεῦμα' (1959)

Schweizer viewed Jesus, not as a 'pneumatic', controlled by the Spirit after the Old Testament fashion, but as 'Lord of the πνεῦμα'.[106] Jesus is also not like 'the pneumatics' who are in the church because he is not the 'object' of the Spirit. He possessed the Spirit from his birth because it was a birth of the Spirit. That Luke

---

[93] *Ibid.*
[94] *Ibid.*
[95] 'hat ... seine Auffassung nicht im Zusammenhang dargestellt'. Hans Conzelmann, *Die Mitte der Zeit: Studien zur Theologie des Lukas* (Tübingen: J.C.B. Mohr, Paul Siebeck, 1962 [1954]), 4.22.
[96] *Ibid.*, 7.
[97] *Ibid.*, 91-92.
[98] 'der Geist kommt als Erwiderung des *Gebets*', *Ibid.*, 167, original italics.
[99] 'der Geist ist in der Kirche; er wird durch ihre Amtshandlungen und Amtsträger übertragen', *Ibid.*, 194.
[100] *Ibid.*, 194-95.
[101] *Ibid.*, 197.
[102] 'unwiederholbar', *Ibid.*
[103] 'Nicht Imitatio, sondern Nachfolge'; 'der Zeit', *Ibid.*, 218.
[104] 'gibt es auch kein Ideal der Imitatio der *Apostel*', *Ibid.*, original italics.
[105] 'übermittelt', *Ibid.*, 204.
[106] 'Pneumatiker'; 'Herr des πνεῦμα', Eduard Schweizer, 'πνεῦμα' (Stuttgart: W. Kohlhammer, 1959), 387-453, 402.

did not compare Jesus' baptism and Pentecost suggests 'that, for Luke, the Spirit gifting of Jesus lies on a totally different level as that of the church'.[107] The Lukan Spirit is drawn from 'the typical Jewish concept of the Spirit as the Spirit of prophecy'.[108] Miracles are never linked to the Spirit, but with a variety of other factors mostly related to Jesus, including Jesus' δύναμις. In this, Luke distinguished between δύναμις and πνεῦμα, whereas elsewhere he treated the terms almost as synonyms.[109] The Spirit is primarily 'the Spirit of prophecy' and this fact 'prevents' Luke from attributing healing and ethical activities to the Spirit.[110] All of Luke's baptised believers have the Spirit and this is 'visible and tangible'.[111] As for the Day of Pentecost, it was likely viewed in terms of Sinai and renewal of the covenant.[112] Now, 'All the members of the end-time church are prophets'.[113] However, the Spirit does not always manifest in ways 'outwardly bizarre'.[114] What the Spirit does is enable individual believers to accomplish Christian mission. The Spirit neither creates faith, forms the model community, nor saves.[115] Regarding Spirit-reception, Schweizer emphasized the Spirit's freedom. He can come before, or even without baptism, and usually comes apart from handlaying. Samaria is 'singular'.[116] Nevertheless, baptism normally imparts the Spirit,[117] while prayer is an even more important preparation for Spirit-reception than baptism.[118]

Frederick Dale Bruner, *A Theology of the Holy Spirit: The Pentecostal Experience and the New Testament Witness* (1970)

Bruner, responding to the early Pentecostal movement, argues, 'baptism of the Holy Spirit joins men to Christ in such a way that the recipients become *his*, i.e., Christians',[119] because Acts 1:8, refers to 'my witnesses'. In Jesus' instructions, there were no conditions save to wait in Jerusalem. That they did pray was not out of necessity. Against von Baer, the prayer is sufficiently separated in the text from the Spirit's coming so that it will not be seen as a cause. Therefore, prayer is not a condition of baptism in the Spirit.[120] Bruner states, 'there is no record in

---

[107] 'die Pneumatiker'; 'Objekt'; 'daß die Geistbegabung Jesu für Lukas auf ganz anderer Ebene liegt als die der Gemeinde', *Ibid.*, 403.
[108] 'die typisch jüdische Auffassung des Geistes als des Geistes der Prophetie', *Ibid.*, 405.
[109] *Ibid.*
[110] 'der Geist der Prophetie'; 'hindert', *Ibid.*, 407.
[111] 'sichtbar und fühlbar', *Ibid.*, 408.
[112] *Ibid.*
[113] 'Propheten sind alle Glieder der Endgemeinde', *Ibid.*, 409.
[114] 'äußerlich absonderlich', *Ibid.*, 410.
[115] *Ibid.*
[116] 'singular', *Ibid.*, 412.
[117] *Ibid.*, 410.
[118] *Ibid.*, 411.
[119] Bruner, *Theology*, 160, original italics.
[120] *Ibid.*, 162.

Acts of men praying that they might receive the Holy Spirit'.[121] Luke 11 is addressed to Christians and is not relevant for the initial Spirit-reception. Of Jesus praying at his baptism, he simply writes, 'prayer and baptism should not be played off at each other's expense'.[122]

'Repentance is being baptized.'[123] Repentance is *'enabled* through both preaching and baptism'.[124] In his discussion of baptism, Bruner thoroughly mixes in Pauline scriptures to make his point: 'to become *his* means, by definition, to receive his Spirit (1:8; cf. I Cor. 6:17; Rom. 8:9)'.[125] Baptism simultaneously imparts forgiveness of sins and the Spirit.[126] Waiting in Jerusalem was a one-time thing, not repeated in Acts. Instead, people need only be baptised. 'Henceforth, baptism is Pentecost.'[127] Preaching is the preparatory means of grace to water baptism. Both together convey the Spirit.[128] The only evidence of Spirit-reception is baptism.[129]

In relation to the Samaria case, Bruner emphasizes οὐδέπω, 'not yet', to say that this word definitively links the future coming of the Spirit to the past water baptism.[130] This was an exceptional case that the Spirit did not come in the actual water:

> The Spirit is temporarily suspended from baptism here 'only' and precisely to teach the church at its most prejudiced juncture, and in its strategic initial missionary move beyond Jerusalem, that *suspension cannot occur*.[131]

Luke did not say the apostles' hands themselves were the medium of transmission of the Spirit. That was what Simon erroneously thought.[132] In light of Ananias in Acts 9: 'The laying on of hands is not an apostolic or episcopal prerogative.'[133] In discussing why Saul did receive the Spirit though the text does not explicitly say so, Bruner observes: 'it is Luke's fashion to summarize in one predicate the whole of a promise to avoid repetition (cf. 2:38-40 with 2:41)'.[134]

In Acts 10 and 11, tongues were a sign to the Jews. 'Tongues were a sign not because they were expected, required, or usual, but precisely because they were unexpected, unrequired, and unusual – resembled only by Pentecost.'[135] Bruner

---

[121] *Ibid.*, 171.
[122] *Ibid.*
[123] *Ibid.*, 166.
[124] *Ibid.*, original italics.
[125] *Ibid.*, 167, original italics.
[126] *Ibid.*, 167, 168.
[127] *Ibid.*, 168.
[128] *Ibid.*, 169.
[129] *Ibid.*, 170.
[130] *Ibid.*, 178.
[131] *Ibid.*, original italics.
[132] *Ibid.*, 181.
[133] *Ibid.*, 190.
[134] *Ibid.*
[135] *Ibid.*, 192.

emphasizes the group nature of the event and claims that in all three cases where people spoke in tongues in Acts, it was always as a group, not as individuals.[136] Cornelius' house is a prime example of the equation of conversion with Spirit-reception.[137] With Cornelius, the Ephesians and Pentecost, the Spirit came before, after, and in baptism, but nevertheless, the Spirit is always given in the water.[138] To help his case, Bruner leaves the text of Luke-Acts behind and appeals to Ephesians, I Corinthians, John, and Titus. Similarly to the early Dunn, he argues that the apostles were not converted until Pentecost because in Acts 11:17 Peter seems to say that is when they believed.[139] For Bruner, 'repentant faith' is 'made actual in baptism'.[140] Bruner argues from Acts 15:8-9 that, 'The cleansing of the heart, faith, the gift of the Holy Spirit are then essentially all *one act of God* and not three moral conditions, or two moral conditions and a result.'[141]

Apollos was a believer in Jesus who simply did not know about Christian baptism.[142] The Ephesian Twelve had not believed in Jesus, but only in 'a Messianic figure'[143] preached by John. Water baptism normally has laying on of hands associated with it.[144] However, Paul did not ask about having hands laid on them, but if they had been baptised, and, therefore, handlaying belongs to baptism and must not be separated into a different rite. Luke set Peter and Paul in parallel, both in general and with regard to handlaying. However, Bruner denies any special apostolic handlaying requirement. Samaria and Ephesus are 'unusual' cases.[145]

Luke presented only one reception or work of the Spirit, not two, as in Pentecostal teaching. Again, he steps away from Luke-Acts to link this with Titus 3:5-6, John 3:5 and 1 Corinthians 6:11.[146] He argues from Acts 22:16 that prayer was a part of baptism.[147] Jesus' baptism is a 'prototype' for baptism today.[148] Bruner argues from Mark 1:10 that 'immediately' indicates Jesus' reception of the Spirit and the water are so close together as to be inseparable. He does not here argue his case from Luke.[149] He approvingly cites Lampe: 'Christian Baptism is a re-presentation of the Baptism of Jesus'.[150]

---

[136] *Ibid.*
[137] *Ibid.*, 193.
[138] *Ibid.*, 193-94.
[139] *Ibid.*, 196.
[140] *Ibid.*, 197.
[141] *Ibid.*, 200, original italics.
[142] *Ibid.*, 206.
[143] *Ibid.*, 209.
[144] *Ibid.*
[145] *Ibid.*, 212.
[146] *Ibid.*, 213.
[147] *Ibid.*, 217.
[148] *Ibid.*, 220.
[149] *Ibid.*
[150] *Ibid.*, 222; Cf. Lampe, *Seal*, 45.

James Dunn, *Baptism in the Holy Spirit: A Re-examination of the New Testament Teaching on the Gift of the Spirit in Relation to Pentecostalism Today* (1970)

Dunn's work represents the beginning of what has been termed, 'the Dunn Debate', an ongoing discussion between Dunn and various interlocutors, especially those of Pentecostal or Charismatic persuasion. For Dunn, Jesus' reception of the Spirit at his baptism, 'is in fact the event which begins the new covenant for Jesus – it initiates the messianic age and initiates Jesus into the messianic age'.[151] There is a sense in which, though he was God's son from birth, he also becomes God's son at his baptism.[152] Dunn, in later works, while continuing to discuss the idea of Jesus' sonship, may be seen to downplay it and to increase the emphasis upon Jesus' inspiration and empowerment.[153] Jesus' baptism/Spirit-reception is 'typical' of all Christians' experience.[154] Jordan and Pentecost are parallel.[155] Power for witness is a corollary to initiation into the new age, the latter being the primary purpose.[156] 'Christian conversion-initiation' is a 'complex' event because it involves both human and divine action. The human expresses repentance in the act of baptism and God consequently grants the Spirit.[157]

Ezekiel 36:27 and Jeremiah 31:33 undergird an understanding of the Spirit as 'the agent of the new covenant and its supreme blessing'.[158] Sinai and the giving of the law serve as background to Pentecost, and the 'essence of the new covenant' is the Spirit.[159] Dunn previously insisted that the apostles were not genuine believers until they received the Spirit at Pentecost. It was, 'only at Pentecost that their faith reached the level of Christian committal, only then that they became Christians in the NT sense of that word'.[160] However, he has since modified this stance: 'Pentecost may not have been when they first believed in Jesus, but it was when their belief was granted the response that Peter/Luke assumed to be the

---

[151] James D.G. Dunn, *Baptism in the Holy Spirit: A Re-examination of the New Testament Teaching on the Gift of the Spirit in Relation to Pentecostalism Today* (London: SCM, 1970; reprint, Philadelphia: Westminster, n.d.), 25.
[152] *Ibid.*, 28.
[153] James D.G. Dunn, *Jesus and the Spirit: A Study of the Religious and Charismatic Experience of Jesus and the First Christians as Reflected in the New Testament* (London: SCM., 1975), 191; James D.G. Dunn, *Christology in the Making: An Inquiry into the Origins of the Doctrine of the Incarnation* (London: SCM, 1989 [1980]), 140.
[154] Dunn, *Baptism*, 32.
[155] *Ibid.*, 40.
[156] *Ibid.*, 32.
[157] *Ibid.*, 37.
[158] *Ibid.*, 48.
[159] *Ibid.*, 49.
[160] *Ibid.*, 52.

norm.'[161] At Samaria, Dunn originally argued the Samaritans' faith was 'defective' and that is why they did not receive the Spirit. He has since withdrawn from this position also.[162]

Saul's conversion was an extended process.[163] Because Luke did not specifically say when Saul received the Spirit, we cannot know.[164] Regarding Cornelius' experience, Dunn argues from the fact of the Spirit being given precisely when Cornelius and company heard Peter preach on forgiveness of sins, that the Spirit must have been 'the bearer' of forgiveness. 'The Spirit was not something additional to God's acceptance and forgiveness but constituted that acceptance and forgiveness.'[165] Based on Acts 15:8-9, Dunn argues similarly to Bruner, that 'God's giving of the Holy Spirit is equivalent to his cleansing of their hearts; these two are one – two ways of describing the same thing.'[166] The Apollos and Ephesian stories are parallel. Apollos was a Christian who had the Spirit.[167] The Ephesians had made some 'act of commitment at some stage in the past. In short, they are disciples, but do not yet belong to *the* disciples; that is, they are not yet Christians'.[168] Dunn argues from Paul's question about baptism that there must be a logical connection between baptism and Spirit-reception.[169] He deals with the Sacramentalist issue of handlaying as a separate rite by saying, 'baptism and the laying on of hands here are the *one* ceremony'.[170]

In his summary of conversion-initiation, Dunn begins with the argument that Acts 2:38 was 'probably' the 'pattern and norm' for Luke.[171] Dunn states that, 'we may assume', exceptional cases aside, the rest of the conversion-initiations in Acts follow this pattern.[172] As Turner will later argue, it is therefore not necessary for Luke to specifically state that the converts received the Spirit, nor to state that they were water baptised. Such was the norm.[173] Dunn recognizes the Spirit's activity before the moment of trust in Jesus,[174] but he argues that the gift

---

[161] James D.G. Dunn, '"The Lord, the Giver of Life": The Gift of the Spirit as Both Life-giving and Empowering', I. Howard Marshall, Volker Rabens, and Cornelis Bennema, (eds), *The Spirit and Christ in the New Testament and Christian Theology* (Grand Rapids: Eerdmans, 2012), 15-16.

[162] James Dunn, 'Baptism in the Spirit: A Response to Pentecostal Scholarship on Luke-Acts', *The Christ and The Spirit:* Volume 2 *Pneumatology* (Edinburgh: T&T Clark, 1998), 228, 240.

[163] Dunn, *Baptism*, 77.
[164] *Ibid.*, 78.
[165] *Ibid.*, 80.
[166] *Ibid.*, 81-82.
[167] *Ibid.*, 88.
[168] *Ibid.*, original italics.
[169] *Ibid.*, 86.
[170] *Ibid.*, 87, original italics.
[171] *Ibid.*, 90.
[172] *Ibid.*, 93.
[173] *Ibid.*
[174] *Ibid.*, 94.

of the Spirit, 'comes neither before nor after conversion but *in* conversion'.[175] How then do faith, the Spirit and baptism relate? He answers:

> In the case of the Ephesians the sequence of Paul's questions indicates that πιστεῦσαι and βαπτισθῆναι are interchangeable ways of describing the act of faith: baptism was the necessary expression of commitment, without which they could not be said to have truly 'believed'.[176]

Dunn continues to explain the heart of his thesis: 'Properly administered water-baptism must have been the climax and act of faith, the expression of repentance and the vehicle of commitment.'[177] Dunn makes clear that the water itself does not impart forgiveness, however.[178] Dunn uses Acts 8 to disprove that water baptism automatically brings the Spirit.[179]

In his other writings, Dunn addresses the issue of the Spirit and experience more fully. 'Spirit not merely causes an ecstatic experience, he/it is himself that experience. So particularly Acts 2:33.'[180] In Acts 2:33, 'the gift of the Spirit is actually described as the ecstatic behaviour and glossolalia of the disciples on the day of Pentecost'.[181] While rejecting the initial evidence doctrine, Dunn nevertheless argues that the single, 'decisive', 'coming of the Spirit was, in Luke's conception, something tangible and visible, most typically (but not solely) in inspired, prophetic speech'.[182] Furthermore, 'the Spirit of the New Testament period was first and foremost an *experience* – an experience almost tangible in quality'.[183] For Dunn:

> the presence or absence of the Spirit in a person's (or community's) life was directly knowable and perceptible – not the Spirit as such, of course, but his presence; the Spirit's presence or absence could be ascertained not just indirectly as a deduction from some rite or formula, but immediately.[184]

Gonzalo Haya-Prats, *Empowered Believers: The Holy Spirit in the Book of Acts* (French edition, 1975)

One could easily think that the Spirit and the gift of prophecy or glossolalia are equivalent. However, this would be erroneous as the Spirit is more than charisms

---

[175] *Ibid.*, 95, original italics.
[176] *Ibid.*, 96.
[177] *Ibid.*, 97.
[178] *Ibid.*
[179] *Ibid.*, 100.
[180] James Dunn, 'Rediscovering the Spirit (1)', *The Christ and the Spirit:* Volume 2, *Pneumatology* (Edinburgh: T&T Clark, 1998), 46.
[181] James Dunn, 'They Believed Philip Preaching (Acts 8:12)', *The Christ and the Spirit:* Volume 2, *Pneumatology* (Edinburgh: T&T Clark, 1998), 217.
[182] Dunn, 'Response', 241.
[183] Dunn, 'Rediscovering', 45, original italics.
[184] *Ibid.*

and cannot be equated with them.[185] Nevertheless, 'Luke presents glossolalia as the typical manifestation of the Spirit.'[186] The phrase, '*the Promise* refers to the collected blessings announced for the messianic age'.[187] The gift of the Spirit is one of those blessings. Contrary to Dunn, the Spirit does not bring forgiveness. Rather, faith, forgiveness, and 'usually' baptism precede the gift of the Spirit.[188] Faith is a 'precondition' for the Spirit.[189] Handlaying, not baptism, is the 'ordinary' means of imparting the Spirit, but this happens 'in close proximity' to baptism.[190] Acts 8, 'does not deny that in the baptism administered by Philip the Samaritans could have received the Holy Spirit in an interior, invisible, sanctifying form'.[191]

David Petts, *The Baptism in the Holy Spirit in Relation to Christian Initiation* (1987)

Petts demonstrates in his literature review that, though Pentecostals believe Baptism in the Holy Spirit (BHS) is subsequent to conversion, they generally believe in 'immediate subsequence'.[192] While delay sometimes occurs, BHS should follow immediately upon conversion so that it is virtually, 'viewed as part of the conversion process'.[193] He finds the same concept in his exegesis of Acts. While he critiques Dunn for overlooking BHS as an empowerment for service,[194] he holds, with Dunn, that Acts 2:38 provides a norm.[195] He denies that Spirit-reception is 'automatic' but also rejects the idea that it is, 'merely available'.[196] Rather, 'at the very least it is to be expected'.[197] Petts holds two concepts in tension. One can be a Christian without BHS, though conversion, 'is not complete without it, but here I am using "conversion" in a wider sense than "regeneration"'.[198] Petts

---

[185] Gonzalo Haya-Prats, trans. Scott A. Ellington, ed. Paul Elbert, *Empowered Believers: The Holy Spirit in the Book of Acts* (Eugene: Cascade, 2011), 52-53. The original Spanish dissertation was first published in French: trans. José J. Romero and Hubert Faes, *L'Esprit, Force de l'Église: Sa nature et son activité d'après les Actes des Apôtres* (Paris: Cerf, 1975).
[186] *Ibid.*, 120, cf. 140.
[187] *Ibid.*, 69, original italics.
[188] *Ibid.*, 138.
[189] *Ibid.*, 144.
[190] *Ibid.*, 52.
[191] *Ibid.*, 150.
[192] David Petts, *Baptism in the Holy Spirit in Relation to Christian Initiation* (M.Th. dissertation, University of Nottingham, 1987), 25.
[193] *Ibid.*, 29. For similar Charismatic views see 33, 35.
[194] *Ibid.*, 50-51.
[195] *Ibid.*, 59.
[196] *Ibid.*, 60.
[197] *Ibid.*
[198] *Ibid.*

requires 'charismatic enduement' for BHS, but he does not here specifically advocate tongues as the *sine qua non* of BHS.[199]

However, in a later work, he affirms tongues as the evidence of Spirit baptism.[200] The immediate subsequence idea continues in Samaria, for there the anomaly is that the Spirit was not received immediately after baptism.[201] Cornelius' house, though different, is not seen as contradicting the normal procedure.[202] The Ephesian disciples illustrate, especially through Paul's question as to whether they received the Spirit 'when' they believed, that belief and Spirit-reception need not be simultaneous.[203] The delay between the Ephesians' baptism in Jesus' name and their receiving the Spirit via Paul's handlaying also fits into Petts' view of 'immediate subsequence'.[204] Petts places BHS clearly within Christian initiation and even within salvation understood more broadly than mere forgiveness of sins.[205]

Robert P. Menzies, *Empowered for Witness: The Spirit in Luke-Acts* (1991)

In contrast to what Turner will later write, Menzies argues that 'Luke never attributes soteriological functions to the Spirit.'[206] Moreover, 'Luke consistently portrays the Spirit as the source of prophetic inspiration, which ... empowers God's people for effective service.'[207] He reasons first that during the intertestamental period, the Spirit was almost entirely separated from salvation. The Spirit was a '*donum superadditum*' that produced prophecy.[208] Second, he argues that Luke worked within this inter-testamental period concept and attributed neither salvific, nor miracle qualities to the Spirit. For Menzies, the early church saw the Spirit as 'charismatic', Paul saw the Spirit as 'soteriological', but Luke saw the Spirit as 'prophetic'.[209] Third, he argues for subsequence and the initial evidence doctrine.[210]

In his analysis of Luke's theology, he separates the Spirit from 'power': 'although Luke can speak of πνεῦμα as the source of δύναμις, the two terms are not synonymous'.[211] John the Baptist's prophecy is understood as originally referring to, 'a deluge of messianic judgment ... the righteous would be separated from

---

[199] *Ibid.*
[200] David Petts, *The Holy Spirit: An Introduction* (Mattersey: Mattersey Hall, 1998), 75.
[201] Petts, *Baptism*, 66.
[202] *Ibid.*, 71.
[203] *Ibid.*, 74.
[204] *Ibid.*, 76.
[205] *Ibid.*, 86-87.
[206] Menzies, *Empowered*, 44.
[207] *Ibid.*
[208] *Ibid.*
[209] *Ibid.*, 45.
[210] *Ibid.*
[211] *Ibid.*, 115.

the wicked by a powerful blast of the Spirit of God, and the latter would be consumed by fire'.[212] Menzies then ties this prophecy to the activity of the post-Pentecost church. 'Luke clearly interprets the sifting activity of the Spirit of which John prophesied to be accomplished in the Spirit-directed mission of the church and its Spirit-inspired proclamation of the gospel.'[213] Furthermore, John's prophecy, 'refers neither to the means by which the individual is purified nor to an event which initiates one into the blessings of the messianic kingdom'.[214]

Luke did not link Jesus' baptism to his Spirit-reception, but rather linked the Spirit to his prayer.[215] The Spirit is not Jesus' 'sonship or messiahship' but the means by which he 'is equipped for his messianic task'.[216] The use of Isaiah in the Nazareth sermon makes no connection between the Spirit and miracles.[217] It, 'highlights preaching as the primary product of Jesus' anointing and the pre-eminent aspect of his mission'.[218] Regarding Jesus' Luke 11 teaching on prayer for the Spirit, Menzies concludes, 'Since it is addressed to Christians, the promise cannot refer to an initiatory or soteriological gift.'[219] Menzies explains Jesus' promise of the Spirit at the end of Luke and beginning of Acts in terms of his separation of Spirit and power: 'δύναμις is mediated by the Spirit but not equivalent to it'.[220]

Regarding Pentecost, Menzies distinguishes his view of the Spirit as 'principally an endowment of power for mission'[221] from other views:

> The disciples receive the Spirit, not as the source of cleansing and a new ability to keep the law, not as a foretaste of the salvation to come, nor as the essential bond by which they (each individual) are linked to God; indeed, not primarily for themselves. Rather ... the disciples receive the Spirit for others.[222]

Contrary to Turner, Sinai is not a background for Pentecost.[223] In addressing the influence of Acts 2:38 on Christian initiation, Menzies believes that Spirit-reception is preceded, under typical circumstances, by repentance and water baptism, and that this was the time when the Spirit was typically received.[224]

Regarding Samaria, Menzies writes that, 'Luke considered the Samaritans to be Christians (i.e. converted) before they received the Spirit.'[225] He sees Luke

---

[212] *Ibid.*, 130.
[213] *Ibid.*, 131.
[214] *Ibid.*
[215] *Ibid.*, 134.
[216] *Ibid.*, 137.
[217] *Ibid.*, 150.
[218] *Ibid.*, 156.
[219] *Ibid.*, 160.
[220] *Ibid.*, 172.
[221] *Ibid.*, 175.
[222] *Ibid.*, 174-75.
[223] *Ibid.*, 189-201.
[224] *Ibid.*, 204.
[225] *Ibid.*

here in contradistinction to other NT writers: 'Luke's account betrays a pneumatology decidedly different from Paul or John, neither of whom could conceive of baptized believers being without the Spirit.'[226] The Spirit is not the *sine qua non* of being a Christian, but rather it is a 'supplementary gift' which members of the church receive after their initiation.[227] Handlaying is a distinct rite intended mainly to commission or to heal, but it can also effect Spirit-reception. Similarly to Lampe, he argues that in Acts 8, handlaying is a 'commissioning ceremony' to 'incorporate the Samaritans, not into the church, but into the missionary enterprise of the church'.[228] In Acts 9, Saul received the Spirit through handlaying and this was commissioning for ministry.[229]

In Acts 10, Menzies argues that Dunn incorrectly identifies the Spirit with μετάνοια, since in Acts 2 repentance comes before Spirit-reception, and the two are separated in 5:31-32.[230] Dunn has no argument in Acts 15:8-9, since it is just a case of 'premise' and 'deduction' and because 'Luke always attributes forgiveness ... to Jesus – never to the Spirit.'[231] Menzies argues that the primary fault with Dunn's equation lies in the fact that Luke made the Spirit a 'gift of prophetic inspiration'.[232] Menzies deals with the Apollos and Ephesus accounts by arguing that Apollos was a Christian who had been a disciple of John and had neither received baptism in Jesus' name, nor learned about Pentecost. The Ephesians were converts of Apollos. Handlaying is commissioning for evangelistic work and impartation of the Spirit.[233] As to Paul's first question, it is Luke's construction and the epistolary Paul would never have asked it.[234] Menzies concludes from Acts 19 that for Luke, the Spirit is not, 'a necessary element in conversion'.[235] Faith/repentance/forgiveness is the meaning of conversion, not Spirit-reception, or baptism. The significance of the Spirit was missionary empowerment: 'The bestowal of the Spirit is God's response to Paul's incorporation of the Ephesians into the missionary enterprise of the church (accomplished through the laying on of hands).'[236] The Ephesian Twelve were part of the Ephesian elders whom Paul exhorted in chapter 20, and therefore the Spirit is presented as equipping them for service. This is the same as at Pentecost, Samaria, Damascus, and Caesarea.[237]

---

[226] *Ibid.*, 206.
[227] *Ibid.*, 211.
[228] *Ibid.*, 212.
[229] *Ibid.*, 214-15.
[230] *Ibid.*, 216.
[231] *Ibid.*, 217.
[232] *Ibid.*, 218.
[233] *Ibid.*, 220.
[234] *Ibid.*, 223.
[235] *Ibid.*, 224.
[236] *Ibid.*
[237] *Ibid.*, 225.

Finally, Menzies addresses subsequence and initial evidence. 'Luke's pneumatology is *different* from – although *complementary* to – that of Paul.'[238] For Luke, the Spirit is a prophetic gift which is not part of conversion-initiation. This is the heart of Menzies' argument. 'The judgment that the gift is distinct from conversion is rooted in the gift's function: it provides power for witness, not justification or cleansing.'[239] Regarding the initial evidence of Spirit baptism, Menzies appeals to systematic theology and writes that it is not a biblical-theology question, nor a question which the New Testament asks. Though Luke tightly links the Spirit to inspired speech,[240] no New Testament writer makes an argument for tongues as the initial evidence. However, 'if we ask the question concerning 'initial physical evidence' of Luke, tongues-speech uniquely 'fits the bill' because of its intrinsically demonstrative character'.[241]

Max Turner, *Power from on High: The Spirit in Israel's Restoration and Witness in Luke-Acts* (1996)

In Part I, Turner does an extensive literature review. Out of that review, two key issues related to this book's goals arise: (1) 'Did all really manifest naked supernatural power?'[242] (2) Is the Spirit a *donum superadditum*?[243] For Turner, however, the primary question is different:

> Is the Spirit received as the source of eschatological 'life' and 'sonship' (accommodating Jesus' baptismal experience to what Paul would probably say of ordinary Christian conversion/initiation), or is the Spirit received as the empowering of the Christian mission (accommodating the apostles' experience at Pentecost, and that of all future Christians at their baptism, to Jesus' baptismal anointing with the Spirit)?[244]

He also asks whether Luke presented the Spirit as a person to be experienced. Sub-questions to that are: Did Luke go beyond the OT literature? Was Luke any different from rabbinic literature?

Turner's answer to the meaning of personal language about the Spirit is that it is, 'a metaphorical way of referring to the *inception* of a specific new activity, or coherent set of activities, believed to be initiated in and through the person concerned'.[245] For Luke, no one receives the Spirit 'as a person'.[246] Jesus himself had two distinct 'receivings' of the Spirit, and Turner argues that the Christian experience is different from both.

---

[238] *Ibid.*, 238, original italics.
[239] *Ibid.*, 239.
[240] *Ibid.*, 250.
[241] *Ibid.*, 251.
[242] Turner, *Power*, 25.
[243] *Ibid.*, 21.
[244] *Ibid.*, 35.
[245] *Ibid.*, 47, original italics.
[246] *Ibid.*

Given that receiving the Spirit means a new set of activities, Turner then asks again whether these activities relate to sonship or to missional empowerment.[247] Turner considers Dunn's argument and sums up his evaluation with asking whether Ezekiel 36 forms a foundational source for Luke. Turner answers that it does not. Luke rather based his understanding on Isaiah 61:1-2, which, 'looks much more like an "empowering" to effect salvation for others, than the means of Jesus' own enjoyment of "new covenant life" and "sonship"'.[248] Joel 3 (MT; LXX) forms the source material for the disciples and the Spirit. Ultimately, 'Dunn has read Luke's pneumatology through Pauline spectacles.'[249] Turner surveys a variety of other scholars, but the question to which he always returns is whether the Spirit functions ethically and soteriologically, or whether the Spirit functions as empowerment for mission. He does not see this problem resolved in the literature.

In Part II, Turner reviews the literature of Judaism with respect to the concept of the 'Spirit of prophecy', and concludes that Menzies and Schweizer understand the Spirit of prophecy too narrowly. It does have social, ethical, and soteriological connotations. In Part III, Turner engages the New Testament narrative and presents a corporate, rather than merely individual, concept of salvation:

> 'salvation' (for Luke) is not merely entry to the remnant messianic community, release from guilt, and assurance of life in some new creation beyond this one … but also ongoing participation in the worship, life and witness of the restored Davidic community which is increasingly cleansed and transformed in history to become a 'light to the Gentiles'.[250]

From this analysis, he asks if the Spirit is soteriologically necessary. Turner presses the argument against Menzies from Luke 1:35. In Jesus' birth accomplished by the Spirit, there is both the Spirit as miracle working power, and the Spirit as ethical influence, for Turner understands the passage to mean that because of the Spirit's involvement in the birth, Jesus will be called 'holy'.[251] Turner repeatedly points out the significance of this miracle of the Spirit being at the beginning of Luke's narrative.[252] Turner argues that the prophetic declarations of Luke 1-2 praise God 'for salvation *already* wrought' and that therefore the idea of Luke 1-2 as the first part of a three stage history of salvation is not possible.[253] Turner does not accept the idea that Luke 1-2 represents prophecy renewed. Rather it is normal prophetic activity for Judaism.[254]

---

[247] *Ibid.*
[248] *Ibid.*, 52.
[249] *Ibid.*
[250] *Ibid.*, 145.
[251] *Ibid.*, 158.
[252] *Ibid.*, 158, 162.
[253] *Ibid.*, 163, original italics.
[254] *Ibid.*, 164.

Turner rejects the Classical Pentecostal view of the Spirit as a *donum superadditum*, as well as the sacramental view that the Spirit is imparted in the water.[255] Jesus' experience of the Spirit is not his 'Spirit baptism', since Turner understands that as an act of cleansing the nation.[256] Jesus' temptation is a New Exodus type experience in which the Spirit actively aids him.[257] Jesus' Nazareth sermon is also New Exodus and a 'fusion of Davidic, servant and Mosaic Christologies'.[258] The sermon, 'most probably means the Spirit-anointed Isaianic Soteriological Prophet inaugurates the "New Exodus"'.[259] Turner, similarly to von Baer,[260] sees New Exodus Moses-like liberation rather than avoidance of Spirit as miracle worker in the Luke 11:20 'finger of God' saying.[261] The actual healings of 7:21, plus the link back to the Nazareth sermon in 7:22, clearly connect the Spirit to physical miracles, not just preaching.[262] Acts 10:38 further supports this reading.[263] Turner distinguishes himself from Dunn, arguing that Jordan was not Jesus' own entrance into the new covenant, but was his reception of power enabling him to bring New Exodus deliverance to Israel.[264]

Sinai forms a background to the Pentecost story.[265] From Pentecost on, the Spirit mediates the presence of the ascended Jesus.[266] Were the disciples 'saved' at Pentecost, as Dunn had argued? Turner answers no. Pentecost 'was the *continuation* of what Jesus 'began' to do and to teach (cf. Acts 1.1) with greater power, rather than a decisive new beginning'.[267] The disciples, in fact, experienced the Spirit indirectly before Pentecost in the ministry of Jesus. But the power and authenticity of this mediated experience of the Spirit Turner does not wish to diminish.[268] He affirms the Pentecostal emphasis upon the Spirit as power for witness. However, the Spirit also does other activities besides witnessing. Turner rejects the position that assigns the Spirit solely to the task of witness. Correspondingly, empowerment was not the main effect of the Spirit upon all believers.[269]

A key concept for Turner is that 'salvation' extends beyond forgiveness of sins and even beyond belonging to the body of redeemed believers. Rather,

---

[255] *Ibid.*, 175-76.
[256] *Ibid.*, 201.
[257] *Ibid.*, 204.
[258] *Ibid.*, 248.
[259] *Ibid.*, 249.
[260] Von Baer, though, does not reference a 'New' Exodus, *Geist*, 135-36.
[261] Turner, *Power*, 255-59.
[262] *Ibid.*, 260-61.
[263] *Ibid.*, 264.
[264] *Ibid.*, 266.
[265] *Ibid.*, 279-89.
[266] *Ibid.*, 306.
[267] *Ibid.*, 331-32, original italics.
[268] *Ibid.*, 333-37.
[269] *Ibid.*, 343-45.

it means the inbreaking kingdom of God, God's self-revealing reconciling and redeeming presence in strength bringing to fulfillment the liberating, radical cleansing and transformation of Israel in accordance with Isaianic hopes for Israel's New Exodus.[270]

He sees the language of Acts 2:4 as indicating a moment of '*invasive* inspiration of the Spirit'.[271] Tongues cannot be argued as 'paradigmatic and normative'.[272] Acts 2:38-39 is the norm. The Spirit is normally given 'to those who repent and are baptized'.[273]

In regards to Samaria, Turner rejects a number of positions: the idea of poorly edited sources, the claim that the Samaritans did not really believe, the argument that it was only the charismata of the Spirit that were given through the apostles, Quesnel's argument for 'two historically distinct initiation paradigms',[274] a narrative argument for a '"forerunner-culminator" typology', and the Pentecostal power to witness as a *donum superadditum*. Samaria is 'anomalous' but not impossible, since the Samaritans were experiencing the salvation wrought by the Spirit in the ministry of Philip.[275] In Acts 9, Turner sees no subsequence, because he distinguishes between 'christological faith' and 'conversional *commitment*'.[276] He also argues that the laying on of hands was no commissioning of Saul, but was probably for healing and not for Spirit-reception, which took place at baptism, as in Acts 2:38.[277]

Regarding Cornelius' house, there is scholarly agreement that Luke compared the Gentile Spirit experience with the day of Pentecost. Turner disagrees with Dunn, arguing that the Spirit is not the same as forgiveness. Forgiveness is the Acts 2:38 'condition' for impartation of the Spirit.[278] However, he draws upon 15:8-9 to affirm Dunn and the soteriological necessity of the Spirit for the Gentiles.[279] Regarding Apollos and the Ephesians, Apollos had the Holy Spirit[280] and the Ephesians were only John's disciples, and not Christians in any sense.[281] Paul's question is seen to reinforce the Acts 2:38 norm. Turner affirms that, 'Luke expects this matter of having received the Spirit *to be a matter of immediate perception*.'[282] The specific moment of reception of the Spirit during conversion-initiation could be expected to have had no particular marker and the recipient would not have been aware of it *because the whole conversion event is such*

---

[270] *Ibid.*, 346.
[271] *Ibid.*, 357, original italics.
[272] *Ibid.*
[273] *Ibid.*, 358.
[274] *Ibid.*, 369.
[275] *Ibid.*, 173-75, cf. 374.
[276] *Ibid.*, 375, original italics.
[277] *Ibid.*, 376-77.
[278] *Ibid.*, 382.
[279] *Ibid.*, 387.
[280] *Ibid.*, 389.
[281] *Ibid.*, 390.
[282] *Ibid.*, 392, original italics.

a powerful experience.[283] Tongues, while they may evidence the Spirit and can be 'an' evidence, and can be viewed as normal, are not 'the' evidence, not normative, because the text does not say that every Ephesian spoke in tongues, only that the group manifested the phenomena. Again, since tongues and prophecy are both mentioned, there is no single normative phenomenon. He sides with Dunn in that,

> conversion, baptism and reception of the 'Spirit of prophecy' formed a single 'conversion-initiation' unit of closely related *theologoumena*. Within it, baptism was the central rite through which the person who repented and came to faith expressed and crystallized these.[284]

The water itself does not effect the transfer of the Spirit, 'rather the Spirit is given to conversional faith, expressed in baptism'[285] with allowance made for the exceptional impartation of the Spirit before or after water baptism. If faith and water baptism do not impart the Spirit then that constitutes an 'anomalous' situation to be rectified.[286] He argues specifically against Classical Pentecostal subsequence, saying that salvation encompassed the broader life of the community and that the Spirit was part-and-parcel with this community life and therefore necessary for salvation so defined.[287] Finally, he again argues that in Luke-Acts, tongues are not the *normative* initial evidence of Spirit-reception, because the argument for this is 'largely inferential' and the evidence 'fragmentary'.[288]

Ju Hur, *A Dynamic Reading of the Holy Spirit in Luke-Acts* (2001)

Hur undertakes a narrative critical reading of the Spirit in Luke-Acts. He aims to uncover, 1) 'the literary traits of the Holy Spirit', 2) 'the literary repertoire' for Luke's citations from the Hebrew Scriptures, 3) 'the theological significance of the Spirit in Luke-Acts', and 4) the significance of 'the interaction between (implied) author/narrator, text and (implied) reader'.[289] Hur cautions, however, 'it would be inappropriate to look at Luke-Acts as a theological treatise about the doctrine of the Holy Spirit'.[290] Hur reviews the Hebrew Scriptures and the Dead Sea Scrolls (DSS) to find the literary repertoire of the Spirit. In the Hebrew Scriptures, the Spirit belongs to YHWH, is given to certain leaders, produces a variety of phenomena including prophecy and miracles, is presented 'as *the source or sustaining power for the Israelites' religio-ethical life*', and is a future promise

---

[283] *Ibid.*, 448.
[284] *Ibid.*, 397.
[285] *Ibid.*, 398.
[286] *Ibid.*
[287] *Ibid.*, 445.
[288] *Ibid.*, 447.
[289] Hur, *Reading*, 33-34.
[290] *Ibid.*, 28.

The Timing, Mechanism & Manifestation of Spirit Reception in Luke-Acts

for the Messiah as well as the Israelite nation.²⁹¹ In the DSS, the Spirit only occasionally is a source of prophetic inspiration, 'but the DSS regard the Spirit as the essential (soteriological?) gift in every member of the community'.

Hur addresses the issue of reliability which becomes methodologically significant for drawing conclusions from the narrative. Luke's narrator is reliable and authoritative for three reasons. He is aligned with God, with Jesus God's Messiah, and with the Holy Spirit. Luke's ideology is theocentric, christocentric, and pneumocentric.²⁹² Hur writes, 'if any characters' speeches or actions are approved or sanctioned by the narrator, the readers, consciously or unconsciously, consider them reliable and authoritative'.²⁹³

Hur only rarely touches upon the matter of initiation. However, he does assert that, 'there is no consistent relationship between the endowment of the Spirit and baptism or laying on of hands'.²⁹⁴ Prayer is significantly related to Spirit-reception, but does not cause it.²⁹⁵ The Spirit is sovereignly bestowed by God apart from 'human efforts'.²⁹⁶ Employment of A.J. Greimas' actantial model has God as Sender, reception of the Spirit as Object, people of God as Receiver, 'Jewish believers' preoccupation and reluctance?' as Opponent, the will of God as Subject, and God 'in response to prayer' as Helper.²⁹⁷ Hur explicitly rejects Menzies' view that the Spirit is given to the Samaritans as missionary empowerment.²⁹⁸

Hur again utilizes Greimas to analyse the key Spirit-reception passages (Acts 8, 10-11, 15, 19). Moving forward from Acts 2, '*the Spirit also begins to function as verifying certain group-characters (unnamed) as incorporated into God's (eschatological) community*'.²⁹⁹ Hur asserts that in these stories, tongues, prophecy, and praise, because they remind the reader of Pentecost, 'serve to signify (to reliable characters [i.e. Peter and John; Peter; Paul] and readers) that they receive the Spirit and are thus accepted by God'.³⁰⁰ Acts 2:38-39 is the 'governing passage' that helps the reader know that all groups who receive the Spirit are validated as God's people.³⁰¹

Based upon the discussion of theocentric, christocentric and pneumocentric ideology and upon actantial analysis, Hur draws the following series of conclusions. The Christian implied reader 'may be led to expect' that the Spirit would provide 'charismatic gifts', help in persecution, and establish community leadership. 'Readers may also be led to recognize that they are saved or verified as

---

²⁹¹ *Ibid.*, 72-73, original italics.
²⁹² *Ibid.*, 98-101.
²⁹³ *Ibid.*, 113.
²⁹⁴ *Ibid.*, 270.
²⁹⁵ *Ibid.*
²⁹⁶ *Ibid.*, 270-71.
²⁹⁷ *Ibid.*, 271.
²⁹⁸ *Ibid.*, 240.
²⁹⁹ *Ibid.*, 276, original italics.
³⁰⁰ *Ibid.* Brackets [ ] original in text.
³⁰¹ *Ibid.*

God's people through their personal experience of "baptism in the Holy Spirit" in some extraordinary ways, e.g. speaking in tongues or prophesying.'[302]

Friedrich Avemarie, *Die Tauferzählungen der Apostelgeschichte: Theologie und Geschichte* (2002)

While not every report of conversion in Acts includes a baptism, baptism is simply understood. Baptism is the normal situation for Christians, and it is deviance from this which Luke tended to mention.[303] Individually, baptism is a rite of passage, understood 'as admission into a new life-context'.[304] Contrary to Turner, the Ephesians were Christians who had only received John's baptism. Avemarie differed greatly from Dunn in that he argued, 'Belief and baptism in Jesus' name normally belong close together, but remain in their togetherness differentiated from one another.'[305] In the early church, a 'baptism of John' for repentance was practiced which did not impart the Spirit, as well as the regular baptism in Jesus' name.[306] Whereas Apollos had the Spirit and was not rebaptised, the Ephesians lacked the Spirit and therefore had to be rebaptised. However, this episode has no normative value. It is an exception.[307]

Acts 2:38-39 were seen to be paradigmatic. Moreover, 'that [Acts 2:38-39] also delivers the model for the connection between baptism and Spirit-reception'.[308] Since Luke did not explicitly describe the coming of the Spirit on the 3000 baptised converts, Avemarie, contrary to Turner, did *not* see it as necessarily implied that they received the Spirit.[309] Instead, 'paradoxically', Acts 8, 10, and 19 show that Luke believed Spirit-reception in fact 'belongs' to water baptism.[310] In the complex event of conversion and initiation, it is baptism which is associated with the giving of the Spirit. Paul's question to the Ephesians about their baptism supports this.[311]

In response to the Pentecostal argument that tongues and prophecy accompany Spirit-reception, and that the Spirit is for missionary empowerment, Avemarie asked in return whether the association of Spirit-reception with water baptism automatically excludes this empowerment emphasis.[312] He affirmed the prophetic, charismatic nature of the Spirit in Acts. But, he did not expect all to be

---

[302] *Ibid.*, 284.
[303] Avemarie, *Tauferzählungen*, 44.
[304] 'als Eintritt in einen neuen Lebenskontext', *Ibid.*, 49.
[305] 'Glaube und Taufe auf Jesu Namen gehören normalerweise eng zusammen, bleiben aber in ihrer Zusammengehörigkeit voneinander unterschieden', *Ibid.*, 73.
[306] *Ibid.*, 78-79.
[307] *Ibid.*, 81.
[308] 'dass [Acts 2:38-39] auch für die Verbindung von Taufe und Geistempfang das Modell liefert', *Ibid.*, 139.
[309] *Ibid.*, 139. Similarly, John F. MacArthur Jr., *Charismatic Chaos* (Grand Rapids: Zondervan, 1992), 217.
[310] Avemarie, *Tauferzählungen*, 140.
[311] *Ibid.*, 143.
[312] *Ibid.*, 144.

missionaries, since Luke did not describe all as missionaries. In particular, at Ephesus, Caesarea, and Samaria there was no missionary thrust.[313] Tongues are not unintelligible, but rather known languages.[314] They are not evidence of Spirit-reception, since Luke did not consistently repeat the connection between Spirit-reception and xenolalia.[315]

Avemarie challenged Dunn's assertion that Spirit impartation and forgiveness of sins are equated. The function of the Spirit to produce visions, dreams and prophecy indicates that the Spirit is not the medium of forgiveness. For such a serious claim, Avemarie expected 'clear text-signals', and, he wrote, there are not.[316] He addressed Dunn's argument from the Cornelius story, especially 15:8-9, saying that, 'the gift of the Spirit is not equated with the salvation event'.[317] Instead, salvation is located in the grace of the Lord Jesus.[318]

Avemarie next asked about the validity of Turner's broader definition of salvation as the New Exodus restoration of Israel and arrival of the kingdom of God, and whether Spirit-reception is therefore necessary to salvation. He raised fundamental concerns regarding Turner's thesis, asserting: 'the thesis appears afflicted with certain methodological and content weaknesses'.[319] He argued that it is careless to accept Turner's thesis without more in-depth examination, but that he was unable to carry out such a complete evaluation of the thesis within the confines of his work. However, he requested proof that Luke intended to discuss a 'collective' concept of salvation as well as an individual concept.[320]

He did not accept Menzies' argument for a separation of Spirit empowered words from non-Spirit empowered deeds. Comparison of Luke 4:18 and Acts 10:38 disproved that.[321] However, that Jesus, anointed with the Spirit, brought salvation to others, does not require Christians to have the Spirit in order to experience salvation when just a few Spirit anointed preachers could bring salvation to them. He recognized the role that the theme of salvation for Israel plays, and found it inappropriate to limit Luke's discussion of salvation to simply that of the individual. However, he did not find a direct connection between the work of the Spirit and this national salvation in the Gospel of Luke, though there is a connection in the book of Acts.[322] Avemarie did see a sense in which the Spirit is soteriologically necessary: 'the Spirit represents the future salvation'.[323] He

---

[313] *Ibid.*, 145-46.
[314] *Ibid.*, 146.
[315] *Ibid.*, 147.
[316] 'eindeutige Textsignale', *Ibid.*, 151.
[317] 'die Geistgabe mit dem Rettungsgeschehen nicht gleichgesetzt wird', *Ibid.*, 152.
[318] *Ibid.*
[319] 'die These mit gewissen methodischen und inhaltlichen Schwächen behaftet scheint', *Ibid.*, 154.
[320] *Ibid.*
[321] *Ibid.*, 155.
[322] *Ibid.*, 156.
[323] 'repräsentiert der Geist das künftige Heil', *Ibid.*, 160.

wrote, 'it is indeed not the salvation itself, it also does not anticipate it, nevertheless it leads preparatively to it and can, in this sense, also be conceived of as 'necessary' to the salvation'.[324] He could not see that Luke intended to portray every normal baptismal Spirit-reception as an equipping for witness and participation in salvation history.[325] Nor is the Spirit the cause of miracles in Acts.[326] Salvation and healing are attributed to the name of Jesus.[327]

Avemarie was ultimately uncertain when it comes to the question of baptism and laying on of hands. With which, exactly, is the coming of the Spirit connected? In regards to Ephesus, both the sequence of the report, and the presence of the genitive absolute indicate that Luke linked the impartation of the Spirit to handlaying. Uncharacteristically, Avemarie was somewhat unclear when speaking of Acts 8. He reasoned, 'In the Samaria-pericope this connection is without question',[328] and then went on to say that in reporting Simon's observation that the Spirit was given by laying on of hands, Luke simply gave Simon's viewpoint, not his own theology.[329] He noted – though with the caution that it is difficult to determine the relationship between Jesus' baptism and that of Christians – that both for Jesus and the Samaritans, the Spirit was given in connection with prayer.[330] However, he did not see the presence of prayer and handlaying as in any way disturbing the link between baptism and Spirit-reception.[331] Water and handlaying both, at the same time, lead to Spirit-reception and this fact defeats the confirmationist position.

Avemarie understood that Dunn no longer held to his argument against subsequence in Samaria, and therefore quickly summarized Dunn's old argument and refuted each point briefly.[332] He questioned the position that the Samaritans did not receive the Spirit because Philip was not an apostle. Ananias was also not an apostle, yet through his ministry the Spirit came to Saul. It does not logically follow to say that because Simon observed that through apostles' hands the Spirit was given, only apostles can give the Spirit.[333] Avemarie continued to wrestle with the question of why the Spirit was not given immediately in baptism. If it was to reconcile the Samaritan with the Jewish church, then why did not Luke also delay the baptism until apostles could be present? He was unsatisfied with

---

[324] 'er ist zwar nicht das Heil selbst, antizipiert es auch nicht, doch führt er vorbereitend darauf zu und kann in diesem Sinne auch als 'notwendig' zum Heil begriffen werden', *Ibid.*

[325] *Ibid.*

[326] *Ibid.*, 161-62.

[327] *Ibid.*, 162.

[328] 'In der Samaria-Perikope steht diese Verbindung außer Frage', *Ibid.*, 165.

[329] *Ibid.*

[330] *Ibid.*, 165-66.

[331] *Ibid.*, 166.

[332] *Ibid.*, 199-70.

[333] *Ibid.*, 172.

any attempt to explain it. He simply acknowledges that Luke himself accepted it as a fact.[334]

The case of the separation of baptism and Spirit-reception at Cornelius' house Avemarie saw as a much simpler problem. If Acts 2:38 is the model, then Acts 10 is in fact 'deviant', but it is explainable because of the direct intervention of God. If Saul received the Spirit through Ananias' handlaying then that is also a divergence from Acts 2:38. He concluded that the sequence of baptism and Spirit-reception may be secondary. Luke could have used the sequence of Acts 2:38 because it was a pattern common to him. However, Avemarie added that Acts 2:38 really represents Luke's theological position.[335]

Youngmo Cho, *Spirit and Kingdom in the Writings of Luke and Paul: An Attempt to Reconcile these Concepts* (2005)

Cho uses the topic of the kingdom of God to compare the views of Luke and Paul on the Spirit. He argues that for Paul, the Spirit is 'the means by which all may participate in the blessings of the kingdom in the present'.[336] For Luke, however, 'the Spirit inspires the proclamation of the kingdom of God and in this way, the Spirit makes it possible for people to enter the kingdom of God'.[337] In Cho's analysis of the baptism of Jesus he finds that Luke focused upon Jesus' prayer and portrays the Spirit in a physical manifestation. The Spirit endows Jesus with power for ministry. The Spirit is not the means by which he calls God his Father.[338]

Cho addresses the relationship between conversion and Spirit-reception in Acts. In Acts 2:38-39, repentance and baptism are prerequisites to the gift of the Spirit and therefore, the Spirit is to be understood as given to the already converted, rather than part of conversion. Moreover, Acts 8 and 10 separate the Spirit from baptism and therefore, 'any attempt to forge a link between the bestowal of the Spirit and conversion experience from Acts 2:38 is unwarranted'.[339] Acts 2:38 is not 'a paradigm for a conversion-initiation pattern'.[340] Cho looks at Lukan redactions of Peter's Pentecost speech to identify what is the 'promise of the Father'. He notes that in 2:17, λέγει ὁ θεός identifies the Joel promise as God's promise. The addition of μου in 2:18 indicates that the gift is given to *God's* male and female servants. In 2:18, καὶ προφητεύσουσιν emphasizes the prophetic nature of the gift of the Spirit. Cho therefore argues that Luke identified the promise of 2:39 specifically with 'the promise of prophetic power'.[341]

---

[334] *Ibid.*, 173.
[335] *Ibid.*, 174.
[336] Youngmo Cho, *Spirit and Kingdom in the Writings of Luke and Paul: An Attempt to Reconcile these Concepts* (Milton Keynes: Paternoster, 2005), 12.
[337] *Ibid.*
[338] *Ibid.*, 115-16.
[339] *Ibid.*, 142.
[340] *Ibid.*
[341] *Ibid.*, 145.

With regards to Samaria, Cho argues that it is positive evidence that the Spirit is not part of salvation, but a subsequent event. Cho argues that the Acts 8 separation of baptism from receiving the Spirit is not atypical of Luke, but typical, and cites Luke 3:21-22, Acts 9:17-19 and Acts 10:44-48. Acts 19:1-7 is also cited as distinguishing conversion from the Spirit.[342] Regarding Damascus, Cho views the Spirit falling when Ananias laid hands upon Saul and questions the link between Saul's salvation and his receiving the Spirit. Rather, the Spirit was given to empower Saul.[343]

Caesarea shows the separation of Spirit and baptism. Cho is uncertain about the precise moment of the Gentiles' conversion and the function of the Spirit in that conversion. Cho finds the clear element is the prophetic, Spirit-prompted speech and this is what Luke presented as being comparable to Pentecost. The Ephesians Cho finds to be 'an eschatological community of believers in Jesus'. He argues that, 'the direct motivation for the disciples' re-baptism is not 'believing in the Messiah', but rather 'believing in the Spirit-giving Messiah' in the end time'.[344] Thus, the Spirit is not tied to conversion.

Randall A. Harrison, *L'Esprit dans le Récit de Luc: Une Recherche de Cohérence dans la Pneumatologie de L'Auteur Implicite de Luc-Actes* (2007)

Harrison seeks to show that Luke was coherent in his presentation of the Spirit in Luke-Acts, though he is careful to say that Luke did not directly teach on the Spirit, and his doctrine must be inferred from the text.[345] Given Luke's skill and interest in the Spirit, there is no reason to believe that he would leave incoherent data in the text.[346] For Harrison, the main point of incoherence is the apparent discrepancy between Peter's assurance that the Spirit will be given upon repentance and baptism, and the various other cases in Acts where the Spirit arrives subsequent to repentance and baptism. This is only problematic if we take Acts 2:38-39 as a 'norm'. This happens because interpreters wrongly import the theologies of Paul and John into Luke.[347] He labels Dunn with this error. Turner's support for a 'norm' is attacked as an argument from silence. Harrison argues that the other Spirit-reception stories in Acts do not follow this "norm," and therefore Luke did not have a 'norm'. Recognizing that Luke understood the Spirit as able to come either at the moment of faith or subsequent to faith eliminates the incoherence in Luke-Acts. It is not possible to reconcile Luke with John and Paul, and Luke should simply be understood on his own terms.[348] Harrison does not hold to tongues as initial evidence, viewing tongues as supplemented by various other manifestations, but he does argue that the Spirit in Luke-Acts is

---

[342] *Ibid.*, 148.
[343] *Ibid.*, 149-50.
[344] *Ibid.*, 159.
[345] Harrison, *L'Esprit*, 383.
[346] *Ibid.*, 341.
[347] *Ibid.*, 308.
[348] *Ibid.*, 395.

always perceptible.³⁴⁹ Harrison reads Turner as putting forward a non-perceptible argument based on the idea of automatic reception of the Spirit at conversion and argues that this introduces incoherence into Luke's work and therefore must be discarded.³⁵⁰ As to the means of receiving the Spirit, handlaying is one means, but not the only necessary means.³⁵¹

Clayton David Robinson, *The Laying on of Hands: With Special Reference to the Reception of the Holy Spirit in the New Testament* (2008)

Pentecost and Cornelius' house are exceptional cases, but descriptions of conferral of the Spirit represent regular practice. In these regular descriptions, 'at no time does Luke give an example of Spirit bestowal in baptism *apart* from handlaying'.³⁵² Robinson raises the possibility, though 'tenuous', that Jesus' upraised hands in Luke 24 were a corporate handlaying which effected the coming of the Spirit at Pentecost.³⁵³ Robinson asks how, if the Spirit in Acts is soteriological, could it be conferred by a later ritual handlaying? He answers that the Spirit could therefore not be soteriological, but must be distinct from conversion. The grammar of Acts 2:38 requires salvation to be a 'prerequisite' to Spirit-reception.³⁵⁴ Acts 2:38 does not guarantee automatic Spirit-reception because, 'Luke does not establish a direct link between baptism and the Spirit elsewhere in Acts.'³⁵⁵

Regarding Samaria, Spirit-reception was not, 'automatic with either faith or baptism'.³⁵⁶ Robinson tries to view the situation from the perspective of readers already familiar with handlaying initiation.³⁵⁷ He has no answer as to why Philip did not lay hands on the Samaritans, nor does he want to convey the idea of apostles having control over the Spirit. Rather, he sees handlaying as, 'somewhere between an efficacious symbol and an intensified form of prayer'.³⁵⁸ Since Luke gave no indication that handlaying was an exceptional practice, it must be seen as normal and typical.³⁵⁹ With Saul's case, Robinson sees him reaching faith prior to being prayed for by Ananias. The text does not indicate that, 'Luke felt the usage of the gesture was unusual.'³⁶⁰ Therefore, for Luke's time, handlaying was 'normal'. Ananias was not an apostle and, thus, others than apostles could

---

³⁴⁹ *Ibid.*, 283.
³⁵⁰ *Ibid.*, 300-302.
³⁵¹ *Ibid.*, 371-72.
³⁵² Clayton David Robinson, *The Laying on of Hands: With Special Reference to the Reception of the Holy Spirit in the New Testament* (Ann Arbor: ProQuest, 2008), 208, original italics.
³⁵³ *Ibid.*, 210.
³⁵⁴ *Ibid.*, 213-14.
³⁵⁵ *Ibid.*, 215.
³⁵⁶ *Ibid.*, 237.
³⁵⁷ *Ibid.*, 237-38.
³⁵⁸ *Ibid.*, 239.
³⁵⁹ *Ibid.*, 260.
³⁶⁰ *Ibid.*, 242.

lay on hands for Spirit-reception.[361] In the Ephesian case, Robinson again argues for the normality of handlaying: 'the natural manner by which Luke relates handlaying without further comment implies that he expected the reader to understand handlaying was normally performed after baptism to bestow the Spirit'.[362] He continues, 'while a separation between faith, baptism, and the gift of the Spirit might hypothetically exist, the separation would be more in theory than actual practice, as initiates would receive handlaying for the Spirit *as part of their Christian-initiation*'.[363] Robinson applies the same narrative exegesis to the question of how regularly charisma manifested. He notes that Luke did not give any signal of surprise at the charismata manifesting and therefore such manifestations must have been normal.[364]

Randal J. Hedlun, *The Social Function of Glossolalia in Acts with Special Attention to the Ephesian Disciples Pericope (Acts 18:24-19:7)* (2009)

Hedlun asserts that 'the Jesus movement increasingly understood glossolalia as a pre-eminent new marker of qualification for inclusion in the purity in-group and, therefore, that circumcision serves sociologically as an interpretive paradigm of glossolalia'.[365] Luke was attempting to legitimate the acceptance of the Gentiles over against a Judaizing Christian group which did not allow Gentiles to receive the Holy Spirit evidenced by glossolalia.[366]

He argues that in the revelation to Zecharias in the Temple, 'God's initiation of the Jesus movement can be traced to this point in the Israelite symbolic universe.'[367] The Temple played a highlighted role in Luke-Acts.[368] The temple's initial validity is affirmed but then, 'The Pentecost account in the first chapters of Acts narrates the relocation of the divine presence to the collectivity of the Jesus group.'[369] Hedlun sees this in legitimation terms, not just as a transition.[370] He writes, 'How did Luke resolve the conceptual dissonance generated by changes in Yahweh's nexus and mode of interaction with creation? He addresses the perceived dissonance with Israel's history by locating speech events at key points in the narrative.'[371]

He further argues that 'the mark of purity classification is glossolalia, which in the Cornelius episode clearly superseded circumcision as the boundary

---

[361] *Ibid.*
[362] *Ibid.*, 255.
[363] *Ibid.*, original italics.
[364] *Ibid.*, 258.
[365] Randall J. Hedlun, *The Social Function of Glossolalia in Acts with Special Attention to the Ephesian Disciples Pericope (Acts 18:24-19:7)* (Ph.D. dissertation, University of South Africa, 2009), 35.
[366] *Ibid.*, 34.
[367] *Ibid.*, 66.
[368] *Ibid.*, 63-64.
[369] *Ibid.*, 64.
[370] *Ibid.*
[371] *Ibid.*, 83.

marker'.[372] This was especially so for Gentile converts, and this explains why glossolalia was not recorded with the Samaritans or Saul, since they were all already circumcised.[373] 'Just as circumcision qualified a Gentile Yahwism convert for initiation into the social world of the Israelites, so glossolalia qualified Gentile converts to the Jesus movement for similar initiation.'[374] Hedlun restates Peter in 10:47, 'These have already crossed our boundaries into contact with holiness. How can we refuse to ritually solemnize what is already their obvious and God-ascribed status as in-group members?'[375] In short, Hedlun argues that glossolalia is a boundary marker.[376]

William P. Atkinson, *Baptism in the Spirit: Luke-Acts and the Dunn Debate* (2011)

As the title explains, Atkinson reviews the debate surrounding Pentecostal responses to Dunn's exegesis of Luke-Acts. Atkinson disagrees with Dunn regarding the meaning of Jesus' Spirit-reception. It is not Jesus' entry into the new covenant, but rather his anointing for service. In this limited sense, then, Jesus' anointing is a pattern for Christians, who are anointed by the Spirit for ministry to the world.[377] Dunn's argument that the disciples only entered the new covenant at Pentecost is undermined by Turner who shows disciples experiencing 'new covenant blessings' before Pentecost.[378]

Just as von Baer noted the structural importance of Acts 1:8,[379] Atkinson emphasizes its narratological importance as even surpassing that of Acts 2.[380] Contrary to Turner, Atkinson sees all Christians as needing empowerment and being called to evangelize.[381] He praises Menzies' observation that Luke redactionally emphasized '*my* servants' in Acts 2, thus making the Spirit a gift to individuals already within the people of God – thus emphasizing the Pentecostal doctrine of subsequence. Moreover, Luke added, 'and they will prophesy', emphasizing the charismatic function of the gift.[382] To demonstrate further Lukan separation of belief and Spirit-reception, he appeals not just to Samaria, where Dunn has to some degree capitulated, but, following Petts, also to Paul's first question to the Ephesians.[383] However, he does not see Spirit-reception as here represented apart

---

[372] *Ibid.*, 115.
[373] *Ibid.*, 118.
[374] *Ibid.*, 119.
[375] *Ibid.*, 120.
[376] *Ibid.*, 134.
[377] William P. Atkinson, *Baptism in the Spirit: Luke-Acts and the Dunn Debate* (Eugene: Pickwick, 2011), 30, 63, 124.
[378] *Ibid.*, 64.
[379] Von Baer, *Geist*, 85.
[380] Atkinson, *Baptism*, 124.
[381] *Ibid.*, 130.
[382] *Ibid.*, 52-53.
[383] *Ibid.*, 44, 65.

from Christian initiation.[384] He rejects the Pentecostal attempt to find subsequence in the case of Saul's conversion.[385] He rejects Dunn's equivalence of Spirit and cleansing/repentance/forgiveness, following Menzies that repentance is the precondition for Spirit-reception, and not identical with it.[386]

For Atkinson, Spirit baptism belongs to Christian initiation. He recognizes 'Christian beginnings' as being a process, but not one that would last for months. Such delays are atypical and in need of correction. Though he sees Spirit baptism as typically occurring around the time of water baptism, he does not see the water itself as communicating the Spirit.[387] Atkinson does not accept arguments for tongues as the initial evidence, but argues that, 'any appropriate charismatic activity or ability is surely sufficient evidence that [individuals] have experienced their "personal Pentecost"'.[388] Like Turner, Atkinson does not believe that Luke conceived of 'ongoing, active Christian life' without the Spirit.[389] However, unlike Turner, he understands the workings of the Spirit in the beginning of Christian conversion and life as distinct, in Luke's writing, from Spirit-reception: 'the Spirit was soteriologically involved, but the Pentecostal reception of the Spirit was not soteriological: it was charismatic and missionary'.[390]

After reviewing the many-faceted debate, Atkinson gives his own synthesis of Luke, John, and Paul. First, John knew two distinct comings of the Spirit, whereas Luke and Paul only spoke of one distinct coming. Second, Luke described, 'prior works of the Spirit',[391] prior, that is, to the official reception of the Spirit. Herein lies the solution to the apparent contradictions between New Testament authors. John, and to some degree, Luke, made room for the systematic theological possibility that Luke and Paul could have been using the same terminology for different Spirit experiences. Paul used Spirit-reception terms for the work of the Spirit on the heart at the beginning of the Christian walk, while Luke employed the same language to refer to an empowering experience.[392] Atkinson cautions that we must avoid simplistic harmonization of the biblical authors. The text itself contains a range of Spirit experiences which, 'can be clustered in a "soteriological" nexus and a "charismatic" nexus'.[393]

---

[384] *Ibid.*, 41.
[385] *Ibid.*, 64-65.
[386] *Ibid.*, 54, 65, 124.
[387] *Ibid.*, 125.
[388] *Ibid.*, 135.
[389] *Ibid.*, 125.
[390] *Ibid.*
[391] *Ibid.*, 117.
[392] *Ibid.*, 119.
[393] *Ibid.*, 120.

Heidrun Gunkel, *Der Heilige Geist bei Lukas: Theologisches Profil, Grund und Intention der lukanischen Pneumatologie* (2015)

For Gunkel, the gift of the Spirit is both initiatory and empowering for mission and is given to the entire church.[394] The Spirit is the identity marker of belonging to the church, the people of God, and replaces circumcision.[395] Jesus is the only mediator of the Spirit, the rite of baptism and the cases of handlaying by apostles only prepare the way for the Spirit to come from Jesus.[396] This means there is nothing that humans can do to facilitate the coming of the Spirit.[397]

Summary of Key Issues

The key issues for this book regard how the Spirit is related to faith and rituals of initiation, and whether the Spirit is in any way evidenced during those rituals. Concomitantly, one's view on Spirit-reception as subsequent to saving faith tends to correspond to one's perspective on mediation of the Spirit through ritual. Regarding mediation, the review shows the following breakdown, with the Spirit given via: handlaying (Gunkel, Adler, Haya-Prats, Robinson); water baptism (von Baer, Conzelmann, Bruner); normally water baptism but sometimes handlaying (Büchsel, Avemarie); sometimes handlaying (Menzies, Harrison); faith, prayer and water baptism (Schweizer). Adler and Haya-Prats allow for the Spirit to come in an initial way in baptism. Dunn, however, does not see the Spirit mediated, but as coming in response to faith which is actualized in baptism. Lampe appears contradictory, early on arguing for baptism as imparting the Spirit, but later categorically rejecting any mediation of the Spirit. Turner sees the Spirit as coming during conversion initiation, in response to faith. Atkinson and Petts see the Spirit coming normally around the time of water baptism, with Petts introducing the concept of 'immediate subsequence'. For Cho, the Spirit is not part of initiation. Gunkel (Heidrun) sees no human mediation.

Regarding manifestation of the Spirit, Gunkel and Dunn see the Spirit as tangible and linked to charismata. Von Baer opposed this view. Schweizer viewed the Spirit as manifesting perceptibly. Haya-Prats recognizes the Lukan Spirit 'typically' manifests charismatically. Turner rejects any normative evidence of the Spirit, but understands the Spirit as immediately perceptible, though within the entire powerful experience of conversion it might pass unnoticed. Bruner and Lampe explicitly reject the Spirit as tied to experience. Avemarie recognized that charismata can accompany the giving of the Spirit in Acts, but denied that glossolalia is necessary evidence of the Spirit. Harrison and Atkinson see the Spirit

---

[394] Heidrun Gunkel, *Der Heilige Geist bei Lukas: Theologisches Profil, Grund und Intention der lukanischen Pneumatologie* (Tübingen: Mohr Siebeck, 2015), 129, 142, 161.
[395] *Ibid.*, 223-24.
[396] *Ibid.*, 125, 135, 206, 208, 212-13.
[397] *Ibid.*, 199.

manifesting in a variety of ways without any normative experience. Of the writers reviewed, only Hedlun and Petts affirm tongues as the evidence of Spirit-reception in Lukan theology. Menzies, though he believes Luke linked inspired speech to the Spirit, and though he believes in tongues as the evidence of 'Spirit baptism', does not believe that Luke taught this doctrine.

CHAPTER 2

Methodology

Introduction

A Brief Background Sketch of the Narrative Critical Method

'The study of the Bible as literature'[1] in the 1940s was conducted by those outside the realm of biblical criticism such as E. Auerbach, and is still represented by, for example, Leland Ryken.[2] Robert Alter's work in the early 1980s was also a significant contribution to this approach. In the 1960s the parables began to be analysed with literary techniques[3] and, in 1969, J. Muilenburg delivered a presidential lecture to the Society for Biblical Literature encouraging literary approaches.[4] Then, as explained in Mark Allan Powell's concise handbook on narrative criticism, biblical scholars began in earnest to employ modern literary tools to analyse the biblical text after 1977, when Don Michie, of the Carthage College English department, demonstrated reading Mark as a short story to a Bible class belonging to fellow Carthage lecturer David Rhoads.[5] The resulting method, which Rhoads termed 'narrative criticism', has continued to be gainfully employed at the hands of Biblical interpreters both in North America and Europe.[6] Israeli exponents of a literary/narrative approach such as Adele Berlin and Yairah Amit, find their inspiration in Meir Sternberg, whose narrative critical work pre-dates Michie and Rhoads.[7] However, Sönke Finnern, in his recent work, *Narratologie und biblische Exegese*, has taken the narrative critical approach currently

---

[1] Dennis L. Stamps, 'Rhetorical and Narratological Criticism', Stanley E. Porter (ed.), *Handbook to Exegesis of the New Testament* (Leiden: Brill, 1997), 219-39; 228.
[2] Stanley E. Porter, 'Literary Approaches to the New Testament: From Formalism to Deconstruction and Back', Stanley E Porter and David Tombs (eds), *Approaches to New Testament Study* (Sheffield: Sheffield Academic, 1995), 77-128; 79.
[3] Stamps, 'Criticism', 228.
[4] Porter, 'Approaches', 80.
[5] Mark Allan Powell, *What is Narrative Criticism?* (Minneapolis: Fortress, 1990), 6.
[6] Francoise Mirguet, 'The Francophone Appropriation and Continuation of Narrative Criticism Applied to the Bible: The Example of Point of View', *PoeT* 30:2 (Summer, 2009), 353-62.
[7] Meir Sternberg, *The Poetics of Biblical Narrative, Ideological Literature and the Drama of Reading*. (Bloomington: Indiana University Press, 1987), cf. the review of Sternberg's journal articles dating to the late 1960s in the preface, xi. Adele Berlin,

employed in the English speaking world to task for, with just a few exceptions, not incorporating the advances made in the field of narratology over the last 30 years since Seymour Chatman's *Story and Discourse*.[8] Classicists, however, have invested considerable resources in narratological endeavours. Irene de Jong's analysis of the Odyssey,[9] and her acclaimed study of the Iliad, *Narrators and Focalizers*,[10] as well as Grethlein and Rengakos' *Narratology and Interpretation*,[11] illustrate this.

Specific Methodological Tools of the Book

This book will follow in the narrative critical tradition, but will attempt to utilize current narratological/literary techniques as well as principles from discourse analysis and rhetorical criticism to approach the question of Spirit-reception in Luke-Acts. Narratological/literary/discourse approaches to Luke-Acts are neither new, as Tannehill, Kurz, Shepherd, Sheeley, Witherup, Hur, Green, Turner, and others have shown, nor lacking in recent application, as the narratological works on Acts by Eisen, Cornils and Harrison,[12] along with Green's application of discourse analysis to baptism,[13] demonstrate. Others have applied a narrative/literary method to specific questions, such as the role of 'outcast characters',[14] the Holy Spirit and suffering,[15] 'wealth and possessions',[16] and Luke's pneumatology.[17] Therefore, the use of these methods *per se* is not the source of the book's originality. However, the book will make original arguments. As no claim is being made to originality in method, no exposition of the general principles of discourse analysis, narratology, or literary analysis will be made. These are well established fields and introductions to them are readily available. The specific aspects of discourse analysis and narratology that will be employed will be identified and discussed.

Poetics and Interpretation of Biblical Narrative (Sheffield: Almond, 1983). Yairah Amit, trans. Yael Lotan, *Reading Biblical Narratives: Literary Criticism and the Hebrew Bible* (Minneapolis: Fortress, 2001).

[8] Sönke Finnern, *Narratologie und biblische Exegese, Eine integrative Methode der Erzählanalyze und ihr Ertrag am Beispiel von Matthäus 28* (Tübingen: Mohr Siebeck, 2010), 24.

[9] Irene de Jong, *A Narratological Commentary on the Odyssey* (Cambridge: CUP, 2001).

[10] Irene J. F. de Jong, *Narrators and Focalizers: The Presentation of the Story in the Iliad* (London/New York: Bristol Classical, Bloomsbury Academic, 2004).

[11] Jonas Grethlein and Antonios Rengakos, *Narratology and Interpretation: The Content of Narrative Form in Ancient Literature* (Berlin: Walter de Gruyter, 2009).

[12] Eisen, *Poetik*; Cornils, *Geist*, Harrison, *L'Esprit*.

[13] Green, 'Baptism', 157-72.

[14] S. John Roth, *The Blind, the Lame and the Poor: Character Types in Luke-Acts* (Sheffield: Sheffield Academic, 1997), 11.

[15] Mittelstadt, *Suffering*.

[16] Metzger, *Consumption*, 1.

[17] Turner, *Power*.

The book will not attempt to analyse every literary aspect of the text. Characterization will not be dealt with, nor will there be an in-depth study of setting, nor a disclosure of all the intricacies of Luke's plot, nor an appreciation of the aesthetics of Luke's work. Rather, it will attempt narrowly to follow the development of just one of Luke's concepts, Spirit-reception, through the Spirit-reception scenes, with an emphasis upon careful observation of the sequence in which those scenes occur in the narrative, and what aspects of each scene are presented to the reader for special attention. To do this it will employ tools which may initially seem rather disparate but upon closer examination reveal themselves to be aptly suited to explicate initiation ritual in Luke-Acts. The three primary tools are the idea of narrative progression/sequential reading from discourse analysis and literary theory, the principle of presupposition pools/ERs from discourse analysis, and the concept of focalization from narratology. The ancient rhetorical technique of amplification will be shown to reinforce the first two modern analytical methods. Analysis of type-scenes, which are related, though not equivalent to, ERs, will also be employed. These three strands of investigation complement each other: a reader works through a story in sequence and as one reads, one accumulates information, especially noting what has been focused upon in the text.

Narrative Progression/Sequential Reading – The Fruit of Literary and Discourse Analysis

Progressive/Sequential Reading

Progressive/sequential reading is reading a narrative in the sequence in which it was written and observing how the story naturally progresses and develops. Reading in sequence and realizing narrative progression are thus two aspects of one narrative reality. No sweeping claim that scholarship in general has failed to read progressively/sequentially will be made. Commentaries, generally, work sequentially through biblical texts and seek to remain cognizant of the impact of prior context upon a given passage. Nor will the book prioritize progressive/sequential reading above other aspects of narrative critical analysis. As discussed below, the initial reading will be integrated with subsequent readings. However, the initial reading does play a role. Any attempt to analyse a story without regard for how the author laid out information for the reader/hearer to encounter and build up a storyworld misses the positive reading benefits that a sequential reading can provide. Written communication, whether read or heard, encourages one to access it from beginning to end, sequentially. As George A. Kennedy writes, 'the rhetorical qualities inherent in the text were originally intended to have an impact on first hearing'.[18]

---

[18] George A. Kennedy, *New Testament Interpretation Through Rhetorical Criticism* (Chapel Hill: University of North Carolina Press, 1984), 6.

Aurality and Sequential Reading

The question may be raised as to whether the oral-aural nature of experiencing a text in the ancient world negates any attempt to link episodes in Luke-Acts. Would not a hearer forget past episodes and therefore only be able to consider the episode currently being read? Is it not impossible to assume that an audience listening to Luke-Acts being read, not in its entirety, but piecemeal as the congregation has occasion to meet, will keep in mind what was read on previous occasions? Is not the assumption of a narrative context larger than the immediate episode erroneous?

One response to this objection is to consider the extensive parallelism in Luke-Acts. Discussion of Luke's structural artistry occupies several book length treatments.[19] If Luke went to such lengths to craft his work, then surely he expected his audience to be able to appreciate it. Second, as William David Shiell describes, ancient lectors (readers) were highly trained to deliver a text to their audience, and audiences, in turn, were accustomed to hearing texts performed.[20] Hearing a book such as Acts read aloud was normal. This was a fundamentally different mode of accessing information than that of the individual scholar with a book in hand who has the liberty of moving back and forth in the text.

Sequential Reading, the Second Reading, and Luke's Implied Reader

Rereading

If we ought to read progressively/sequentially (henceforth, simply 'sequentially') – and certainly an ancient audience which heard a lector read Luke's work listened to it sequentially – what then should be made of the rereader, of the 'second hearing'? Does not the second-time reader have the ability from the outset of a narrative to make connections back to front? Does that not contravene the whole idea of sequential reading? As Iser observed, the repeat reader is aware of the real significance or insignificance of the various details of the story.[21] This differs

---

[19] Classic examples include Charles H. Talbert, *Literary Patterns, Theological Themes, and the Genre of Luke-Acts* (Missoula: Scholars and Society of Biblical Literature, 1974); Gudrun Muhlack, *Die Parallelen von Lukas-Evangelium und Apostelgeschichte* (Frankfurt am Main: Peter Lang, 1979); G.W. Trompf, *The Idea of Historical Recurrence in Western Thought: From Antiquity to the Reformation* (Berkeley: University of California Press, 1979), especially 121-29; cf. Douglas S. McComiskey's evaluation of Talbert in, *Lukan Theology in the Light of the Gospel's Literary Structure* (Milton Keynes: Paternoster, 2004), 76-162. McComiskey concludes, 'He has demonstrated conclusively that Luke composed his Gospel using detailed individual and structured parallels' (161-62). More recently see, Clare K. Rothschild, *Luke-Acts and the Rhetoric of History: An Investigation of Early Christian Historiography* (Tübingen: Mohr Siebeck, 2004), 99-141.

[20] William David Shiell, *Reading Acts: The Lector and the Early Christian Audience* (Leiden: Brill, 2004), 33

[21] Wolfgang Iser, *The Implied Reader: Patterns of Communication in Prose Fiction from Bunyan to Beckett* (Baltimore: Johns Hopkins University Press, 1974), 281. The first-time reader reflects upon the past in light of new facts and this functions as a kind of

from the first-time reader for, as Thomas M. Leitch points out, no reader has the capability of being totally aware of all the aspects and implications of a narrative upon first reading: 'only successive readings will allow us to focus on the development of events and characters, significant patterns of imagery and ideology, modulations of tone, and whatever else makes the story act on us as it does'.[22] Moreover, when a reader does reread, s/he experiences the story differently. Reading a detective story the first time conveys a different pleasure from reading it a second time. The foreknowledge of who committed the crime allows the reader to focus, not on trying to solve the mystery, but on appreciating how the author masked the truth and dropped clues.[23] As Menakhem Perry relates, 'A second reading of a text is a sort of conscious reconstruction of the naive reading.'[24]

The Implied Reader of Luke-Acts
This raises the question of what kind of reader (this term will be understood to include a listening audience as well as a single 'reader') Luke wrote for – a first-time reader or a rereader. When we ask about the kind of reader a writer aims at, we ask about the implied reader. To begin with, we must be careful not to mistake the implied reader for the narratee. The narrator narrates the story to the narratee and the implied reader, the one for whom the book is actually written, overhears what is said. For example, imagine a story ostensibly told by a rather serious sounding narrator to one of Stalin's faithful minions with the apparent purpose of giving encouragement in the extermination of some unhelpful and hapless group of people. The reader soon discovers that, not only does s/he not identify with the narrator and Stalin's minion, but that the dialogue between said narrator and minion portrays them, and the ideology they espouse, as buffoonish. Clearly the story is satirical, and the narratee is not the same as the implied reader (neither is the narrator the same as the implied author). On the other hand, one could equally construct a story in which the interests of the narratee and the implied reader were similar, and the two seemed almost indistinguishable (though they are, technically, always distinguishable).

So then, with what kind of narratee/implied reader relationship are we dealing with in Luke-Acts? Troy M. Troftgruben writes that there is virtually no indication anywhere in Acts that the two are distinguishable.[25] This may be true, but it

---

'rereading', cf. José Angel García Landa, 'Rereading (,) Narrative (,) Identity (,) and Interaction', *Interculturalism: Between Identity and Diversity*, Beatriz Penas Ibáñez and Mª Carmen López Sáenz (eds) (Bern: Peter Lang, 2006), 212.

[22] Thomas M. Leitch, 'For (Against) a Theory of Rereading', *MFSt* 33.3 (Fall, 1987), 491-508; 493-94.

[23] *Ibid.*, 492.

[24] Menakhem Perry, 'Literary Dynamics: How the Order of a Text Creates its Meanings [With an Analysis of Faulkner's "A Rose For Emily"]' *PoeT* 1.1/2 (Autumn, 1979), 35-64 + 311-61; 357.

[25] Troy M. Troftgruben, *A Conclusion Unhindered: A Study of the Ending of the Acts Within Its Literary Environment* (Tübingen: Mohr Siebeck, 2010), 42.

must be confirmed. In Luke's story, the narrator has full and exact knowledge, and the narratee has partial knowledge but is being further instructed by the narrator. It is therefore implied that the reader will learn along with Theophilus, thus initially aligning the implied reader with the narratee. Theophilus may be Luke's patron, but he is also a character who learns from Luke. What we do not know at the outset of the story is whether Luke's implied reader will continue to be aligned with Theophilus, or whether later signals in the story will indicate that the two part company. As with Stalin's minion, the implied reader could diverge strikingly from the narratee. However, Theophilus is the starting point for constructing the implied reader. It is an initial setting which, if not contradicted, indicates that Theophilus does in fact represent the implied reader. We must therefore look for deviations from the norm. Does the text indicate that Luke's implied reader is more informed or less informed than Theophilus, or does the narrative confirm that Theophilus is a character representative of the implied audience?

What signals, then, would we look for? R. Alan Culpepper, seeking to uncover the implied reader of the Gospel of John, proposed identifying as known to the implied reader all things which the narrator does not explain, and vice versa. He looks specifically at the five categories of, 'persons (or characters), places, languages, Judaism, and events'.[26] Joseph B. Tyson goes to considerable length applying Culpepper's method to reconstruct Luke's ideal reader from allusions that the reader is expected to recognize, characters given minimal introduction, geographic references, and various other aspects of the text that indicate the authorial assumption of knowledge on the part of the reader.[27] He concludes that Luke wrote to a Gentile Godfearer who is not a Christian.[28] However, William Kurz critiques the method as 'wooden' because it does not consider other literary factors, such as irony or plot, for why the author does not supply information.[29]

Kurz takes the opposite view, that the implied reader is a Christian. Key points in his argument are: the 'us' in Luke 1:2; 'instructed' in Luke 1:4; Paul's prophecies of the church after his departure (Acts 20:29-30), which correspond to Jesus' provisions for the church in terms of the Eucharist, apostolic leadership and prophetic warnings (Luke 22:19-20, 29-32, 35-37); Jesus' prophecies in Luke 21, which would relate to Christians' persecution and vindication at the destruction of Jerusalem; Jesus' return for his own and his admonition to be prepared

---

[26] R. Alan Culpepper, *Anatomy of the Fourth Gospel: A Study in Literary Design* (Philadelphia: Fortress, 1983), 212. Culpepper does not distinguish between narratee and implied reader in John, 206.
[27] Joseph B. Tyson, *Images of Judaism in Luke-Acts* (Columbia: University of South Carolina Press, 1992), 23.
[28] *Ibid.*, 35, 182-183.
[29] William S. Kurz, 'Images of Judaism in Luke-Acts', *JAAR* 61.2 (Summer, 1993), 388-90; 389.

for his return. Kurz emphasizes the cumulative weight of all these arguments together.[30]

Does, then, Luke's preface give any quick, easy answers? The 'us' that Kurz argued from could just mean the narrator and the narrator's Christian associates, not necessarily including Theophilus. It likewise does not necessarily mean that the implied reader belongs to the 'us', though that is not impossible. Loveday Alexander addresses the question of whether κατηχήθης in Luke 1:4 means 'have been instructed' or 'have been informed', concluding that from the immediate context, either is equally possible, but her study of the preface in light of ancient scientific writing suggests to her the former.[31] But a suggestion is not conclusive. So, no, the preface does not give a definite answer about the narratee, or about the implied reader. Again, it only provides a starting point.

Kurz, however, notes that the evidence a narrative critic looks for to identify the implied reader is the same evidence which historical and redaction critics have long used.[32] Robert Maddox highlighted some of that evidence. Luke cited the Hebrew Scriptures as proof of arguments, something which would be persuasive only for a reader who accepted the authority of the Hebrew Scriptures. Luke's allusions to Hebrew Scriptures would only be grasped by an insider (e.g. Luke 8:9-10 and Luke 9:28-36). Luke's terminology such as 'kingdom of God' or 'Son of Man' goes unexplained. Maddox argued further that a significant number of Jesus' parables are for his followers: Luke 11:5-8; 12:35-48; 16:1-9; 17:7-10; as well as 8:9-15; 12:1-12. He notes that Jeremias is reported to have asked whether Luke would have included the Lord's Prayer and the institution of the Lord's Supper for non-Christians.[33] To this could be added Menzies' study of the sending of the Seventy, where he observes that Jesus' missional instructions were not mentioned by Luke as a mere historical curiosity, but as a model for a post-Pentecost church.[34]

In addition to this rapidly accumulating evidence for a Christian implied reader, we find that Peter, in Luke 12:41, asks the very question about the implied audience that we are asking. He says, 'Lord, do you say this parable to us or also to all?' Jesus responds with a question about who is the faithful and wise steward, indicating that the parable is addressed, not to outsiders, but insiders. Must we read this as requiring the implied reader be more than a Christian, but also a

---

[30] William S. Kurz, *Reading Luke-Acts, Dynamics of Biblical Narrative* (Louisville: WJKP, 1993), 13-15.
[31] Loveday Alexander, *The Preface to Luke's Gospel: Literary Convention and Social Context in Luke 1.1-4 and Acts1.1* (Cambridge: CUP, 1993), 139, 141-142.
[32] Kurz, *Reading*, 13.
[33] Robert Maddox, *The Purpose of Luke-Acts* (Edinburgh: T&T Clark, 1982), 12-15, 28.
[34] Robert Menzies, 'The Sending of the Seventy and Luke's Purpose', Paul Alexander, Jordan Daniel May, and Robert G. Reid (eds), *Trajectories in the Book of Acts* (Eugene: Wipf and Stock, 2010), 87-113; 89-90, 112.

Christian in a position of responsibility? This is possible, but lacks sufficient textual indicators for certainty. Luke's implied reader is simply one entrusted with the kingdom. A Christian.

Thus, Luke's implied reader does not deviate from the image of Theophilus, the narratee. However, Luke-Acts on at least one occasion depicts partially initiated individuals (Acts 8:16). Could Luke's implied reader be such, a Godfearer convert who knows the Hebrew scriptures, recognizes all the Biblical allusions, but has only experienced water baptism and not Spirit baptism? Again, Peter's question in Luke 12:41 reflects an implied reader already entrusted with the kingdom, not a partially initiated convert. Moreover, Luke's address to Theophilus, while presuming his need for better, more complete and accurate instruction, does not indicate any major deficiency in his initiation. That Theophilus had received instruction does not necessarily mean that he was a recent convert. A socially respectable individual who had some position in the church comfortably combines both Luke 12:41 and Luke 1:3-4. For these reasons, Luke's implied reader, being aligned with Theophilus, should be considered fully initiated. We find Kurz's position substantiated by the evidence which Maddox supplied, as well as by the dialogue in Luke 12:41. Thus, the implied reader of Luke-Acts is knowledgeable of scripture, a 'faithful steward', a fully initiated member of the church, a Christian.

Rereading, Again

Returning then, to the question of rereading, since we conclude that Luke intended his work to be read by Christians in the Christian community, it does not seem likely he would have expected only one reading.[35] Even if he expected it to be read in private by someone like 'Theophilus', it does not seem realistic that he would expect it to be ignored after only one reading. Given that he writes ostensibly to someone who occupies the role of learner, instructed in Christian faith, with the purpose of lending exactitude to what has been previously learned, it is reasonable to think Luke's ideal reader is expected to study his literary work with a conscientiousness corresponding to the care with which it was composed.[36] It is not unreasonable to assume that the lector would at least peruse the text before performing it, and this could lead one towards seeing the lector as studying the text deeply and the listening audience simply applauding a performance. While one might be tempted to propose two implied readers of Luke-Acts,[37] the simple churchgoer/hearer who merely enjoys the story and a more sophisticated reader who picks up on all the LXX allusions, Brian Richardson

---

[35] On public reading of books, cf. Shiell, *Reading*, 33.

[36] Discussion of Luke's structural artistry occupies several book length treatments. Cf. footnote 19 above.

[37] The question regarding the unity of Luke and Acts will be taken up below.

cautions not over-hastily to find multiple implied readers when one will do.[38] Could not Luke's thoughtful reader both enjoy and understand? We conclude that while Luke must have been aware that his work would be read in a congregation and heard by individuals of varying levels of competence, he did not display a clear multi-tiered target audience. One implied reader/audience suffices for Luke-Acts.

But if Luke's implied reader is a rereader and previously familiar with the basic Christian story, then are we not justified in discarding linearity and analysing the story from every angle? It may seem so. However, even a first-time reader reflects back upon the story already read, thus 'rereading'.[39] Consider again the rereader of the detective story. Knowing the end in advance, the rereader can contrast her/himself with a reader, namely her/his former self, who does not know the outcome. That very contrast is part of the pleasure of superiority, of insider knowledge. So being a second-time reader eliminates neither understanding of, nor interaction with, how a first-time reader reads. Leitch, in fact, suggests that one scholarly approach to rereading is to analyse the means a story employs to 'achieve its initial effects'.[40] How does the story generate initial suspense or create surprise for the implied first-time reader? Thus, we cannot jettison linear, sequential reading, because the rereader remains aware of how the first-time reader is 'supposed' to be surprised, frightened, enlightened, or otherwise impacted by the story. The implied, first-time reader remains a part of the second-time reading experience.

There is yet another reason why we cannot be done with sequential reading. Stories have a power to enforce typical responses even upon multiple readings. Granted, in certain types of literature, such as the detective story, there can be a distinct shift in type of enjoyment, namely from surprise at the final twist in plot, to anticipation of rereading that final twist in the plot. But at the same time, stories are able to preserve a surprising continuity of experience upon rereading due to a particular phenomenon of human nature. Richard Gerrig points out that people have the ability to experience, as if for the first time, a story where the outcome is known. The hero will live, of this one is sure, but one still feels suspense at her/his precarious plight. Gerrig calls this 'anomalous suspense' and explains it as a 'cognitive illusion' in which normal cognitive processes are tricked genuinely to expect a unique outcome to the well-known story.[41] His is one of a variety of competing explanations for what is known as the 'paradox of suspense'.[42]

---

[38] Brian Richardson, 'Singular Text, Multiple Implied Readers', *Sty.* 41.3 (Fall, 2007), 259-74; 267. For a classic review of the implied reader, see, Robert M. Fowler, 'Who is "The Reader" in Reader Response Criticism?' *Se.* 31 (1985), 3-30.
[39] Cf. García Landa, 'Rereading', 212.
[40] Leitch, 'Rereading', 494.
[41] Richard J. Gerrig, 'Reexperiencing Fiction and Non-Fiction', *JAAC* 47.3 (Summer, 1989), 277-80; 279.
[42] Aaron Smuts, 'The Paradox of Suspense', *SEP* (Fall, 2009), 1-15. Cf. Aaron Smuts, 'The Desire-Frustration Theory of Suspense', *JAAC* 66.3 (Summer, 2008), 281-90;

While there is no consensus resolution to the problem of how suspense can occur despite a narrative situation, such as rereading, where the outcome is known,[43] the reality of the phenomenon is confirmed not just by anecdotal evidence, but by empirical research. For example, in one study in which 56 participants watched a suspenseful film once and then again two weeks later, and their suspense levels were measured throughout the course of both viewings: 'Results show that surprise and suspense attenuate with repeated exposure, but the characteristic development of the suspense experience – peaks, spikes etc. within the curve progression – remains the same.'[44] The points in the narrative at which participants responded, and the outline of their response, did not change. Only the intensity decreased. So while rereading can create new pleasures, it does not eliminate old ones. The tenacity of 'anomalous suspense' must be reckoned with when attempting a dispassionate scholarly analysis of Luke-Acts. Even though a repeat reader is able to make connections between disparate points in a narrative sequence that a first-time reader cannot, the power of a story emotionally to affect a reader in a similar way each time remains. We are not in error to include genuine suspense as part of the analysis of Luke's text.

But what then of the scholar who seeks critical detachment in order properly to analyse the text? Cannot an objective approach reveal chiasms and parallels that might be missed by a more casual review? Certainly, so long as that analysis considers the impact the narrative is designed to have on its implied reader. This 'implied impact' is a textual artefact to be studied along with the chiasms and parallels.[45] This book's approach aligns with that of Jeannine K. Brown, who, after reviewing the concept of implied reader, 'affirms there is a textually-derived implied reader who responds appropriately to the text's goals and this implied

---

Christy Mag Uidhir, 'The Paradox of Suspense Realism', *JAAC* 69.2 (Spring, 2011), 161-171; Robert J. Yanal, *Paradoxes of Emotion and Fiction* (University Park: Pennsylvania State University, 1999).

[43] Anthony J. Sanford and Catherine Emmott, *Mind, Brain and Narrative* (Cambridge: CUP, 2012), 230.

[44] Jella Hoffmann and Andreas Fahr, 'Re-experiencing Suspense and Surprise: Processes of Repeated Exposure to Narrative Fiction'. Lecture at the 'Panel Exploring the Cognitive and Affective Effects of Narrative' (57th Annual Conference of the International Communication Association, 2007, San Francisco, USA). For earlier experimentation see, William F. Brewer, 'The Nature of Narrative Suspense and the Problem of Rereading', Peter Vorderer, Hans Jürgen Wulff, Mike Friedrichsen (eds), *Suspense: Conceptualizations, Theoretical Analyses, and Empirical Explorations* (Mahwah: Lawrence Erlbaum, 1996), 107-28.

[45] No comment is intended regarding whether or not the actual reader helps construct the implied reader. Cf. Iser, *Reader*, xii; Wolfgang Iser, *The Act of Reading: A Theory of Aesthetic Response* (Baltimore: Johns Hopkins University Press, 1978), 34; cf. Wolf Schmid's discussion of the translation of Iser's term 'impliziter Leser' in, 'Implied Reader', Peter Hühn et al (eds), *The Living Handbook of Narratology* (Hamburg: Hamburg University Press, 2013), paragraph 25, URL = hup.sub.uni-hamburg.de/lhn/index.php ?title=Implied Reader &oldid=2015 [view date: 20 March, 2013].

reader is a valid aim of narrative criticism'.[46] This is not simply the first-time reader, for the implied author constructs the implied reader on three levels: the initial progressive reading experience which includes the construction of hypotheses about the nature of the story and its final outcome; the retrospective comprehension from the vantage point of the completed story; and the rereader who knows the end from the beginning and re-experiences the progression in the text with that knowledge.

Sequential Reading and the Unity of Luke and Acts

Michael F. Bird, at the conclusion of his review of the state of the question of Luke-Acts unity, argues that if one assumes 'Luke-Acts' to be a whole, then one must be able to demonstrate that claim and provide, 'a description of the exact nature of the unity between the two volumes and a justification of its hermeneutical significance'.[47] Since this book reads Luke and Acts sequentially, assuming a relationship, the parameter of what constitutes unity sufficient for a sequential reading must be identified.

First, C. Kavin Rowe argues that based upon the extensive research of Andrew F. Gregory and his own contributions,[48] we have little (Gregory) to no (Rowe) evidence of Luke and Acts ever being read together. Therefore, they were likely never read together at any point in their reception history. Consequently, 'our interpretations of Luke-Acts may not reflect the practice of the earliest readers after all'.[49] Rowe takes Luke Timothy Johnson to task for presuming, in his commentary on Acts, to know from literary analysis what actual readers of Luke's writings would have thought.[50] However, Luke and Acts need never have been read together by actual readers for us to observe that Luke's implied reader reads them together. That we have virtually no evidence of ancient readers reading Luke and Acts together says nothing about how the actual author expected his books to be read (a historical question), nor about how the implied author expects his works to be read (a narratological question). Additionally, as Johnson points out, contrary to Rowe, neither does it allow us to conclude that they were not

---

[46] Jeannine K. Brown, *The Disciples in Narrative Perspective: The Portrayal and Function of the Matthean Disciples* (Leiden: Brill, 2002), 125.

[47] Michael F. Bird, 'The Unity of Luke-Acts in Recent Discussion', *JSNT* 29.4 (2007), 425-48; 442.

[48] Andrew Gregory, *The Reception of Luke and Acts in the Period Before Irenaeus* (Tübingen: Mohr Siebeck, 2003); C. Kavin Rowe, 'History, Hermeneutics, and the Unity of Luke-Acts', Andrew F. Gregory and C. Kavin Rowe (eds), *Rethinking the Unity and Reception of Luke and Acts* (Columbia: University of South Carolina Press, 2010), 43-65. Cf. Andrew Gregory, 'The Reception of Luke and Acts and the Unity of Luke-Acts', *JSNT* 29.4 (2007), 459-72.

[49] Rowe, 'History', 49.

[50] Rowe cites Johnson, *The Acts of the Apostles* (Collegeville: Michael Glazier, Liturgical, 1992), 476.

read and heard together by the first readers and audiences (again, a historical matter).[51] Rowe only offers an argument from silence.

Second, Luke and Acts need not be shown to have been composed at the same time for one to read them sequentially. Against Rowe and with Johnson, a time gap in composition is irrelevant to literary connectedness.[52] Third, they need not be exactly the same genre. To read sequentially, a reader need only perceive Acts to be a sequel to the Gospel of Luke. The sequel may take up different themes, may differ stylistically, and may be readable standing by itself, but as long as the reader is led to believe that it is connected to the initial story by the same author, or even by someone known to be imitating the same author, sequential reading will go on. Readers read intertextually even when authors differ – witness how the New Testament draws freely upon the 'Old'. So with just a modicum of justification, such as Acts 1:1, a reader will expect connections between stories. Jacob Jervell's argument that the preface to Luke does not apply to Acts because of an assumed gap in time between writing, and because the works are assumed to be different kinds of literature, does not consider the aforementioned proclivity of readers to make intertextual connections and of authors to expect such connections to be made (cf. Mark 13:14 and Matthew 24:15, 'let the reader understand').[53] As Bird makes clear, it is not at issue that the same person wrote Luke and Acts, nor is it being questioned that the books are connected by numerous literary links. Rather only the intensity of that connection is under scrutiny.[54] As Alexander observes, in Acts Luke gives, 'a continuation of a story already halfway through'.[55] Thus, with the same authorship, with literary ties recognized, and with Luke even, as Jervell acknowledges, 'recapitulating' his forward,[56] thereby explicitly encouraging his implied reader[57] to read Acts in the light of what has gone before, there is more than a minimum amount of unity for sequential reading.

Yet, someone might object that if sequential reading is based upon Luke's claim to write sequentially (καθεξῆς), and if there is doubt about whether all the aspects of Luke's first preface can be applied to his second volume (for example, Alexander cites Luke's assertion that 'many' have already written on his topic and that he is the recipient of a tradition)[58] then there is doubt about the sequential

---

[51] Luke Timothy Johnson, 'Literary Criticism of Luke-Acts: Is Reception History Pertinent?' Andrew F. Gregory and C. Kavin Rowe (eds), *Rethinking the Unity and Reception of Luke and Acts* (Columbia: University of South Carolina Press, 2010), 66.

[52] *Ibid.*, 67.

[53] Jacob Jervell, *Die Apostelgeschichte: Übersetzt und erklärt* (Göttingen: Vandenhoeck & Ruprecht, 1998), 57.

[54] Bird, 'Unity', 425-26.

[55] Loveday Alexander, *Acts in its Ancient Literary Context: A Classicist Looks at the Acts of the Apostles* (London: T&T Clark, 2005), 25.

[56] Jervell, *Apostelgeschichte*, 57.

[57] His narratee, Theophilus, is not his implied reader, but the implied reader is influenced by what is said to the narratee.

[58] Alexander, *Acts*, 24.

reading method. In answer, Luke's ideal reader reads sequentially whether Luke exerted extra care to arrange his material in order or not. Finally, Bird's challenge to identify the hermeneutical significance of unity between Luke and Acts will not be taken up here in its entirety, but the significance of the implied reader reading sequentially from Luke to Acts will be discussed below.

Sequential Reading and Accumulation

Perry emphasizes the role of sequence and accumulation in creating meaning within, 'the literary text':

> Its verbal elements appear one *after* another, and its semantic complexes (e.g., scenes, ideas, characters, plot, value-judgments) build up 'cumulatively,' through adjustments and readjustments.
>
> The ordering and distribution of the elements in a text may exercise considerable influence on the nature, not only of the *reading process*, but of the *resultant whole* as well.[59]

Peter M. Phillips summarizes the theory of sequential reading in his work on John's Gospel, *The Prologue of the Fourth Gospel: A Sequential Reading*.[60] He points out that literary theory, discourse linguistics, and semiotics all propound the same principle of reading a text sequentially. For example, in literary theory, Iser argued that narrative ambiguity leads a reader to seek to disambiguate textual gaps in knowledge, and the reader is guided in this process by structures within the text.[61] Iser's work expressed what Phillips calls, 'sequential disclosure, the gradual unfolding effect of the text upon the reader's interpretation of the narrative world'.[62] Drawing upon Gerard Genette's emphasis on the linear nature of narrative, Phillips critiques modern biblical methods which may be insensitive to this linearity:

> In a field of study dominated by critical readings, it is important to remember that texts are experienced sequentially. Most commentaries seem to deal with texts sequentially, since they work through the texts verse-by-verse, sometimes even word-by-word. However, even though they follow the sequence of the text, commentators constantly introduce interpretive elements from the rest of the text, or from other associated texts or from other general sources. This process of metatextual gap-filling disables sequential disclosure.[63]

---

[59] Perry, 'Dynamics,' 35, original italics.
[60] Peter M. Phillips, *The Prologue of the Fourth Gospel: A Sequential Reading* (London: T&T Clark, 2006), 25-26.
[61] Wolfgang Iser, 'Interaction Between Text and Reader', Susan R. Suleiman and Inge Crosman (eds), *The Reader in the Text: Essays on Audience and Interpretation* (Princeton: Princeton University Press, 1980), 106-19; 111-12. See, also, Iser, *Reader*, 288; Iser, *Act*, 116-18, 169.
[62] Phillips, *Prologue*, 26.
[63] *Ibid.*, 27.

This book will *not* join Phillips in making such broad criticism of 'most commentaries'. It will, however, assert the usefulness of sequential reading. Phillips also finds the same principle of sequential disclosure in the discourse linguistics of Catherine Emmott's *Narrative Comprehension: A Discourse Perspective*,[64] and the semiotics of Umberto Eco.[65] Phillips himself employs it in a phrase-by-phrase analysis of John's prologue. This book will not attempt such a microanalysis of sequential disclosure in Luke-Acts, but will utilize the principle in the macro-analysis of Spirit-reception scenes. Such a course has already been charted by Kari Syreeni, who conducted a sequential analysis of Matthew's Peter scenes.[66] The book seeks to avoid the metatextual fallacy and approach Luke-Acts with a sensitivity to the disclosure structure devised by Luke without neutralizing Luke's creative presentation.

Similarly to Phillips, S. John Roth succinctly states how sequential reading affects the reader:

> An audience-oriented analysis of Luke-Acts will, therefore, be guided by two questions that stem from the nature of narrative: What is the immediate effect on the reader during the reading process? And, what is the rhetorical significance of the placement of episodes and the sequence of events in the narrative?[67]

A sequential macro-analysis of initiation scenes in Luke-Acts will not ignore Roth's two points. In terms of rhetorical significance of episode sequences, one must ask about their cumulative effect upon the reader, as well as whether later episodes answer questions that earlier scenes raise. Johnson emphasizes the sequential reading concept when, in reference to the prologue to Luke's Gospel, he writes: '"In order" is an especially revealing term. The sequence of the story is significant in Luke-Acts to a remarkable degree. How one thing follows after another seems almost as important as the things themselves.'[68]

---

[64] Emmott, *Comprehension*, 75-87.
[65] Phillips, *Prologue*, 28-30.
[66] Kari Syreeni, 'Peter as Character and Symbol in the Gospel of Matthew', David Rhoads and Kari Syreeni (eds), *Characterization in the Gospels: Reconceiving Narrative Criticism* (Sheffield: Sheffield Academic, 1999), 106-52; 120-52.
[67] Roth, *Blind*, 64. Cf. Robert L. Cohn's analysis of the linear and cumulative logic within a series of Elijah episodes, 'The Literary Logic of 1 Kings 17-19', *JBL* 101.3 (1982), 333-50; Robert Polzin's synchronic analysis of three Genesis stories, '"The Ancestress of Israel" in Danger', *Se.* 3 (1975), 81-98; Richard Edwards, 'Uncertain Faith: Matthew's Portrait of the Disciples', Fernando F. Segovia, ed., *Discipleship in the New Testament* (Philadelphia: Fortress, 1985), 47-61; 48; Pamela Shellberg, *From Cleansed Leapers to Cleansed Hearts: The Developing Meaning of* Katharizo *in Luke-Acts* (Ph.D. dissertation, Marquette University, 2012), 154.
[68] Luke Timothy Johnson, *Scripture and Discernment: Decision Making in the Church* (Nashville: Abingdon, 1996), 77.

Sequential Reading and Discourse Analysis

In the same vein, Green's application of discourse analysis to the problem of baptism in Luke-Acts emphasizes the need for sequential reading: 'one proceeds in the narrative from start to finish. What comes before constrains the possible meaning of what comes after, within the text'.[69] This is an aspect of point two of four implications of discourse analysis for baptism in Luke-Acts for which Green argues.

The first is 'normality'. The audience will, 'attribute coherence to Luke's narrative unless it is forced to infer otherwise. Even in those cases where a change in normal practice is perceived, the analysis of "language in use" presumes that change to be minimal'.[70] Green cites Gillian Brown and George Yule in support of this point.[71] They draw upon Teun A. van Dijk:

> An important COGNITIVE condition of semantic coherence is the ASSUMED NORMALITY of the worlds involved. That is, our expectations about the semantic structures of discourse are determined by our KNOWLEDGE about the structure of worlds in general and of particular states of affairs or courses of events. For abnormal worlds, we need specific indicators.[72]

Van Dijk gives the illustration of someone whose work desk is clean and ready for work, 'but' the person does not feel like working. A communicator must insert the indicator 'but' to signal that despite normal conditions, there is abnormal behaviour.[73]

Brown and Yule reason that we expect to happen what normally happens:

> We assume that our muscles will continue to move normally, that doors which normally open will continue to open, that hair grows on heads, that dogs bark, that towns retain their geographical locations, that the sun will shine, and so on.[74]

Communication occurs in light of normal expectations. Furthermore, Brown and Yule cite K.R. Popper, who argued that humans are born with an innate tendency to expect and to recognize regularity.[75] Popper wrote, 'we are born with expectations; with "knowledge" which, although not *valid a priori*, is *psychologically or genetically a priori*, i.e. prior to all observational experience. One of the most

---

[69] Green, 'Baptism', 160. See also, Joel B. Green, 'Internal repetition in Luke-Acts: contemporary narratology and Lucan historiography', Ben Witherington (ed.), *History Literature and Society in the Book of Acts* (Cambridge: CUP, 1996), 283-99.
[70] Green, 'Baptism', 160.
[71] *Ibid.*; Gillian Brown and George Yule, *Discourse Analysis* (Cambridge: CUP, 1983), 62.
[72] Teun A. van Dijk, *Text and Context: Explorations in the Semantics and Pragmatics of Discourse* (New York: Longman, 1977), 99, original emphases.
[73] *Ibid.*, 98-99.
[74] Brown and Yule, *Analysis*, 62.
[75] *Ibid.*

important of these expectations is the expectation of finding a regularity'.[76] Thus, as individuals recognize regularities, they become able to predict what will happen in a given situation.[77] This applies to baptism (and concomitantly, to Spirit-reception) in Luke-Acts. The reader will not expect chaos and incoherence on Luke's part. If Luke told slightly different stories, the reader will not immediately expect them to represent divergent documents poorly edited, nor will the reader assume that Luke is incoherent, but will look for some way to make sense of them within the storyworld. Progression in a story is not the same as confusion. The reader expects Luke to be dependable as a writer and expects his storyworld to be true to the normal functioning of the universe as s/he knows it.

Luke also does not seek to prove to his reader the existence of a supernatural realm. This indicates that Luke's implied reader accepts supernatural events and beings as part of reality. However, that Luke's reader believes in the existence of angels and accepts their appearance as within the realm of possibility does not mean that Luke's reader believes in the *regular* appearance of such beings. Angels may be normal in the sense of 'part of reality' but not normal in the sense of 'everyday occurrence'. Thus, Luke's story retains a sense of the extraordinary when he tells of Gabriel's visit to Zacharias in the Temple, or Peter's angelic deliverance from prison. In both of these cases, textual signals indicate that the event was not ordinary. Gabriel explains his unique identity as one who stands before God who had come with a special announcement. Peter thought he was seeing a vision, and not a 'real' angel. Thus, normality does *not* equal typicality. This distinction is useful when discussion whether certain behaviours such as tongues or handlaying would be considered extraordinary or regular. *Mere narration proves neither regularity nor exceptionality*, and, unfortunately, there are no simple criteria for making such a determination. It can only be identified by evaluating the literary devices within each story.

Second, Green appeals to 'presupposition pools':

> Presuppositions derive partially from one's experience before and outside of the text, but these are sometimes negated, reformed and/or replaced by a narrative text, and always expanded as the narrative unfolds. Privilege of meaning is consequently allocated to the lexicon that is supported by and developed within the narrative as one proceeds in the narrative from start to finish. What comes before constrains the possible meaning of what comes after, within the text.[78]

Brown and Yule speak of the concept of presupposition pools, drawing upon the work of Vennemann. He discusses the:

> 'presupposition pool' which does not belong to individual sentences only but to entire discourses or, at least, stretches of discourses. The information contained in

---

[76] K.R. Popper, *Conjectures and Refutations: The Growth of Scientific Knowledge* (London: Routledge & Kegan Paul, 1963), 47, original italics.

[77] Brown and Yule, *Analysis*, 62-63.

[78] Green, 'Baptism,' 160.

this pool is constituted from general knowledge, from the situative context of the discourse, and from the completed part of the discourse itself.[79]

Similarly, Robert C. Tannehill writes:

> Resonance is a cumulative experience in reading. Connections among narrative materials build up, so that more and more are available as background for exploring those nodal points of narrative where many connecting lines cross.[80]

When applied to the analysis of written texts, the concept of 'presupposition pool' may refer to extra-textual knowledge with which a reader comes to the text, or to the accumulation of intra-textual knowledge. While we may not know how a real flesh and blood reader will make connections among bits of data in the presupposition pool,[81] and we do not have certain access to the extra-textual presupposition pool of Luke-Acts, we can determine the intra-textual presupposition pool that has accumulated at any point along the development of the narrative. So, as discussed above, Luke's implied reader has gone through some level of Christian indoctrination. But we do not know if that instruction included teaching on the history of the church. We cannot say that the implied reader at the beginning of Luke-Acts necessarily knows that there will be a character named Saul who will persecute Jesus' followers. The implied reader reading the story at the beginning of Acts 8 does know about Saul, but does not necessarily know that Saul will soon be converted and become a preacher himself. What the analyst can know is that within the storyworld, the implied reader's knowledge of the story as it is being presented, versus as s/he may be expected to know from extra-textual sources, grows with the discourse. The 'resonance' increases as the story unfolds. The *novum* is Luke's unique presentation of the possibly well-known story.

Vennemann discusses a second aspect of presupposition pools which is directly relevant to Luke-Acts interpretation:

> Each participant of a discourse is operating with his own presupposition pool. His pool grows as the discourse proceeds. Each utterance made by another participant adds information to the pool; in particular, each statement that is not challenged becomes presuppositional for the remainder of the discourse.[82]

Thus, as Luke introduced statements of fact through, for example, narrative asides, or his narrative spokespersons, as long as those statements are unchallenged, they have an ongoing presuppositional impact on the narrative. Again, mere narration of something does *not* establish it as a regular procedure. The Spirit caught away Philip and Luke's reader is expected to believe that such an event happened. However, Luke gave no signals in the text either to indicate that

---

[79] Vennemann, 'Topics', 313-28; 314.
[80] Robert C. Tannehill, *The Narrative Unity of Luke-Acts, A Literary Interpretation*, Vol. 2, *The Acts of the Apostles* (Minneapolis: Augsburg Fortress, 1990), 76.
[81] Cf. Tannehill, 'resonance is not entirely controllable by an author', *Ibid.*
[82] Vennemann, 'Topics', 314.

this was a regular procedure or an irregular procedure. It enters the reader's intratextual presupposition pool as something possible, that is all. With casting lots, Luke gave no immediate textual signal indicating that lot casting was or was not customary among the disciples of Jesus. However, Zacharias was chosen by lot to go into the temple (Luke 1:9), indicating that lots were in use as a selection tool in at least one religious context in Judea relatively close to the time of Acts 1. Jesus' clothes were divided by lot among soldiers (Luke 23:34), direct evidence that lot casting was in use in Judea, at least among soldiers, at precisely this time. So, while Luke did not explicitly say that casting lots was a regular practice of Jesus' disciples, the reader has no reason to think the apostles' activity to be extraordinary and does have grounds to think it typical. Luke said nothing about lots being required, or normative. The arrival of the Spirit presents itself as a major plot development that suggests lots ceased to be necessary and explains the fact that they are not used again. In this regard, von Baer attributed the use of lots to the lack of the presence of the Spirit and observed that, in contrast to the choice of deacons in chapter 6, fullness of the Spirit is not a criterion, and handlaying to impart spiritual power is not practiced.[83] Singular, occasional, and intermittent events are constructed as such by the story. If something is to be read as a standard procedure, the story itself must construct it as such. The book makes no claim to a universally applicable method for distinguishing the regular from the occasional. Each story must be evaluated in terms of the literary devices employed.

Third, Green discusses the role of 'intertextual frames': 'we make sense of the Lukan portrait of baptism in Acts on the basis of what we have seen and heard before'.[84] Frames are related to the 'general knowledge' aspect of presupposition pools. Deborah Tannen identifies the basic principle behind a variety of related terms such as 'schema', 'script', and 'frame', as:

> what R.N. Ross (1975) calls 'structures of expectations,' that is, that, on the basis of one's experience of the world in a given culture (or combination of cultures), one organizes knowledge about the world and uses this knowledge to predict interpretations and relationships regarding new information, events and experiences.[85]

So, when one goes to a wedding, one has an expectation that a specific series of events will unfold. Deviations from the standard wedding 'script' or 'frame' might make a statement about the couple's values, or be variously funny, shocking, or tragic. But we interpret the deviation based upon our expectations of what we understand to normally happen at a wedding. Tannen emphasizes, however, that frames need not be conceived of as static repositories of data, but, quoting Frederic Bartlett, as 'active, developing patterns'.[86] In terms of Luke-Acts, we

---

[83] Von Baer, *Geist*, 83. Similarly, Dunn, *Baptism*, 45-46.
[84] Green, 'Baptism', 161.
[85] Deborah Tannen, 'What's in a Frame?' Deborah Tannen (ed.), *Framing in Discourse* (Oxford: OUP, 1993), 14-56; 16.
[86] *Ibid.*, 16.

do not have certain access to the frames which Luke expected his reader to have (i.e., which his implied reader had). For example, we simply do not know in advance of reading Luke-Acts what expectations the implied reader would have had with regard to water baptism. We do, however, have the frames which are created within the narrative. These frames may be 'active, developing patterns', but they influence our expectations as we proceed through the narrative. At the end of reading Luke-Acts, we can say what Luke expected his reader to know about water baptism.

Fourthly, Green discusses narrative/audience response: 'discourse theorists would be concerned with how persons within the narrative respond to the message of baptism'.[87] The same interest applies to how Luke's audience would respond to the message, and Green cites Luke 7:29-30 as an example.[88] There Luke divided the nation of Israel into two groups, one that submitted to God's will in being baptised by John, 'all the people' and the tax gatherers, and one which did not, the Pharisees and lawyers. This aspect of discourse theory relates to the didactic intent contained in the narrative. Submitting to John's baptism was the will of God, who was for Luke, the ideological standard, the ultimate normative spokesperson, and therefore, to submit to the rituals of John's successors in the narrative, the apostles of Jesus, is to submit to God. Luke was prescriptive, not merely descriptive.

In actuality, all four of Green's points can be subsumed under Phillips' rubric of sequential reading. Reading in sequence one expects normality, one builds up a presupposition pool, one utilizes prior information/frames to understand new contexts, and one gauges how the author expects one to react by how normative characters react. Phillips' and Green's work has significant implications for study of Christian initiation in Luke-Acts, particularly in answering the methodological concern raised by Beverly Gaventa when she objects to using Acts 2:38 as paradigmatic for Luke's 'scheme of conversion',[89] and to making it 'the basis for analysing conversions that occur elsewhere in Acts',[90] because, 'it selects one small pattern in the garment and seeks to make the rest of the garment conform to that pattern'.[91] Gaventa does not consider the role of sequential development in a narrative. The initial presentation that a reader experiences *does* contribute to the reader's growing conception of an idea. Placed at the beginning of a narrative, a 'pattern' is not merely 'one small pattern in the garment', but the beginning of a presupposition pool which readers use for interpreting what comes later in the text. Initial patterns are influential. Deviations from the initial setting may

---

[87] Green, 'Baptism', 161.
[88] *Ibid.*
[89] Beverly Roberts Gaventa, *From Darkness to Light: Aspects of Conversion in the New Testament* (Philadelphia: Fortress, 1986), 96.
[90] *Ibid.*, 97.
[91] *Ibid.* Cf. Beverly Roberts Gaventa, 'Toward a Theology of Acts: Reading and Rereading', *Interp.* 42.2 (April, 1988), 146-57; 149.

occur, but they cannot be read in isolation from what the reader initially encounters. One must only be careful, therefore, to find the initial scene and read forwards from that initial scene. In this regard, Green observes that since Luke precedes Acts, and presupposition pools develop sequentially, therefore, 'this requires that 'baptism' as this is portrayed in Lk. 3.1-20 figure prominently in our analysis of baptism in Acts'.[92] To this may be added Luke 3:21-22. Similarly, Daryl D. Schmidt writes:

> A narrative study by nature must keep track of an expanding network of contexts when it isolates any one feature for particular attention. For example, first impressions established in the narrative have an ongoing effect throughout the rest of the narrative, even as they are modified and revised.[93]

This means that Acts 2:38 cannot be the sole foundation stone of Christian initiation in Luke-Acts, but must be interpreted in light of what has gone before. This is true even though the theological content of baptism is modified over the course of the story from repentance and admission to the community waiting for an unnamed Messiah, to repentance and submission to Jesus as Messiah and entrance into the Jesus community. In other words, in the change from John's baptism to baptism in Jesus' name, the theological content is modified to reflect the identity of Jesus as resurrected, exalted Messiah, but it remains an immersion rite,[94] and its function to demonstrate repentance remains unchanged, as does its association in Luke's storyworld with empowerment by the Holy Spirit. The so called contradictions, or 'exceptional' cases, when no longer compared just to Acts 2:38, but viewed in terms of progressive development from Luke 3, especially Luke 3:21-22, onwards, lose their scandalous character and cease to be contradictory. Acts 2:38 remains significant, however, because of its placement at the beginning of volume 2 of Luke-Acts. It is consequently programmatic for Luke-Acts – a foundational aspect of the Luke-Acts presupposition pool.

Entity Representations

In her analysis of the mental activity of reading, Catherine Emmott discusses 'entity representations' (ERs). As we have already mentioned in the introduction, ERs are the mental constructs developed linearly through the text as the reader accumulates data about characters, objects, circumstances, procedures, etc.[95] When new information about any particular subject comes along in the narrative,

---

[92] Green, 'Baptism', 160-61.
[93] Daryl D. Schmidt, 'Anti-Judaism and the Gospel of Luke', William R. Farmer (ed.), *Anti-Judaism and the Gospels* (Harrisburg: Trinity, 1999), 63-96; 65.
[94] The debate concerning the nature of the baptism rite will not be engaged here. The term 'immersion' will be used to clarify the distinction between baptism as a ceremony composed of several possible ritual elements, such as water, prayer, handlaying(?), and the specific aspect of the baptism ritual associated with *water*. Whether the water ritual was sprinkling, pouring, or immersing is irrelevant to the thesis.
[95] Emmott, *Comprehension*, 81-84.

a reader will fit it into the network of associations s/he already has in mind about that subject. The idea here is similar to Vennemann's presupposition pools, only more topic specific and primarily intra-textual. A presupposition pool could be seen as the accumulation of all knowledge from within and without the text relevant to understanding the story, whereas an ER would be all the, primarily, text-generated knowledge relevant to understanding a particular aspect of the story, a character named Tom, or a place called Smallville, and so on. It is in the interest of the exegete to observe the development of ERs from the perspective of a first-time reader, not attempting to understand any segment of a narrative in isolation from the narrative development which has gone before. All the principles of sequential reading discussed by Phillips, Roth, Johnson, and Green apply in the progressive development of ERs. ERs form the basis for normality; they are essential ingredients of presupposition pools; they make up the frames by which one interprets new data; they contain the responses to the message of the author which serve as normative standards for the reader.

In analysing Spirit-reception in Luke-Acts, careful attention will be paid to the formation of the ER for initiation. The fact that Luke-Acts mentions various elements somehow related to initiation, such as belief, repentance, water, prayer, handlaying, and Holy Spirit, is nothing new. What has not been done, however, is to observe the development of the association of these elements. Just how are they linked together, and how did they come to be linked together in the progressive unfolding of the narrative? Moreover, after they have been presented, perhaps multiple times over the course of the narrative, what is the ER for initiation that the reader is left with? Thus the cumulative impact of the entire series of initiation scenes, from Jesus' baptism in Luke 3 to Paul's initiation of the Ephesian disciples in Acts 19, must be evaluated. Only then can Luke's conception of Spirit-reception be understood. The initiation ER thus has various sub-components, including ERs for Spirit-reception, baptism, prayer, and handlaying. The book will deal with these subordinate ERs in the process of addressing the initiation ER.

Focalization

The approach to focalization employed here will be that of the dualistic external/internal focalization as found in Michael Toolan, Mieke Bal, Wolf Schmid, and Irene de Jong.[96] For reasons not to employ Gerard Genette's older triadic

---

[96] Toolan, *Narrative*; Mieke Bal, *Narratology: Introduction to the Theory of Narrative* (Toronto: University of Toronto Press, 2009); Wolf Schmid, *Narratology: An Introduction* (Berlin: De Gruyter, 2010); de Jong, *Narrators*. For recent views on focalization see, Peter Hühn, Wolf Schmid, Jörg Schönert (eds), *Point of View, Perspective, and Focalization: Modeling Mediation in Narrative* (Berlin: Walter de Gruyter, 2009), and Burkhard Niederhoff, 'Focalization', Peter Hühn, et al. (eds), *The Living Handbook of Narratology* (Hamburg: Hamburg University Press), URL = hup.sub.uni-hamburg.de/lhn/index.php ?title=Focalization &oldid=1561 [view date: 19 June, 2012].

model, Schmid offers a detailed discussion in his introduction to narratology.[97] What then do we mean when we speak of 'focalization'? When narrators tell a story from the perspective, or point of view, or 'orientation',[98] of a character, they 'focalize' through that character. For example, 'Young Tom eyed the large chocolate bar sitting on the counter'. The narrator speaks, but she describes things from young Tom's orientation. This is termed internal focalization because Tom is inside the story. Alternatively, the narrator could have said, 'A large chocolate bar sat on the counter.' In this case, the narrator tells the reader a fact without focalizing it through a character within the narrative. This is termed external focalization because the narrator stands outside the story. In both cases, the chocolate bar is the thing focalized.

Specifying the object towards which the reader's attention is directed, that is, the 'focalized', helps the analyst to identify the referent of a particular discourse. If, for example, a subsequent sentence read, 'Tom checked to see if he had enough to buy it', the 'it' could not be the counter, though 'counter' is also a noun and theoretically could be bought. The focalization of the previous sentence delimits the antecedent of the pronoun. In the same way, focalization also enables the reader/viewer to understand what is being identified in a particular scene. For example, in a documentary film an archaeologist holds up a stone artefact, and the camera zooms in for a close-up from several angles. The narrator then explains, 'This is the evidence that researchers have been looking for'. The narration works together with the camera's focalization to specify the referent to 'this' as the stone artefact, and then to make an identification of the artefact with the looked-for evidence. The same phenomenon of focalization followed by identification will be observed in Luke-Acts.

Other Literary Devices

The vast field of literary studies which goes under such headings as poetics, narrative criticism, narratology, and stylistics will not be reviewed here. Aspects of literary theory which are employed later in the book will be highlighted.

Metalepsis and Narrative Asides

Metalepsis is the shift from one narrative level to another.[99] If a narrator has one of her characters tell a story, then there is a 'story within a story', or a sublevel

---

Cf., also, Monika Fludernik, trans. Patricia Häusler-Greenfield and Monika Fludernik, *An Introduction to Narratology* (London: Routledge, 2009 [German, 2006]).
[97] Schmid, *Narratology*, 91-95.
[98] Toolan, *Narrative*, 60.
[99] John Pier, 'Metalepsis', Peter Hühn, et al. (ed.), *The Living Handbook of Narratology* (Hamburg: Hamburg University Press), Paragraph 2. URL = hup.sub.uni-hamburg.de/lhn/index.php ?title=Metalepsis &oldid=1509 [view date: 11 October, 2012]. See also, Anja Cornils, 'La métalepse dans les *Actes des Apôtres*: un signe de narration fictionnelle?' John Pier and Jean-Marie Schaeffer, ed., *Métalepses: Entorses au pacte de la représentation* (Paris: Éditions de l'EHESS, 2007), 95-107.

of narration. If the narrator stops telling the story and starts to tell the reader why s/he picked this story to tell and why she thinks the reader will like it – in other words, she holds a direct conversation with the reader about the story – then she has left the level of the narrative and gone up to the level of narrator/reader. When the narrator starts off with, 'My dear reader, you should know that…', this kind of shift in narrative level is quite clear. Sometimes, it is not so overt and more care must be paid to the narrative to identify such shifts, for they bear significance to the interpretation of the story.

Narrative asides are the form of metalepsis relevant to this study. Steven M. Sheeley writes: 'Narrative asides may be defined as parenthetical remarks addressed directly to the reader which interrupt the logical progression of the story, establishing a relationship between the narrator and the narratee which exists outside the story being narrated.'[100] Sheeley continues: 'Perhaps the most important role [of the asides is to] provide a means by which the narrators guide the readers into the correct interpretation of events.'[101] Eckart Reinmuth also underscores the role of *kommentierende Textteile*, or narrative asides: 'Especially illuminating are phrases, with which an author directly places her/himself in connection with the intended addressee, in which s/he elucidates, comments, assesses something.'[102] Thus, in the process of identifying what Luke directly taught, and not merely described, narrative asides play a significant role. For example, Luke explained in Acts 10:46 how the Jews who had come with Peter recognized the Gentiles had received the Spirit – they heard them speak with tongues and magnify God.

Functional Redundancy

To say that redundancy is important contributes nothing new. Susan Suleiman writes, 'it is by means of redundancy that plural meanings and ambiguities are eliminated and a single 'correct' reading imposed'.[103] Clearly redundancy has a function. Ronald D. Witherup draws upon Sternberg's extensive discussion of repetition in biblical narrative[104] to coin the term, 'functional redundancy', and apply it to Acts. The key element of Sternberg's theory utilized by Witherup is his short section on how repetition can vary. Sternberg lists five basic varieties

---

[100] Steven M. Sheeley, *Narrative Asides in Luke-Acts* (Sheffield: Sheffield Academic, JSOT, 1992), 36.

[101] Sheeley does not comment on glossolalia and narrative asides, *ibid.*, 175, cf. 13, 176.

[102] 'Besonders aufschlussreich sind hier Formulierungen, mit denen ein Autor sich direkt mit den intendierten Adressaten in Verbindung setzt, indem er etwas erläutert, kommentiert, bewertet'. Eckart Reinmuth, *Hermeneutik des Neuen Testaments: Eine Einführung in die Lektüre des Neuen Testaments* (Göttingen: Vandenhoeck und Ruprecht, 2002), 19-20.

[103] Susan Rubin Suleiman, 'Redundancy and the "Readable" Text', PoeT 1.3 (1980), 119-42; 120. See also, Janice Capel Anderson, 'Double and Triple Stories, the Implied Reader, and Redundancy in Matthew', Se. 31 (1985), 71-89.

[104] Sternberg, *Poetics*, 365-440, esp. 390-92.

of repetition: (1) expansion or addition; (2) truncation or ellipsis; (3) change of order; (4) grammatical transformations; (5) substitution. Sternberg argues that these types of repetition are not present in the biblical text merely for stylistic reasons, but serve practical functions in the narrative. Witherup demonstrates this in his analysis of the three call/conversion stories of Paul, showing that the role of Paul's companions and Ananias progressively decreases, while the brilliance of the revelatory light and direct instructions from Jesus increases.[105] He also analyses the repetition of the Cornelius episode demonstrating that it functions to advance the plot, increase suspense, interweave characterization and plot, and establish thematic unity.[106]

As the Spirit-reception scenes of Luke-Acts have some elements repeated and some omitted, we must ask how these repetitions and omissions are functioning cumulatively in the narrative and not immediately assume that Luke was inconsistent. An awareness of functional redundancy allows one to recognize that the purpose of the scenes may vary. In a sequence of scenes, the basic structure may be repeated but the first scene may emphasize one aspect of Spirit-reception while the second emphasizes another and omits what was emphasized before. For example, the Pentecost story repeatedly focalizes xenolalia with no mention of handlaying, whereas the Samaria story focalizes handlaying and does not mention xenolalia. Functional redundancy raises the possibility (other factors would be necessary to confirm that possibility) that Pentecost is addressing the nature of Spirit-reception while Samaria speaks to a means.

Action Peaks and Didactic Peaks

Robert E. Longacre employs the term 'peak' in his analysis of narrative discourse: 'I use the term *peak* to refer to any episode-like unit set apart by special surface structure features and corresponding to the climax or denouement in the notional structure'.[107] He breaks the concept of 'peak' into subsets, the action peak and the didactic peak, and illustrates the distinction from the Genesis flood story where the water reaches a high point, an action peak (Gen. 7:17-24), and then where God blesses Noah and makes a covenant, a didactic peak (Gen. 9:1-17).[108] Longacre writes, 'A didactic peak is a special elaboration of some episode which precedes or follows the action peak. Essentially action ceases at a didactic peak and participant(s) speak out in a monologue/dialogue which develops the theme of the story'.[109]

Longacre identifies a variety of features which mark peaks. With 'rhetorical underlining' the author slows down narration producing the heightening effect

---

[105] Ronald D. Witherup, 'Functional Redundancy in the Acts of the Apostles: A Case Study', *JSNT* 48 (1992), 67-86; 84.
[106] Ronald D. Witherup, 'Cornelius Over and Over Again: "Functional Redundancy" in the Acts of the Apostles', *JSNT* 49 (1993), 45-66; 64-65.
[107] Robert E. Longacre, *The Grammar of Discourse* (New York: Plenum, 1996), 37.
[108] *Ibid.*, 37.
[109] *Ibid.*, 37-38.

of a slow-motion segment of a film.[110] 'Concentration of participants' fills the narrative 'stage' with actors.[111] 'Heightened vividness', Longacre writes, 'may be obtained in a story by a shift in the nominal-verbal balance, by a tense shift, by shift to a more specific person, or by shift along the narrative-drama parameter'.[112] By 'narrative-drama parameter', Longacre means a continuum from narrative to pseudo-dialogue (apostrophe and rhetorical questions) to dialogue to drama. He particularly notes the use of rhetorical questions as peak markers.[113] 'Change of pace' involves 'variation in the size of constructions and variation in the amount of connective material'.[114] 'Change of vantage point and/or orientation' refers to focalization, i.e., 'through whose eyes do we view the story?'[115] Finally, changes in the number of particles and the use of onomatopoeia can indicate a peak.[116]

In application to Luke-Acts, Longacre's 'peaks' can be useful in sorting through what has typically been a disputed area – the matter of didactic intention. That Luke is a theologian is not seriously in dispute. But, *how* can we identify his theological points? Didactic peaks, drawn from discourse theory, can serve as a useful tool in helping to pinpoint exactly what Luke was emphasizing for didactic purposes. Johannes Panagopoulos employs this principle, though apart from Longacre's terminology, to Acts, observing: 'that one cannot separate the theological statements, which for the most part are located in the speeches, from their frame. The Pentecost speech, for example, has no meaning when one separates it from the Pentecost experience and vice versa'.[117]

Type-Scenes

Matthew Clark states that, 'One of the most important aspects of the Homeric epics is the use of type-scenes; that is, recurring situations which are narrated according to a more or less fixed pattern'.[118] Mark W. Edwards, in his extensive review of the literature on Homeric type-scenes, points to Walter Arend as having early on identified common 'typischen Scenen'.[119] Arend described a wide variety of type-scenes: the arrival, the visit, the embassy, the dream, the sacrifice,

---

[110] *Ibid.*, 39.
[111] *Ibid.*, 40.
[112] *Ibid.*
[113] *Ibid.*, 42
[114] *Ibid.*, 43.
[115] *Ibid.*, 45-46.
[116] *Ibid.*, 47.
[117] 'daß man die theologischen Aussagen, die sich zum größten Teil in den Reden befinden, von Ihren Rahmen nicht trennen kann. Die Pfingstrede, z.B. hat keinen Sinn, wenn man sie von dem Pfingstereignis trennt und umgekehrt'. Johannes Panagopoulos, 'Zur Theologie der Apostelgeschichte', *NT* 14.2 (April, 1972), 137-59; 139.
[118] Matthew Clark, 'Formulas, metre and type-scenes', Robert Fowler (ed.), *The Cambridge Companion to Homer* (Cambridge: CUP, 2004), 117-38; 134.
[119] Mark W. Edwards, 'Homer and Oral Tradition: The Type-Scene', *OT* 7.2 (1992), 284-330.

the meal, the landing of a ship, the wagon journey, the chariot ride, the arming of the warrior, the putting on of clothing, sleep, deliberation, the gathering, oath-taking, the bath. Each of these type-scenes has standard elements. For example, in the visit: (1) the guest comes to the entrance of the central hall; (2) someone present sees the guest; (3) gets up from his place and hurries to the guest; (4) takes the guest by the hand and greets the guest; (5) leads the guest into the hall; (6) encourages the guest to take a seat and prepares a seat for the guest, usually a seat of honour; (7) brings food and invites the guest to eat; (8) the meal is described and finished with a formulaic saying.[120] There are variations, though. For example, a character could be a human, or could be a god, and there will be other variations accordingly. Though elements are standard, they are not identical. Edwards writes, 'Like Greek temples, instances of a type-scene are similar in structure but always different in scale and in details.'[121] Type-scenes may be abbreviated to a few lines, or expanded over one or two pages, as suits the poet. Amplification is not done at random, though. It is purposeful emphasis of some feature of the story.[122]

In terms of biblical studies, Robert Alter is recognized as having introduced the principles of type-scenes.[123] Alter, drawing upon the advances made in Homeric research, first listed the classic Biblical type-scenes:

> the annunciation ... of the birth of the hero to his barren mother; the encounter with the future betrothed at a well; the epiphany in the field; the initiatory trial; danger in the desert and the discovery of a well or other source of sustenance; the testament of the dying hero.[124]

---

[120] Walter Arend, *Die Typischen Scene bei Homer* (Berlin: Weidmannsche Buchhandlung, 1933), 34-35.

[121] Mark W. Edwards, *Homer: Poet of the Iliad* (Baltimore: John Hopkins University Press, 1987), 72.

[122] *Ibid.*, 74.

[123] Robert Alter, 'Biblical Type-Scenes and the Uses of Convention', *CI* 5.2 (Winter, 1978), 355-68; popularized in Robert Alter, *Art of Biblical Narrative* (n.pl.: Basic Books, 1981), see chapter 3, 'Biblical Type-Scenes and the Uses of Convention', 47-62. Cf. Leland Ryken, *Words of Delight: A Literary Introduction to the Bible* (Grand Rapids: Baker, 1992), 50-51; Leland Ryken, *How to Read the Bible as Literature and Get More Out of It* (Grand Rapids: Zondervan, 1984), 192-93.

[124] Alter, *Art*, 51. Since Alter, many others have utilized a type-scene approach, e.g. recently, Jonathan Kruschwitz, 'The Type-Scene Connection between Genesis 38 and the Joseph Story', *JSOT* 36.4 (2012), 383-410; Thomas E. Grafton, 'Just As It Was Spoken: Annunciation Type-Scenes and Faithful Response in Luke's Birth Narrative', *CBibW* 31 (2011), 143-61; Benjamin J.M. Johnson, 'What Type of Son is Samson? Reading Judges 13 as a Biblical Type-Scene', *JETS* 53.2 (June, 2010), 269-86; 269; Min Suc Kee, 'The Heavenly Council and its Type-scene', *JSOT* 31.3 (March, 2007), 259-73; Brian Britt, 'Prophetic Concealment in a Biblical Type Scene', *CBQ* 64.1 (2002), 37-58; Robert H. O'Connell, 'Proverbs VII 16-17: A Case of Fatal Deception in a "Woman and the Window" Type-Scene', *VT* 41.2 (April, 1991), 235-41.

Like Arend, Alter found standard elements in each type-scene. For example, in the well type-scene: the man comes from a foreign land; draws water from the well; the woman hurries away to her family to tell the news; the man eats with the family; and they marry.[125] However, biblical type-scenes are not as highly stylized as in Homer.

Thus, the type-scene generally, as Mary Therese DesCamp observes, differs from simple repetition of actions or words in that it is a more complex phenomenon. Yet, repetition and type-scenes, while different, both function as frames. She writes:

> the occurrence of a single part of the type-scene results in the cognitive retrieval of the entire frame. Type-scenes are not merely literary mechanisms; they are first and foremost conceptual mechanisms, and their presence alerts a reader to activate a conceptual frame.[126]

This is highly significant, for it eliminates the tedious duty of having to repeat every detail every time a typical scene appears and it enables a writer economically to allude to a concept. But this also means that if the reader is not familiar with the type-scene, s/he will miss the allusion.

In making the transition from Homer to biblical studies, and given that the type-scene is a concept familiar from modern cinema, some terminological clarification is needed. Tannehill defines a type-scene as, 'a basic situation which recurs several times within a narrative'.[127] This does not have the emphasis upon repetitive elements that Arend and Alter have, but does catch the idea of a repetitive scene. However, Joel F. Williams critiques Tannehill's use of the term 'type-scene' for scenes that are similar within a particular narrative, but do not reflect a convention that the reader is familiar with from literature in general. Williams prefers the term 'narrative analogies' for Tannehill's phenomenon.[128] While a type-scene can be understood as belonging to the general cultural conventions about how a story should be told (for example in the Hollywood 'chase scene', a fruit stand is inevitably upended), Tannehill has not strayed far from Arend's seminal work which was a study of type-scenes within Homer with a comparison to Apollonius and Virgil. In other words, a single author can have scenes typical within her/his work and this is just as much a type-scene as when we find a scene common in popular literature or cinema. Moreover, Williams overlooks the ability of a narrative to construct a new scene with which the audience is unfamiliar, and then repeat that scene with its constituent elements, thus

---

[125] Alter, *Art*, 52.
[126] Mary Therese DesCamp, *Metaphor and Ideology: Liber Antiquitatum Biblicarum and Literary Methods Through a Cognitive Lens* (Leiden: Brill, 2007), 81.
[127] Robert C. Tannehill, *The Narrative Unity of Luke-Acts: A Literary Interpretation* Volume 1: *The Gospel According to Luke* (Philadelphia: Fortress, 1986), 170.
[128] Joel F. Williams, *Other Followers of Jesus: Minor Characters as Major Figures in Mark's Gospel* (Sheffield: Sheffield Academic, 1994), 38.

making it recognizable as a type-scene. For example, having read one annunciation scene, and then encountering a scene with similar features, a reader will compare the two scenes. Upon encountering a third, or fourth annunciation scene, a reader will by then have expectations about how annunciation scenes will turn out. Those expectations may then be met, or subverted, but the type-scene is present nonetheless.

This kind of intertextuality is at work when New Testament writers draw upon conventional scenes from the Hebrew Scriptures, often altering them or playing upon them, as with the annunciation not to Elizabeth, but to Zacharias, and Jesus' encounter with the woman at the well. The level of detail and stylization of a type-scene may also vary, but each type-scene provides a framework within which various typical elements can be configured and reconfigured. Standard features can be rearranged while still retaining the typicality of the scene.[129] Homer may depict the arming of a human or of a god. For the modern cinematic 'hero and hero's companion ride off into the sunset' scene, the hero may go off on a horse, or car, or speedboat, or rocket ship, and the companion may be a 'sidekick' or a significant other. The story remains the same; only the discourse changes.

Thus, Tannehill's definition is perfectly suitable for literary analysis purposes and allows us, for example, to consider Jesus' baptism as belonging to the baptism scenes found in Acts. From the perspective of the rereader, the basic elements of Jesus' baptism, namely ritual immersion in water, prayer and Spirit experience, appear in various forms and configurations in Acts baptism scenes. Prayer, for example, can be found in Acts 8, but with modification. There it is stated that the initiators pray. Prior prayer also features in the Cornelius episode, both on the part of Cornelius (Acts 10:2, 30) and Peter (Acts 10:9). In Acts 19, Paul does not pray, but he lays hands upon the Ephesians, an act which Acts 8:15-17 has already associated with prayer. The experiential quality of Jesus' Holy Spirit encounter finds its counterpart in later stories where visions and other tangible manifestations are characteristic of Pentecostal experience (e.g. Acts 2:2-4, 17; 10:46; 19:6). That a literary analysis categorizes Jesus' baptism and Spirit experience with the 'Christian' baptism of Acts has theological significance.

Not only can a narrative construct a type-scene by repetition, but we may also arrive at a type-scene when an experience common to characters in the narrative or to the implied reader is portrayed. For example, Luke presented John the Baptist's baptism as a virtually universal experience for Palestinian Jewry. When Jesus is baptised he partakes of the common experience. The reader, both initial and rereader, expects to see an example of a Johannine baptism. But Luke made it more. Luke's reader is informed of the baptism of the people (Luke 3:21). Luke's picture of Jesus' baptism builds upon this typical experience by adding the coming of the Spirit and the voice from heaven. His baptism was like, and

---

[129] Cf. George Savran, 'Theophany as Type Scene', *PTX* 23.2 (Spring, 2003), 119-49; 125-26.

yet unlike, that of any of John's other baptisands, as befits one whom the reader knows is God's son. Furthermore, in addition to being a type-scene by virtue of its commonality with other characters in the narrative and by having elements in common with Acts baptism scenes, Jesus' baptism is a type-scene because the implied reader recognizes it as an example of something common to her/his own experience. As discussed above, the implied reader is familiar with Christianity and with Christianity's standard features: water baptism and Spirit experience. Jesus' baptism is therefore a typical scene, not because it is precisely and exactly like the Christian baptism known to the implied reader, but because it has common, recognizable elements.

To this someone will surely object that Jesus' experience and Christian baptism have too many differences to be considered parallel: Jesus was baptised by John, whereas Christian converts are baptised by Christians; Jesus received the Spirit directly from heaven, whereas at Pentecost the Spirit is given by Jesus; Jesus was anointed as Messianic deliverer, but Christians experience the Spirit as members of the church. However, as stated above under the discussion of Homeric scenes, identical repetition is not a feature of type-scenes. A type-scene provides a structure containing recognizable elements. The elements consist of typical scenery, roles and plot, but the instantiation of those elements may differ considerably without in the least detracting from the typicality of the scene. In a modern 'boy meets girl by accident' type-scene, the accident could be that they bump into one another in a school hallway. Or, their cars crash into each other. There are an infinite number of possible forms for the encounter, yet all would be easily recognizable as 'boy meets girl by accident'. In the biblical 'boy meets girl at well' type-scene, the 'boy' could alternately be Jacob, or Abraham's servant, or Moses, or Jesus.[130] Thus, who does the baptising, who gives the Spirit and the functional nexus of Spirit activity may differ depending upon the particular discourse, but the type-scene remains the same.

Rhetorical Criticism and Amplification

Not all the techniques of ancient rhetorical criticism will be studied here in relation to Luke-Acts. Such would be a book in itself. However, αὔξησις or 'amplification', one of the basic tools of communication learned by ancient students of rhetoric,[131] will be employed because it corresponds so closely with the modern approaches of sequential reading and presupposition pools. Malcolm Heath identifies amplification as, 'the techniques used to increase the perceived importance

---

[130] James G. Williams, 'The Beautiful and the Barren: Conventions in Biblical Types-Scenes', *JSOT* 17 (1980), 107-19; 109, 113.
[131] Malcolm Heath, 'Invention', In Stanley E. Porter, ed., *Handbook of Classical Rhetoric in the Hellenistic Period 330 B.C.–A.D. 400* (Leiden: Brill, 1997), 89-119, 95.

of some fact that is taken as given'.[132] Kennedy writes, 'Amplification is a rhetorical device whereby a speaker dwells on a thought and thus gives it greater emphasis'.[133] He states further that:

> Most of what goes on in rhetorical composition is *amplification* of the basic thesis of the speaker by means of the topics which he has chosen to utilize in support of it.[134]

> The speaker must therefore develop his subject repeating his basic ideas several times in different words, illustrating what he means, relating it in some way to the experience of his audience.[135]

Richard Burridge writes that it, 'involves developing at length or repeating a certain theme or idea to ensure that the audience understands its importance'.[136] The unknown[137] author of *On the Sublime*, a first century A.D. treatise on communication, wrote:

> Closely associated with the part of our subject we have just treated of[138] is that excellence of writing which is called amplification, when a writer or pleader, whose theme admits of many successive starting-points and pauses, brings on one impressive point after another in a continuous and ascending scale.[139]

First century writer Quintilian stated:

> Accumulation of words and sentences identical in meaning may also be regarded under the head of amplification. For although the climax is not in this case reached by a series of steps, it is none the less attained by the piling up of words.[140]

Kennedy writes, 'A speech is linear and cumulative, and any context in it can only be perceived in contrast to what has gone before.'[141] Witherington argues that Acts uses the rhetorical technique of amplification/accumulation, not just within individual speeches, but across the series of speeches:

> The 'Christian' speeches in Acts must be examined in the context of the ongoing and developing narrative, as they are meant to have a cumulative effect. By this I

---

[132] *Ibid.*, 95.
[133] Kennedy, *Criticism*, 53.
[134] *Ibid.*, 21, original italics.
[135] *Ibid.*, 22.
[136] Richard A. Burridge, 'The Gospels and Acts', Stanley E. Porter (ed.), *Handbook of Classical Rhetoric in the Hellenistic Period 330 B.C.–A.D. 400* (Leiden: Brill, 1997), 507-32, 524.
[137] R. Dean Anderson Jr., *Ancient Rhetorical Theory and Paul* (Leuven: Peeters, 1999), 84.
[138] Section X discusses selection and combination of examples. Longinus, *On the Sublime*, trans. H.L. Havell (London: Macmillan, 1890).
[139] *Ibid*.
[140] Quintillian, trans. H.E. Butler, *The Institutio Oratoria of Quintilian* (Cambridge: Harvard University Press, 1921), 279. Cf. Jeanne Fahnestock, *Rhetorical Style: The Uses of Language in Persuasion* (Oxford: OUP, 2011), 394.
[141] Kennedy, *Criticism*, 5.

mean that after Acts 2 sometimes Luke will repeat themes in speeches, but only allusively, because he has already established the theme in an earlier speech. These speeches, as we find them now in Acts, are meant to have a cumulative effect on the audience and should not be seen as isolated phenomena, however they functioned in the original historical setting.[142]

Malcolm Heath points out that though there is no specific rhetorical term for amplification within a single work over the course of a series of speeches, there is the case 'of Cato, who (reportedly) ended all his speeches on any subject by saying that Carthage should be destroyed'.[143] Given that an ancient author had control over her/his work[144] just as an ancient speaker had control over her/his speech, Witherington's approach, namely that Luke employed amplification over the course of his work, cannot be viewed as unreasonable. Richard P. Thompson shares Witherington's method, understanding that ancient rhetoric produces a 'cumulative effect' within the whole narrative, not just the speeches.[145] The only point of adjustment would be that accumulation did not start with Acts, but with Luke's Gospel. Specifically in regards to the Saul conversion stories, Witherington writes: 'the later speeches are meant to amplify and add to the earlier narrative, or put the other way around, the later speeches presuppose what has been said in the earlier narrative and in various ways reinforce its major thrusts'.[146]

Witherington's application of amplification to the speeches of Acts corroborates the modern techniques of sequential reading and presupposition pools. The speeches of Luke-Acts build upon one another. Thus, to understand Acts 2, one must read the story of Jesus' Jordan experience. One must ask how Luke accumulated his concept of Spirit-reception over the course of his entire work. How did he build the picture? Thus, for example, the Spirit-reception scene of Acts 19 ought not to be analysed in isolation from all the Spirit-reception scenes that have come before, but rather, as the last Spirit-reception scene of the series (Acts 22:16 is not a Spirit-reception scene and mentions only part of what 9:17-18 reports), all the reader's accumulated understanding of Spirit-reception comes to bear upon it. Being last in a series does *not* make a scene the final exemplar. However, it is impacted by all that has gone before. Modern literary and discourse approaches are therefore not at odds with the rhetoric of ancient composition.

Identifying Didactic Intent

Reformed commentator H.N. Ridderbos, writing of the 'apostolic, authoritative character' of the speeches in Acts, stated that, 'they are directed not only to the

---

[142] Ben Witherington, *New Testament Rhetoric: An Introductory Guide to the Art of Persuasion in and of the New Testament* (Eugene: Cascade, 2009), 52.
[143] Malcolm Heath, private email, 04/01/2013.
[144] *Ibid.*
[145] Richard P. Thompson, *Keeping the Church in Its Place: The Church as Narrative Character in Acts* (New York: T&T Clark, 2006), 15.
[146] Witherington, *Rhetoric*, 76.

original audience, but to all who read them'.[147] But speeches could be viewed differently than stories. How, then, are we to treat Luke's narrative sections? As William and Robert Menzies, Arie W. Zwiep and Douglas A. Blanc have pointed out, the Evangelical community recognizes that narrative portions of scripture can communicate theology.[148] For example, Grant Osborn affirms that, 'Biblical narratives contain theology.'[149] Klein, Blomberg and Hubbard, in addressing the genre of Acts state, 'If theological biographies [sic] best captures the essence of the Gospels, then *theological history* – a narrative of interrelated events from a given place and time, chosen to communicate theological truths – best characterizes Acts.'[150] David S. Dockery recognizes the historical value of Luke's material, but views it as, 'primarily theological'.[151] Anthony C. Thiselton writes that Acts is, '*both* theology *and* history'.[152] David G. Peterson calls Acts, 'theological history'.[153]

Luke's didactic intentions are not seriously in question. Moreover, after the work of Roger Stronstad on keeping the theologies of Luke and Paul distinct,[154] it is widely recognized, though perhaps not always practiced, that Luke cannot be read through the lens of Paul's letters. The issue now revolves around how Luke's theology can be identified. Gordon Fee was sceptical this could be done, but he put the question well: 'how does one unpack or discover Luke's *theological* interests in his individual narratives, and how does one distinguish those he *intends* to be normative from those he does not, without his giving us some clue

---

[147] H.N. Ridderbos, *The Speeches of Peter in the Acts of the Apostles* (Leicester: Tyndale, 1962), 28.

[148] William W. Menzies and Robert P. Menzies, *Spirit and Power, Foundations of Pentecostal Experience* (Grand Rapids: Zonderva, 2000), 42; Arie W. Zwiep, *Christ, the Spirit and the Community of God: Essays on the Acts of the Apostles* (Tübingen: Mohr Siebeck, 2010), 102; Douglas A. Blanc, for American Baptists specifically, *A Theological Construction of Spirit Baptism: Seeking a Consensus Between Baptists and Pentecostals in the USA* (Ph.D. dissertation, University of Wales: Trinity St. David, 2012), 272.

[149] Grant R. Osborn, *The Hermeneutical Spiral: A Comprehensive Introduction to Biblical Interpretation* (Downers Grove: IVP, 2006), 220.

[150] William W. Klein, Craig L. Blomberg, Robert L. Hubbard, *Introduction to Biblical Interpretation* (Nashville: Thomas Nelson, 1993), 418, original italics.

[151] David S. Dockery, 'The Theology of Acts', *CTRev* 5.1 (1990), 43-55; 45.

[152] Anthony C. Thiselton, *The Holy Spirit: In Biblical Teaching, Through the Centuries, and Today* (London: SPCK, 2013), 50, original italics; similarly, Anthony C. Thiselton, *The Hermeneutics of Doctrine* (Grand Rapids: Eerdmans, 2007), 449. Cf. the ground-breaking work of Marshall, *Luke*.

[153] David G. Peterson, *The Acts of the Apostles* (Grand Rapids: Eerdmans, 2009), 26-27.

[154] Cf. especially Roger Stronstad, *The Charismatic Theology of St. Luke* (Peabody: Hendrickson, 1984), 9-12. But, cf. G.D. Kilpatrick's similar caution, 'The Spirit, God, and Jesus in Acts', *JTS* 15 (1964), 63; 63.

in the text itself.¹⁵⁵ Redaction criticism and a literary approach offer a way forward.¹⁵⁶

A number of commentators have identified specific narrative elements which communicate didactic intent, and their suggestions merit evaluation. Peterson lists nine literary and rhetorical factors that might have 'hortatory implications'.¹⁵⁷ These are: 'editorial summaries', 'inclusions', 'use of key terms, often in contextually limited ways', 'use of scripture', 'speeches with patterns of repetition', 'narrative repetition', 'parallel accounts', 'contrasting accounts', and 'significant geographical, cultural, and social indicators'.¹⁵⁸ Cole states more generally that narratives, 'may include didactic elements as actors in the narrative comment or command'.¹⁵⁹

Witherington suggests three ways that didactic intent can be identified:

> (1) look for positive repeated patterns in the text, or (2) look for when there is only one pattern, or (3) look for when there is a clear divine approval or disapproval in the text for some belief or behaviour or experience or religious practice.¹⁶⁰

Klein, Blomberg and Hubbard reason similarly:

> Primarily, we need to study the entire book to determine if specific events form a consistent pattern throughout or if the positive models Luke presents vary from one situation to another. The former will suggest that Luke was emphasizing a normative, consistent principle; the latter, that applications *may* change from one time and place to the next.¹⁶¹

Allan T. Loder likewise asks, 'Does Luke offer a *consistent pattern* of Spirit-baptism in Acts *in order to teach* that the experience (or experiences) described should be *re*-experienced in the life of every Christian?'¹⁶² Avemarie and Keener required, but did not find, consistent repetition to make tongues normative.¹⁶³ So too, Rick Walston writes, 'Something must be repeated to establish a norm (a

---

¹⁵⁵ Gordon D. Fee, *Gospel and Spirit: Issues in New Testament Hermeneutics* (Grand Rapids: Baker Academic, 1991), 91, original italics.
¹⁵⁶ Menzies and Menzies, *Spirit*, 41.
¹⁵⁷ Peterson, *Acts*, 42.
¹⁵⁸ *Ibid.*, 42-47.
¹⁵⁹ Cole, *Life*, 206.
¹⁶⁰ Ben Witherington, *The Acts of the Apostles: A Socio-Rhetorical Commentary* (Grand Rapids: Eerdmans, 1998), 100.
¹⁶¹ Klein, Blomberg and Hubbard, *Interpretation*, 424, original italics.
¹⁶² Thomas A. Loder, 'An Examination of The Classical Pentecostal Doctrine of The Baptism in The Holy Spirit: In Light of the Pentecostal Position on the Sources of Theology' (M.A. thesis, Providence Theological Seminary, 2000), 72, original italics; similarly, Craig L. Blomberg, *From Pentecost to Patmos: An Introduction to Acts through Revelation* (Nashville: B&H, 2006), 10.
¹⁶³ Avemarie, *Tauferzählungen*, 147. Craig S. Keener, *Acts, An Exegetical Commentary* (Grand Rapids: Baker Academic, 2012), 1.830; Craig S. Keener, 'Why does Luke use Tongues as a Sign of the Spirit's Empowerment?' JPT 15.2, 177-84; 183.

'have-to pattern'). Furthermore, this 'thing' must be consistent each time it is repeated'.[164]

In evaluating these proposals, we observe that Peterson wisely indicates multiple factors in the communication of theology, and Cole understands the power of narrative asides. Witherington's third point fits neatly into the fourth point of discourse principles advocated by Green, the function of characters, by their responses to ideology presented in the narrative, to influence the audience either for or against that ideology. The concept of normative spokespersons fits into this category. However, the approaches of Witherington, Klein, Blomberg and Hubbard, Loder, Avemarie, Keener, and Walston also assume that a 'repeated' or 'consistent' pattern is necessary in order to communicate authorial intention regarding the prescription of behaviour.[165] Yet, the mere repetition of a particular pattern, while suggestive, does not answer the question of whether the author would have presented a different pattern in a different circumstance. In other words, suppose that in every case in Luke-Acts that Spirit-reception was mentioned, the individuals involved were also said to have spoken in tongues. Six out of six, including Jesus at the Jordan, or seven out of seven, depending upon whether Acts chapter 4 is included as an initial reception of the Spirit, is one hundred percent. So at first blush one might think Luke was absolutely communicating an intention about tongues as evidence of Spirit-reception. However, what if tongues simply happened to occur in the stories that Luke told? Had he told a seventh or eighth story, tongues may not have been included. Moreover, six or even seven is a small sample to base a doctrine on. It would seem that one needs more than repetitious patterns to establish authorial intent.

This then raises the question of 'incidental' details in a story. David Trobisch cites apparent discrepancies and improprieties in Luke's story of the ascension, in Saul's conversion, and in the abrupt transition from 'Saul' to 'Paul' and concludes: 'Because of the poor literary quality of Acts, it does not seem appropriate to base an argument on details but instead to concentrate on the major lines of the overall concept'.[166] However, Trobisch does not even mention the careful literary analysis of the three Saul conversion stories by Witherup, and what he deems poor editing may simply be due to ancient literary conventions being different from modern ones. On the other hand, Johnson writes, 'The more one reads

---

[164] Rick Walston, *The Speaking in Tongues Controversy: The Initial, Physical Evidence of the Baptism in the Holy Spirit Debate* (USA, n.p.: Xulon, 2003), 146.
[165] Cf. Dockery, 'Theology', 46.
[166] David Trobisch, 'The Book of Acts as a Narrative Commentary on the Letters of the New Testament: A Programmatic Essay', Andrew F. Gregory and C. Kavin Rowe (eds), *Rethinking the Unity and Reception of Luke and Acts* (Columbia: University of South Carolina Press, 2010), 119-27, 125.

Luke-Acts, the more intricate and subtle appear the traces of the author's creativity in every phase of the narrative'.[167] Going a step further, Witherington doubts that incidental details even exist:

> One of the things Luke as a rhetorical historian is unlikely to do is offer interesting but rhetorically irrelevant or insignificant details in his narrative. Everything is included with the view to persuading the audience about various matters. In short, the material is purpose-driven and tendentious in shape.[168]

When viewed from this perspective, then, a repetitious pattern would not be happenstance, but a product of the author's crafting. Patterns do express authorial intent when Witherington's point is granted that the total literary work is the result of careful arrangement and construction. The opposing view, that Luke simply recorded historical events without any ulterior theological motives, naturally does not allow patterns to be significant for understanding the author's communication. As has already been discussed, the question of Luke as a theologian is settled. This means that patterns must be viewed as communicatively significant. What it does not mean, though, is that the *only* way Luke could have communicated is through repetition. Where this is assumed there remains the possibility that other means of communication besides repetition have been overlooked.

So how then do literary devices, including repetition and 'patterns', divulge to the reader the author's intent? They do so by separating aspects of a narrative which pertain to the narrative itself from aspects which pertain to the intended audience. Taking a simple, but clear example, in a sports-shoe commercial featuring a running athlete, the athlete may be wearing a blue shirt, but the camera does not focus on the shirt; it focuses on the shoes. The brand of shirt is not mentioned, but the famous shoe company has its name clearly presented. The blue colour is not likely by chance, as everything in a commercial can be expected to be carefully scripted; however, no overt attempt is necessarily being made to persuade the audience to wear blue. An observer of the commercial can only conclude that its creator intends for the audience to be influenced by the choice in footwear of the athlete. If the audience is also persuaded to wear blue, that could be seen as 'collateral influence' not especially intended, but unavoidable. In literary terms, the athlete is a 'normative spokesperson', and the shoe is 'focalized'. Identifying the item being sold in the commercial is thus not a matter of guesswork. The intuitive understanding of the commercial can be definitively analysed.[169]

---

[167] Luke Timothy Johnson, *The Literary Function of Possessions in Luke-Acts* (n.pl.: Scholars, 1977), 14.
[168] Witherington, *Rhetoric*, 78.
[169] The literature on analysis of advertising and of visual media in general is extensive, but some examples include: Guy Cook, *The Discourse of Advertising* (London: Routledge, 2001); Gunther Kress and Theo van Leeuwen, *Reading Images: The Grammar of Visual Design* (London: Routledge, 2006); Theo van Leeuwen and Carey

Focalization, then, is a crucial aspect of determining didactic quality. But, what is a normative spokesperson? This is a construct of the author, a character the implied audience is expected to sympathize with, believe, and even imitate.[170] The actual audience may, in fact, not like the character at all, but it will understand that the author wants it to like the character. The narrative spokesperson functions further to identify what is to be taken as normative for the audience. After the action scene, does the spokesperson turn to the audience and encourage a healthy lifestyle, or does s/he somehow emphasize a certain brand of footwear? That is, is there an action peak followed by a didactic peak? In terms of Luke-Acts, does the normative spokesperson make a statement about what has been narrated? For example, after describing how people experienced the promised Holy Spirit, Luke had Peter instruct his audience that if they would repent and be baptised they would receive the aforementioned gift of the Spirit. Or, the narrator himself may turn to the audience and make a statement about some previously narrated event, as in Acts 10:45-47, which informs the reader, 'This is how the early leaders, Peter and his fellows, knew people had received the Spirit.' One reads against the grain to acknowledge such a narrative aside, but then to say that it only had relevance for the characters in the story, and not for the audience. Luke did not add a qualifying statement such as, 'uniquely on this occasion', or, 'but things are done differently now'. The procedure used by early church leaders is established as normative for the audience by two literary devices, the influence of a normative spokesperson and a narrative aside.

A counter example is Peter's prayer on the housetop (Acts 10:9). Though Peter is a normative spokesperson, and his example influential for the reader, there is no narrative aside saying, 'God met him because he was on the housetop', or, 'all the faithful were regularly ascending the housetops to pray', or, 'the apostles knew that he was acceptable to God because he prayed on the housetop'. Housetop prayer is not a regular practice of Luke's heroes (though Jesus likes to pray on mountains, Luke 6:12; 9:28) nor does Luke especially praise housetop prayer. There is no textual signal to guide the reader into believing that Luke is 'selling' housetop prayer. *The mere fact that an event is narrated does not make it normative* nor suggest that there is didactic intent on the part of the author. The athlete in the commercial wears a blue shirt, Peter prays on the housetop, etc. Those things are not being promoted, though by virtue of the power of suggestion, the audience may in fact be influenced to wear a blue shirt, or pray on a rooftop (or mountaintop). However, the combination of focalization and normative spokespersons, especially speeches by normative spokespersons ('I only use product X'), as well as comments by the narrator spoken directly to the implied audience

---

Jewitt, *The Handbook of Visual Analysis* (London: SAGE, 2001); Barbara J. Phillips and Edward F. McQuarrie, 'Beyond Visual Metaphor: A New Typology of Visual Rhetoric in Advertising', *MarT* 4 (June, 2004), 113-36.

[170] On imitation, see Petri Merenlahti, *Poetics for the Gospels? Rethinking Narrative Criticism* (London: T&T Clark, 2002), 52.

('Remember, that is how the apostles did it'), are well able to identify what is intended to be didactic.

Didactic intent is therefore not inferred from narrative in the sense of reaching an inductive conclusion, no matter how repetitive a pattern may be. It is directly identified by the analysis of focalization, normative spokespersons, action/didactic peaks, presupposition pools/entity representations, repetition, and patterns. For this reason, counting the times a particular word, phrase or phenomenon occurs throughout a narrative may indirectly indicate what might be important to an author, but it does not directly divulge didactic intent. That must be determined by study of literary devices. Analysis of Luke-Acts based upon the numbers, that is, so many occurrences of handlaying, of tongues, of repentance, etc., does not consider significant data sets, namely focalization, position in the narrative, presupposition pools/entity representations, and structures of repetition, and therefore does not present the full picture of Luke's work. A prime example of this is Walston's argument that, 'less than twelve percent of the people who were saved throughout the book of Acts spoke in tongues'.[171] One must ask how the narrative focalizes the various phenomena, what normative spokespersons and the narrator say about the focalized, what position the focalized phenomena have in the narrative's sequential development, whether any structures of repetition communicate the author's viewpoint, and what information accumulates in the presupposition pool generally, and specifically in the entity representations for particular themes. If such a broader analysis were to indicate that tongues-speaking was a part of the ER for initiation, then, like baptism itself (e.g. Acts 13:43) and like reception of the Spirit (Acts 2:41), it would not need to be explicitly mentioned in every account of conversion. That is, all the information in a particular ER need not be repeated in every instantiation of it. A single reference could be sufficient to evoke the entire ER, as happens at Acts 2:41 where only water baptism is mentioned but Spirit-reception is understood because Peter has specifically promised the Spirit upon water baptism.

Conclusion

By sequential reading, as advocated by Perry, Phillips, Green, et al., the interpreter can avoid disambiguating the text prematurely and spoiling the intended rhetorical effect. Instead, sequential analysis draws upon the insights of discourse analysis by recognizing expected normality, utilizing presupposition pools and intertextual frames, and looking for narrative/audience response. Luke also employed a variety of literary devices to shape his actual reader's thinking. One of the most significant is focalization, the lens through which the reader experiences the story. The thing focalized is the object, or idea, or person, or phenomenon which Luke's narrative camera shows, sometimes close up, sometimes from multiple angles, and which becomes imprinted upon the reader's mind, taking its

---

[171] Walston, *Controversy*, 153.

place in the reader's general presupposition pool and in the reader's ER for some particular topic. Metalepsis and narrative asides function to disclose the author's intent and may therefore function in tandem with focalization, the latter drawing the reader's attention to something and the former clarifying its significance. Functional redundancy means that the repetition for which Luke is well known is not merely a product of his particular style, but has meaning in its own right. Where an initial scene may raise more questions than it answers, further similar yet distinct scenes serve to clarify those questions. Discourse analysis provides yet another means of grasping narrative intent through Longacre's discourse 'peaks'. Didactic peaks are naturally of special interest in interpreting Lukan narrative and show that the job of finding authorial, didactic intent is not a hopeless game of guesswork and subjective opinion, but can be grounded in objective discourse principles. Type-scenes serve as a literary complement to the study of ERs. They allow an author to play upon typical expectations as well as to evoke an entire scene with an allusion to just a part of a type. They also allow for variation within a standard framework. The ancient rhetorical critical method of amplification, when applied to Luke's speeches as a whole, as Witherington argues, adds support to the modern methods of sequential reading and presupposition pools. If the ancients expected arguments to be piled one on top of another in an accumulating fashion, then it makes sense to follow the accumulation as it takes place in the narrative and carefully observe the final aggregation. Appeal to amplification undercuts the objection that sequential reading and presupposition pools, as modern constructs, have no validity for an ancient document.

That Luke was indeed a theologian and that he did set out to communicate his own theological views is widely agreed. The challenge lies in identifying Luke's theology, and for that the foregoing tools of narratological/literary/ discourse analysis provide the means of explicating the theology embedded in Luke's ex-tensive narrative. This is not primarily a task of inference, as if Luke had written a history from which certain events might suggest certain theological predispo-sitions on Luke's part. It is not a matter of counting the number of times a par-ticular phenomenon appears and deriving conclusions from the consensus. Ra-ther, determining Luke's theology means analysing his literary devices to deter-mine where he focused reader attention and what comments he and his narrative spokespersons made about the focalized object.

CHAPTER 3

Jesus' Baptismal Praying and Spirit Experience in Luke's Gospel

Introduction

Having discussed the question of methodology, we now begin to apply the narrative and discourse tools studied to the story of Jesus' experience of the Spirit at his baptism. While this is not the first mention of Spirit experience in Luke-Acts, it is the first Spirit-reception within an initiatory type-scene. The chapter addresses whether Jesus' Jordan experience is archetypal of Christian initiatory experience and, if it is, whether it has any bearing upon the implied reader's understanding of later initiation scenes in Luke-Acts. The research addresses the Dunn-Turner debate and concludes that Turner's case against Dunn is unrelated to the narrative process by which significant elements of the Jordan experience enter the reader's ER for Spirit-reception. Moreover, the possibility that Jesus had a private visionary experience not seen by bystanders does not change the fact that the reader views the vision with Jesus, and thus the vision is 'real' and 'objective' for the reader, and therefore, the contents of the vision enter the reader's ER for Spirit-reception and influence how the reader understands later similar stories.

The component of the Jordan story that has potentially serious implications for the reading of later stories is the differentiation between water and prayer within the one unitary baptism ceremony and the association of Spirit-reception with the act of prayer. That is, prayer belongs integrally to the baptism ceremony, which, in its totality, is an appeal for the Spirit; but, within that ceremony, water and prayer may be distinguished with Spirit-reception attached explicitly to the latter and the former serving as preparation for Spirit-reception. This, along with the association of Spirit-reception with prayer in Luke 11:13, would indicate that a reader who comes to Acts 2:38 will not expect the Spirit to be communicated to new converts in the water of immersion, but *immediately* afterwards during baptismal prayer. No subsequence from initiation is in view. This is highly significant because it virtually eliminates one of the supposed inconsistencies of Luke-Acts, namely the assumed dissonance between Acts 2:38 and those cases where Luke portrays the Spirit coming by human impartation/facilitation distinct from the water of the baptismal ceremony (Acts 8 and 19). The question of how Acts 10 fits into the ER for Spirit-reception will be dealt with in chapter 6.

Jesus' Jordan Experience

Jordan and Pentecost

Turner writes, 'I think I myself have been guilty of pressing the qualitative distinctions between the gift of the Spirit to Jesus and the gift of the Spirit to the disciples a little too sharply at a number of points.'[1] While he recognizes commonality with Acts, with respect to Dunn's view, which will be elaborated below, he views Jesus' Jordan experience as unique and non-paradigmatic.[2] Turner's position that Jordan is non-paradigmatic (with respect to Dunn's argument) does not challenge the conclusions presented in this book. Namely, Jesus plays a leading role in the narrative and is, from a literary perspective, a normative spokesperson; the scene of Jesus' baptism is a type-scene which occupies a significantly initial position within the narrative; and finally, sequentially constructed ERs accumulate information and carry it forward in the narrative. Jesus' Jordan experience impacts the implied reader's understanding of Pentecost.

Standard Views

Turner identifies three standard views on whether Jesus' baptism was paradigmatic. First, there is the view that Jordan is the paradigm of a *donum superadditum*, an empowering gift given in addition to salvation.[3] In support of this approach Menzies argues that the πλήρης πνεύματος ἁγίου of Luke 4:1 ties Jesus' experience to that of the church and signals the empowering that both needed to fulfil the tasks given them by God.[4] Similarly, James B. Shelton denies any qualitative difference between Luke 3 and Acts 2 based on the fact that the Holy Spirit acts in both cases.[5] Stronstad argues that, 'Luke parallels the Spirit baptism of the disciples with the inaugural anointing of Jesus by the Holy Spirit',[6] and supports his argument with Talbert's parallels between Jordan and Pentecost.[7] Talbert has the following similarities: Prayer precedes the coming of the Spirit; there are physical manifestation(s) of, or related to, the Spirit; and the Spirit experience is located just before a ministry (Jesus'/the apostles') beginning with a

---

[1] Max Turner, '"Empowerment for Mission"? The Pneumatology of Luke-Acts: An Appreciation and Critique of James B. Shelton's *Mighty in Word and Deed*', *VoxEv* 24 (1994), 103-22; 112.

[2] Max Turner, 'Luke and the Spirit: Renewing Theological Interpretation of Biblical Pneumatology', Craig G. Bartholomew, Joel B. Green, Anthony C. Thiselton (eds), *Reading Luke: Interpretation, Reflection, Formation* (Milton Keynes: Paternoster, 2005), 267-93, 275.

[3] *Ibid.*, 274.

[4] Menzies, *Empowered*, 142.

[5] James B. Shelton, *Mighty in Word and Deed: The Role of the Holy Spirit in Luke-Acts* (Peabody: Hendrickson, 1991), 49.

[6] Stronstad, *Theology*, 51.

[7] *Ibid.*; cf. Talbert, *Patterns*, 16. Menzies follows the same procedure, Robert P. Menzies, 'Luke's Understanding of Baptism in the Holy Spirit: A Pentecostal Dialogues with the Reformed Tradition', *JPT* 16.2 (April, 2008), 86-101; 94.

programmatic sermon.⁸ Parsons' argument, that Luke's employment of ekphrasis at Jesus' baptism and at Pentecost conceptually links Jesus and the disciples, could also be adduced to support Talbert's parallels.⁹

The second major view understands Jordan as a paradigm of what happens to Christians when they are baptised, namely their entrance into the new covenant where they are now 'sons' of God.¹⁰ In 1928, Hans Windisch wrote:

> The figure of Christian baptism can also come into play here – baptism, water, Spirit, new birth, being a child of God are also the main ideas of Christian baptism, cf. Rom. 8:15; Gal. 4:6; Tit. 3:5; John 3:5 – and the baptism of Jesus is to be understood as paradigm and as initiation of the general Christian baptism: Jesus, the first Christian who was baptized.¹¹

Dunn has advanced and expanded this view. Jesus is the first human to experience the new covenant, manifested in Jesus' Spirit experience which is a Spirit baptism and a model for the Spirit baptism which every Christian experiences.

> The baptism in the Spirit, in other words, is not primarily to equip the (already) Christian for service; rather its function is to initiate the individual into the new age and covenant, to 'Christ' (= anoint) him, and in so doing to equip him for life and service in that new age and covenant. In this Jesus' entry into the new age and covenant is the type of every initiate's entry into the new age and covenant.¹²

Third, 'Jesus' experience of the Spirit is unique, even if important elements of it are carried over into the church after Pentecost'.¹³ 'The parallels highlight significant common elements, not identity of meaning.'¹⁴ This is Turner's own view. He reasons that: 'Luke 1:35 and 3:21-22 ['probably'] denote unique and

---

⁸ Talbert, *Patterns*, 16.
⁹ Parsons, *Acts*, 38. Cf. Heidi J. Hornik and Mikeal C. Parsons, 'Philological and Performative Perspectives on Pentecost', Steve Walton, et al. (eds), *Reading Acts Today: Essays in Honour of Loveday C. A. Alexander* (London: T&T Clark, 2011), 137-53; 140. On ekphrasis, see Ruth Webb, *Ekphrasis, Imagination and Persuasion in Ancient Rhetorical Theory and Practice* (Farnham: Ashgate, 2009); Christopher M. Chinn, 'Before Your Very Eyes: Pliny *Epistulae* 5.6 and the Ancient Theory of Ekphrasis', *CP* 102.3 (July, 2007), 265-80.
¹⁰ Turner, 'Renewing', 275.
¹¹ 'Kann auch der Typus der christlichen Taufe hier hineinspielen – Taufe, Wasser, Geist, Neugeburt, Gotteskindschaft sind auch die tragenden Ideen der Christentaufe, vgl. Rom. 8:15; Gal. 4:6; Tit. 3:5; Joh. 3:5 – und die Taufe Jesu ist als Paradigma und als Initiation der allgemeinen Christentaufe zu verstehen: Jesus der erste Christ, der getauft ward', Hans Windisch, 'Jesus und der Geist nach Synoptischer Überlieferung', Shirley Jackson Case (ed.), *Studies in Early Christianity* (New York: Century, 1928), 215.
¹² Dunn, *Baptism*, 32. Similarly, Lampe, *God*, 70. Cf. G.R. Beasley-Murray, *Baptism in the New Testament* (London: Macmillan, 1962), 65.
¹³ Turner, 'Renewing', 275.
¹⁴ Turner, *Power*, 434; cf. Max Turner, 'The Spirit and Salvation in Luke-Acts', Graham N. Stanton, Bruce W. Longenecker, and Stephen C. Barton (eds) *The Holy Spirit and Christian Origins* (Grand Rapids: Eerdmans, 2004), 103-16; 110.

unrepeated actions of the Spirit, rather than being paradigmatic.'[15] That is, they do not represent a first experience of the Spirit followed by a subsequent Spirit baptism; nor does Jordan represent Jesus as the first, and only, individual to experience the Spirit in a supposed second epoch of salvation history (old covenant, ministry of Jesus, church age).

The present book, in focusing upon the timing, mechanism, and manifestation of Spirit-reception, makes no argument regarding the essential quality of Jesus' experience vis-à-vis that of the disciples. That is, no claim will be made concerning the similarity or dissimilarity of the nature of Jesus' Spirit experience to that of the disciples at Pentecost. *No* claim is made that Jesus' experience is archetypal in the sense of Jesus being the first to experience the Spirit under the new covenant/messianic age. Turner, then, will be followed in that he argues that elements of Jesus' experience do carry over to Pentecost. Jesus' experience at the Jordan provides, not the complete paradigm, but still a foundational aspect of the ER for initiation which is constructed sequentially through the narrative, accumulating concepts and associations as the various initiation scenes are presented. The complete paradigm is only found in the fully accumulated ER (which is *not* equivalent to the final scene).

Jordan as Influencing the Reader's View of Pentecost: Objections and Responses

Objections
In terms of implied reader theory, we must ask how the Theophilus-like implied reader, who, as already discussed,[16] is a Christian who has been baptised and has a Spirit experience, would respond to this scene? Let us evaluate the possibilities. First, would the implied Christian reader view the scene as totally alien because it is ostensibly Johannine baptism and not Christian baptism? One could argue that the reader is personally familiar only with Christian baptism, and that Jesus' baptism was performed by John, even if Luke did not explicitly show John baptising Jesus. Moreover, here the Spirit comes from heaven to Jesus, but with Christian baptism, Jesus dispenses the Spirit. For these two reasons one might argue that the reader would be unable to see any connection between the two baptisms/Spirit experiences.

However, the fact that Jesus experiences the Spirit during baptismal prayer sets his experience apart from the rest of those baptised by John. Jesus' baptism is not an ordinary Johannine baptism. It possesses the element distinctive to Christian baptism – Spirit experience. But someone might reiterate the objection that this supposedly distinctive Christian element is not given by Jesus, but received by Jesus, and that this constitutes an absolute difference. It was a Spirit experience, but it was not the same kind of Spirit experience, nor the distinctive

---

[15] Turner, 'Renewing', 276.
[16] Cf. Methodology.

Christian experience. Moreover, one might object that Jesus' experience possesses another element dissimilar to Christian baptism in Luke-Acts, namely his experience of the Father's voice and approbation. Plus, unlike the experience of Christians, Jesus' experience was a vision, and it was not his first encounter with the Spirit (cf. Luke 1:35).

Responses
Aside from the fact that the book is interested not in qualitative differences or similarities between Jesus' experience and that of his followers, but in the ritual structure of their experiences, the straightforward literary response to all of these objections is that this baptismal/Spirit-reception scene is a type-scene, as discussed under Methodology. As with Homeric type-scenes, identical repetition is not a feature of biblical type-scenes. A type-scene provides a structure containing recognizable elements. The elements consist of typical scenery, roles and plot, but the instantiation of those elements may differ considerably without in the least detracting from the typicality of the scene. Thus, who does the baptising, who gives the Spirit, and the functional nexus of Spirit activity may differ depending upon the particular discourse, but the type-scene remains the same. The Christian reader sees in Jesus' experience her/his own experience. Jesus' baptism may not encompass all that a baptism in the Christian community entails, for the entire narrative lies before the reader. Luke will build upon Jordan. But, nonetheless, here is a significant *beginning* of Luke's picture of what baptism in the church looks like. Does this make every event in Jesus' life 'normative' or 'prescriptive'? Certainly not. Normativity is *not* automatic for everything a protagonist does or experiences. It must be constructed by the story.

That Luke presented Jesus as unique is clear from the storyline. The voice affirms him as God's Son and this has royal overtones (Psalm 2:7). It also is allusive of the prophet-like-Moses. In Numbers 12:6, God tells Aaron and Miriam that he speaks to ordinary prophets in visions and dreams, but he speaks to Moses directly, verbally. But in recognizing Jesus' uniqueness, we cannot overlook the archetypal way in which the type-scene renders him. His was an extraordinary experience, yet it was also much like that of the ordinary Christian. The visionary quality of Jesus' Spirit experience brings it in line with the standard type from Acts where the rereader knows that visions are typical of Spirit generated experience (Acts 2:17). Jesus is simply the greater, superior prophet-like-Moses in contrast to ordinary prophets who have only visions and dreams. Moreover, the rereader knows that he teaches his followers to pray to their Father for the Spirit (Luke 11:13), behaviour that recalls his own prayer. While one might object that Luke 3:21-22 does not say that Jesus prayed for the Spirit, only that he prayed, Luke 11:13 retrospectively gives significance to his prayer. Unique as Luke portrayed him, he is not the only one who can call God Father or pray and receive the Spirit.

That this may not have been Jesus' first experience of the Spirit (Luke 1:35) also does not affect the type-scene as multiple experiences of the Spirit are part of Luke's storyworld. Jesus' followers experienced the Spirit before Pentecost (Luke 11:13; cf. 9:1; 10:1; and Numbers 11:16-30). In literary terms, the hero may have ridden off into the sunset before; the man may have met other women at the well. The elements of a type-scene are malleable. It is the core configuration of immersion in water/praying/Spirit experience which allows one to recognize the type-scene here presented. Jesus, pious as the multitude praying outside the temple (Luke 1:10), undergoes the common purification ritual, prays and has a Spirit experience. Luke's implied reader, knowing from the preface that the origins of Christianity are being presented, recognizes in the type-scene a depiction of the origins of Christian baptism. This is because the reader sees, for the first time, the combination of water and Spirit experience that marks later baptisms in Acts. This is not to say that the implied reader would think this is a full, complete, and final picture of Christian baptism – the story is only beginning – but the raw elements are present: water, praying, Spirit. These are all that is necessary for the first-time reader to draw parallels to church life, and more than sufficient for a second-time reader to find explicit parallels with later Lukan story elements. Luke presented a type-scene which functions prototypically in the narrative. Modifications will be applied later.

How then does reading Luke 3:21-22 as a type-scene impact the implied reader going forward in the narrative? First and foremost it links Spirit-reception to baptismal praying.[17] This is not *post*-baptismal prayer, but prayer at the time of immersion, *possibly* while still in the water (as will be discussed below). Prayer is the element of the type-scene directly linked to Spirit experience. If later instantiations of this type-scene appear in abbreviated form, the reader has a fuller version, though not the fullest, given early in the narrative with which to make comparison and fill in any gaps. If Jesus, the protagonist, received the Spirit while praying, then no implied reader will expect baptism to be prayerless. The Spirit is expected to come during the praying which accompanies immersion. The water itself, though an act of submission to God which could, in this sense be understood as a prayer, is still differentiated by Luke from the act of praying to which the coming of the Spirit is attached. Luke could, without difficulty, have added a scene in which converts are explicitly depicted as receiving the Spirit in the water without prayer, and this would have expanded the type-scene to include two elements linked to Spirit-reception, prayer and water. But Luke did not present us with such a scene. On the contrary, he later has Jesus teach that the Father will give the Spirit to those who ask (Luke 11:13). This prayer teaching, while not part of an explicit initiatory type-scene, e.g., there is no mention of water, reinforces the Luke 3 connection between prayer and Spirit-reception. For Jesus, the Spirit is not received in water, but in prayer. The Lukan link between prayer and the Spirit means that Acts 2:38-39 can be fully understood as an adumbration of the already present type-scene without suggesting that Luke associated Spirit-

---

[17] Odette Mainville agrees that the Spirit comes as a result of Jesus' praying, *L'Esprit dans l'oeuvre de Luc* (N.pl: Fides, 1991), 214, as did von Baer, *Geist*, 61.

reception directly with the water. It does not state that the Spirit will be received *in* the water, but simply that if one repents and is immersed, one will receive the Spirit. The timing is not made explicit. Based upon the previous Jordan River type-scene, the implied reader will not expect the converts of Acts 2:38-39 to receive the Spirit in the water of their immersion, but will expect them to pray during the baptismal ceremony, just like Jesus did. This prayer does not constitute a separate ceremony from baptism, but belongs to the baptism type-scene.

The Possibility of a Vision

Turner also views Jesus' Jordan experience as a vision. Turner, following Fritzleo Lentzen-Deis, has argued that this was a vision, and not a publically visible event.[18] Alfred Loisy suggested that Luke presented it as occurring without witnesses, arguing that 'Our author himself does not venture to say expressly that the crowd saw the miracle, which would have obligated him to explain why "the people" had not immediately recognized Jesus as Christ.'[19] Turner, in consideration of the parallel with Peter's vision, writes, 'the 'descent' of the Spirit as a dove, and the heavenly voice, are thus to be taken as mutually interpretative elements in a private visionary experience'.[20] Nevertheless, Turner clarifies the implications of his position by writing:

> To say that Luke understood Jesus' seeing of a dove and hearing of a voice as elements of a visionary phenomenon does not mean, however, that there was no corresponding 'event' (Luke clearly believes there was a corresponding endowment which this vision interprets).[21]

Turner reads the text as saying that *something* did occur. Again, he writes, 'the messianic endowment received at the time of his baptism was a markedly powerful presence of the Spirit that was to come to strong (and observable) expression in and through him'.[22] Turner's recognition of a 'corresponding "event"' is the relevant fact for narrative analysis, for, regardless of whether Luke portrayed

---

[18] Turner, *Power*, 195. Cf. Fritzleo Lentzen-Deis, *Die Taufe Jesu nach den Synoptikern: Literarkritische und gattungsgeschichtliche Untersuchungen* (Frankfurt am Main: Josef Knecht, 1970), 105-22. Cf. Kosnetter, who argues for 'an objective, perceptible process', 'ein objektiv wahrnehmbarer Vorgang', Johann Kosnetter, *Die Taufe Jesu: Exegetische und religionsgeschichtliche Studien* (Wien: Verlag Mayer, 1936), 198.

[19] 'Notre auteur lui-même ne s'aventure pas à dire expressément que la foule a vu le miracle, ce qui l'aurait obligé à expliquer pourquoi « le peuple » n'avait pas tout de suite reconnu Jésus comme Christ'. Alfred Loisy, *L'Évangile Selon Luc* (Paris: Émile Nourry, 1924), 142. Similarly, Kosnetter says only Jesus and John saw the supernatural event, *Taufe*, 210.

[20] Max Turner, 'Jesus and the Spirit in Lukan Perspective', *TynB* 32 (1981), 3-42; 12. Similarly, Carl R. Holladay, 'Baptism in the New Testament and Its Cultural Milieu: A Response to Everett Ferguson, *Baptism in the Early Church*', *JECS* 20.3 (Fall, 2012), 343-69; 350-51.

[21] Turner, *Power*, 196.

[22] *Ibid.*, 202; cf. 199.

the event as a private vision or as a happening visible to other characters in the narrative, the reader vicariously experiences the event. The reader sees the vision just as clearly as the reader sees the other happenings in the storyworld, and the reader equally includes the information gathered from the vision or the 'natural' happening into her/his growing understanding of the storyworld.

Differentiation between Immersion and Prayer within the One Baptismal Ceremony

But given that Jesus' baptismal experience forms a part of the Lukan presupposition pool and the ER for baptism in Luke-Acts, how is Jesus' prayer related to his baptism? Martin Dibelius wrote, 'The mention of the prayer of Jesus tears the connection between baptism and Spirit endowment.'[23] Mason affirmed the idea of separation, as did Dom Gregory Dix.[24] However, W.F. Flemington stated that for Jesus, 'baptism with water coincided with the descent of the Holy Spirit'.[25] G.W.H. Lampe, concluding his chapter on Jesus' baptism, wrote:

> the fact that Christian Baptism is a re-presentation of the Baptism of Jesus implies that it is through Baptism in water, and not through any other ceremony, such as a physical anointing, that the believer enters into the possession of the Spirit which is imparted through his membership of Christ.[26]

Certainly, as has been argued above, a reader of Luke would see many similarities between the two baptisms, but the development of the idea of baptism must be carefully followed through all of Luke-Acts, rather than extracted solely from the beginning of Luke. Jesus' baptism is prototypical, but it is not the final portrait. Even Acts 19:1-7 cannot be viewed on its own, but only in light of the accumulated ER for initiation.

Lampe's defence of the Spirit/water connection over against a separation of water and Spirit in the Gospels must be examined. He argues that Jesus' 'coming up from the water' was not a leaving of the water and going onto the land, but simply an emerging after being immersed. Thus, Jesus remained in the water and therefore the connection between water and Spirit is not severed.

The several texts read as follows:

βαπτισθεὶς δὲ ὁ Ἰησοῦς εὐθὺς ἀνέβη ἀπὸ τοῦ ὕδατος· καὶ ἰδοὺ ἠνεῴχθησαν [αὐτῷ] οἱ οὐρανοί, καὶ εἶδεν [τὸ] πνεῦμα [τοῦ] θεοῦ καταβαῖνον ὡσεὶ περιστερὰν [καὶ] ἐρχόμενον ἐπ' αὐτόν· (Matt. 3:16)

---

[23] 'Die Erwähnung des Gebetes Jesu zerreißt den Zusammenhang zwischen Taufe und Geistesbegabung', Martin Dibelius, *Die urchristliche Überlieferung von Johannes dem Täufer* (Göttingen: Vandenhoeck & Ruprecht, 1911), 60.
[24] Mason, *Confirmation*, 15; Dom Gregory Dix, *The Theology of Confirmation in Relation to Baptism* (Westminster: Dacre, 1946), 30.
[25] W.F. Flemington, *The New Testament Doctrine of Baptism* (London: SPCK, 1964), 42.
[26] Lampe, *Seal*, 45.

καὶ εὐθὺς ἀναβαίνων ἐκ τοῦ ὕδατος εἶδεν σχιζομένους τοὺς οὐρανοὺς καὶ τὸ πνεῦμα ὡς περιστερὰν καταβαῖνον εἰς αὐτόν· (Mark 1:10)

Ἐγένετο δὲ ἐν τῷ βαπτισθῆναι ἅπαντα τὸν λαὸν καὶ Ἰησοῦ βαπτισθέντος καὶ προσευχομένου ἀνεῳχθῆναι τὸν οὐρανὸν καὶ καταβῆναι τὸ πνεῦμα τὸ ἅγιον σωματικῷ εἴδει ὡς περιστερὰν ἐπ᾽ αὐτόν (Luke 3:21 – 22a)

Luke had only two activities, baptism and praying,[27] and Luke omitted Mark's ἀναβαίνων ἐκ τοῦ ὕδατος, thus *apparently* leaving Jesus in the water (Luke does not explicitly state that Jesus was still in the water). One could argue that because βαπτισθέντος is an aorist participle, the action must have been completed before the heavens opened and therefore Luke implied that Jesus ascended out of the water. Such is not the case. Completion of the act of immersion does not equate to leaving the water. Moreover, an aorist does not automatically indicate action antecedent to the main verb. It could equally be action coincident with the main verb as in Turner's rendering: 'when Jesus too was baptized – and while he was actually praying – heaven opened'.[28] On this reading, prayer is an integral part of the baptism itself, not a subsequent event. The various views will be discussed below.

Von Baer noted that of the synoptic writers, only Luke recorded Jesus' prayer.[29] Furthermore, von Baer observed Luke's association of Jesus' praying with significant events such as his choice of disciples, his questioning of Peter, his transfiguration, and his passion. He observes a similar pattern of prayer preceding a significant event in Acts such as with Pentecost, Acts 4:31's Spirit-reception, and the Samaritans' Spirit-reception. 'On the basis of this observation we can assume that Luke is of the opinion that the prayer of Jesus during the Jordan baptism and the following Spirit-reception are to be set in relation to one another'.[30] It must be observed that von Baer, while attaching the Spirit to Jesus' prayer, does not separate the prayer from the baptism, prayer occurs 'during' the baptism. Walter Grundmann saw the gift of the Spirit as the Father's response to Jesus' prayer.[31] Dunn writes: 'For Luke the Spirit is given in response to prayer,

---

[27] Hee-Seong Kim, *Die Geisttaufe des Messias: Eine kompositionsgeschichtliche Untersuchung zu einem Leitmotiv des lukanischen Doppelwerks* (Frankfurt am Main: Peter Lang, 1993), 53-54; John Michael Penney, *The Missionary Emphasis of Lukan Pneumatology* (Sheffield: Sheffield Academic, 1997), 37.

[28] Turner, *Power*, 195.

[29] Von Baer, *Geist*, 60.

[30] 'Auf Grund dieser Beobachtung können wir annehmen, daß Lukas der Meinung gewesen ist, das Gebet Jesu während der Jordantaufe und die darauf erfolgte Geistesempfängnis seien zueinander in Beziehung zu setzen', *Ibid.*, 61; similarly, Frederick W. Danker, *Jesus and the New Age: A Commentary on St. Luke's Gospel* (Philadelphia: Fortress, 1988), 95; so too, Peter Böhlemann, *Jesus und der Täufer: Schlüssel zur Theologie und Ethik des Lukas* (Cambridge: CUP, 1997), 91.

[31] Walter Grundmann, *Das Evangelium Nach Lukas* (Berlin: Evangelische Verlagsanstalt Berlin, n.d.), 2.107-108. So too, F. Godet, trans. E.W. Shalders, *A Commentary on the Gospel of St. Luke* (Edinburgh: T&T Clark, n.d.), 1.186. Cf. Bart J. Koet, *Dreams and Scripture in Luke-Acts: Collected Essays* (Leuven: Peeters, 2006), 17.

and neither in nor through baptism'.[32] This differentiation between prayer and baptism puts Dunn at odds with von Baer, though the two are in agreement on the prayer/Spirit link. Donald L. Gelpi wrote, 'Very likely Luke separates Jesus' vision and the descent of the Breath from the event of the baptism itself lest his readers misinterpret John's baptism as the cause of Jesus' messianic anointing'.[33] Voss, Tannehill, Hur, and Marshall also see the link to prayer.[34] In contrast to Gelpi's separation of baptism and prayer, John R. Levison, in commenting on the general association of prayer and the Spirit, writes, 'Jesus receives the spirit [sic] at his baptism while he is praying (3:21-22)'.[35] This is similar to Turner as quoted above. Though Turner writes, 'The baptismal narrative *separates* Jesus' water baptism *from* (but also loosely *joins* it *to*) a subsequent prayer experience involving a vision of the dove-like Spirit's descent',[36] he cannot be understood to say that the prayer experience was entirely separate from the baptism ceremony, as if it were a modern confirmation. For Turner, the prayer experience remains *joined to* the baptism.

To evaluate these conflicting views, we must turn our attention to a more detailed analysis of Luke 3:21-22. First, as noted above, Luke did not have Jesus ascending out of the water, thus apparently leaving the activity of prayer to be understood as taking place while Jesus is still in the waters of Jordan. Second, the phrase, Ἰησοῦ βαπτισθέντος καὶ προσευχομένου, is a genitive absolute construction. Yet, the precise timing of the events remains a subject of interpretation. The aorist passive participle could be viewed as either antecedent to the action of the main verb, ἀνεῳχθῆναι, or coincident. Robertson cautions, 'it must not be forgotten that the aorist part does not in itself mean antecedent action, either relative or absolute',[37] and he points the interpreter to context. This is also true for Attic Greek (though no claim that Luke was an Atticist is made here).[38] Guy L.

---

[32] Dunn, *Baptism*, 33-34. Also, Heinz Schürmann, *Das Lukasevangelium, Erster Teil: Kommentar zu Kap. 1,1-9,50* (Freiburg: Herder, 1969), 197.

[33] Donald L. Gelpi, 'Breath-Baptism in the Synoptics', *Charismatic Experiences in History* (Peabody: Hendrickson, 1985), 15-43, 29.

[34] Gerhard Voss, *Die Christologie der Lukanischen Schriften in Grundzügen* (Paris: Desclee de Brouwer, 1965), 83-84; Tannehill, *Luke*, 56; Hur, *Reading*, 207-208; I. Howard Marshall, *The Gospel of Luke: A Commentary on the Greek Text* (Exeter: Paternoster, 1978), 152.

[35] John R. Levison, *Filled with the Spirit* (Grand Rapids: Eerdmans, 2009), 231. So too, Everett Ferguson, *Baptism in the Early Church: History, Theology, and Liturgy in the First Five Centuries* (Grand Rapids: Eerdmans, 2009), 101; Joan Taylor, *John the Baptist Within Second Temple Judaism: A Historical Study* (London: SPCK, 1997), 4; Francois Bovon, *Luke the Theologian: Fifty-five Years of Research (1950-2005)*, (Waco: Baylor University Press, 2006), 268.

[36] Turner, 'Renewing', 274, original italics.

[37] A.T. Robertson, *A Grammar of the Greek New Testament in the Light of Historical Research* (Nashville: Broadman, 1934), 860.

[38] Cadbury suggests, 'the vocabulary of Luke ... is not so far removed from the literary style of the Atticists as to be beyond comparison with them', Henry J. Cadbury, *The*

Cooper writes, 'About the previous time usually expressed by aorist participles it must be observed that this is a notion of previous action which, while real, must in many or most cases hardly be translated with any great specificity.'[39]

The fact that the aorist participle is passive, suggesting an action done to Jesus, and the present participle is middle, suggesting an action performed by Jesus himself, does not automatically disambiguate the syntax. Jesus could have prayed while the act of immersion was being carried out and the heavens would then have opened at precisely that time. The aorist participle would then be understood as perfectly coincident with the main verb. However, a general coincidence, 'at the time he was baptised' allows Jesus to pray *at the time* he was immersed, without stressing any idea of underwater prayer. Or Luke could have meant that Jesus prayed after he was immersed. The grammar cannot force a conclusion either way. Both 'after having been baptised and while praying' and 'when baptised, and while praying' are equally acceptable translations.

However, the immediate move from being immersed to praying, as well as possibly Luke's aforementioned omission of ἀναβαίνων which could be understood as leaving Jesus in the water (the argument does not rest upon this), suggests that, even if Luke wished to express that the prayer was subsequent to the immersion, *it was viewed as part of the overall experience*. One strains the text to find any lengthy gap between the act of immersion and the act of praying. As Jacob Kremer notes, observing the genitive absolute with aorist and then with present participles, 'The baptism of Jesus itself he cites together with the prayer of Jesus ... so to say as prerequisite for the following event'.[40] That immersion and prayer were together prerequisite for the heavens opening is reasonable. One cannot, however, require a temporal gap between prayer and heaven opening, as the present tense 'praying' is clearly coincident with heaven opening. What Luke's redactional addition of 'while praying' emphasizes is that the opening of the heavens and the descent of the Spirit were linked to the prayer element of the baptismal experience. One cannot exclude the water element and say it has nothing to do with the Spirit, but neither can one deny the impact of Luke's redaction. Luke tied the Spirit to prayer, not immersion. Rather, the whole baptismal experience, immersion *and* prayer, leads to reception of the Spirit. Baptismal prayer, then, finds association with Spirit experience early in Luke-Acts.

Style and Literary Method of Luke (New York: Kraus, 1969 [OUP, 1920]), 38. However, Albert Wifstrand concluded, 'the Gospel of Luke neither is nor tries to be classicizing or Atticistic in style', *Epochs and Styles* (Tübingen: Mohr Siebeck, 2005; Sweden: Mailice Wifstrand, 2005), 26.

[39] Guy L. Cooper, after K.W. Krüger, *Attic Greek Pose Syntax* (Ann Arbor: University of Michigan Press, 1998), 1.846.

[40] 'Die Taufe Jesu selbst nennt er zusammen mit dem Gebet Jesus ... sozusagen als Voraussetzung der folgenden Geschehnisse', Jacob Kremer, *Pfingstbericht und Pfingstgeschehen: Eine exegetische Untersuchung zu Apg 2, 1-13* (Stuttgart: Verlag Katholisches Bibelwerk GmbH, 1973), 205.

Praying for the Spirit and Preventing Repossession: Jesus on Initiatory Prayer

As background for Jesus' teaching on prayer (Luke 11), Turner points out that the sending of the 72 in chapter 10 invokes the Exodus story of Moses imparting the Spirit to 70/72 elders (Numbers 11:16-30).[41] In terms of developmental sequence, the reader has just seen Moses and Elijah on the mount with Jesus in chapter 9 and now the reader encounters 72 disciples. Transfer of the Spirit is thus part of the cotext, and though Numbers 11 does not mention prayer for the Spirit, Elisha did specifically request Elijah's spirit (2 Kings 2:9).

Turner correlates the serpents and scorpions of 11:11-13 with Jesus' prior teaching (10:19-20) on power over demon spirits represented as serpents and scorpions, and then incisively concludes that Jesus is teaching that the Father will not give a demonic spirit, but a 'good' Spirit (πνεῦμα ἀγαθόν, a textual variant suggested by Turner).[42] Immediately afterwards Jesus is accused of exorcism through Beelzebub to which Luke's Jesus retorts that he does it by the 'finger of God'. When seen in connection with the immediate discussion of evil spirits and with the recent mission of the Seventy-Two, it functions as a Lukan indicator that the disciples experienced, if only indirectly, the Spirit prior to Pentecost.[43]

But just as Jesus, the stronger one, can evict the weaker demons, so too, a group of demons can repossess their former property if it is not kept by a stronger power (Luke 11:21-26). What then is the stronger power that would have protected the hapless man? From the preceding cotext, the reader knows that the man could have prayed to the Father for the Spirit. Patrick McNamara's observation of Jesus' ministry (drawing on the parallel Matthew 12:43-45 passage), 'Positive possession protects against demonic possession',[44] certainly applies to the Lukan Jesus. Having read about Jesus casting out demons by the finger of God, thus recalling the Exodus power encounter with Pharaoh's magicians, and then reading about the man out of whom a demon departed, the reader will not conclude that the man is an isolated case, but rather typical of people Jesus cast demons out of. Luke depicted the exorcised and delivered individual as personally responsible to maintain her/his deliverance by earnestly entreating the heavenly Father for the Spirit at the time of her/his exorcism/deliverance. Edward J. Woods writes:

> Also before the Beelzebub pericope, Luke's form of the Lord's Prayer does not include the words, 'but deliver us from evil'. This omission appropriately anticipates the Beelzebub pericope, and especially vv. 24-26, where evil is *persistent* in its attempt to gain a re-entry into man. This could suggest that Luke understands

---

[41] Turner, *Power*, 338; cf. Menzies, 'Seventy', 87-113; 96-99.
[42] *Ibid.*, 340.
[43] *Ibid.*, 339-341.
[44] Patrick McNamara, *Spirit Possession and Exorcism: History, Psychology and Neurobiology*, Volume 1, *Mental States and the Phenomenon of Possession* (Santa Barbara: Praeger, 2011), 136.

Jesus' intent that prayer *by itself* is not ultimately sufficient to overcome evil. It could also suggest that persistent prayer is needed to overcome evil, as well as obtain God's best gifts, chief of which is the Holy Spirit (Luke 11.5-13). This point could be significant, coming just *before* the Beelzebub pericope (Luke 11.14-26).[45]

Beasley-Murray reasons that because the context is one of teaching on prayer for those already believers, this prayer for the Spirit must actually have been prayer for the gifts of the Spirit as well as prayer for the Spirit himself by new converts.[46] However, Beasley-Murray does not analyze the full context which includes not just the Lord's Prayer, but also the extended discussion of demons and demon possession. Therefore he misses that the real context is that of deliverance/exorcism and thus of the incorporation of individuals recently delivered from Satan's power into Jesus' kingdom. Moreover, the last time someone in Luke's storyworld prayed and received the Spirit was at Jesus' baptism. Any talk of prayer for the Spirit cannot be seen in isolation from that key event in Luke's narrative. Initiation is the ER to which Jesus' teaching on prayer for the Spirit most naturally attaches.[47]

The reader must also ask whether Jesus meant this teaching only for demoniacs, or for all who have been delivered by Jesus' Moses-like ministry. Jesus describes himself as 'gathering' (11:23). Surely it is not only demoniacs whom he gathers. Rather for Luke, all Jesus' followers are being delivered in this New Exodus. Thus Luke's Jesus taught an unmediated, pre-Pentecost experience of the Spirit not just available, but highly necessary for recently cleaned and delivered individuals, both former demoniacs and all others who had previously been under Satan's power. Luke presented this prayer for the Spirit as properly taking place at the time of deliverance from Satan, which, as 11:23 suggests, is conceived more broadly than just exorcism. But if the recently demonized person should pray to her/his Father for the Spirit, then surely s/he also should learn the prayer to the Father which Jesus taught his followers. Thus, the implied reader, having already been instructed in the faith, is not learning a new prayer, but hearing an etiological story which locates the learning of the Lord's Prayer within initiation in association with prayer for the Spirit and exorcism.

How then are we to understand the disciples' experience of the Spirit in the period of Jesus' earthly ministry? Let us clarify what Luke did not say. Luke did not depict the disciples praying at baptism to receive the Spirit. That Luke thought the disciples were baptised can be concluded from Luke 7:29-30, which

---

[45] Edward J. Woods, *The 'Finger of God' and Pneumatology in Luke-Acts* (Sheffield: Sheffield Academic, 2001), 184, original italics.
[46] G.R. Beasley-Murray, *Baptism*, 119.
[47] No attempt here is being made to connect Luke's storyworld with the liturgical practice of the later church which taught catechumens the Lord's Prayer possibly around the time of the renunciation of Satan and exorcism. Cf. Alistair Stewart-Sykes (ed.), *Tertullian, Cyprian and Origen on the Lord's Prayer* (St Vladimir's Seminary Press, 2004), 22; Willy Rordorf, 'The Lord's Prayer in the Light of its Liturgical Use in the Early Church', *StLi* 14.1 (1981-81), 1-19; 2-5.

states that all the people and the tax gatherers, in contrast to the Pharisees and lawyers, were baptised by John. So, for those disciples already baptised by John, their prayer for the Spirit, inspired by Jesus' Luke 11:13 teaching, would come subsequently to their baptism.

Turner argues that since the setting for the teaching on prayer is, 'the pre-Easter missions of Jesus and his disciples', therefore, 'God's Spirit (or a spirit of power from God) is portrayed as a pre-Pentecost possibility available to some of Jesus' followers'.[48] He continues:

> Even though it goes against his tendency to present Jesus as the unique bearer of the Spirit in the period of the ministry, Luke has not suppressed this older perception – perhaps because it does not involve experiencing the Spirit as the gift of the 'Spirit of prophecy', but merely as God's liberating power at work through the disciples.[49]

Menzies' approach to the passage is different. Similarly to F.F. Bruce, who writes, 'Possibly Luke understands the future tense 'will give' of the post-Pentecostal situation',[50] Menzies applies it strictly to the post-Pentecost community. He makes three points: 1) Only after Pentecost will the gift of the Spirit be available, 2) The gift is not 'initiatory or soteriological' because it is promised to people already disciples, i.e. Christians, 3) Based on Luke's use of πνεῦμα ἅγιον in other passages, it must here refer to 'an endowment of prophetic power'.[51]

Taking Menzies' third point first, it is not necessary that just because in other contexts the Holy Spirit is understood as the Spirit of prophecy, it is so understood here. As the quote from Turner shows, he finds no indication of Spirit of prophecy usage in this passage. While the Numbers 11 passage, to which, as Turner recognizes, allusion is made in the sending of the Seventy-Two, contains prophecy as a manifestation of the Spirit, the mission of the Seventy-Two does not involve ecstatic prophecy, but healing the sick and exorcism (10:9, 17). The nearness of the kingdom the Seventy-Two proclaim is understood by the fact of the healings they perform (10:9).[52] Thus, the emphasis is not upon verbal proclamation, which could be understood as prophecy, but on the demonstration of the kingdom's presence, on power.

Looking at Menzies' first point, one can argue that the 'prevention of repossession' teaching would have been understood by Luke's implied reader as applying not to pre-Pentecost believers, but only to post-Pentecost believers. However, these options of pre- and post-Pentecost are not mutually exclusive. While there is no reason why Luke's implied reader would not import Jesus' 'then' teaching into her/his 'now' situation, Luke still presents Jesus as teaching a protective Spirit experience to his followers to be received immediately after exorcism, or after a more generally conceived 'deliverance' from Satan. Menzies'

---

[48] Turner, *Power*, 340.
[49] *Ibid.*, 341.
[50] F.F. Bruce, 'Luke's Presentation of the Spirit in Acts', *CrThR* 5.1 (1990), 15-29; 17.
[51] Menzies, *Empowered*, 160.
[52] Turner, *Power*, 338.

first point assumes the matter he is trying to establish. The question at hand is when, in fact, did the Father begin giving πνεῦμα ἅγιον to people who ask? Turner is more accurate in recognizing a pre-Pentecost role for the Spirit.

Menzies' second argument that because the saying is addressed to believers it cannot be initiatory overlooks the nature of initiation as a process. For example, no one would question that water baptism is an initiatory rite, yet, in Luke's conception, the act of immersion in water does not coincide exactly with belief and repentance, as the Luke 3 story of John's immersing the multitudes with Luke's emphasis upon moral change, not immersion *per se*, and the sequence of belief, repentance and immersion in Acts 2:37-38, show.

Moreover, the simple fact that Jesus' instruction is not addressed to a select few leaders, but to his followers generally indicates that this is initiatory. If all are to pray for the Spirit, then anyone who has not yet prayed for the Spirit has not done what the rest of the group has done and, unless the Spirit was obtained some other way than prayer, is lacking what all members of the group have. This universality of Spirit experience, and prayer for that experience, indicates an initiatory context. Additionally, Menzies has not considered the cotext of exorcism which also suggests an initiatory setting, as well as the ER for initiation which is activated by mention of prayer for the Spirit. That is, the last time someone prayed and the Spirit came was in an initiatory context. Menzies, therefore misses two key aspects of the story when he applies the Luke 11:13 saying strictly to the post-Pentecost believer and then only to a post-conversion, non-initiatory setting.[53]

How does the growing initiation ER influence a reader's understanding at this point? Luke 3:21-22 depicts praying happening at the time of immersion and Spirit-reception being linked to that prayer. The Luke 11 depiction of exorcism/deliverance followed immediately by prayer for the Spirit, builds on this picture by suggesting that when one begins to follow Jesus, one should pray for the Spirit. Menzies cannot use Luke 11 to argue for Pentecostal subsequence for it is not 'directed to the members of the Christian community'.[54] It describes new converts, individuals recently delivered from 'Egypt' by Jesus' Moses-like ministry, and the implied reader understands it as directed towards candidates for initiation into the Christian community. The 'repetitive character of the exhortation to pray',[55] which Menzies rightly derives from the grammar of 11:2 and 11:10, therefore indicates not repetitive prayer in the normal life of the believer, but persistent prayer for the Spirit by the candidate at initiation. This reinforces the 3:21-22 link between prayer and Spirit-reception. Finally, Luke indicated that Jesus' disciples did experience the Spirit before Pentecost.

---

[53] Menzies and Menzies, *Spirit*, 116-17.
[54] *Ibid.*, 116.
[55] *Ibid.*, 117.

Conclusion

The chapter has noted several objections to viewing Jesus' baptismal experience as having a narrative impact upon the Pentecost story. The chapter then discussed objections to these arguments using type-scene analysis. Jesus' baptism belongs to the larger type-scene of baptism and Spirit experience. The rereader recognises this type-scene immediately. The initial reader will recognise Jesus' baptism as 1) being an example, though with extraordinary qualities, of an experience common among Israelites during the ministry of John, and 2) containing elements similar to her/his own initiatory experience, namely, water and Spirit experience. Regarding the visionary nature of Jesus' experience, the reader shares it vicariously with Jesus. Moreover, for Luke's storyworld, visions of the spirit world are anything but unreal. The spirit world is seen to be just as objectively real as the 'natural' world, and even the location of the presently reigning king of Israel. The key way in which the Jordan story would affect later stories is in its association of Spirit-reception with prayer aspect of the baptismal ceremony. This remains true whether one takes the aorist passive participle as antecedent or coincident with the main verb. To this is added the reinforced link between Spirit-reception and prayer in Luke 11:13. Thus, the reader of Acts 2:38 would expect new converts to pray at their baptisms – prayer is understood an integral element of the baptismal experience – and would associate reception of the promised Spirit not simply with immersion, but specifically with prayer at the time of immersion. The chapter has also addressed Jesus' teaching on prayer for the Spirit. This prayer is seen as protection against repossession in cases of exorcism. Its association with the transference of individuals from Satan's kingdom to that of Jesus indicates that it was initiatory. The prayer for the Spirit also demonstrates the disciples experienced the Spirit prior to Pentecost.

CHAPTER 4

Xenolalic Experience: An Evaluation of its Prominence and Potential in the Pentecost Story

Introduction

Having studied the ER for baptism in Luke's Gospel, we now turn to its development within Acts. In following a narrative critical approach, this chapter employs analysis of focalization to specify the referent to Peter's Spirit discourse. This analysis produces surprising results, indicating that Luke focused reader attention upon a particular experience, namely xenolalia. Narrative analysis supports the claim of Benny C. Aker that Acts chapter two 'pivots around' tongues speech, but potentially undermines his rejection of tongues as a 'boundary marker'.[1]

The focalization of xenolalia begins with the narrative directing the reader forward in the story, not on tongues, but on Spirit-reception. At the end of Luke and the beginning of Acts, the reader is caused to anticipate the coming 'promise of the Father' (Luke 24:49), the experience of being baptised in the Spirit (Acts 1:5). When the day of Pentecost arrives, two phenomena precede the arrival of the Spirit, wind and fire. Given that Moses, Elijah, and the Exodus are already prominent motifs in the story, objections to a Sinai/Horeb allusion cannot be sustained. Wind and fire are preliminary phenomena anticipating the arrival of a divine voice, which occurs as the Spirit gives utterance through the believers. Thus, the reader's expectations are resolved in a surprise twist – the voice of God neither thunders nor whispers to a solitary prophet, but speaks out from the mouths of a whole gathering of prophets.[2]

The narrative next focuses backward in the story upon the xenolalia. The questions and mockery of the crowd revolve, not around the wind and fire, but around the speaking in languages that is loud enough to draw a crowd. In the Pentecost

---

[1] Benny C. Aker, 'Acts 2 as a Paradigmatic Narrative for Luke's Theology of the Spirit' (A paper presented at an Evangelical Theological Society session on Luke-Acts, no date [posted to web 10/30/2001, https://www.agts.edu/faculty/faculty_publications/articles/aker_acts2.pdf]), 13.

[2] On the connection between Moses' wish in Numbers 11 and the Spirit on all God's people at Pentecost, cf. D. Karl Bornhäuser, *Studien zur Apostelgeschichte* (Gütersloh: Verlag C. Bertelsmann, 1934), 21.

story with its various phenomena, Luke used the questions of the crowd to focalize the xenolalia experience, marking it as the referent of his Spirit discourse. This is not arbitrary reductionism, selectively picking one manifestation out of the many Pentecostal phenomena, because Luke's crowd did not ask what the wind or the fire meant, it asked what the languages meant. Since the reader knows the crowd is curious, the reader has an expectation that the crowd would ask about the phenomena if it knew about them. For an inquisitive multitude to view fire sitting upon the disciples' heads and not to inquire about it is incongruous. Because the crowd does not ask about the wind or the fire, the reader knows that the crowd is not aware of these initial phenomena.

Speaking out strange sounds loudly in a public space is certainly not normal behaviour. This conclusion is buttressed by the accusation of some members of the crowd that the speakers are drunk. Therefore the tongues-speaking can be reasonably linked with dissociative behaviour – 'linked' for Peter himself either was not affected by the tongues, or the effects wore off quickly enough for him to deliver a coherent sermon. Despite the link with dissociative behaviour, Luke affirmed that the utterances are real languages and not nonsense. The utterances can be described as dissociative xenolalia.

When Peter speaks about the Spirit, the tangible referent to his discourse is the singular phenomenon which the crowd inquires about – the xenolalia going on before the eyes and ears of the audience. Peter says, 'this is what was spoken'. When he says 'this' we know, because Luke has focalized it through the crowd's questions and mockery, that the thing to which he refers – the referent to his discourse – is the people speaking in tongues. Tongues speaking is the referent to his discourse on the Spirit. Peter, the normative spokesperson, then makes a double identification: the focalized dissociative xenolalia experience is the prophesied eschatological Spirit experience; the promised Spirit experience is the dissociative xenolalia. This is not a synecdoche, with xenolalia standing in for the Spirit, but an identification of experiences – the xenolalia experience identified as the promised Spirit experience and vice versa.

Furthermore, the identification is framed positively and not negatively. That is, Peter does *not* say 'xenolalia and nothing else' is the promised Spirit experience; he simply identifies what the xenolalia is, namely the promised Spirit experience. He also states the converse – the promised Spirit is identified as what the audience sees and hears, which is not wind or fire, but dissociative xenolalia. The reader may ask whether any other manifestation, or perhaps no manifestation, could also be identified as the promised Spirit experience. This would not be a questioning of the authority of Peter (or Luke), but of the completeness of Peter's exposition. Do Peter's first two Pentecost identifications tell us *all* there is to know about the manifestation of the Spirit? The initial reader cannot be sure because there remains the possibility that Luke will identify some other phenomenon, or lack thereof, as the promised Spirit experience later in the narrative. That is, Luke has not yet exclusively identified tongues speaking as the promised Spirit experience.

However, within the context of this particular discourse about Jesus and the Spirit, xenolalia is the only manifestation under discussion. Therefore, when Peter states that upon repentance and baptism, his audience will receive the gift of the Spirit, the reader expects the audience to experience the same manifestation which they repeatedly asked about and which Peter repeatedly explained. This is Peter's third identification: both now and in the future, what all will receive is the promise; the promise is identified as manifesting in what they see and hear; what they see and hear is dissociative xenolalia.

The chapter discusses how best to interpret this data. There are two basic approaches. The first would be that because the immediate referent to 'gift of the Spirit' and 'the promise of the Spirit' within this discourse is xenolalia, this third identification actively restricts what the first two identifications had left open. That is, the topic under discussion has been the xenolalia phenomenon and what it means; therefore, when the crowd is guaranteed the Spirit, it must be in terms of the phenomenon under discussion. This would leave no room for suggesting that some other manifestation, or that the lack of any manifestation, could be identified as the promise of the Spirit which all are to receive.

The second approach would be to recognize that Luke has genuinely identified xenolalia as a manifestation of the Spirit, and has certainly given it prominence by focalizing it and locating it within his programmatic Pentecost story. However, while acknowledging that the referent being discussed is the xenolalia phenomenon, Luke did not state that this phenomenon is the only manifestation of the promise. The thing guaranteed to all is 'the promise' not a particular manifestation of the promise and though, with the discourse referent being xenolalia, the reader has a genuine expectation that xenolalia will accompany Spirit-reception, the implied reader is aware that Luke could choose to subvert this initial impression. Thus the debate turns upon whether an explicit statement both *identifying* xenolalia as the expected manifestation of the Spirit *and excluding* other phenomena from that role is required to assert *sine qua non* status for xenolalia. The whole ER for initiation must accumulate before a clear answer can be found.

Narrative Focus Forward on Spirit-Reception

Anticipation and Suspense

Luke generated anticipation of Spirit-reception through the final instructions of Jesus but then unexpectedly resolved that anticipation in a xenolalic experience. This surprise twist in the story jolts the reader into asking what this experience means, while foreshadowing allusions to Sinai and Horeb have already provided a partial answer. The reader draws upon information already in the ER for Spirit experience to understand what this coming promise is going to be like. The reader's anticipation is generated[3] by Jesus' command to the Eleven and their associates to await the 'Father's promise' in the last chapter of Luke's Gospel

---

[3] Cf. Kurz, *Reading*, 21.

(Luke 24:49) and the first chapter of Acts (Acts 1:4-5).[4] The reader recalls that Jesus assured his disciples of the Father's willingness to give the Holy Spirit (Luke 11:13).[5] The reader learns that Jesus had already instructed the disciples about this promise, and that it was the fulfilment of the Baptist's prophecy that the Coming One would baptise with the Spirit. Luke's Jesus omits the reference to fire. This raises the question in the reader's mind of where the 'fire' went. Thus, the reader anticipates the coming Spirit as a special 'Father's Promise,' but remains in suspense because the text next relates the replacement of Judas (1:12-26), something seemingly unrelated to the Spirit's imminent coming.

It must be noted that Luke employed 'baptised with the Holy Spirit' co-referentially with receiving the Father's promise, mitigating any attempt within Lukan material to separate an initial Spirit-reception from a subsequent Spirit baptism.[6] Not that Luke on multiple occasions did not reference what Atkinson identifies as 'prior' works of the Spirit,[7] as well as later 'fillings'. But, Luke did not conceive of two distinct Spirit-receptions.

Expectations

Expectations of Isaianic New Exodus Restoration for Israel
At Jesus' final instructions to his disciples, Luke used the phrase 'power from on high' (ἐξ ὕψους δύναμιν Luke 24:49) evoking Isaiah 32:15 (LXX) 'Spirit from on high' (πνεῦμα ἀφ' ὑψηλοῦ). Isaiah makes this outpouring of the Spirit upon Israel the beginning point of restoration for the destroyed nation. In Acts 1:8, Jesus speaks a phrase identical to Isaiah 49:6 (LXX): ἕως ἐσχάτου τῆς γῆς. Luke 3:4-6 has already explicitly cited Isaiah 40:3-5 (LXX), the introduction to a section of Isaiah pregnant with themes of Israel's salvation portrayed as a new Exodus. David Pao, Turner, and Matthias Wenk have argued that Luke employed this concept extensively.[8]

Avemarie critiqued Turner's use of the Isaianic New Exodus to make salvation 'collective' instead of 'individual', saying that this is fundamentally flawed.[9] He objected that it requires that, 'Luke's intended reader must have had the state

---

[4] On the narrative link between Luke and Acts, see Von Baer, *Geist*, 78, and Mainville, *L'Esprit*, 143.
[5] Robert C. Tannehill also suggests Lk 11:13 as background for Lk 24:49 and Acts 1:4-5, *Acts*, 12.
[6] Cf. A.T. Lincoln, 'Theology and History in the Interpretation of Luke's Pentecost', *ET* 96 (1984-1985), 204-209. See also, James D.G. Dunn, 'Baptism in the Holy Spirit ... yet once more', *JEPTA* 18 (1998), 3-25, 17.
[7] Atkinson, *Baptism*, 81.
[8] David W. Pao, *Acts and the Isaianic New Exodus* (Grand Rapids: Baker Academic, 2002; Mohr Siebeck, 2000); Turner, *Power*; Wenk, *Power*; cf. Peter Mallen, *The Reading and Transformation of Isaiah in Luke-Acts* (London: T&T Clark, 2008).
[9] Avemarie, *Tauferzählungen*, 154.

of knowledge and expectations horizon free from Christian influence of a contemporary Palestinian Jew'.[10] Avemarie was right that Luke's intended reader *was* influenced by existing Christianity. But, he did not support his claim that Luke's reader did not have the 'expectations horizon' of a Palestinian Jew. Moreover, he posited an antithesis between collective and individual salvation which is not Turner's. Avemarie acknowledged that he did not evaluate Turner's entire thesis.[11] Furthermore, he wrote before Pao's seminal work. More recently, Andrew Perry has argued against finding a new Exodus in Isaiah 58 and 61, and Luke 4.[12] He sees only Jubilee imagery. However, he does not seek to evaluate whether there is New Exodus usage elsewhere in Luke-Acts.[13] Luke's clear use of Exodus imagery will be discussed from a narratological perspective below. The restoration of Israel must be considered as part of the expectations which Luke's reader has of the Spirit's imminent arrival.

Expectations of the Promise of the Father
What then does the reader expect this 'Father's promise' to look like? Luke's reader remembers the birth narratives where prophetic speech, sometimes loud prophetic speech, was the sudden consequence of being 'filled' with the Spirit. Luke's reader also remembers the Baptist's words that the Mightier One will baptise with the Holy Spirit and fire (Luke 3:16).[14] Though Jesus, in his Acts 1:5 reference to John's prophecy, did not mention fire, his statement evokes the memory of the Baptist's prophecy of Spirit and fire baptism (see discussion below). Alongside prophetic speech and fire, Luke's reader remembers the voice of God which spoke out of heaven at Jesus' baptism (3:21, 22). Luke associated this with Jesus praying after his baptism and the Spirit descending bodily upon him in the form of a dove. Additionally, Luke's reader anticipates power for witness (Acts 1:8). This is not something entirely new, as Jesus had already given his apostles (Luke 9:1-2) and the Seventy-Two (Luke 10:1, 9, 19) power and authority for healing and exorcism in order to proclaim the kingdom; so whatever power was to come must be extraordinary indeed. Thus, Luke can expect his reader to anticipate that the disciples will experience miraculous power, and either prophesy, and/or experience some kind of fire, and/or see a dove, and/or hear the audible voice of God when the Father's promise arrives. The restoration of desolated Israel also belongs to these quickened hopes. Next, allusions to Sinai and Horeb further strengthen and focus these expectations.

---

[10] 'Lukas' intendierter Leser müsse den von christlichen Einflüssen freien Kenntnisstand und Erwartungshorizont eines zeitgenössischen palästinischen Juden haben', *Ibid.*
[11] *Ibid.*
[12] Andrew Perry, *Eschatological Deliverance: The Spirit in Luke-Acts* (Ph.D. dissertation, University of Durham, 2008), 200.
[13] Perry, *Deliverance*, 196.
[14] Tannehill, *Acts*, 26.

Expectations Intensified

Fire. On the day of Pentecost, Luke recorded the manifestations of wind and fire. Regarding the fire and John the Baptist's earlier saying, von Baer objected that, 'Despite the tongues of fire mentioned in the Pentecost report, Luke has, in this event, obviously not seen the fulfilment of the prophecy about the fire baptism, rather only about the Spirit baptism.'[15] On the other hand, Leisegang argued that Luke, as author of both the Gospel and Acts, developed the fire motif in the Pentecost story.[16] Kremer, Gerhard Schneider, and Morna D. Hooker also link the Baptist's prophecy to Pentecost.[17] The book's focus upon timing, mechanism, and manifestation, calls for further evaluation of the fire motif as to whether Luke viewed it as a manifestation of Spirit-reception.

When John's prophecy was mentioned, John had already been introduced as Isaiah's priestly voice in the wilderness for Luke contrasted the appearance of 'John the son of Zacharias in the wilderness' (Luke 3:2) with high priests Annas and Caiaphas,[18] and his Luke 3:4-6 quote from Isaiah 40:3-5 (LXX) is prefaced in the LXX by 40:2a, 'Speak, you priests, to the heart of Jerusalem'.[19] From Luke 1:17 the reader already understands John as Malachi's promised Elijah (Malachi 4:6).[20] Where Luke 3:17 portrays unrepentant Israelites as 'chaff' (ἄχυρον), burned in judgment by the Coming One, Malachi 4:1 speaks of wicked Israelites as 'straw' or 'stubble' (καλάμη) being burned. So, there is similarity in the idea of judgment. But is Luke 3:17's fire of judgment the same as the Coming One's baptism of Spirit and fire (Luke 3:16)?

Von Baer argues that it is, and he cites the Gospels' use of the imagery of fire as judgment in support (e.g., Mt 3:10, 12; 5:22; 7:19; 13:40, 42, 50; 18:8; 25:41; Mark 9:43-49; Luke 9:54; 17:29; John 15:6):

> On the basis of this appraisal, it is completely impossible to see something other than the judgment-fire in the Baptist's saying of Matthew 3:11; Luke 3:16, especially because in Matthew 3, 10, 12 as well as Luke 3, 9, 17, the mentioned fire is explicitly bound to the thought of judgment.[21]

---

[15] 'Trotz der in dem Pfingstbericht erwähnten Feuerzungen hat Lk. in diesem Ereignis offenbar nicht die Erfüllung der Weissagung von der Feuertaufe, sondern nur von der Geistestaufe gesehen', Von Baer, *Geist*, 162.

[16] Leisegang, *Pneuma*, 74, 132.

[17] Kremer, *Pfingstbericht*, 114. Gerhard Schneider, *Apostelgeschichte 1,1-8,40* (Freiburg: Herder, 2002 [1980]), 249. Morna D. Hooker, 'John's Baptism: A Prophetic Sign', Graham N. Stanton, Bruce W. Longenecker, Stephen C. Barton (eds), *The Holy Spirit and Christian Origins* (Grand Rapids: Eerdmans, 2004), 22-40; 32.

[18] Perry, *Deliverance*, 264.

[19] *Ibid.*

[20] Turner, *Power*, 151.

[21] 'Auf Grund dieser Feststellung ist es ganz unmöglich etwas anderes wie das Gerichtsfeuer in dem Täuferwort Mt. 3, 11; Lk. 3, 16 zu sehen, besonders da in Mt. 3, 10, 12 sowie Lk. 3, 9, 17 das erwähnte Feuer ausdrücklich mit dem Gerichtsgedanken verbunden wird', Von Baer, *Geist*, 161.

Perry, however, argues that since Luke drew on Malachi and Malachi portrays non-destructive priestly purification,[22] Luke's fires are different. There will be a fire of purification and later a fire of judgment. In evaluation of Perry, Luke 1:76 (cf. Luke 7:27) did roughly cite Malachi 3:1 making John the one who goes before the face of the Lord who is coming suddenly to his temple to purify the priests who have corrupted themselves (Malachi 1:6-2:9, 3:2-3). Also, Malachi ends with the wicked burned as stubble (4:1). But is this burning of the wicked different than the Lord's refining fire? Dunn thinks so.[23] There would then be two fires in Malachi corresponding to the ideas of purification and judgment. One could counter Dunn by arguing that judgment is how the Lord will purify the priests. A definitive resolution does not come easily. However, whether Malachi's priests are purified by the death of some of their number, or by some less severe means, they are purified. The uncertainty over the precise relationship of purification and judgment in Malachi does not alter the fact that Malachi contains both purification and judgment imagery. Consequently, evaluation of any Lukan reference or allusion to Malachi must recognize not only the imagery of destruction, but also the motif of purification. Therefore, read in light of both of Malachi's motifs, there is the possibility that Luke's Baptist promises a Coming One who will not just destroy, but will also purify. The question then becomes how Luke understood this purification to be accomplished.

Dunn sees it as originally having three aspects: 1) it was a metaphor drawn from John's water rite: 'the Spirit and fire are clearly the elements into which people would be plunged',[24] 2) it had to do with the initiation of the new age and initiates entrance into the new age,[25] 3) it meant both judgment and purification: 'purgative, purifying those who repented, destructive, consuming those who did not'.[26] However, Dunn also writes that the metaphor was transformed, first by Jesus to mean that he himself must experience a baptism of fire (cf. Luke 12:49-50) and then by the early Christians who applied it to their Pentecostal experiences. Luke recorded their new view.[27] Turner argues that the Baptist's actual utterance referenced no personal Spirit experience, but rather an experience of national transformation as the Spirit anointed Coming One purges the repentant and destroys the wicked.[28] This is in line with the priestly purification/destruction of the wicked motif. Turner also sees Luke reapplying John's prophecy to the Pentecost event. He concludes that,

---

[22] Perry, *Deliverance*, 256, 258. Cf. David L. Peterson, *Zechariah 9-14 & Malachi: A Commentary* (London: SCM, 1995), 224, who also sees Malachi's fires as distinct.
[23] Dunn, *Baptism*, 12.
[24] James Dunn, 'The Birth of a Metaphor – Baptized in the Spirit', in *The Christ and the Spirit:* Volume 2, *Pneumatology* (Edinburgh: T&T Clark, 1998), 103-17; 107.
[25] *Ibid.*, 107.
[26] *Ibid.*, 106.
[27] *Ibid.*, 112.
[28] Turner, *Power*, 185.

The expression 'baptize in Holy Spirit-and-fire' in Luke-Acts so far has two denotations (the Pentecost event, and the end-time deluge which it foreshadows, both in its character and in its intensity), but one basic connotation (an eschatological and overwhelming experience of God's Spirit).[29]

Thus, one can argue that Luke's Acts reader would find in the description of 'tongues like fire' at Pentecost the Lukan fulfilment of John the Baptist's prophecy. That is, regardless of whether John's prophecy originally referenced strictly judgement, or purification and judgment, or purification alone, Luke has brought fire into contact with believers, thereby suggesting that Luke has applied the purificatory aspect of the prophecy to his Pentecost story.

On the other hand, one could argue that the fire has nothing to do with John's prophecy, which concerned judgment, not purification, but is simply part of the theophany; the absence of fire from Acts 1:5 is conclusive evidence that Luke excluded the judgment connotations of fire from Pentecost. The weakness in this argument is the aforementioned presence of allusions, in Luke's gospel, to Malachi, a book containing both judgment and purification. It becomes difficult to argue that Luke 3:16 is strictly judgment without a hint of purification.[30]

Sinai and Horeb. Stronstad argues that Pentecost 'echoes'[31] the theophanies of Sinai and Horeb in that:

> (1) They all take place on the mountain of God, Mount Zion also being God's mountain.
> (2) There is a common temporal pattern of:
>> a. Celebration of the Passover
>> b. An intervening period of weeks
>> c. A number of days for preparation
>> d. A morning time theophany
> (3) The Pentecost theophany is a combination of the Sinai and Horeb theophanies.

Stronstad also notes a difference in that Pentecost created a 'community of prophets', whereas Sinai created a kingdom of priests.[32]

Contrary to Stronstad, Jon Ruthven argues that this theophanic language should not be considered a reference to Mount Sinai, but rather to Is. 59:19, 20 (LXX). He points especially to the presence of βίαιος in both Acts 2:2 and Is.

---

[29] Max Turner, 'Spirit Endowment in Luke/Acts: Some Linguistic Considerations', *VoxEv* 12 (1981), 45-63; 52.
[30] The theological implications of Pentecost fire as purificatory are intriguing, but the dissertation's focus upon timing, mechanism, and manifestation will not allow further pursuit of this subject.
[31] Roger Stronstad, *The Prophethood of All Believers: A Study in Luke's Charismatic Theology* (Cleveland: CPT, 2010 [1999]), 52.
[32] *Ibid.*, 52-53.

59:19.³³ Considering Luke's intensive use of Isaiah, Ruthven correctly sees a connection. But he errs in excluding reference to Sinai/Horeb. Perry rejects a Sinai reference, preferring allusions to Babel, the Red Sea, and Isaiah 6.³⁴ Avemarie was also unpersuaded.³⁵ But, neither Ruthven, Perry, Avemarie, nor Menzies considers the persistent presence of the Exodus ER in the text.

Menzies argues that Luke did not use the wind and fire to reference Sinai or covenant renewal. First, the rabbinic association of the giving of the Law with Pentecost is late, covenant renewal in *Jubilees* is limited to the Noahic and Abrahamic covenants with only 'minor' links to Sinai, the Qumran scrolls also do not evidence linkage to Sinai, and the New Testament itself makes no such connections.³⁶ Next, he argues that the various key words and phenomena of Pentecost, wind, fire, voice, etc., while finding parallels to Sinai accounts in Philo and Targum Pseudo-Jonathan, are not 'unique to Sinai traditions',³⁷ since a variety of other biblical and extra-biblical texts have similar imagery. Luke's usage is simply 'characteristic of theophanic language in general'.³⁸ Moreover, 'Luke associates the Spirit rather than the voice of God with the wind and fire imagery'.³⁹ Rabbinic stories of language miracles are not sufficiently parallel and are most likely late.⁴⁰ Finally, Acts 2:33, unlike Ephesians 4:8, does not draw upon Psalm 67:19 (LXX) and is not 'a Christian counterpart to rabbinic exegesis of Psalm 67'⁴¹ in which Jesus, as the new Moses, ascends to heaven to receive the Spirit, instead of the Torah, and to give it to the waiting people. Tellingly, Menzies writes, 'The absence of any reference to Moses, the law or the covenant in Acts 2 speaks decisively against this proposal'.⁴² Menzies' argument is opposed by Turner and Wenk⁴³ who both present the case for deliberate Lukan Sinai/Pentecost association with Jesus as the new Moses. Their arguments will not, for the most part, be repeated here. Rather, a narratological response with be utilized.

Menzies is correct that late Rabbinic writings cannot inform the New Testament text and that terminology common to theophanic literature cannot persuade. However, narratological analysis identifies Menzies' last statement as indicating

---

33 Jon Ruthven, '"This Is My Covenant with Them": Isaiah 59.19-21 as the Programmatic Prophecy of the New Covenant in the Acts of the Apostles (Part I)', *JPT* 17 (2008), 32-47; 36-38.
34 Perry, *Deliverance*, 246-49.
35 Avemarie, *Tauferzählungen*, 209.
36 Menzies, *Empowered*, 190-92.
37 *Ibid.*, 195.
38 *Ibid.*, 196.
39 *Ibid.*, 195.
40 So too, W. Grundmann, 'Der Pfingstbericht der Apostelgeschichte in seinem theologischen Sinn', *Studia Evangelica Volume II: Papers Presented to the Second International Congress on New Testament Studies*, Part I: *The New Testament Scriptures* (Berlin: Akademie-Verlag, 1964), 584-94; 592.
41 Menzies, *Empowered*, 198.
42 *Ibid.*, 200.
43 Turner, *Power*, 279-89; Wenk, *Community Forming Power*, 246-51.

a foundational error. Neither he, nor Ruthven, nor Perry, nor Avemarie recognizes that Moses' and Elijah's appearance on the Mount of Transfiguration talking about Jesus' coming 'departure' (ἔξοδον, Luke 9:30, 31),[44] established an ER for the Exodus motif which drew upon the Elijah imagery in the Nazareth sermon (4:25-26) and that remained with the reader through the narrative all the way to Pentecost. Moses *is* in the narrative, and the Exodus too, because the context of the narrative is not limited to the few verses immediately peripheral to any given text, but consists of the accumulated experiences of the reader, especially those experiences of climactic moments like the transfiguration and Jesus' inaugural sermon. Moreover, once the reader moves on to Acts 3:22, he reads that Luke explicitly identified Jesus as the new Moses and this further modifies and reinforces his already existing Exodus understanding of Pentecost. The Isaianic New Exodus and new covenant imagery of Moses/Elijah, Sinai/Horeb, form the primary narrative backdrop for Acts 2:2-4, not Is. 59:19. Additionally, Wenk points out the threefold repetition in Acts 2 of the collocation, 'signs' and 'wonders' (σημεῖα καὶ τέρατα or vice versa in 2:19, 22, and 43). These are attributed to Jesus in 2:22, as Menzies himself notes.[45] This is narratologically significant because they are deeply associated with Moses, the Exodus, and Mount Sinai, the very thing which Menzies denies (cf. Ex 7:3; 11:9-10; Deut. 4:34; 6:22; 7:19; Is. 8:18),[46] and even taken up by Isaiah and related to Jerusalem, Mount Zion.

The rest of Menzies' objections are invalidated by the Exodus ER. The terminology of Pentecost is not mere generic language of theophanies, because it is undergirded by the presence of Moses, Elijah, and the Exodus. The Exodus imagery cannot be isolated to earlier chapters. It moves forward in the narrative with the reader. The reader does not forget about Moses and Elijah and therefore, when theophany-like language appears in Acts 2, the implied reader does not attach this language to just any theophany in the Hebrew Scriptures or intertestamental literature, but specifically to the theophanies that accompanied the characters previously given prominence in the narrative – Moses and Elijah.

This focus upon Sinai need not exclude allusions to other specific theophanies. G.K. Beale argues that Sinai was a 'prototypical' theophany which other latter theophanies reflected.[47] 'The manner in which God's presence comes to fill the tabernacle, temple and church enhances the plausibility that Luke is describing Pentecost as the temple for this new age.'[48] Beale finds specific parallels between

---

[44] Cf. Ralph P. Martin, 'Salvation and Discipleship in Luke's Gospel', *Interp.* 30 (1976), 366-80; 370.

[45] Robert P. Menzies, *The Language of the Spirit: Interpreting and Translating Charismatic Terms* (Cleaveland: CPT, 2010), 26-27.

[46] Wenk, *Community*, 250.

[47] G.K. Beale, *The Temple and the Church's Mission: A Biblical Theology of the Dwelling Place of God* (Downers Grove: IVP, 2004), 205. Beale acknowledges drawing upon Jeffrey J. Niehaus, *God at Sinai: Covenant and Theophany in the Bible and Ancient Near East* (Grand Rapids: Zondervan, 1995), 371.

[48] *Ibid.*, 211.

Pentecost and 2 Chronicles 7:1, 3. Both have fire, something filling the "house", praise by God's servants, and praise by onlookers.[49] Earlier in the story (2 Chronicles 5:12) we read of 120 priests who blew trumpets. It is not impossible that Luke conflated elements of the Solomonic Temple theophany with that of Sinai in his Pentecost story. But these are allusions to specific, related theophanies, not to generic theophany.

Menzies also does not address the *sequence* of the theophanic terms. The stylized progression wind/storm, fire, voice belongs specifically to Mount Horeb and Elijah, and generally to Mount Sinai and Moses.[50] Menzies also misses the preliminary nature of wind and fire to the φωνὴ τοῦ θεοῦ both at Sinai and Horeb. Luke did not parallel his account with Philo or the Targums,[51] but directly with a blended Sinai/Horeb, the epitome of covenant and covenant renewal. The forty days of Jesus' appearances add to the Sinai/Horeb allusions.

Expectations Resolved
Thus, as Luke's reader arrives at Acts 2:4, s/he is anticipating prophetic speech, a dove, or a mighty voice from heaven, or perhaps a 'still small voice'. Surprisingly, for the Lukan story context though not for the wider literary context of Philo,[52] s/he hears various languages, spoken from the disciples themselves (λαλεῖν ἑτέραις γλώσσαις), as the Spirit was giving them ἀποφθέγγεσθαι, 'to express orally'.[53]

BDAG's definition of the word, 'to express oneself orally, w. focus on sound rather than content, *speak out, declare* boldly or loudly (of the speech of a wise man ... but also of an oracle-giver, diviner, prophet, exorcist, and other inspired persons)',[54] conforms to the expectation of loud prophecy. It cannot be taken to mean that the utterance had no content and was mere gibberish simply because

---

[49] *Ibid.*

[50] Luke did not insert an earthquake to make it an absolutely perfect parallel. But on the narrative relationship between Horeb and Sinai, especially the proposal that they share a common type-scene, see, Britt, 'Concealment', 44-46. For a list of parallels between Sinai and Horeb, see, Jörg Jeremias, 'Die Anfänge der Schriftprophetie', *ZThK* 93.4 (December, 1996), 481-99; 486, and Stronstad, *Prophethood*, 53. Theodor Seidl denies direct literary dependence, but suggests a common tradition, 'Mose und Elija am Gottesberg. Überlieferungen zu Krise und Konversion der Propheten', *BZ* 37.1 (1993), 1-25; 20. James Nohrnberg argues that the Moses story reflects Elijah, *Like unto Moses: The Constituting of an Interruption* (Bloomington: Indiana University Press, 1995), 329.

[51] Turner, *Power*, 283.

[52] Cf. Philo, 'The Decalogue', trans. Charles Duke Yonge, *The Works of Philo Judaeus, the Contemporary of Josephus, Translated from the Greek* (London: H.G. Bohn, 1854-1890), sections 32-35.

[53] Walter Bauer, rev. and ed. Frederick William Danker, et al., *A Greek-English Lexicon of the New Testament and other Early Christian Literature* (Chicago: University of Chicago Press, 2000), 125.

[54] *Ibid.*, 125, original italics. So too, Kramer, *Pfingstbericht*, 123-24.

the definition states that the focus is on sound. That the utterance had linguistic content was already stated in the text, ἑτέραις γλώσσαις.

But did all the gathered believers utter words by the Spirit? Donald Guthrie's appeal to the preliminary phenomena is pertinent:

> The infilling of the Spirit extended to *all* believers. Not only does Luke say that 'they were all filled with the Holy Spirit' (Acts 2:4), but that the tongues of fire distributed and rested on 'each one of them' (2:3). The Spirit's coming is, therefore, seen as both corporate and individual. There is certainly no room for the idea that any believers were excluded from this initial experience.[55]

The fire sat ἐφ' ἕνα ἕκαστον αὐτῶν (2:3) and in this way Luke brought the individual believers into focus so that in the next breath when he says all πάντες were filled with the Spirit and began to speak in other tongues one cannot complain that Luke did not repeat the word 'all', and therefore we do not know for certain if 'all' actually spoke in tongues. Luke's camera has already individualized the phenomena occurring so a repetition of the word 'all' is not necessary. Was the 'all' just the apostles?[56] No, the 'all' who were together (2:1) and the 'all' who were filled (2:4) have their antecedent in the men and women who had been praying (1:13-14), which Luke expanded to include a group of 120 (1:15).[57] Dieter Schneider aptly expresses how Luke joined the two aspects of Pentecost – the individual and the group:

> Two principles of Spirit bestowal are here already clear ...The one is the principle of *individuation* (= the Spirit comes on every individual), the other is the principle of *sociality* (= the Spirit comes on all together). Both principles stand in correlation to one another and therefore do not exclude one another.[58]

---

[55] Donald Guthrie, *New Testament Theology* (Leicester: IVP, 1981), 537, original italics. Similarly, Wilfried Eckey, *Die Apostelgeschichte: Der Weg des Evangeliums von Jerusalem nach Rom, Teilband I 1,1-15,35*, (Neukirchen-Vluyn: Neukirchener Verlagsgesellschaft mbH, 2011), 2.135.

[56] For 'all' as a narrative emphasis upon the apostles, cf. Jacob Kremer, 'Was Geschah Pfingsten? Zur Historizität des Apg 2, 1-13 berichteten Pfingstereignisses', *WuW* 3 (1973), 195-207; 197; Nelson P. Estrada, *From Followers to Leaders: The Apostles in the Ritual of Status Transformation in Acts 1-2* (London: T&T Clark, 2004), 47, 204-207.

[57] Similarly, Eduard Lohse, *Die Einheit des Neuen Testaments: Exegetische Studien zur Theologie des Neuen Testaments* (Göttingen: Vandenhoeck & Ruprecht, 1973), 179; Rudolf Pesch, *Die Apostelgeschichte: 1. Teilband, Apg 1-12* (Köln: Benziger Verlag; Neukirchen-Vluyn: Neukirchener Verlag des Erziehungsvereins GmbH, 1986), 282; Atkinson, *Baptism*, 62. Cf. I. Howard Marshall, 'The Significance of Pentecost', *SJTh* 30 (1997), 347-69; 352-53.

[58] 'Zwei Prinzipien der Geistverleihung werden hier schon deutlich ... Das eine ist das Prinzip der *Individuation* (= der Geist kommt auf jeden einzelnen), das andere das Prinzip der *Sozialität* (= der Geist kommt auf alle gemeinsam). Beide Prinzipien stehen in Korrelation zueinander und schließen sich darum gegenseitig nicht aus'. Dieter Schneider, *Der Geist, der Geschichte macht: Geisterfahrung bei Lukas* (Neukirchen-Vluyn: Aussaat Verlag, 1992), 36.

Narrative Focus Backward on the Xenolalia Experience
The Initial Redundant Focalization of the Xenolalia Experience

After Luke employed the literary devices of foreshadowing, suspense, and allusion to focus his reader's attention on what is, as will be shown, dissociative xenolalia, he used redundant focalization to direct the reader back toward the dissociative xenolalic experience, then interpreted the focalized dissociative xenolalic experience in terms of the anticipated Spirit-reception. That is, he used repeated focalization to identify the referent for his Spirit discourse. First, after the Spirit begins to give the disciples prophetic utterance, the movement of the crowd towards 'this voice/sound' τῆς φωνῆς ταύτης directs the reader's attention to it (2:6). That something is being focalized is clear,[59] but what? While Keener and Peterson identify the 'sound' with the disciples' tongues speech,[60] von Baer was uncertain whether the wind or the tongues is the subject of the crowd's interest.[61] Heidrun Gunkel thinks that Luke 'left open' the question of which phenomenon drew the crowd, and suggests it was possibly both.[62] Jon Ruthven equates τῆς φωνῆς ταύτης with the ἦχος of the wind.[63] However, the immediate antecedent to φωνή is the speaking of the believers, not the sound of the wind. As to the fact that Luke spoke of 'the voice' singular, Luke could easily have been presenting the group as making a unified sound, either from theological reasons (emphasizing the singular voice of the Spirit speaking) or from practical reasons (the various voices of a group would blend together to make a unified sound[64]) or both. Moreover, when the crowd arrives, they are bewildered, not because they hear a wind, but because they hear their own languages being spoken. One could argue that perhaps they initially heard the wind, but when they arrived, the wind had ceased and they only heard the sound of languages. Or perhaps the languages were more interesting than the wind and that is why they did not ask about the wind. Or perhaps they did ask about the wind and Luke never mentioned it. However, these interpretations, aside from being speculative arguments from silence, have the textual problem that the disciples uttering languages is the immediate antecedent to τῆς φωνῆς ταύτης, not the wind. The order

---

[59] 'In 2:6-13 the narrator permits the crowd to become a focalizing character. That is, we are experiencing the event through the perceptions, thoughts, and feelings of the crowd' (Tannehill, *Acts*, 28-29). Robert W. Funk briefly analyzes focalization in Acts 2:1-6. *The Poetics of Biblical Narrative* (Sonoma: Polebridge, 1988), 111.

[60] Craig S. Keener, *The Spirit in the Gospels and Acts: Divine Purity and Power* (Peabody: Hendrickson, 1997), 195. Peterson, *Acts*, 135.

[61] Von Baer, *Geist*, 87. So too, David S. Morlan, *Conversion in Luke and Paul: Some Exegetical and Theological Explorations* (PhD Durham University, 2010), 148; Kremer, 'Pfingsten?' 199; W.F. Burnside, *The Acts of the Apostles* (Cambridge: CUP, 1916), 87.

[62] Gunkel, *Geist*, 149.

[63] Jon Ruthven, 'Covenant', 42.

[64] So Gerald Hovenden, *Speaking in Tongues: The New Testament Evidence in Context* (London: Sheffield Academic, 2002), 68.

of events in Luke's story places languages after the wind, and the gathering crowd after the languages.

A related, and as will become apparent later, a narratively significant matter, is whether the crowd saw the fire. One could argue that the fire was still continuing when the crowd arrived. However, the story actively excludes such a reading because, despite there being a reason within the story for the crowd to ask about the fire, namely its marvellous character, the crowd makes no inquiries. This is *not* an argument from silence, for the extraordinary nature of the manifestation – tongues of fire resting upon the disciples' heads – calls for a response from the characters within the story. For the characters, who, as will be seen, are presented as inquisitive, to know about the marvellous fire and to ignore it is incongruous. Thus, the reader is required by the story itself to conclude that the crowd was not witness to the fire, for had it been, it would have been amazed and inquired of its significance.

The crowd's reactions to languages being spoken by persons not normally able to speak them rivet the reader's attention. Luke presented an explanatory statement from himself, then, from the characters, three honest inquiries, one positive statement, and one piece of ridicule about the language utterances. Luke focalized through the crowd upon the speakers as well as upon the utterance: a) 'They were hearing, each one in his own dialect, them speaking' (2:6); b) 'Look, are not all these who speak Galileans?' (2:7); c) 'And how is it that we hear, each in our own language in which we were born?' (2:8); d) 'we hear them speaking in our own tongues the great things of God' (2:11); e) 'What does this mean?' (2:12); f) 'They are full of new wine' (2:13). Luke emphasized the xenolalic experience by repeating in the dialogue what he had just narrated.[65]

Now redundancy comes into play. The crowd's positive reactions are framed by what Sternberg calls 'repetition with variation'.[66] 'Amazed and marvelled' (7); and 'amazed and perplexed' (12); highlight the majority's attitude toward the miraculous speaking of the Galileans. The crowd neither asks nor expresses amazement about wind or fire, it asks and marvels about the speaking in languages. The crowd is presented as curious, and therefore the reader has the expectation that, if they knew about the mighty wind or the fire resting on the disciples' heads, they would inquire. That they do not ask is active proof, not an argument from silence, that they do not know of these initial phenomena.

The crowd is the focalizer and the dissociative xenolalia the focalized. Carson, in his interaction with Classical Pentecostals, does not utilize a narrative approach when he asks why they arbitrarily pick tongues as normative and not wind and fire. While Luke vividly presented preliminary phenomena to the arrival of the Spirit, the questions which the crowd asked and his normative spokesperson

---

[65] Cf. Robert Alter on literal word for word repetition in *Art*, 77.
[66] Sternberg, *Poetics*, 391-92.

answered were not about the wind or fire, but only about the dissociative xenolalia.[67] Kremer recognizes what Luke was not doing: 'The Pentecost sermon, on one hand, does not have to do with the phenomena portrayed in v. 2 and v. 3 (at least not explicitly).'[68] But, he fails to analyse the focalization of tongues for he continues, '[The Pentecost sermon] also does not consider specifically the speaking in foreign languages.'[69] However, he does recognize the role of the visible nature of the believer's experience in the Pentecost sermon, 'On the other hand, it assumes an exceptional, observable-to-all-behaviour of the disciples, which could be misperceived as a consequence of drunkenness.'[70]

Some have suggested, however, that the wonder of Pentecost was not a miracle of speaking, but a miracle of hearing. Gregory Nazianzen (ca. 325-391[71]) raised the possibility and then rejected it because the miracle would then be in the hearers and not the speakers.[72] It was discussed by John Calvin and Theodore Beza and rightly rejected for the same reason as Gregory.[73] In the twentieth century, Gustav Hoennicke rejected it because ἑτέραις excludes ecstatic speech as in 1 Corinthians 14.[74] George Barton Cutten argued against it because Luke's idiom, 'tongues speaking', emphasizes a miracle in the tongue and not the ear.[75] Recently, Keener rejected it because, 'Luke reports their speaking 'other languages' before mentioning that anyone hears them (2:4).'[76]

However, Jenny Everts, whose arguments are followed by Menzies, has renewed the case for the hearing miracle view.[77] Everts suggests first that, despite

---

[67] Carson, *Spirit*, 142. Anthony A. Hoekema similarly asked why wind and fire are not evidence. *Tongues and Spirit-Baptism, A Biblical and Theological Evaluation* (Grand Rapids: Baker, 1972), 68.
[68] 'Die Pfingstpredigt geht einerseits nicht auf die v.2 und v.3 geschilderten Phänomene ein (jedenfalls nicht ausdrücklich)', Kremer, *Pfingstbericht*, 178.
[69] '[Die Pfingstpredigt] berücksichtigt auch nicht eigens das Reden in fremden Sprachen', *Ibid.*
[70] 'Andererseits setzt sie ein außergewöhnliches, allen wahrnehmbares Verhalten der Jünger voraus, das als Folge von Trunkenheit mißdeutet werden konnte', *Ibid.*
[71] Philip Schaff and Henry Wace (eds), *A Select Library of Nicene and Post-Nicene Fathers of the Christian Church* (Grand Rapids: Eerdmans, n.d.), 7.188, 199.
[72] Gregory Nazianzen, 'Oration XLI On Pentecost', Philip Schaff and Henry Wace (eds), *A Select Library of Nicene and Post-Nicene Fathers of the Christian Church* (Grand Rapids: Eerdmans, n.d.), 7.378-85; paragraph XV, 384.
[73] John Calvin, *Acts* (Wheaton: Crossway, 1995 [Vol. 1, 1552; Vol. 2, 1554]), 31; Theodore Beza, trans. L. Tomson, *The New Testament of our Lord Jesus Christ, translated out of Greeke by Theod. Beza* (Dort: Isaac Canin, 1603), 108.
[74] Gustav Hoennicke, *Die Apostelgeschichte* (Leipzig: Verlag von Quelle & Meyer, 1913), 29. D. Erwin Preuschen agreed that ἑτέραις excludes ecstatic speech, *Die Apostelgeschichte* (Tübingen: Verlag von J.C.B. Mohr, Paul Siebeck, 1912), 11.
[75] George Barton Cutten, *Speaking with Tongues Historically and Psychologically Considered* (New Haven: Yale University Press, 1927), 18.
[76] Keener, *Acts*, Volume 1, 823.
[77] Jenny Everts, 'Tongues or Languages? Contextual Consistency in the Translation of Acts 2', *JPT* 4 (1994), 71-80; cf. Robert P. Menzies, 'The Role of Glossolalia in Luke-

Acts 2:11, διαλέκτῳ in Acts 2:6, 8, is contrasted with ἑτέραις γλώσσαις of 2:4. Second, she concludes from τῇ ἰδίᾳ διαλέκτῳ in 2:6, 8, that, 'These two verses would imply that each individual heard the entire group of disciples speaking the individual's native language.'[78] She argues further that only some of the crowd were given the hearing miracle. The rest heard what was actually being spoken – ecstatic, non-intelligible utterances. She argues that had they really been speaking in foreign languages, no one would have thought them drunk.[79]

Yet, visionary and/or Spirit experience in Luke has never, up to this point in the narrative, resulted in non-intelligible utterance, but rather in loud prophecy (Luke 1:42) and praise (Luke 1:46, 68). Without some signal from the text, there is no reason to read otherwise. Gregory's argument remains valid, for Luke did not say the Spirit came upon the crowd, or that the Spirit enabled understanding.[80] Keener's cogent argument also speaks against a hearing miracle. Moreover, the mockery does not require non-language, but dismissal of what was being said[81] as well as an indication of the dissociative nature of the speech. Incongruously loud speech would also explain the charge of drunkenness.

Furthermore, that τῇ ἰδίᾳ διαλέκτῳ (2:6) is singular and therefore is better understood to modify ἤκουον εἷς ἕκαστος than λαλούντων αὐτῶν does not necessitate that a miracle of hearing took place, only that Luke emphasized the evidential nature of the crowd's experience. The crowd was hearing the prophetic speech which Luke had already depicted as understandable. Thus Christopher Forbes rightly argues against a hearing wonder: 'in view of the comments of the crowd and the parallel use of ἑτέραις γλώσσαις and διάλεκτος in vv. 4, 6, 8 and 11'.[82] However, Everts' argument for consistency in translating γλώσσαις throughout Acts is significant from a narratological perspective.[83] Instead of consistently reading it as unintelligible speech, the connotation of intelligible language that Luke initially gave to γλώσσαις remains in the narrative unless specifically modified; as will be shown, it is not. The implied reader consistently reads xenolalia.

Acts', *AJPS* 15.1 (2012), 47-72; 52-53. Menzies (52) acknowledges his indebtedness to Everts. Hovenden is sympathetic to Everts, but ultimately sides against her, Hovenden, *Tongues*, 64-72.

[78] Everts, 'Tongues?' 75.
[79] *Ibid.*
[80] Watson E. Mills, *A Theological/Exegetical Approach to Glossolalia* (New York: University Press of America, 1985), 62.
[81] Cf. Marshall, 'Pentecost', 361.
[82] Christopher Forbes, *Prophecy and Inspired Speech in Early Christianity and its Hellenistic Environment* (Tübingen: J.C.B. Mohr, Paul Siebeck, 1995), 48.
[83] Everts, 'Tongues?' 76-77.

The Triple Identification

First Identification
Luke's stage has been full of crowds rushing and actors pointing, all focusing the reader's attention upon the phenomenon of dissociative xenolalia, and all pushing forward the question of its meaning. In Longacre's discourse grammar terms, the 'concentration of participants', 'heightened vividness', use of rhetorical questions, and focalization or 'change of vantage point', indicate a discourse 'peak'.[84] At this peak moment, Luke brought forward an actor to give a speech in response. It is not just any actor. Peter[85] stands with the eleven other apostles, normative spokespersons all, and speaks out (ἀπεφθέγξατο αὐτοῖς) as their leader, delivering Luke's answer[86] to the mockery and the honest questions concerning tongues speech. This fits what Longacre terms a 'didactic peak': 'a special elaboration of some episode which precedes or follows the action peak. Essentially action ceases at a didactic peak and participant(s) speak out in a monologue/dialogue which develops the theme of the story.'[87]

Peter's point one: they are not drunk (2:15). Point two: the tongues speech experience is the promised prophetic experience of the Spirit spoken of by Joel, 'this is what has been spoken' τοῦτό ἐστιν τὸ εἰρημένον (2:16, cf. Joel 2:28-32). Here Luke made a direct identification, the dissociative xenolalia experience is the scripturally foretold experience of the end-times prophetic Spirit. One might ask whether a New Testament writer would ever think in terms of direct identification. Is that not a modern concept and anachronistic to apply to Luke-Acts? However, this kind of identification is consonant with E. Earle Ellis' observation of LXX exegetical terminology, 'In the Greek Old Testament οὗτος ἐστίν translates terms that introduce the explanation of divine revelation through a divine oracle (Isa 9:14f.), parable (Ezek 5:5), vision (Zech 1:10, 19; 5:3, 6), dream (Dan 4:24, [21]) and strange writing (Dan 5:25f.).'[88] In Ellis' examples, the verb is sometimes understood. For Daniel, Ellis used Theodotion, who is post-NT period and therefore not admissible as evidence bearing upon Lukan usage. However, Dan 2:28 LXX is another example Ellis missed. His point is well taken. Richard Longenecker also points out that this is a standard method of biblical interpretation at Qumran called pesher ('solution', 'interpretation'), in which a biblical text is understood to have been intended specifically for the Qumran community.[89] In addition to Acts 2:16, Longenecker lists Peter's identification in Acts 4:11, and

---

[84] Longacre, *Grammar*, 37-48.
[85] Tannehill identifies Peter as a 'reliable spokesman for the implied author, having been instructed by Jesus and inspired by the Spirit' (*Acts*, 15).
[86] Not just any answer. Tannehill writes that, 'The Pentecost speech is one of the most carefully constructed speeches in Acts' (*Ibid.*, 41).
[87] Longacre, *Discourse*, 38.
[88] E. Earle Ellis, *The Old Testament in Early Christianity: Canon and Interpretation in the Light of Modern Research* (Tübingen: J.C.B. Mohr, Paul Siebeck, 1991), 83.
[89] Richard Longenecker, *Biblical Exegesis in the Apostolic Period* (Grand Rapids: Eerdmans, 1975), 38-39.

his application of scripture to Judas in Acts 1:20 and to Jesus in 2:25 and 3:22, as examples of pesher.[90] Grammatically and conceptually, there is thus no issue with understanding Peter as saying that the dissociative xenolalia experience is to be identified as the 'pouring out of the Spirit' experience spoken of by Joel. What cannot be done at this point is to assert that 'this', *and nothing else but* 'this', is the promised experience. Luke has stated the identity of the xenolalia experience, but Luke has not qualified the xenolalia experience as the *only* possible expression of the promised Spirit experience.

Moreover, we must consider that there is more to the identification than mere pouring out the Spirit. Included in that pouring out is the idea of prophecy, which is understandable as being fulfilled in the xenolalia. That is, Peter asserts that the prophetic activity promised by Joel is fulfilled in the supernaturally spoken languages to which they are all witnesses. Xenolalia *is* prophecy.[91] Peter goes on to speak of visions and dreams, and then repeats the idea of prophecy, thus bracketing the visions and dreams with prophecy. This is not unlike Numbers 12:6, which identifies visions and dreams as the means of God's communication to prophets. Luke suggested that visions and dreams are grouped together in the general category of prophecy, which is fulfilled in the xenolalia.[92]

But, what of the apocalyptic signs? These are also part of the identification. Are they supposed to be fulfilled in the xenolalic utterances of a few believers? Stronstad argues that the wind, the fire, and the tongues correspond to the signs in heaven above and earth below: 'the explicit "this is that" perspective of Peter (Acts 2.16) ought to cause interpreters to identify the wonders and signs on the day of Pentecost with the wonders and signs which Joel announced' and not with the phenomena at the crucifixion.[93] He argues that Luke's mention of fire above the believers implies there was smoke that accompanied the fire, and that this explains the darkening of the sun and moon with a red bloodlike hue.[94]

Stronstad has gone beyond the text in arguing for implied smoke with its accompanying effects. In Luke's presentation, the crowd only asks about what the languages mean, not about fire. As discussed above, it is incongruous for characters who are presented as inquisitive to ignore strange and marvellous manifestations. It is not an argument from silence to state that because the characters do not ask about the phenomena, the implied reader knows they are not aware of the phenomena. Luke's implied reader, however, is certainly aware of the epiphenomena, and s/he may be expected to link them to Peter's citation of signs, and in this way Stronstad's view can be substantiated, but not directly. There is, however, no problem in understanding the languages as an instantiation of the

---

[90] *Ibid.*, 100-101. Cf. Marshall, 'Pentecost', 362.
[91] So too, William S. Kurz, *Acts of the Apostles* (Grand Rapids: Baker Academic, 2013), 46.
[92] Stronstad also sees tongues as 'prophetic speech', *Prophethood*, 64.
[93] *Ibid.*, 50.
[94] *Ibid.*, 50-51.

prophetic signs. What the crowd sees and asks about is the promised Spirit experience and also a sign. The alert reader will also remember the darkness and rending of the Temple veil before Jesus' death (Luke 23:44-45), and Luke explicitly mentioned the wonders and signs done by Jesus (2:22). So at one level, Luke answered the crowd's question that the dissociative xenolalia is the promised eschatological outpouring of the Spirit, inclusive of prophecy, visions and dreams, and is also a sign in accordance with the Joel prophecy. At another level, Luke linked into the reader's memory of Jesus' miraculous deeds and the cosmic signs at his death, which is a clever segue into the sermon on Jesus' murder and resurrection.

But, unless Luke specifically stated that *only* the xenolalia phenomenon was to be equated with the promised Spirit experience, we cannot be certain that other phenomena might equally have been capable of being equated with the Spirit experience, or that Spirit-reception might be possible with no accompanying phenomena at all. While recognizing the implied reader understands Pentecost as a monumentally significant event and therefore precedent-setting, without Luke's *explicit restriction* of Spirit-reception to xenolalia, the reader cannot be certain that xenolalia is the sole experience of Spirit-reception. What if, later in the narrative, God does it differently? We will therefore be careful to observe whether, through some structure within the story, Luke made an explicit restriction of Spirit-reception to xenolalia. At this point, Luke has fashioned no such restriction.

Another objection to absolutely identifying xenolalia with Spirit-reception is the possibility that this apparent identification could simply be a synecdoche for the Spirit. Just as one who buys a new car says, 'I've just bought a motor',[95] so too, could not Luke be using tongues speech to represent the Spirit? This would not be a claim that there was a fixed idiom where one said, 'I've got tongues', and thereby meant, 'I've got the Spirit.' Rather this would be the tongues image in the story standing in for a full description of the Spirit. The implication of this argument is that any other manifestation, such as praise or prophecy, could equally function as a synecdoche for the Spirit. However, Luke did not use tongues to represent the Spirit as one uses a motor to represent a car. Luke identified the tongues experience with the promised experience of the Spirit, not with the Spirit *per se*. The tongues were the pouring out of the Spirit, they were prophecy. They were not the Spirit. But could not Luke have equally inserted some other manifestation for the 'experience of the Spirit'? In other words, could tongues be a synecdoche for the experience of the Spirit? At this point he has not, and it remains to be seen whether he will do that.

For Luke, participation in the prophetic Spirit signifies participation in the eschatological people of God which has been developing since John. As Zwiep writes, 'In Acts, the Spirit plays a decisive role in the formation of the Christian community. It cannot be doubted that, for Luke, the Spirit is the *identity-marker*

---

[95] US idiom would be, 'I've got wheels'.

*of the New People of God.'*⁹⁶ Menzies, though, has a different perspective. For him, καί γε ἐπὶ τοὺς δούλους μου καὶ ἐπὶ τὰς δούλας μου (Acts 2:18) indicates that reception of the Spirit, as a gift to people who are already God's servants, must always be a gift subsequent to belonging to God, to being a member of God's people: 'membership in the community of salvation is not dependent on the gift of the Spirit; rather, the former is a presupposition for the latter. The Spirit of prophecy is given to those who already are the servants of God.'⁹⁷

Against Ansgar Wucherpfennig, who argues that the Acts 2 Spirit *makes* people into God's servants,⁹⁸ Menzies rightly identifies the Spirit as coming to the already existing people of God. However, what Menzies overlooks is the transition from the Spirit coming upon current members of the people of God to the Spirit coming upon *new* members of the people of God. Peter's citation of the prophecy applies Spirit-reception to what was observed to be happening to the current disciples of Jesus and then promises that as others join the community of Jesus' followers, they too will receive the Spirit. At this point, Spirit-reception becomes an aspect of initiation and Menzies' point no longer has the same strength. The decision to become a member of God's people still precedes Spirit-reception, but the decision is not sufficient to be accepted into the community; one must be baptised and only thereafter can one expect to receive the Spirit. Thus Spirit-reception belongs to the process of joining the community and is not expected to be experienced post-initiation.

Dunn has in the past argued that the apostles had not come to genuine faith until Pentecost, because Peter said that God gave the apostles the gift of the Spirit, '*when* we believed [πιστεύσασιν] in the Lord Jesus Christ' (11:17).⁹⁹ Turner writes, 'to insist that this must mean a punctiliar act of belief, coincident with the gift of the Spirit, is simply abuse of the aorist'.¹⁰⁰ Most recently, Dunn has withdrawn from this position, saying, 'Pentecost may not have been when they first believed in Jesus, but it was when their belief was granted the response

---

⁹⁶ Arie W. Zwiep, 'Luke's Understanding of Baptism in the Holy Spirit: An Evangelical Perspective', *PeSt* 6.2 (2007), 127–49; 133, original italics. So too, Jacob Jervell, 'Sons of the Prophets: The Holy Spirit in the Acts of the Apostles', *The Unknown Paul: Essays on Luke-Acts and Early Christian History* (Minneapolis: Augsburg, 1984), 96-121; 99; Jacob Jervell, 'Das Volk des Geistes', Jacob Jervell and Wayne A. Meeks, ed., *God's Christ and His People* (Oslo: Universitetsforlaget, 1977), 87-106; 87; Robert W. Wall, '"Purity and Power" According to the Acts of the Apostles', *WTJ* 34.1 (Spring 1999), 64-82; 71.

⁹⁷ Robert P. Menzies, *The Development of Early Christian Pneumatology with Special Reference to Luke-Acts* (Sheffield: Sheffield Academic, 1991), 219. Cf. Atkinson, *Baptism*, 52-53.

⁹⁸ Ansgar Wucherpfennig, 'Acta Spiritus Sancti: Die Bedeutung der vier Sendungen des Geistes für die Apostelgeschichte, *In memoriam* Fredrich Avemarie', *ThPh* 88 (2013), 194-210; 201.

⁹⁹ Dunn, *Baptism*, 52, original italics.

¹⁰⁰ Turner, *Power*, 343.

that Peter/Luke assumed to be the norm.'[101] Thus, to receive the prophetic Spirit is neither forgiveness of sins, nor something additional to salvation.[102] As Hui points out, Luke's conception of salvation was not mere forgiveness, but also, 'healing, exorcism, physical deliverance, peace, joy, resurrection hope, and eternal life'.[103] Moreover, while Luke certainly had a concept of individual salvation (cf. Zaccheus, Luke 19:9), Luke also had a corporate concept of salvation (cf. Zacharias, Luke 1:67-79).[104] The Isaianic restoration of Israel is underway.[105] Salvation encompasses the restoration and to participate in *that* is to experience Lukan salvation in the corporate sense.

Second Identification
In 2:33 Luke presented the converse of what he stated in 2:16. Whereas 2:16 reads that the dissociative xenolalia is to be identified as the promised Spirit experience, in 2:33 Luke pictured the promise of the Spirit as the dissociative xenolalia. This second direct identification made by Luke comes at the climactic point of Jesus' exaltation to the Father's right hand and his reception of the Spirit. While Turner affirms that what 2:33 refers to is 'the Pentecostal phenomena',[106] the specific phenomenon which Luke himself focalized through the questions (and mockery) of the crowd is dissociative xenolalia. For Luke, there was only one phenomenon functioning as a referent to his (Peter's) Spirit discourse. The interaction between Peter and the crowd has not been about any phenomenon except the tongues speaking. As discussed above, it is no argument from silence to observe that Luke's crowd does not hear the wind or see the fire. The crowd has been presented as curious and therefore the reader would expect it to have inquired about those phenomena, had it been aware of them. The reader has an expectation that the crowd will behave consistently with the qualities which the narrator has ascribed to it. Luke has presented the crowd as inquisitive. Therefore the reader knows that had the crowd seen fire resting atop the disciples' heads, the crowd would have asked about it. Consequently, the reader knows the crowd did not see the fire. The same applies for the wind. The referent to 'what you see and hear' can only be dissociative tongues speaking. The Father's promise of the

---

[101] Dunn, 'Lord', 1-17; 15-16.
[102] Rebecca Denova affirms receiving forgiveness of sins and the gift of the Spirit as aspects of belonging to the 'remnant' of Israel that God is restoring. *The Things Accomplished Among Us, Prophetic Tradition in the Structural Pattern of Luke-Acts* (Sheffield: Sheffield Academic, 1997), 156.
[103] Archie Wang Do Hui, *The Concept of the Holy Spirit in Ephesians and its Relation to the Pneumatologies of Luke and Paul* (Ph.D. dissertation, University of Aberdeen, 1992), 240-41.
[104] Cf. Max Turner, 'Interpreting the Samaritans of Acts 8: The Waterloo of Pentecostal Soteriology and Pneumatology?' *Pn.* 23.2 (Fall, 2001), 265-86; 269.
[105] On restoration more generally, cf. Bo Reicke, *Glaube und Leben der Urgemeinde: Bemerkungen zu Apg. 1-7* (Zürich: Zwingli-Verlag, 1957), 53.
[106] Turner, *Power*, 276.

Ritual Water, Ritual Spirit

Spirit poured out by Jesus is manifested as the people speaking in different languages.

However, though Luke has clearly emphasized tongues speaking, he has not normativized dissociative xenolalia as the *singular* experience of the Spirit. That is, the promise is manifested as tongues speaking on this programmatic occasion, but that does not mean that God could not, on some other occasion, have the promise manifest in some other fashion. Two aspects to the narrative must be recognized. There is a narrative emphasis, in a programmatic story, on tongues speaking. However, the implied reader has not been told that tongues is the *exclusive* manifestation of the Spirit.

Though Dunn cites Acts 2:4, 33; 8:17-18; 10:44ff.; 19:6 and states that Luke has a 'rather crude concept of Spirit as almost identical with glossolalic and prophetic inspiration',[107] Dunn clearly does *not* see Luke restricting the manifesting phenomena to glossolalia. Haya-Prats similarly writes that this looks like an equation of the Spirit with charismatic phenomena. With reference to 2:33 he writes that

> there is a certain interchangeability between the Holy Spirit and its charismatic manifestation: 'this that we both see and hear.' This might lead one to believe that the gift of the Holy Spirit can be reduced to the charisma of glossolalia or of prophecy. Such a minimalist interpretation would, at the very least, contradict the importance that the author attributes to the Pentecostal episode.[108]

Haya-Prats goes on to argue, 'The consequences of this abiding fullness of the Spirit surpass the *strictly* prophetic manifestations; at times they will be manifested as power, other times as wisdom, as joy, as comfort, and as testimony'.[109] Thus, while he grants that, 'Luke presents glossolalia as the typical manifestation of the Spirit',[110] and affirms that, 'Glossolalia and the rest of the exultant manifestations of the Spirit have a place in the ritual of initiation – baptism and the laying on of hands – or in the community meetings',[111] he argues that, 'it is a shortsighted consideration which limits itself to that which the biblical authors had presented as an exterior sign of the presence of the Spirit'.[112] In other words, for Haya-Prats, there is no *sine qua non* manifestation of the Spirit.

Haya-Prats is right that the Spirit is too expansive in Acts to be equated with charismatic phenomena, but this fact obscures for him what Luke did identify, namely, the experience of a certain charismatic phenomenon with the experience of the Spirit. That is not the same as saying the Spirit *is* the phenomenon. The identifying power of 2:33 which Haya-Prats recognizes but dismisses can be properly understood in terms of the identification of experience. It is certainly

---

[107] Dunn, *Jesus*, 122.
[108] Haya-Prats, *Believers*, 52, cf.106.
[109] *Ibid.*, 53, original italics.
[110] *Ibid.*, 120.
[111] *Ibid.*
[112] *Ibid.*, 54.

true that Luke would later describe other modes of experiencing the Spirit, cf. being physically transported, Acts 8:39, experiencing communication from the Spirit Acts 13:2; 15:28; 16:6, not to mention all sorts of visions and dreams which Luke attributed to the Spirit, Acts 2:17. Yet, visions are not what the crowd asks about. The sole phenomenon repeatedly focalized by Luke is dissociative xenolalia. The referent to Peter's Spirit discourse is not wind or fire, but xenolalia. Luke's narrative identifications are that the dissociative xenolalic experience is the experience of the Spirit and the experience of the Spirit is the dissociative xenolalia.

Though Luke did mutually identify the xenolalia and the experience of the Spirit, thus suggesting absolute equation, caution requires that without some narrative structure excluding other possible experience, the reader cannot absolutely equate the experience of the Spirit with xenolalia. Luke has, at this point in the narrative, *not* explicitly restricted the Spirit experience to tongues. He has not yet written, 'tongues and only tongues'. However, neither has he indicated that there is any other experience that could be identified as the promised Spirit experience. The crowd did not ask, nor did Peter answer, why people were dreaming or having visions. The crowd did not even ask why people were prophesying. They had to be told that the phenomenon they were witnessing was prophecy. Within the context of the Pentecost narrative, the only thing that Peter has addressed has been what the crowd had seen and heard, the dissociative xenolalia. The only the referent within the story for the experience of the Spirit has been tongues.

Someone could object that the idea of the experience of the Spirit as a physical, versus purely spiritual, event is inappropriate? Haya-Prats is not alone in sensing 2:33 has something to say about experience. Kremer concluded, 'When Luke writes about Spirit-reception, he postulates an observable experience.'[113] As cited above in the literature review, Dunn writes, 'Spirit not merely causes an ecstatic experience, he/it is himself that experience. So particularly Acts 2:33.'[114] In another article, Dunn writes of Acts 2:33, 'the gift of the Spirit is actually described as the ecstatic behaviour and glossolalia of the disciples on the day of Pentecost'.[115] Dunn argues that the single, 'decisive', 'coming of the Spirit was, in Luke's conception, something tangible and visible, most typically (but not solely) in inspired, prophetic speech'.[116] He states, 'the Spirit of the New Testament period was first and foremost an *experience* – an experience almost tangible in quality'.[117] He continues:

> the presence or absence of the Spirit in a person's (or community's) life was directly knowable and perceptible – not the Spirit as such, of course, but his presence; the

---

[113] 'Wenn Lukas über Geistempfang schreibt, setzt er eine wahrnehmbare Erfahrung voraus', Kremer, *Pfingstbericht*, 201.
[114] Dunn, 'Rediscovering', 46.
[115] Dunn, 'Philip', 216-21; 217.
[116] Dunn, 'Response', 222-42; 241.
[117] Dunn, 'Rediscovering', 43-61; 45, original italics.

Spirit's presence or absence could be ascertained not just indirectly as a deduction from some rite or formula, but immediately.[118]

Even more, Dunn writes that, 'Christians are expected not merely to possess the Spirit, but to possess it 'visibly and tangibly' (Schweizer)'.[119]

From these quotes it is clear that concluding Luke focalized tangible experience is not new or radical. However, Dunn and Haya-Prats take a broader, mixed view of experientiality, that many experiences evidence the Spirit, and have missed that Luke, in this instance, took a narrow view, coupling a specific experience to Spirit-reception – dissociative xenolalia. This is the sole referent for Luke's Spirit discourse. Luke's taking a 'narrow' view is not to be equated with Menzies' argument that the Spirit in Luke is restricted to prophetic speech. Luke's view of the activity of the Spirit is broad indeed. In relation to Spirit-reception, however, Luke specified, by means of focalization, a particular phenomenon. Luke did not, at this point in the narrative, direct the reader to observe any other phenomena. Luke focused reader attention upon one phenomenon and then discussed the significance of that phenomenon. This then raises the question as to whether this focus is a result of historical circumstance and whether Luke will modify his presentation later in the narrative. That it happened this way once, and that Luke accurately recorded the way it happened this one time, does not mean that it must necessarily happen the same way other times. As Keener recognizes, Luke used tongues as evidence of Spirit baptism. But, Keener denies that Luke made it the normative evidence.[120] Any claim for tongues as the *normative* experience of Spirit-reception requires more than these two identifications.

Third Identification
The response of Peter, the normative spokesperson, to the crowd's question, 'What should we do?' is straightforward: repent, be baptised and they will receive the gift of the Holy Spirit (2:38). What they will receive is what all will receive (2:39). While Kremer recognized the close link, even the non-differentiation, between the Spirit experience of the newly baptised and that of the disciples, he implied that the new converts would *not* receive an observable experience: 'Because this Spirit-reception of the baptised is not differentiated from the observable one of the disciples, there exists, to all appearances, between both kinds a close relationship.'[121] However, Windisch observed a different implication of Peter's promise: 'When Peter at Pentecost promises all repentant the gift of the Holy Spirit, they should all, therefore, themselves experience what they

---

[118] *Ibid.*, 45.
[119] *Ibid.*
[120] Keener, *Acts*, 1.830-31. Cf. Keener, 'Tongues', 183.
[121] 'Da dieser Geistempfang der Getauften von dem wahrnehmbaren der Jünger nicht unterschieden wird, besteht allem Anschein nach zwischen beiden Arten eine enge Beziehung', Kremer, *Pfingstbericht*, 179.

just then from the disciples had heard and seen: glossolalia and tongues speech 2:33, 38 cf. 4:31.'[122]

Douglas C. Bozung finds Pentecostal arguments for tongues as the necessary evidence of Spirit baptism lacking because they have no explicit statement that what is narrated is also to be understood as normative.[123] However, here, in a third direct identification (2:39), it appears, *at first blush*, that Luke stated the dissociative xenolalia experience is what all will receive, not just all the people present on that particular occasion, but 'as many as the Lord our God will call'. Whereas Loisy argued that 'the promise' refers to the Spirit because of the prior reference in verse 33, Penney states: 'The "promise" (2:39) here refers not simply to the Holy Spirit, but to the benefits of salvation as a whole, of which the Holy Spirit is supreme.'[124] Jens Schröter, arguing that the gift of the Spirit is to be differentiated from forgiveness of sins, and that 'the promise' is for all converts, therefore concludes, 'The ἐπαγγελία is thus not limited to the gift of the Spirit.'[125] Schröter's conclusion does not follow from his premises, however. More accurately, Hans Jörg Sellner links 2:33 to 2:39, 'the reader *can* do absolutely nothing else except identify the ἐπαγγελία which is here addressed with the ἐπαγγελία τοῦ πνεύματος τοῦ ἁγίου'.[126] In other words, converts receive *both* forgiveness of sins *and* the promise. Luke has already twice (2:16 and 2:33) identified the dissociative xenolalia experience as the promised experience of the Spirit. Wind and fire have been excluded as possible referents. The only referent in the Spirit discourse is tongues speech. The implied reader is presented with an apparently tight argument. The dissociative xenolalia experience is the experience of the prophetic Spirit foretold by Joel (2:16). The experience of the promise of the Father spoken of by Jesus is manifested in the dissociative xenolalia experience (2:33). The promise is what all will receive (2:39). Luke has provided no other discourse referent for ἡ ἐπαγγελία except xenolalia.

---

[122] 'Wenn Petrus zu Pfingsten allen Bußfertigen die Gabe des heiligen Geistes verheißt, so sollen sie alle an sich erfahren, was sie soeben von den Jüngern gehört und gesehen haben: Glossolalie und Zeugenreden 2 33.38 vgl. 4 31', Hans Windisch, *Taufe und Sünde im ältesten Christentum bis auf Origenes: Ein Beitrag zur altchristlichen Dogmengeschichte* (Tübingen: J.C.B. Mohr, Paul Siebeck, 1908), 93.

[123] Douglas C. Bozung, 'The Pentecostal Doctrine of Initial Evidence: A Study in Hermeneutical Method', *JMT* (Spring, 2004), 89-107; 98.

[124] Alfred Loisy, *Les Actes des Apôtres* (Paris: Émile Nourry, 1920), 215. Penney, *Emphasis*, 91.

[125] 'Die ἐπαγγελία ist demnach nicht auf die Gabe des Geistes beschränkt'. Jens Schröter, 'Die Taufe in der Apostelgeschichte', David Hellholm, et al. (eds), *Ablution, Initiation and Baptism: Late Antiquity, Early Judaism and Early Christianity* (Berlin: Walter de Gruyter, 2011), 557-86; 563.

[126] '*kann* der Leser gar nicht anders, als die hier angesprochene ἐπαγγελία mit der ἐπαγγελία τοῦ πνεύματος τοῦ ἁγίου zu identifizieren', Hans Jörg Sellner, *Das Heil Gottes: Studien zur Soteriologie des lukanischen Doppelwerks* (Berlin: Walter de Gruyter, 2007), 263, original italics.

At this point in the narrative, one way of interpreting the data is that Luke has not 'merely narrated', but directly taught that every initiate would experience the dissociative xenolalic gift of the Spirit. While the identifications of 2:16 and 2:33 left open the possibility that some other manifestation (or non-manifestation) could be identified as the experience of the Spirit, 2:39 guarantees the referent under discussion to every convert in perpetuity. This could be seen as effectively *restricting* the initiatory manifestation to xenolalia. While the Spirit can still manifest in other ways, one specific mode has been identified as that which always accompanies initiation and is promised to all initiates. The book has raised this argument as one possible interpretation of the narrative data uncovered by a study of focalization.

A narrative objection to this argument is that Luke has not explicitly negated other manifestations. That is, Luke has not said, 'xenolalia and only xenolalia'. The converts were promised 'the promise' and despite the programmatic expectation of xenolalia which is not to be denied, Luke has not closed the door on other manifestations signalling the arrival of the promise. At this point in the narrative, Luke still has the possibility of modifying the expectations generated by Acts 2:16, 33, 38-39. The rereader knows that Luke modified the sequence of the undeniably programmatic 2:38 in 10:47-48. If Luke modified the sequence of immersion and Spirit-reception then he can also modify the expectation of xenolalia.

There are also other objections to tongues as the *sine qua non* manifestation of Spirit-reception. Carson states: 'The reception of the Holy Spirit promised by Peter (2:38) and presumably received by the three thousand was not, so far as we are told, attested by tongues.'[127] Ernst Haenchen concludes that, at Luke's time, not every Christian experienced the '*ecstatic* Spirit' because Luke did not mention tongues in verse 41.[128] Andrew Das observes similarly that after the crowd is baptised, the Pentecost phenomena are not repeated and specifically, they do not speak in tongues.[129] These observations appear to contradict the idea that every initiate who receives the Spirit speaks in tongues. Similarly, Bozung argues that Luke could not have taught tongues as the initial evidence because he did not consistently mention tongues at every Spirit-reception.[130] Bozung's argument applies from the perspective of a rereader.

In response, one may observe that Luke also did not explicitly state that the 3000 received the Holy Spirit. As Schuyler Brown objects: 'Baptism with holy spirit [sic] may be promised by Peter to the crowd after the Pentecost speech, but

---

[127] Carson, *Spirit*, 143.
[128] Ernst Haenchen, *The Acts of the Apostles: A Commentary* (Oxford: Basil Blackwell, 1971), 184, original italics.
[129] A. Andrew Das, 'Acts 8: Water, Baptism, and the Spirit', *ConJ* 19.2 (April, 1993), 108-34; 119.
[130] Bozung, 'Doctrine', 98. Cf. Frederick R. Harm, 'Structural Elements Related to the Gift of the Holy Spirit in Acts', *ConJ* 14.1 (January, 1988), 28-41; 29.

it is only conferred at key points in the expansion of the church's mission.'[131] Similarly, James M. Hamilton argues that the Spirit experiences of Acts 2, 8, 10, and 19 are not described elsewhere and are therefore unique, salvation-historical experiences not repeated at every conversion nor intended to be prescriptive of normal conversion experience.[132] Avemarie wrote that it is not conclusively implied that the 3,000 received the Spirit.[133] Howard M. Ervin argued that to assume from 2:41 that the Spirit was given is, 'an appeal to propositional logic rather than to a clearly demonstrable exegetical datum'.[134] Ervin, moreover, argued that baptism was definitely not followed immediately by reception of the Spirit. He reasoned that the 3,000 converts of Peter's Pentecost sermon (2:41) and those who believed after that (2:47) as well as the 5,000 of Peter's second sermon (4:4) all received the gift of the Spirit, not immediately and individually after their baptism, but corporately after the prayer of 4:31. He reasoned that: (1) being 'filled' with the Spirit is a permanent condition because πίμπλημι is a stative verb;[135] (2) since the apostles were permanently filled with the Spirit at Pentecost, they could not again have been filled in 4:31; (3) it must, therefore, have been only new converts who were 'filled' after the prayer.[136]

Brown, Hamilton, Avemarie, and Ervin, however, do not take into consideration the effect of a normative spokesperson. The reason Luke did not say the words, 'and 3000 received the gift of the Holy Spirit', is because his normative spokesperson had already said that would happen upon repentance and baptism. As Shepherd states, 'what a reliable commentator says will happen, will happen'.[137] Luke simply narrated how many were baptised and the reader knows that they therefore received the Spirit.[138] Against Avemarie, this narrative framework is not uncertain, but established by standard literary devices. Against Ervin, this is not an appeal to extra-textual logic, but to the text's own interpretive framework. Therefore, if the converts of Pentecost received the Spirit immediately after their baptism, then Ervin's whole argument falls apart, for, while πίμπλημι may indeed be stative, it is context which determines the duration of that state. The text does not say, 'permanently, unchangingly, forever filled'. On the contrary, Luke gave a circumstance when individuals once filled are filled anew. In 4:31, Luke stated that three events took place, the location where the believers

---

[131] Schuyler Brown, '"Water-Baptism" and "Spirit-Baptism" in Luke-Acts', *AThR* 59.2 (April, 1977), 135-51.

[132] James M. Hamilton, *God's Indwelling Presence: The Holy Spirit in the Old and New Testaments* (n.p.: B&H, 2006), 191-93.

[133] Avemarie, *Tauferzählungen*, 139.

[134] Howard Ervin, *Conversion-Initiation and the Baptism in the Holy Spirit: A Critique of James D.G. Dunn, Baptism in the Holy Spirit* (Peabody: Hendrickson, 1984), 22.

[135] Howard Ervin, *Spirit Baptism: A Biblical Investigation* (Peabody: Hendrickson, 1987), 45-48.

[136] Ervin, *Baptism*, 49-54. Cf. Howard Ervin, *These Are Not Drunken as Ye Suppose* (Plainfield: Logos, 1968), 62-67.

[137] Shepherd, *Narrative*, 143.

[138] Cf. Guthrie, *Theology*, 539.

were was shaken, 'all' were filled, and they were speaking God's word boldly. He did not support Ervin's argument by saying, 'now, all had reached a state of fullness', as if the remainder of unfilled believers had become filled, thus completing the number of the filled. Luke allowed that people can have repeated experiences for which the metaphor of 'filled' is appropriate. Ervin's argument is undermined by the narrative both at 2:41 and 4:31.[139]

The idea that the experience of the apostles at Pentecost was uniquely salvation-historical and not shared by the 3,000 who converted is brought into question by a study of focalization and normative spokespersons. The argument can be made that Luke's Peter promises the same experience of the tongues-speaking apostles to all who convert, thus tying the salvation-historical event of Pentecost to *every* individual initiation. Robert W. Lyon, in arguing that Spirit baptism is the same as Spirit-reception, rebutted the 'salvation-historical' argument and, inadvertently, presented the argument for tongues as the normative evidence of Spirit-reception: 'Peter promised to his hearers the very same experience which they had seen occur in the original outpouring.'[140] But if it was the very same experience which they had seen, then Windisch is right – they received tongues speech.

It can be objected that the crowd did *not* receive everything which the initial disciples had experienced. Luke created no expectation that the new converts would have fire on their heads or hear a rushing mighty wind. Therefore, the experience of the apostles and their companions must be recognized as different from that of the crowd. Once this is recognized, we return to the question of whether the implied reader would expect the crowd to receive the phenomenon which the crowd had asked about and Peter had explained. The book recognizes that one interpretation of the narrative data would be that the promise – identified not as wind and fire, but as dissociative xenolalia – is received by all.

This interpretation would argue that just as Luke did not say every person received the Spirit, but he required it to be so by means of his normative spokesperson, neither did Luke write the words 'and 3000 spoke in other languages'. Nor did he need to explicitly state that tongues speech occurred every time he mentions Spirit-reception for the reader to understand it to be so. The model for Spirit experience has been established, and now all that need be done is refer to it. Green expounds on this principle, but not in reference to tongues:

> This also entails taking with the greatest seriousness the pattern-setting words of Peter in Acts 2.38 – so that even when Luke does not enumerate each item of human response and salvific promise comprised in Peter's pronouncement (and he rarely

---

[139] Thus the experience of Acts 4:31 will not be counted among the scenes of initial Spirit-reception. For detailed discussion of 'filled' as a metaphor, see Max Turner, 'Endowment'. Cf. J.H.E. Hull, *The Holy Spirit in the Acts of the Apostles* (London: Lutterworth, 1967), 120-24.

[140] Robert W. Lyon, 'Baptism and Spirit Baptism in the New Testament', *WTJ* 14.1 (Spring, 1979), 14-26, 18.

does), those responses and salvific gifts are to be presumed present *unless we are given explicit reason to think otherwise*.[141]

Turner reaches almost the same conclusion with a slightly different approach:

> Only on the assumption that 2.38-39 provides something of a 'norm' adequately explains why Luke does not feel obliged to record the reception of the Spirit by the converts who are baptized in 2.41; that is, he could assume the reader would interpret references to people being baptized ... as occasions when they received the Spirit unless (as in 8.16) it is explicitly stated otherwise.[142]

But, it could be argued, when Turner states, 'Luke does not mention that the Pentecost converts received the Spirit with charismatic "initial evidence"',[143] he does not note that the principle he uses for Spirit-reception also applies to the nature of that reception. The narrative principles expounded by Turner and Green could be employed to argue that Luke caused his reader to expect the 3000 to receive the same dissociative xenolalic experience which the crowd had repeatedly asked about and which Peter had repeatedly explained.

As stated above, the great objection to this argument is that Luke did not explicitly exclude other phenomena from serving as manifestations of the Spirit. That is, while one may recognize the rhetorical power of Luke's positive statements about the fact that the Spirit was manifested in a xenolalia experience, and one may even acknowledge narrative force exerted to create programmatic expectation of the same phenomenon occurring in the repentant crowd and all future converts, one must equally acknowledge the Luke has *not explicitly excluded* other possible manifestations (or non-manifestations) of the Spirit. This leaves the narrative door open for Luke to later suggest that the Spirit could manifest his arrival some other way, or even in no visible manner at all. A thoroughgoing exegesis must carefully evaluate both what has been said and what has not been said.

While the manifestation of the Spirit may still be an open question, the gift of the Spirit is not (although it too can be modified in terms of timing, as in the Samaria story, Cornelius' house, and possibly Ephesus). The recognition that converts receive the Spirit as part of their initiation undermines Menzies' position that, 'the gift of the Spirit is given only to those who are members of the community of salvation',[144] and Stronstad's argument that the gift of the Spirit is not part of conversion but given to individuals with an 'antecedent spiritual

---

[141] Green, 'Baptism', 161, original italics.
[142] Turner, *Power*, 359. So, also, Lorenz Oberlinner, 'Das Wirken des Geistes und das Handeln der Menschen: Der Weg der Mission in der Apostelgeschichte', Philipp Müller (ed.), *Seelsorge in der Kraft des Heiligen Geistes* (Freiburg: Herder, 2005), 161-77; 164.
[143] Turner, *Power*, 449. So too, Stott, *Baptism*, 28.
[144] Menzies, 'Understanding', 95. Similarly, Cho, *Spirit*, 141-42.

state'.[145] Though it is true that those already in the people of God received the Spirit on the day of Pentecost, a fact that Menzies' observation of Luke's repeated use of μου (Acts 2:18) to identify the recipients of the Spirit as God's own servants makes clear,[146] those who joined the people of God received the Spirit during the joining process. *The reality of subsequence for the one group does not negate the fact of initiatory experience for the other.* Even when one finds brief subsequence between the moment of faith and the moment of Spirit-reception, that subsequence exists within the structure of initiation. For, while Stronstad is correct in that the 3000 converts believed and were immersed before receiving the gift of the Spirit, and thus temporarily existed in a forgiven state prior to their reception of the Spirit, the gift of the Spirit is tied to repentance and baptism and is therefore experienced during integration into the believing community, and not subsequently to that integration. If the story of Jesus' baptism has any influence upon the reader of Acts 2, the reader might even anticipate the converts receiving the Spirit while they are still standing in the baptismal waters.

In linking Spirit-reception to water baptism,[147] Luke's text evokes the Spirit-reception ER with its imagery of Jesus' baptism in which Spirit-reception occurred after baptism and during prayer. The Spirit-reception ER also contains the associations between prayer and Spirit-reception from Jesus' Luke 11 teaching. Thus, Luke's reader would not expect the water itself to convey the Spirit, but would expect baptismal praying by an initiate according to the model of Jesus' praying at the time of his immersion in the waters of Jordan. Here the concept of initiation as a *process* comes into play. Sharing in the blessings of eschatological salvation does not equate to the decision to accept Jesus as the risen Messiah. Luke distinguished the two because repentance is presented as a prerequisite to the immersion in/after which the Spirit is received. These two elements (repentance and immersion) of Lukan initiation do not temporally coincide.[148] But, neither is there great temporal separation.

Richard N. Longenecker concludes that Acts 2:38 is 'theologically normative'.[149] Avemarie asserted 2:38 is paradigmatic for Luke's understanding of baptism, observing that 'the baptism section of the Pentecost pericope, in several

---

[145] Roger Stronstad, 'Forty Years On: An Appreciation and Assessment of Baptism in the Holy Spirit by James D.G. Dunn', *JPT* 19.1 (April, 2010), 3-11; 10.
[146] Menzies, 'Understanding', 95.
[147] J.H.E. Hull, wrestling with the implication that the baptising of 3,000 would take time and this would mean that some received the Spirit before others, suggested that Luke made, 'willingness to be baptised' the criteria, not literal baptism. But, Luke did not say, 'be willing to be baptised', but, 'be baptised'. The temporal implications remain, Hull, *Spirit*, 94, 99.
[148] Shelton also notes this, *Mighty*, 129.
[149] Richard N. Longenecker, *Acts* (Grand Rapids: Zondervan, 1995), 81.

respects, offers a paradigm of Lukan baptismal understanding'.[150] Daniel Marguerat states, 'Here Luke states the rule: baptism in Acts is accompanied by the gift of the Spirit. The reasoned exceptions arise over the course of the narrative'.[151] Cornils affirms, 'The "normal sequence" is explicitly portrayed by Peter in Acts 2:38'.[152] She, however, recognizes that 2:38 cannot be adopted alone, without considering the modifications made to it later in the narrative.[153] Her understanding will be discussed further in the next chapter.

But how can we justify this normative/paradigmatic role for Acts 2:38? Richard F. Zehnle, following O. Glombitza, added a small, but literarily important point. According to 2:37, all the apostles are questioned. In 2:38, Peter responds. Thus Peter's formulation of initiatory ritual is spoken on behalf of all the apostles.[154] It bears authoritative weight in Luke's narrative. Moreover, it is paradigmatic because Luke combined suspense, surprise, entity representations, intertextual references, focalization, and a normative spokesperson (the major protagonist in this section), at the beginning of his second volume, in the first major speech of the protagonist, early in the development of the reader's conception of initiation. As Gerald L. Stevens writes, 'Luke fronts the narrative for plot development, making Pentecost the controlling narrative event of Acts.'[155] Thus, the narrative evidence works against Cho who states, 'any attempt to forge a link between the bestowal of the Spirit and conversion experience from Acts 2:38 is unwarranted'.[156]

The Timing of Forgiveness and Water Baptism

In seeking to determine precisely when the Spirit is given to new converts, we must address the matter of the timing of forgiveness, which Luke associated, in a way which we will examine below, with Spirit-reception. When, then, is the

---

[150] 'der Taufabschnitt der Pfingstperikope in mehrerlei Hinsicht ein Paradigma des lukanischen Taufverständnisses bietet', Avemarie, *Tauferzählungen*, 34. Cf. L. Goppelt, *Theologie des Neuen Testaments* (Göttingen: Vandenhoeck & Ruprecht, 1980 [1976]), 331-32.

[151] 'Luc énonce ici la règle: le baptême dans les Actes s'accompagne du don de l'Esprit. Des exceptions motivées surgiront au cours du récit', Daniel Marguerat, *Les Actes des Apôtres (1-12)* (Genève: Labor et Fides, 2007), 96.

[152] 'Der „normale Ablauf" wird von Petrus explizit in Apg 2,38 dargestellt', Cornils, *Geist*, 187.

[153] *Ibid.*; cf. 205.

[154] Richard F. Zehnle, *Peter's Pentecost Discourse: Tradition and Lukan Reinterpretation in Peter's Speeches of Acts 2 and 3* (New York: Abingdon, 1971), 36. Otto Glombitza, 'Der Schluss der Petrusrede Acta 2:36-40: Ein Beitrag zum Problem der Predigten in Acta', *ZNW* 52.1-2 (January 1, 1961), 115-18; 117. So too, Haenchen, *Acts*, 183.

[155] Gerald L. Stevens, 'Luke's Perspective on Pentecost in Acts 1–12', AAR/SBL Southwest Regional Meeting, March 17-18, 2001, Dallas, TX, 35. Similarly, Aker, 'Paradigmatic', 13.

[156] Cho, *Spirit*, 142.

moment of forgiveness, in the water or at the time of repentance, or do these two coincide? The text of Acts 2:38 reads:

Πέτρος δὲ πρὸς αὐτούς· μετανοήσατε, [φησίν,] καὶ βαπτισθήτω ἕκαστος ὑμῶν ἐπὶ τῷ ὀνόματι Ἰησοῦ Χριστοῦ εἰς ἄφεσιν τῶν ἁμαρτιῶν ὑμῶν καὶ λήμψεσθε τὴν δωρεὰν τοῦ ἁγίου πνεύματος.

Dunn states that, 'the precise relation between the repentance, baptism and forgiveness of sins is unclear,' but concludes that baptism is 'the medium by which the repentance is expressed'.[157] A.T. Robertson argues the grammar, namely εἰς, does not help to answer this problem: 'only the context and the tenor of N.T. teaching can determine whether 'into,' 'unto' or merely 'in' or 'on' ('upon') is the right translation, a task for the interpreter, not for the grammarian'.[158] Luther B. McIntyre, Jr., however, does see a solution in the grammar. Following J.C. Davis,[159] he grants that εἰς is purposive (for) and not causative (because of). However, based upon pronoun/verb agreement, he argues that, 'the command to be baptized is parenthetical and is not syntactically connected to remission of sins'.[160] In the format given by McIntyre, the relevant lines are:

- μετανοήσατε
    - καὶ βαπτισθήτω
    - ἕκαστος ὑμῶν
- εἰς ἄφεσιν τῶν ἁμαρτιῶν ὑμῶν

McIntyre argues, therefore, that the antecedent to the final ὑμῶν is the crowd given the command μετανοήσατε.[161] In McIntyre's favour, it does not say, 'let him be baptised, each of you ... for the remission of the sins of each', which would clearly link baptism to the individual's forgiveness. However, McIntyre does not overcome the problem of the first ὑμῶν. The crowd, which he argues is the antecedent to the last ὑμῶν, is present in the phrase which McIntyre wants to exclude as strictly parenthetical. There is a smooth conceptual continuity from the command to the crowd to repent, to every individual in the crowd being baptised, to the resulting forgiveness of the crowd's sins. McIntyre would associate

---

[157] James Dunn, *The Acts of the Apostles* (Peterborough: Epworth, 1996), 33.
[158] Robertson, *Grammar*, 592.
[159] J.C. Davis, 'Another Look at the Relationship Between Baptism and Forgiveness of Sins in Acts 2:38', *RestQ* 24.2 (1981), 80-88. For the causal argument, see, R. Bruce Compton, 'Water Baptism and the Forgiveness of Sins in Acts 2:38', *DBSJ* 4 (Fall 1999), 3-32; 29-32.
[160] Luther B. McIntyre Jr., 'Baptism and Forgiveness in Acts 2:38', *BS* 153 (January-March, 1996), 53-62; 57. So too, Stanley D. Toussaint, 'Acts', John F. Walvoord and Roy B. Zuck (eds), *The Bible Knowledge Commentary: An Exposition of the Scriptures* (Colorado Springs: David C. Cook, 1983), 1.359. Craig L. Blomberg and Jennifer Foutz Markley draw upon McIntyre, *A Handbook of New Testament Exegesis* (Grand Rapids: Baker Academic, 2010), 176.
[161] McIntyre Jr., 'Baptism', 57.

forgiveness strictly with repentance, but the grammar associates it with both repentance and baptism. Similarly, Ashby L. Camp, in his cogent rebuttal of McIntyre, argues:

> even if εἰς ἄφεσιν τῶν ἁμαρτιῶν ὑμῶν is syntactically related only to μετανοήσατε, the phrase καὶ βαπτισθήτω ἕκαστος ὑμῶν may be epexegetical and thus be *logically* connected to εἰς ἄφεσιν τῶν ἁμαρτιῶν ὑμῶν.[162]

Camp further argues, 'McIntyre completely ignores the possibility that εἰς ἄφεσιν τῶν ἁμαρτιῶν ὑμῶν modifies *both* μετανοήσατε and βαπτισθήτω.'[163] Moreover, Camp cites Acts 3:26 where ἕκαστον serves as antecedent to ὑμῶν, thus demonstrating an exception to the rule of agreement that McIntyre bases his argument upon. Camp also lists John 7:53, καὶ ἐπορεύθησαν ἕκαστος εἰς τὸν οἶκον αὐτοῦ, which has the singular ἕκαστος corresponding with the third person plural ἐπορεύθησαν, and Revelation 20:13c, καὶ ἐκρίθησαν ἕκαστος κατὰ τὰ ἔργα αὐτῶν, where again the singular ἕκαστος is matched with a plural verb.[164] The syntax of 2:38, therefore, does not support the argument that baptism is parenthetical and forgiveness of sins is attached strictly to repentance.

David S. Morlan, however, downplays the importance of baptism by appealing to the wider Lukan narrative:

> Luke has many conversion stories in his two-volume narrative that have no mention of baptism. This being the case, it seems highly unlikely that he believed the action alone of baptism 'sealed the deal' on conversion since he thought it unnecessary to include it in each conversion case.[165]

Morlan does not consider that Luke was under no compulsion to woodenly repeat his programmatic statements. Yet, Morlan is certainly correct in that immersion was not always necessary to receive the gift of the Spirit (cf. Cornelius' house). But, Cornelius' house makes clear that conversion was *not* finished without immersion. Peter did not say, 'seeing the Gentiles have received the Spirit, there is no need to immerse them'.

Dunn, as already mentioned, takes a different approach. He argues that genuine faith and baptism coincide. Not that the water itself imparts forgiveness, Dunn denies that.[166] Rather, baptism is the act which normally actualizes faith, and in the act of baptism one reaches genuine faith/repentance, but not before. Dunn states:

> Baptism properly performed is for the NT essentially the act of faith and repentance – the actualization of saving faith without which, usually, commitment to Jesus as

---

[162] Ashby L. Camp, 'Re-examining the Rule of Concord in Acts 2:38', *RestQ* 39.1 (1997), 37-42; 38, original italics.
[163] *Ibid.*, 38.
[164] *Ibid.*
[165] Morlan, *Conversion*, 158.
[166] Dunn, *Baptism*, 97.

Lord does not come to its necessary expression. As the Spirit is the vehicle of saving grace, so baptism is the vehicle of saving faith.[167]

Dunn argues from the Ephesians disciples:

> the sequence of Paul's questions indicates that πιστεῦσαι and βαπτισθῆναι are interchangeable ways of describing the act of faith: baptism was the necessary expression of commitment, without which they could not be said to have truly 'believed'.[168]

Summarizing the situation in Acts, Dunn writes, 'Properly administered water-baptism must have been the climax and act of faith, the expression of repentance and the vehicle of commitment.'[169]

But then ought not Peter, and John Baptist before him, to have said, 'be baptised that you may properly repent'? The NA27 text reads μετανοήσατε, [φησίν,] καὶ βατπισθήτω 'repent, he says, and be baptised' thus clearly separating repentance from the water and not allowing Dunn's scheme. Though φησίν is not present in B *pc* Aug[pt], the NA27 text is supported by P[74vid]) AC 81. 945. 1175. 1739. 1891. *pc* vg. C.K. Barrett suggests that, 'φησίν could have been omitted on the grounds that it interrupts the sequence μετανοήσατε καὶ βατπισθήτω'.[170] In this case the interrupting presence of φησίν represents the more difficult, and therefore more likely, reading.

Moreover, Luke has already discussed the meaning of repentance in his pericope on John Baptist. It is the Luke 3 context of the Baptist demanding practical deeds of repentance which allows one to read κηρύσσων βάπτισμα μετανοίας εἰς ἄφεσιν ἁμαρτιῶν and conclude that for Luke, the ritual was not the imparter of forgiveness, but the changed life, the repentance. So too, W. Wilkens, who brings out the importance of the Lukan great commission:

> The baptism speech of Luke 3:7ff shows indeed that John preaches no magically mediated salvation. If one compares Acts 2:38 with Luke 24:47, one recognizes that, overall in the thinking of Luke, the decisive weight does not lie on baptism, but rather on repentance as its condition.[171]

Luke's presentation in Luke chapter 3 leaves no room going into Acts 2 for Dunn's theory that baptism is necessary to actualize repentance. Genuine repentance is the necessary prerequisite for baptism, not the other way around.

---

[167] *Ibid.*, 227.
[168] *Ibid.*, 96.
[169] *Ibid.*, 97.
[170] C.K. Barrett, *A Critical and Exegetical Commentary on the Acts of the Apostles* (London: T&T Clark, 1994), 1.153.
[171] 'Daß Johannes kein magisch vermitteltes Heil predigt, zeigt ja die Täuferrede Luk. 3,7ff. Vergleicht man Apg. 2,38 mit Luk. 24, 47, so erkennt man, daß überhaupt im Denken des Lukas das entscheidende Gewicht nicht auf der Taufe liegt, sondern auf der Umkehr als ihrer Bedingung', W. Wilkens, 'Wassertaufe und Geistempfang bei Lukas', *TZ* 23 (1967), 26-47; 33.

Luke also separated belief and water baptism in Acts 2:41a: οἱ μὲν οὖν ἀποδεξάμενοι τὸν λόγον αὐτοῦ ἐβαπτίσθησαν. The aorist participle construction, 'the ones having gladly received', is prior to, not coincident with, the aorist verb, 'were baptised'. However, Dunn could still argue that while it says they gladly received Peter's message, they had not reached the full level of faith/repentance necessary for salvation until they entered the water and therefore it is actually coincident. But, if this concept of reaching the critical mass of faith was really the case, why did Luke not explain it? Had Luke believed that baptism enables or actualizes forgiveness he could have said something to that effect. To argue for baptism as the only, or even as the typical, act capable of actualizing repentance/faith burdens the text with unnecessary metaphysics. A public act arising from a decision to make a lifestyle change, that is, genuine repentance, and showing submission to and identification with the message of, and the community awaiting, the Messiah's imminent arrival sufficiently explains John the Baptist's ritual. Repentance and submission to/identification with the preaching of the kerygma sufficiently explains the baptism Peter preached. However, Dunn is not wrong in seeing baptism as a ritual act integral to genuine repentance. For Luke, repentance is not equated with baptism, but if one repents, one will be baptised. The clear and precise parsing of the moment of faith/repentance and the moment of baptism must wait until the story of Cornelius' house. There, Luke laid to rest any hint that forgiveness comes in the moment of contact with the water. Forgiveness comes in the moment of belief. So then, does the gift of the Spirit come in the moment of belief? As the discussion of McIntyre's claims has indicated, Luke presented repentance *and baptism* as the apostolic, authoritative teaching on how to receive forgiveness. With baptism being associated with repentance, and with forgiveness associated with the repentance/baptism idea, Luke seemed to present the gift of the Spirit as related somehow to this complex. What then is the precise relationship?

The Timing of Spirit-Reception in Relation to Water Baptism

After Luke's statements regarding repentance, baptism, and forgiveness, he writes: καὶ λήμψεσθε τὴν δωρεὰν τοῦ ἁγίου πνεύματος. When would the converts receive the Spirit experience: at the moment of repentance, in the water of baptism, or thereafter? W. Wilkens pointed out the narrative significance of the distinction between John's baptism of repentance and John's prophecy of Jesus' Spirit/fire baptism for interpretation of Luke's presentation of baptism at Pentecost:

> *If Luke links to this baptism proclamation, this means that: water baptism in the name of Jesus Christ and Spirit-reception take on the separation foundationally*

formulated in the baptism proclamation. It is therefore not possible to so interpret Acts 2:38 that both acts occur together.[172]

Wilkens' argument has appeal, but one could argue that, unlike John's baptism, in Christian baptism the temporal separation is removed and Spirit-reception takes place at the moment of immersion.

If, against the evidence, McIntyre's argument were accepted, that baptism is parenthetical to repentance and forgiveness, then one could easily, though not necessarily, conclude that the Spirit is given at the moment of repentance, *before* baptism. As John R.W. Stott said, the 3,000 'received the forgiveness of their sins and the gift of the Spirit simultaneously'.[173] Gerhard Krodel asserts that, 'in Acts 2:38 the Spirit is given simultaneously with repentance, baptism, and forgiveness'.[174] However, he does not attempt to explain, as Dunn does, how repentance and baptism can occur at the same time. G. Kittel, on the other hand, argued that the promise of the Spirit is added to the instructions for obtaining forgiveness of sins: 'The Spirit baptism is then namely everywhere from the water baptism to be sharply separated, and the Spirit is never given through the mere water baptism'.[175] Luke did not write: 'repent and be baptised ... for the remission of your sins and the gift of the Holy Spirit', but 'repent and be baptised ... for the remission of your sins and you will receive the gift of the Holy Spirit'. The first option would tend towards subordinating both remission of sins and receiving the gift of the Spirit together under baptism. But the addition of 'and you will receive' raises the question as to whether repentance, baptism and forgiveness are all prerequisite for something which follows, either logically or temporally or both.

Chrys C. Caragounis states that in conditional sentences, 'The protasis may be an imperative, in which case the apodosis is introduced by καί.'[176] He cites Ephesians 4:26 ὀργίζεσθε καὶ μὴ ἁμαρτάνετε, and John 2:19 λύσατε τὸν ναὸν τοῦτον καὶ ἐν τρισὶν ἡμέραις ἐγερῶ αὐτόν. Pesch argued that, 'The construction 'imperative + καί + future' marks a conditional structure: repentance and baptism

---

[172] '*Schließt Lukas an diese Täuferverkündigung an, so bedeutet das: Wassertaufe auf den Namen Jesu Christi und Geistempfang nehmen an der in der Täuferverkündigung grundlegend formulierten Diastase teil. Es ist daher nicht möglich, Apg. 2,38 so zu interpretieren, als fielen beide Akte zusammen*', Wilkens, 'Wassertaufe', 30-31, original italics. Contrary to Michel Quesnel, *Baptisés dans L'Esprit: Baptême et Esprit Saint dans les Actes des Apôtres* (Paris: Les Éditions du Cerf, 1985), 51.

[173] Stott, *Baptism*, 29.

[174] Gerhard Krodel, 'The Functions of the Spirit in the Old Testament, the Synoptic Tradition, and the Book of Acts', Paul D. Opsahl (ed.), *The Holy Spirit in the Life of the Church From Biblical Times to the Present* (Minneapolis: Augsburg, 1978), 10-46, 33.

[175] 'Die Geistestaufe ist dann nämlich überall von der Wassertaufe scharf zu scheiden, und der Geist wird niemals durch die bloße Wassertaufe gegeben', G. Kittel, 'Die Wirkungen der christlichen Wassertaufe nach dem Neuen Testament', *ThStKr* 87 (1914) 25-53; 38.

[176] Chrys C. Caragounis, *The Development of Greek and the New Testament: Morphology, Syntax, Phonology, and Textual Transmission* (Tübingen: Mohr Siebeck, 2004), 189.

are conditions of Spirit-reception.'[177] Adler argued that καί located between an imperative and a future verb is consecutive and cited James 4:7, ἀνίστητε δὲ τῷ διαβόλῳ καὶ φεύξεται, as an example. So too, F. Blass and A. Debrunner, who said that the consecutive καί 'is especially frequent after imperatives'.[178] For Acts 2:38, Barrett suggested, 'do this, and in consequence you will receive'.[179] There is no exegetical reason to deny that Acts 2:38 describes a conditional situation. However, that Peter sets conditions for receiving the Spirit does not answer the question as to whether Spirit-reception is temporally coincident with, or subsequent to, fulfilling those conditions. Nor does syntax answer the broader narrative question as to whether these conditions are malleable (cf. Acts 10).

What then, of the matter of timing? Adler argued further that Luke could have associated the Spirit directly with the water if he had wanted to by writing, 'λήμψεσθε ἄφεσιν ... καὶ τὴν δωρεάν'. However, then he would have lost the allusion to Luke 3:3 βάπτισμα μετανοίας εἰς ἄφεσιν ἁμαρτιῶν. More recently, Paul Elbert has argued similarly that if Luke had wanted an immediate water/Spirit link he could have used the imperative plus present participle structure that he employs elsewhere (Luke 6:35; 19:17; 20:31; 21:36). Elbert gives the following example consistent with Luke's usage:[180] μετανοήσατε ... βαπτισθήτω ... τὴν δωρεὰν τοῦ ἁγίου πνεύματος λαμβάνοντες. But, had he so subordinated Spirit to water, he would have contradicted his cotext in which the Spirit is the chief feature, not baptism. The crowd has not been inquiring about baptism, nor has Peter been preaching a homily on baptism.

Adler also employed an argument from syntax:

> When Luke, however, in two different ways places forgiveness of sins and Spirit-reception in connection with baptism, forgiveness of sins with εἰς ἄφεσιν, Spirit-reception, in contrast, with καὶ λήμψεσθε, where he nevertheless had had the opportunity to set both on a common denominator, he surely wants to thereby express that between remission of sins and Spirit-reception there does not exist the same relationship to baptism.[181]

---

[177] 'Die Konstruktion «Imperative + καί + Futur» markiert ein konditionales Gefüge: Umkehr und Taufe sind Bedingung des Geistempfangs', Pesch, *Apg 1-12*, 125. Cf. Barrett, who states that Pesch, 'goes a little too far in treating this as a conditional use of the imperative'. Barrett affirms that, 'Peter is truly issuing a command, or instruction' (Barrett, *Acts*, 154-55).

[178] F. Blass and A. Debrunner, trans. Robert W. Funk, *A Greek Grammar of the New Testament and other Early Christian Literature* (Chicago: University of Chicago Press, 1961), 227.

[179] Barrett, *Acts*, 154.

[180] *Ibid.*, 106.

[181] 'Wenn Lukas aber Sündenvergebung und Geistempfang auf zwei verschiedene Weisen mit der Taufe in Verbindung setzt, die Sündenvergebung mit εἰς ἄφεσιν, den Geistempfang dagegen mit καὶ λήμψεσθε, wo er doch die Möglichkeit gehabt hätte, beides auf den gleichen Nenner zu bringen, so will er damit doch wohl ausdrücken, daß zwischen Sündennachlaß und Geistempfang nicht die nämlichen Beziehungen zu der Wassertaufe bestehen', Adler, *Taufe*, 27.

He concluded, based upon the reading of 2:38, that water baptism is the 'Wirkursache', or 'efficient cause', of forgiveness of sins, but is the 'Voraussetzung', the 'prerequisite', of Spirit-reception.[182] However, it must be noted here that it is possible for something to be *both* prerequisite *and* means. 'Drop the egg and it will break.' The dropping is prerequisite to the breaking, but in a sense it is also the means of the breaking. If water baptism is the efficient cause of forgiveness, why could it not be the efficient cause of Spirit-reception as well? This fault in Adler's logic does not mean his conclusion is wrong, just that the way he arrived at it is not ideal.

This is not to say that Luke here asserted that the Spirit cannot come before baptism and later contradicted himself in the Cornelius story. Baptism is for the remission of sins. But, Luke provided us with no statement that forgiveness can only be available through baptism. If sins are remitted before baptism, then, within Luke's theology, the Spirit can come. That is the clarification of Cornelius' house. However, the course of the narrative up to this point has presented baptism as integrally associated with forgiveness of sins. Peter follows the practice of John the Baptist before him. Baptism is, therefore, not optional. It is required for entrance into the community. It is normal and the gift of the Spirit upon baptism is equally normal. Deviations from this norm can occur, as Luke will later elaborate, but deviations do not obviate the original teaching of the apostle and normative spokesperson, Peter.

We return to the question of timing. In addition to the questionable argument from syntax, Adler made the interesting case that the observers on the day of Pentecost would have been either direct, or at least indirect, witnesses to the Spirit coming upon the waiting disciples; therefore, they would have known that it was an experience out of heaven, and not one received through baptism, since the disciples did not receive the Spirit in connection with baptism. Therefore, baptism would have been seen as a prerequisite and not as the means.[183] Adler's case here is not strong because we do not have direct access to the minds of Peter's original audience. However, his case can be modified using narrative principles so that it becomes significantly more forceful. Luke's *reader* observed the events of Pentecost. Adler's point therefore applies. The reader cannot expect mere water to transmit the Spirit when s/he just saw the Spirit obtained without water. Why would the reader expect immersion to impart the Spirit when s/he has twice now observed the Spirit descend from heaven? S/he has heard Jesus teach on receiving the Spirit and he never once said it was received in the moment of immersion. With such a precedent already in place, Luke would have to provide a textual signal to his reader to indicate a change in the mode of impartation.

---

[182] *Ibid.*, 27-28.

[183] *Ibid.*, 28. Lake argues similarly, Kirsopp Lake, 'Baptism (Early Christian)', James Hastings, et al. (eds), *Encyclopaedia of Religion and Ethics* (New York: Charles Scribner's Sons, n.d.), 2.379-90.

However, Adler is viewing baptism as mere immersion, not as a composite ceremony involving immersion *and* prayer. When baptism is viewed from the perspective of the narrative up to this point (namely, including the story of Jesus' baptismal experience) the reader knows that prayer is an integral part of baptism. Therefore, it is possible for the reader to think that baptism – not merely immersion, but immersion and prayer – is the means of Spirit-reception and not merely the prerequisite. F. Scott Spencer writes, 'Peter established a clear – but *not necessarily simultaneous* – link between repentance, baptism, and Spirit-reception (2.38)',[184] but he, like Adler, is viewing baptism as strictly immersion and not as a complex ceremony. Luke, in Acts 2, did not supply a depiction the 3000 receiving the Spirit. A description (no claim that it is 'the definitive' description will be made) of new converts receiving the Spirit must wait until the Samaria story.

Conclusion

An analysis of characters and story logic has shown that the crowd was not aware of the preliminary phenomena of wind and fire. The implied reader knows this because the crowd is depicted as inquisitive, yet does not ask about phenomena that are marvellous. This is no argument from silence. The incongruity of the crowd knowing, but not asking, *actively* excludes awareness of the wind and fire. Then, through the crowd's repeated questions and mockery, Luke focalized the dissociative xenolalia, identifying it as the solitary referent for Peter's discourse on the Spirit. Peter then identified the dissociative xenolalia experience as the Spirit experience foretold by Joel. Peter then identified the Spirit experience spoken of by Jesus, the 'promise of the Father', as what the crowd sees and hears. The only discourse referent to the seeing and hearing is the dissociative xenolalia. Finally, Peter guarantees the 'gift of the Holy Spirit' upon repentance and baptism and states that this 'promise' is for all who convert, both now and in the future.

This third identification raises the issue of normativity and the book presents two possible responses to the problem. The first possible interpretation of the data is that the third identification does something the previous two did not: it normativizes the dissociative xenolalia. Peter directly asserts that all converts in perpetuity will have *this* experience. Such an authoritative statement cannot be undone by Luke. He can add to it, but not subtract from it. That is, converts may have other experiences of the Spirit, but they cannot be without this *sine qua non* experience.

The second possible way of looking at the data is to recognize the focalization of xenolalia and understand it as the evidence, *on this occasion*, of the Spirit's coming. One may also recognize xenolalia as the referent to Peter's Spirit discourse and even acknowledge there is, therefore, a programmatic expectation that

---

[184] F. Scott Spencer, *Acts* (Sheffield: Sheffield Academic, 1997), 87, original italics.

not only this crowd, but also all future converts, would experience xenolalia. However, despite cognizance of this narrative thrust, this programmatic expectation, one must also recognize that Luke did *not explicitly exclude* other phenomena (or lack thereof) from manifesting the Spirit's arrival. Without explicit exclusion of other phenomena, the door remains open for Luke to alter his initial impression of universal xenolalia and replace xenolalia later in the narrative or even to eliminate it altogether. Only study of the further narrative will determine whether Luke made such alterations/modifications.

What is clear is that Luke ritually linked Spirit-reception to repentance and baptism (2:38). Because the Luke 3:21-22 depiction of Jesus' baptism informs the reader of Acts 2:38, the reader expects the converts to receive the Spirit as Jesus did, during the baptismal prayer which occurs while the initiate is still in the baptismal waters. This is the reader's expectation from the ER for baptism. However, Luke did not explicitly show the 3000 converts being baptised, and so left a gap as to how the Spirit is actually transmitted to them. His first explicit depiction of new converts receiving the Spirit only comes in Acts 8.

Chapter 5

Prayer and Handlaying: What to Do When the Spirit Does not Come

Introduction

Acts 2 described the Spirit coming upon individuals already in relationship with the risen Christ. But Luke did not show the Spirit being received by new converts. The implied reader has an expectation, from Luke 3:21-22, that the Spirit is associated with prayer immediately following the act of immersion and consequently expects prayer at the time of the Pentecost converts' immersion. Acts 8, however, discusses two new rituals – prayer and handlaying by apostles. This chapter will attempt to understand how Luke integrated these new concepts into his ER for initiation.

A sequential approach appropriately reads Acts 2 and 8 in light of Luke 3:21-22, and the early differentiation between immersion and prayer for the Spirit within the one baptismal experience carries forward through the narrative. Yet, Barrett objected, 'It is however precisely the separation of the imposition of hands from baptism, and the attaching of the gift of the Spirit to the imposition of hands rather than to baptism, that constitutes one of the main problems in Acts 8.'[1] However, Luke could have understood *differentiation* between immersion and prayer/handlaying for the Spirit, viewing all these as belonging to the one baptismal ceremony, without having advocated *separation* into multiple ceremonies. Whether that was, in fact, Luke's opinion remains to be seen.

That Luke presented prayer and handlaying as a means of facilitating the coming of the Spirit, does not make it the standard means. The reader is left with the question as to whether Luke intended handlaying to be seen as the exclusive means, or a normal means, or an exceptional means. Or was Samaria a totally unique occurrence? Analysis of focalization and redundancy identify handlaying in combination with prayer by initiators, as the mechanism for Spirit impartation/facilitation used at Samaria. But, that identification does not answer the question. Analysis of the story itself indicates that Luke intended his reader to understand handlaying as a normal procedure to employ when converts have not

---

[1] C.K. Barrett, 'Light on the Holy Spirit From Simon Magus (Acts 8,4-25)', J. Kremer (ed.), *Les Actes des Apôtres: Traditions, rédaction, théologie* (Leuven: Leuven University Press, 1979), 281-95; 284.

received the Spirit through their own belief and immersion. However, the frequency with which it would need to be employed is not established through this one episode. The rest of the Luke-Acts narrative must be evaluated before any determination on frequency can be made.

Was Samaria a 'corporate' experience of the Spirit, as Bruner, Carson, and Alan J. Thompson suggest,[2] or an individual experience? This chapter makes the case for individual. Are we assuming intention to teach about initiation on the part of Luke when he had no such intention at all? As George T. Montague asserts, 'Luke never intended to write a treatise on baptism or on the laying on of hands.'[3] This chapter argues that the care with which Luke discussed initiation indicates that he did intend to communicate theologically about it.

Summary of Acts 8:4-25

Philip preaches to the Samaritans and they are baptised. Udo Smidt asserted that, among the Samaritans, the Spirit had not been able to take his work 'in depth', and the movement was one of 'enthusiasm'.[4] Dunn argued similarly, that the Samaritan's faith was defective, but no longer holds the position and therefore will not be responded to in detail.[5] Thorough rebuttals can be found in Ervin, Turner, and Avemarie.[6] In short, Luke did not indicate to his reader that Philip's preaching was faulty. Rather, the Samaritans were baptised in the name of Jesus Christ. Here Avemarie employed a narratological approach by appealing to the previous course of the narrative to affirm that this baptism is indeed a 'Christian' one: 'The course of the narrative up till now implicitly suggests that already (v. 5, 12).'[7] The apostles at Jerusalem send Peter and John who prayed for the Samaritans to receive the Spirit. Luke specifically explained to his reader why the apostles prayed for the Samaritans to receive the Holy Spirit. They had only been baptised in the name of Jesus and the Spirit had not yet fallen on any of them. Luke showed the apostles laying hands on the Samaritans and causing them

---

[2] Bruner, *Theology*, 192; Carson, *Spirit*, 145; Alan J. Thompson, *The Acts of the Risen Lord Jesus: Luke's Account of God's Unfolding Plan* (Downers Grove: IVP, 2011), 139.

[3] George T. Montague, *Holy Spirit: Growth of a Biblical Tradition* (Peabody: Hendrickson, 1976), 292; similarly, R. Reitzenstein, *Die Vorgeschichte der christlichen Taufe* (Leipzig: B.G. Teubner, 1929), 163.

[4] 'in der Tiefe', 'Begeisterung'. Udo Smidt, *Die Apostelgeschichte Übersezt und ausgelegt* (Kassel: J.G. Onken, 1951), 61.

[5] Dunn, 'Response', 228, 240.

[6] Ervin, *Conversion-Initiation*, 25-35; Turner, *Power*, 362-67; Avemarie, *Tauferzählungen*, 169-70.

[7] 'Implizit legt das schon der bisherige Gang der Erzählung nahe (V. 5, 12)'. *Ibid.*, 31.

thereby to receive the Spirit. Luke then focalized on handlaying through Simon's perspective.[8] Finally, the apostles went to other Samaritan villages.

Focalization of Handlaying

Erasmus claimed the apostles had authority to impart the Spirit which deacons did not have.[9] Paul Volz affirmed handlaying as clearly associated with Spirit-reception in Acts 8:17.[10] Siegfried Schulz asserted that through apostolic handlaying the Samaritan missions-church was brought into the fellowship of the apostolic community which alone possessed the Spirit.[11] Maurice Goguel argued from Simon's request that Luke thought only the apostles had the power to impart the Spirit.[12] A. Schlatter stated the apostles were, 'regarded as in a supreme degree the mediators of the Spirit'.[13] Adler affirmed that the apostles received the Spirit not only for themselves, but also so that they could communicate the Spirit to others through handlaying.[14] Von Baer, though, rejected the idea of the Spirit being transmitted by humans and wrote that Simon misunderstood what was happening: 'The Holy Spirit is, in fact, according to the view of Luke, a free gift of the Lord which does not let itself be simply transmitted, like Simon Magus assumes.'[15] Dunn, working from Jesus' Jordan experience, sees Spirit-reception as solely the work of God, unmediated by any human act, separate from the human ritual of water baptism.[16] Likewise, Hur objects that the Spirit is sometimes given apart from handlaying, and handlaying does not always result in Spirit-reception, and that therefore, it cannot be 'viewed as a necessary means of receiving the

---

[8] 'Nach dem Erzählzusammenhang empfängt auch Simon den Geist'. Martina Böhm, *Samarien und die Samaritai bei Lukas* (Tübingen: J.C.B. Mohr, Paul Siebeck, 1999), 300.

[9] Desiderius Erasmus, trans. Robert D. Sider, *Paraphrase on the Acts of the Apostles* (Toronto: University of Toronto Press, 1995 [1524]), 59.

[10] Paul Volz, *Der Geist Gottes und die verwandten Erscheinungen im Alten Testament und im anschließenden Judentum* (Tübingen: J.C.B. Mohr, Paul Siebeck, 1910), 115.

[11] Siegfried Schulz, *Die Mitte der Schrift: Der Fühkatholizismus im Neuen Testament als Herausforderung an den Protestantismus* (Stuttgart: Kreuz Verlag, 1976), 139.

[12] Maurice Goguel, trans. H.C. Snape, *The Birth of Christianity* (London: George Allen & Unwin, 1953 [*La Naissancce du Christianisme*. Paris: Payot, 1946]), 180. Cf. Cuthbert Hamilton Turner, *Studies in Early Church History: Collected Papers* (Oxford: Clarendon, 1912), 12.

[13] A. Schlatter, 'Holy Spirit', James Hastings, ed., *Dictionary of the Apostolic Church* (Edinburgh: T&T Clark, 1915), 1.573-81; 574. Similarly, H. Wheeler Robinson, 'Hand', James Hastings (ed.), *Dictionary of the Apostolic Church* (Edinburgh: T&T Clark, 1915), 1.521.

[14] Nikolaus Adler, *Das erste christliche Pfingstfest: Sinn und Bedeutung des Pfingstberichtes Apg 2, 1-13* (Münster: Aschendorffsche Verlagsbuchhandlung, 1938), 136.

[15] 'Ist doch der Heilige Geist nach der Anschauung des Lukas eine freie Gabe des Herrn, die sich nicht einfach übertragen läßt, wie es Simon Magus annimmt', Von Baer, *Geist*, 174.

[16] Dunn, *Baptism*, 37.

Spirit'.[17] Rather, the gift of the Spirit to the Samaritans must be attributed to the sovereignty of God exercised 'in response to the prayer of Peter and John (cf. Lk. 11.13). In other words, the bestowing of the Spirit is not considered a human prerogative'.[18] Witherington writes similarly, 'The book of Acts suggests God's sovereignty over the whole matter, not that the matter is in the control of clerics, not even apostles.'[19] Green states, 'we should steer clear of imagining that Luke would allow that the church somehow possesses or dispenses the Spirit as the church wishes'.[20] Barrett vociferously wrote of:

> Luke's fundamental conviction, which is that the Spirit does not respond to certain stimuli, such as the laying on of hands, more or less in the manner of Pavlov's dog, but is given solely *ubi et quando visum est Deo*. It is God, not magicians or even apostles, who gives his own Spirit.[21]

Contrary to Dunn, Hur, Witherington, and Barrett, the text *does* give the prerogative for facilitating the gift of the Spirit to humans, specifically to apostles who have the gift of God (τὴν δωρεὰν τοῦ θεοῦ Acts 8:20) to do so. That is precisely what the story of Simon's greed revolves around, as will be demonstrated in the detailed discussion of focalization below. The fact that handlaying can be used for various rites, such as a commissioning service (6:6; 13:3), or a prayer for healing (Luke 4:40; 13:13; Acts 9:17; 28:8), does not negate the function of handlaying within one particular rite, namely, prayer for Spirit-reception. This does not imply that handlaying is the standard rite, only that it is a rite used by apostles. Nor does this require that the Spirit is transferred from the bodies of the initiators to the bodies of the initiates. The transference view is not impossible for Luke's narrative, but it is not necessary. Samaria can be fully understood in terms of the initiator facilitating the gift of the Spirit from God to the initiate. As Turner states, 'it is simply a matter of prayerful human incorporative invocation of the Spirit'.[22]

That the Spirit is sometimes given without handlaying seems like a serious objection to the position that handlaying is a rite used to facilitate the Spirit. Von Baer argued: 'As Acts 2:1ff.; 4:31; 10:44, as well as the majority of places were the discussion is of a sudden filling of the disciples, show, Spirit-reception is also

---

[17] Hur, *Reading*, 240. Similarly, Guthrie, *Theology*, 542-43; Keith Warrington, *Discovering the Holy Spirit in the New Testament* (Peabody: Hendrickson, 2005), 56.

[18] Hur, *Reading*, 240.

[19] Witherington, *Acts*, 288.

[20] Green, 'Baptism', 170. Similarly, Justo L. Gonzalez, *Acts: The Gospel of the Spirit* (Maryknoll: Orbis, 2001), 109; Richard I. Pervo, *Acts* (Minneapolis: Fortress, 2009), 213.

[21] Barrett, 'Light', 293.

[22] Max Turner, 'The Spirit of Christ and "Divine" Christology', Joel B. Green, Max Turner (eds), *Jesus of Nazareth, Lord and Christ: Essays on the Historical Jesus and New Testament Christology* (Grand Rapids: Eerdmans, 1994), 420.

in no way mechanically bound to handlaying'.[23] Hur argues that it cannot therefore be 'a necessary means' if by that is meant the only means, and looking ahead in the text to the Cornelius story certainly confirms that. The Samaritan story, though, as will be shown under the coming discussion of focalization, directly links the facilitation of the gift of the Spirit to human actions, namely prayer and handlaying by gifted individuals. Luke maintained the sovereignty of God first, in that Luke showed the apostles praying, thus demonstrating their dependence upon God, and second, in that God gives the ability to facilitate to whom he wills. But once given, the human apostles carry out the task of their own accord.

A major narratological objection to this analysis comes from Tannehill, Hur, and Eisen who argue, against Bovon,[24] that Simon's viewpoint, expressed in verse 18, is not that of the authoritative narrator.[25] Eisen writes, 'In the scene of the encounter of Peter and John with Simon Magus, Simon's observation is not narrator opinion (Acts 8:15-24). Much more, the direct speech of Simon betrays his magical misunderstanding (Acts 8:19).'[26] Tannehill and Hur go beyond Eisen in incorrectly identifying the nature of the supposed misunderstanding. Tannehill writes, 'The narrator is telling us how Simon interpreted what he had seen, and this is not to be taken as simple truth. Indeed, Peter corrects this interpretation when he calls the Spirit "the gift of God".'[27] Hur also writes that Luke presented Peter as 'identifying the Holy Spirit as "God's gift"'[28] and states that Simon incorrectly 'thought that to give and/or to receive the Holy Spirit is a human action'.[29] Johnson concurs that the gift here spoken of is the Spirit.[30] However, though Luke elsewhere used the concept of 'gift' in association with the Holy Spirit (e.g., Acts 2:38 τὴν δωρεάν, 11:17 δωρεάν), Peter does not, in this passage, call the Spirit the gift of God.[31] We know this because, in 8:19, Simon asked for

---

[23] 'Wie Acta 2, 1 ff.; 4, 31; 10, 44 sowie die Mehrzahl der Stellen, wo von einem plötzlichen Erfülltwerden der Jünger die Rede ist, beweisen, ist auch der Geistesempfang keineswegs mechanisch an die Handauflegung gebunden', Von Baer, *Geist*, 175.
[24] Bovon, *Luke*, 269.
[25] Von Baer argued the same, though not in narratological terms, *Geist*, 174. For discussion of mixing of viewpoints, see Boris Uspensky, *A Poetics of Composition: The Structure of the Artistic Text and Typology of a Compositional Form* (Berkeley: University of California Press, 1973), 32-43.
[26] 'In der Szene der Begegnung von Petrus und Johannes mit Simon Magus ist Simons Beobachtung ... nicht Erzählermeinung (Act 8,15-24). Vielmehr verrät die direkte Rede des Simon sein magisches Missverständnis (Act 8,19)', Eisen, *Poetik*, 116-17. Similarly, Heidrun Gunkel, *Geist*, 212. Cf. Turner, 'Christology', 420.
[27] Tannehill, *Acts*, 106.
[28] Hur, *Reading*, 136.
[29] *Ibid.*, 135.
[30] Johnson, *Acts*, 149.
[31] Dietrich-Alex Koch attributes this unique usage to 'vorlukanische Traditionsmaterial', 'Geistbesitz, Geistverleihung und Wundermacht Erwägungen zur Tradition und zur lukanischen Redaktion in Act 8 5-25', *ZNW* 77 (1986), 64-82; 76.

τὴν ἐξουςίαν ταύτην that upon whomever he should lay his hands, that person might receive the Holy Spirit. Then, in 8:20, Peter responds to Simon's request for τὴν ἐξουσίαν ταύτην by saying that Simon had falsely supposed that τὴν δωρεὰν τοῦ θεοῦ could be purchased with money. In Luke's narrative, τὴν ἐξουσίαν ταύτην coveted by Simon is τὴν δωρεὰν τοῦ θεοῦ possessed by Peter. The 'gift' is the power to facilitate the Spirit, not the Spirit *per se*.[32] Schneider correctly writes, 'He seeks the ἐξουσία of the apostle to impart the Spirit through handlaying.'[33]

This mistake aside, Tannehill, Hur, Eisen, and Avemarie all raise the question of whether verse 18 represents Luke's opinion or merely Simon's. Hur suggests that Simon is not a reliable character as are Peter and Jesus.[34] Avemarie's concern[35] was similar, namely that by presenting the story from the perspective of Simon Magus, Luke obscured his own theological opinion. However, as Michael Patrick Whitehouse observes: 'Simon is not rebuked in 8:20 for incorrectly seeing a connection between handlaying and the Holy Spirit ... but for thinking that he could purchase such a gift (i.e., the ability to confer the Spirit).'[36] Ulrich Heckel concludes that through Luke's presentation of God fulfilling the apostles' prayer for the Spirit, of the idea 'authority', and of the 'gift of God': 'Therewith Luke affirmed the effectiveness of the handlaying observed by Simon.'[37]

Moreover, with ἰδών Luke affirmed that Simon correctly observed apostolic handlaying as the means of Spirit facilitation.[38] Luke did not write, 'Simon, supposing that the Spirit was given', as if presenting Simon's idiosyncratic idea.

---

[32] Haenchen also distinguishes between the Spirit and the gift of imparting the Spirit, cf. *Acts*, 304; as does Joseph A. Fitzmyer, *The Acts of the Apostles: A New Translation with Introduction and Commentary* (New York: Doubleday, 1998), 406. So too, Klaus Berger, 'Propaganda und Gegenpropaganda im Frühen Christentum: Simon Magus als Gestalt des Samaritanischen Christentums', Lukas Bormann, Kelly Del Tredici and Angela Standhartinger (eds), *Religious Propaganda & Missionary Competition in the New Testament World* (Leiden: Brill, 1994), 313-17; 315. Mitzi J. Smith understands this passage correctly, *The Literary Construction of the Other in the Acts of the Apostles: Charismatics, the Jews, and Women* (Cambridge: James Clarke, 2011), 23; as does Samkutty, *Mission*, 162.

[33] 'Er erstrebt die ἐξουσία der Apostel, durch Handauflegung den Geist zu vermitteln'. Schneider, *Apostelgeschichte 1,1-8,40*, 493.

[34] Hur, *Reading*, 135.

[35] Avemarie, *Tauferzählungen*, 165.

[36] Whitehouse, *Impositio*, 70. So too, Hull, *Spirit*, 105. Similarly, Don Jackson, 'Luke and Paul: A Theology of One Spirit from Two Perspectives,' *JETS* 32.3 (September, 1989), 339.

[37] 'Damit bejaht Lukas die von Simon beobachtete Wirksamkeit der Handauflegung', Ulrich Heckel, *Der Segen im Neuen Testament: Begriff, Formeln, Gesten; mit einem praktisch-theologischen Ausblick* (Tübingen: J.C.B. Mohr, Paul Siebeck, 2002), 329-30.

[38] Cf. Patrick Fabien, who recognizes that ἰδών strengthens the parallel between 14-17 and 18-19, but also sees it as increasing the ambiguity between faith and magic, 'La conversion de Simon le magicien (Ac 8,4-25)', *Bib.* 91.2 (2010), 210-40; 220, cf. 211.

Luke was fully able to identify a character's own perception with some modifier when he wanted to, both when that perception is accurate and when it is false. For example:

1) Acts 27:13
δόξαντες τῆς προθέσεως κεκρατηκέναι, ἄραντες
The sailors supposed they had attained their purpose, but they had not.

2) Acts 16:13
ἐξήλθομεν ἔξω τῆς πύλης παρὰ ποταμὸν οὗ ἐνομίζομεν προσευχὴν εἶναι
Paul's group accurately supposed prayer to be taking place at the river.

3) Acts 16:27
ἤμελλεν ἑαυτὸν ἀναιρεῖν νομίζων ἐκπεφευγέναι τοὺς δεσμίους
The jailer falsely supposed the prisoners had fled.

Furthermore, these interpreters' objections do not take into consideration another aspect of poetics: the function of a character to reinforce the narrator. A number of writers have noted this principle. Witherup gives a classic example where the narrator calls Cornelius εὐσεβὴς καὶ φοβούμενος τὸν θεόν and then characters say he is δίκαιος καὶ φοβούμενος τὸν θεόν. This is simple repetition with substitution: righteous for pious. The servants serve here as normative spokespersons. Witherup also notes how the redundant expression of similar viewpoints by characters in the Cornelius story (Peter in chapter 10, repeated in 11, then Peter and James in 15) reinforces the view of the implied author, and is 'a way of establishing and promoting the one primary ideological point of view from which all others are viewed or evaluated'.[39] Berlin observes the same principle of using direct discourse to confirm narration and notes that the narrator may be either 'confirming the words of the character', or that s/he, 'ironically or not, is adopting the character's viewpoint'.[40]

Alter also discusses this concept. 'When there is no divergence between a statement as it occurs in narration and as it recurs in dialogue, or vice versa, the repetition generally has the effect of giving a weight of emphasis to the specific terms which the speaker chooses for his speech'.[41] He cites the classic case of Asahel running after Abner in which the narrator says, 'He swerved neither to the right nor to the left in his pursuit of Abner', while the dialogue has Abner say, 'Swerve to the right or to the left and seize one of the young men for yourself' (Alter's translation). Functionally, then: 'The common idiom of swerving

---

[39] Witherup, 'Cornelius', 45-66; 53-54.
[40] Berlin, *Poetics*, 64.
[41] Alter, *Art*, 77.

neither right nor left is thus converted through the repetition into a concrete image of the geometry of survival.'[42]

This kind of reinforcing of the narrator's viewpoint can occur even with a character who is a villain. Robert Brawley notes that in Acts 19:26 (read with reference to Acts 17:24), Demetrius the silversmith's accusation of Paul, that 'this Paul' says 'they are not gods, those being made by hands', though ostensibly negative, is correct. Brawley concludes that, 'With intricate interweavings of point of view, even a character who opposes the narrator ideologically may unwittingly express the truth from the narrator's perspective.'[43] The text presents the powerful effect of the apostles' handlaying through the eyes of Simon immediately after Luke narrated it for the reader. As Simon realizes that the apostles can lay hands on people and they will receive the Spirit, he learns experientially what the reader already knows. Thus the axis of the character's knowledge converges with the reader's knowledge just received from the narrator. As Witherup observes, 'The coinciding of narrative points of view helps to establish reliability in the story and also reinforces major messages or ideological stances.'[44]

However, not only did Luke use informational convergence, but he employed progressive repetition with functional variation as well. A.B. Caneday sees this regarding impartation of the Spirit through handlaying: 'Luke labors to make this point, not only by stating it once (8:17) and then restating the cumbersome phrase two more times (8:18, 19), but also by focusing upon Simon Magus' request to buy the apostles' authority.'[45] In fact, the facilitation of the Spirit concept is repeated four times, with a new element progressively added each time. First comes the summary of the situation in verses 14-16: apostles come from Jerusalem; they pray so that the converts may receive the Holy Spirit; the Spirit had fallen on none of the converts; they had only been baptised, albeit in the right name. Second, we learn more detailed information in verse 17 that there was not simply prayer, there was also handlaying which is when the Spirit-reception occurred: 'Then they began laying hands on them and they were receiving the Holy Spirit.' Third, immediately after hearing the handlaying narrated, we experience it vicariously with Simon: 'And Simon, having seen that through the laying on of the hands of the apostles the Holy Spirit was given' (8:18). Luke focalized the con-

---

[42] *Ibid.*
[43] Robert L. Brawley, *Centering on God: Method and Message in Luke-Acts* (Louisville: WJKP, 1990), 21. Cf. Seymour Chatman, *Story and Discourse: Narrative Structure in Fiction and Film* (Ithaca: Cornell University Press, 1978), 156-57.
[44] Witherup, 'Redundancy', 74. Cf. Sternberg, *Poetics*, 512.
[45] A.B. Caneday, 'Baptized in the Holy Spirit: Epochal Theology in Luke-Acts' (paper presented to the annual Upper Midwest region meeting of the Society for Biblical Literature, April 8-9, 1994).
[https://www.academia.edu/1916368/Baptized_in_the_Holy_Spirit_electronic_resource_ epochal_theology_in_Luke-Acts_by_AB_Caneday; accessed on 04/07/14], 25.

cept of apostolic handlaying through Simon's eyes. Fourth, Simon himself specifically asks for this handlaying power, 'that whoever I should lay hands on may receive the Holy Spirit' (8:19).

For Luke, impartation/facilitation of the Spirit through prayer and handlaying was a means of bringing converts into the common experience of the people of God. Simon's lust for this power illustrates its impressive reality, and Peter's rebuke that it is a gift from God not to be purchased with money reiterates the apostolic opinion upon the matter. Peter and John have the gift of facilitating the gift of the Spirit with their hands. Philip, evangelist and miracle worker though he is, apparently does not. We must qualify Philip's status with 'apparently' because Luke did not explicitly exclude Philip from the handlaying activity. Luke's focus was simply on the activity of the apostles, who are unequivocally presented as carrying out the ministry of Spirit impartation. Philip will be discussed at length in the next section.

Thus, in a four part structure, Luke used focalization and functional redundancy to intensify the significance of handlaying for Spirit-reception. He subsumed it under the rubric of prayer. He explicitly coupled it with Spirit-reception. He brought the facilitation mechanism close to the reader through the lens of Simon's wide-eyed desire. Finally, he vocalized the concept of Spirit facilitation as a possessable power/authority – possessable by those worthy of it, that is. For Luke's reader, the connection between gifted hands and facilitation of the Spirit is not in doubt. The question is simply whether Simon will be able to purchase this power for his own hands, and of that there is no chance.

Further Examination of Handlaying

Haenchen, while rejecting the historicity of Acts 8, affirmed that, 'in Luke's community baptism and the laying-on of hands must still have been associated'.[46] Schneider simply affirms that, 'Repentance and water baptism give the Holy Spirit', and then suggests that in extraordinary situations handlaying may be used to portray the unity of the church following a prayer for the Spirit.[47] Johannes Leipoldt recognized that there was a connection between baptism and handlaying in early Christianity, but said that we can no longer determine exactly what that

---

[46] Haenchen, *Acts*, 304. Cf. Otis Carl Edwards, Jr., 'Exegesis of Acts 8:4-25 and Its Implications for Confirmation and Glossolalia: A Review Article on Haenchen's Acts Commentary', *AThR.SS* 2 (September, 1973), 100-112; 110. For a more recent proposal of multiple sources behind Acts 8, cf. Patrick L. Dickerson, 'The Sources of the Account of the Mission to Samaria in Acts 8:5-25', *NT* 39.3 (July, 1997), 210-34; 227. Pesch presents the commentators on the Acts texts related to 'Taufe und Geistempfang in der Apostlegeschichte', but in the end, he offers no solution. Pesch, *Apg 1-12*, 281-85.

[47] 'Umkehr und Wassertaufe geben den Heiligen Geist'. Schneider, *Geist*, 43. Samkutty, though devoting a monograph to the Samaritan mission, states, 'no extensive discussion will be made here to unravel Luke's theology of water-baptism or Spirit-reception', V.J. Samkutty, *The Samaritan Mission in Acts* (London: T&T Clark, 2006), 170.

relationship was.⁴⁸ In contradistinction, one could argue that it belongs in a separate category, apart from baptism, as Adler maintained. Adler wrote:

> The handlaying of the two apostles does not form a part of the baptism or, as Behm says, one of the two 'proper centrepieces of the procedure at the admission into the church' (p. 171), rather a complete, independent act.⁴⁹

Cornils' approach to the baptism/Spirit-reception stories must be given closer attention. She categorizes Spirit related stories in Acts by the level of the Spirit's involvement. She then identifies four prototypical story structures. These are outlined below.

Prototypical Narrative with High Action Potential for Pneuma

1. Prototype: Prophetic Pneuma-Narratives
   Foretelling of the Holy Spirit → speaking / mediation through a person → fulfilment

2. Prototype: Missionary Pneuma-Narratives
   Preparation → speech of Pneuma → mission

Prototypical Narrative with Middle Action Potential for Pneuma

3. Prototype: Pneumatic Baptism Narratives
   Belief → baptism with water → (handlaying) / baptism with Holy Spirit → effect

Prototypical Employment of Pneuma with Low Action Potential

4. Prototype: be 'filled with / full' Pneuma
   Actors + 'full / filled with' Holy Spirit + special qualities / abilities / activities⁵⁰

---

[48] Johannes Leipoldt, *Die urchristliche Taufe im Lichte der Religionsgeschichte* (Leipzig: Verlag von Dörssling & Franke, 1928), 72.

[49] 'Die Handauflegung der beiden Apostel bildete nicht einen Teil der Taufe oder, wie Behm sagt, eines der beiden "ordnungsgemäßen Hauptstücke des Verfahrens bei der Aufnahme in die Gemeinde" (S. 171), sondern eine vollkommen selbständige Handlung'. Adler, *Taufe*, 105-106. Cf. Joseph Coppens, *L'Imposition des Mains et Les Rites Connexes dans le Nouveau Testament et dans L'Église Ancienne: Étude de Théologie Positive* (Paris: J. Gabalda, Éditeur, 1925), 188.

[50] Prototypische Erzählungen mit hohem Aktionspotential von Pneuma
1. Prototyp: Prophetische Pneuma-Erzählungen
Voraussage des heiligen Geistes → Sprechen / Vermittlung durch Person → Erfüllung

2. Prototyp: Missionarische Pneuma-Erzählungen
Vorbereitung → Reden von Pneuma → Mission

The prototypical story structure of interest to this book is the third – Pneumatic Baptism Narratives. While Cornils states that Acts 2:38 presents, 'The "normal sequence"', she also writes that 2:38 cannot be adopted as is, but must be expanded: 'So, in Acts 8:17, between the baptism with water and the reception of, respectively, the baptism with Holy Spirit, occurs the act of handlaying by a mediating person (apostle).'[51] For Cornils, this is no narrative contradiction, only a simple expansion of the fundamental structure, namely,

> Water baptism → Spirit baptism.

She recognizes that this structure can be reversed:

> Spirit baptism → Water baptism.

However, this interchange has a purpose: 'thereby both baptisms also still remain bound inseparably with one another'.[52] If water baptism → Spirit baptism had not already been the established schema, then Peter would have had no reason to offer water baptism to the Gentiles in Acts 10.[53] Against Adler, Cornils suggests handlaying belongs to immersion. Against von Baer, who wrote that, 'To this connection, which is presupposed between baptism and Spirit-reception in Acts 2:38, the report about the activity of Philip, as well as of Peter and John in Samaria, in chapter 8, stands in contradiction',[54] Cornils' work demonstrates that Acts need not be seen as self-contradictory, but can be understood within a narrative framework. To fully substantiate Cornils, the book must finish discussing all the Spirit-reception scenes in Luke-Acts.

Prototypische Erzählungen mit mittlerem Aktionspotential von Pneuma

3. Prototyp: Pneumatische Tauf-Erzählungen
Glaube → Taufe mit Wasser → (Handauflegung) / Taufe mit heiligem Geist → Wirkung

Prototypische Verwendung von Pneuma mit niedrigem Aktionspotential

4. Prototyp: ‚erfüllt von / voll' Pneuma sein
Handlungsträger + ‚voll / erfüllt mit' heiligem Geist + besondere Eigenschaften / Fähigkeiten / Tätigkeiten
Cornils, *Geist*, 184-90.

[51] 'Der ‚normale Ablauf'. 'So erfolgt in Apg 8,17 zwischen der Taufe mit Wasser und dem Empfang von bzw. der Taufe mit heiligem Geist der Akt der Handauflegung durch eine vermittelnde Person (Apostel)', *Ibid.*, 187; cf. 198.
[52] 'damit beide Taufen auch weiterhin untrennbar miteinander verbunden bleiben', *Ibid.*, 205.
[53] *Ibid.* Similarly, Loisy, *Actes*, 452.
[54] 'Zu diesem Zusammenhang, der zwischen Taufe und Geistesempfang in Acta 2, 38 vorausgesetzt wird, steht der Bericht über die Tätigkeit des Philippus, sowie des Petrus und Johannes in Samaria, Kap. 8, im Widerspruch', Von Baer, *Geist*, 172.

Moreover, Acts 8 does not contradict Acts 2, because Acts 2 did not say that the Spirit would be imparted in the water. The reader of Acts 2:38-39 remembers Jesus' immersion where the Spirit was not attached to the immersion, but to the prayer that accompanied the immersion. The implied reader expects the converts of Pentecost to pray when they are immersed. The expectation of prayer at immersion remains present when the reader arrives at Acts 8. Therefore, when Luke stated that Peter and John prayed for the Samaritans because the Spirit had not fallen and the Samaritans were only immersed, a reasonable assumption from the story so far is that no prayer had taken place. Caution must be exercised, however, because Luke did not explicitly exclude prior prayer. Nevertheless, the expectations of the implied reader, generated by past stories, cannot be discarded. For the reader, lack of prayer is a possible, but unconfirmed, explanation. Acts 8 builds upon Acts 2, strengthening the reader's understanding from Jesus' baptism that mere immersion does not impart the Spirit.

The question arises as to whether Philip was able to lay hands effectively upon converts. That Philip was not so gifted is not an argument from silence because there exists within the story a need for the Spirit to be imparted, yet Philip does not meet this need. Peter and John meet the need. Yet Luke was not explicit. Perhaps, when Philip saw that the Samaritans had been immersed and yet the Spirit had not come, he decided, or was told by God, to withhold the application of his ability until the arrival of the apostles. This, however, is merely an argument from silence. All that Luke explicitly stated is that the Spirit did not come until the apostles arrived. It would also be an argument from silence to say that Philip did not participate with Peter and John in the activity of handlaying, for while the text states that Peter and John laid hands upon the Samaritans, and that Simon saw it was through the apostles' hands the Spirit was given, Luke did not explicitly say that Philip did not also lay hands upon people. There is one aspect of the text, tenuous though it may be, that could suggest that Philip began to operate in the gift of facilitation *after* Peter and John arrived. Simon asks, δότε κἀμοὶ τὴν ἐξουσίαν ταύτην 'give also to me this authority'. It could have been that Simon thought Peter and John had given Philip the authority and so requested that he also, that is, he as well as Philip, would be given authority.

A Noticeable Failure

Luke left a 'gap'[55] as to what Simon saw that allowed him to know that people received the Spirit at the apostles' hands. Von Baer argued that there must have been some external sign.[56] Graham Twelftree affirms that there was some 'external evidence'[57] of the Spirit, but does not think this had to be tongues. He writes, 'it could equally have been a falling down or expressions of heightened joy, or

---

[55] Kurz, *Reading*, 85.
[56] Von Baer, *Geist*, 90.
[57] Graham H. Twelftree, *People of the Spirit: Exploring Luke's View of the Church* (London: SPCK, 2009), 88.

some signs of spiritual drunkenness (cf. 2:13; Eph. 5:18)'.[58] Wilfried Eckey, while not making any major contribution to the discussion, still states the obvious: Luke did not say.[59] The reader must fill in this gap using the only material presented so far in the text which is the Pentecost narrative's dissociative, xenolalic depiction of Spirit-reception. Wind and fire would not be considered as possible identifying manifestations of the Spirit in Samaria, because they were not identified as the definitive experience of the Spirit in Acts 2. Luke established a programmatic expectation that xenolalia would be experienced by every baptised convert, and, though the reader may be curious to know whether Luke later made any exceptions to this initial impression, the reader carries this basic understanding forward in the text. Avemarie noted regarding Simon's observation that the Spirit was given through the laying on of hands: 'that he 'sees' it, could be an indication of corresponding manifestations of the Spirit'.[60] Following the Spirit-reception ER and reading the Spirit-reception type-scenes in the order of their occurrence, first Pentecost and then Samaria, allows a narrative approach to confirm the suggestion of Avemarie and be more precise about what 'corresponding manifestation' a reader would identify.

An Individual Experience

Following Bruner,[61] Carson argues that in every instance in Acts where tongues are included or suggested, 'the manifestation of the Spirit's presence in tongues is part of a *corporate* experience. Never in Acts is this the experience of an individual convert'.[62] Zwiep writes, 'I fail to see convincing proof for the systematic individualization of Spirit baptism in Luke-Acts'.[63] Certainly, the initial coming of the Spirit at Pentecost was a corporate affair. But, even then, the Spirit experience which was promised to those who repented and were baptised was received by the new converts individually. All were not baptised at the same moment. Acts 2:38 individualizes reception of the promised Spirit experience, which was, as Acts 2:16 and 2:33 imply, a dissociative tongues experience. Similarly, against Carson and Zwiep, Samaria does not present a corporate experience of charismatic manifestation, but an individual one. Acts 8:17 reads:

> τότε ἐπετίθεσαν τὰς χεῖρας ἐπ' αὐτοὺς
> καὶ ἐλάμβανον πνεῦμα ἅγιον

---

[58] *Ibid.*
[59] Eckey, *Apostelgeschichte 1,1-15,35*, 265.
[60] 'dass er es "sieht", könnte ein Hinweis auf entsprechende Manifestationen des Geistes sein', Avemarie, *Tauferzählungen*, 52.
[61] Bruner, *Theology*, 192.
[62] Carson, *Spirit*, 145, original italics.
[63] Zwiep, 'Understanding', 135.

The verbs are imperfect and may be viewed as ingressive, stressing an action's beginning, 'with the implication that it continued for some time',[64] or iterative, signifying an ongoing, repetitive action.[65] Either view is possible in this context. Henry Barclay Swete said, 'ἐλάμβανον corresponds to ἐπετίθεσαν: as each in turn received the imposition of hands he received also the gift of the Spirit.'[66] Moreover, simple logic informs us that two apostles did not lay hands upon all the Samaritans at once. It was individual, one-person-at-a-time work. Therefore the manifestation, whatever it was which allowed Simon to recognize that through the laying on of the apostles' hands the Holy Spirit was given, was a manifestation associated with the individual, one-person-at-a-time, facilitation of the Spirit. Reception of the Spirit is only corporate in the sense that all fully initiated members of the community have experienced it. It is the common experience received during initiation. Zwiep, however, writes, 'The gift of the Spirit is *intrinsic* to the community, so to speak, hence every believer participates in the life of the Spirit.'[67] However, this is not at all Luke's presentation. For Luke, the community possesses the gift of the Spirit, because every individual within it possesses the gift of the Spirit. Every individual possesses the Spirit because it was received during initiation into the community.

A Mediated Experience

John the Baptist prophesied the Coming One would baptise in the Holy Spirit and fire (Luke 3:16). Turner argues that the Baptist's actual utterance referenced an experience of national transformation as the Spirit anointed Coming One purges the repentant and destroys the wicked. Luke then applied this purging concept at an individual level in Acts 1:5-8 and 11:15-18.[68] Regardless of how one understands the historical John, Luke's narrative links the motif of baptising in the Spirit (the theological significance of the absence of 'and fire' lies outside the narrow focus of this book on the timing, mechanism, and manifestation of Spirit-reception) to Jesus' action with respect to both the apostles/disciples and to the 3000 converts at Pentecost (Acts 1:4-5; 2:33). This is because Luke identifies the 'promise of the Father' as the experience of being 'baptised in Holy

---

[64] Daniel B. Wallace, *Greek Grammar Beyond the Basics: An Exegetical Syntax of the New Testament* (Grand Rapids: Zondervan, 1996), 544.

[65] On the iterative imperfect, *ibid.*, 546. Cf. Robertson, *Grammar*, 884. Caneday, also, views this as an iterative imperfect, 'Baptized', 27. Similarly, R.J. Knowling, 'The Acts of the Apostles', W. Robertson Nicoll (ed.), *The Expositor's Greek Testament* (London: Hodder and Stoughton, 1900), 2.217; Cf. Frederic Henry Chase, *Confirmation in the Apostolic Age* (London: Macmillan, 1909), 26.

[66] Henry Barclay Swete, *The Holy Spirit in the New Testament: A Study of Primitive Christian Teaching* (London: Macmillan, 1931), 91. So too, Mason, *Confirmation*, 19. Cf. David Pawson, *The Normal Christian Birth: How to Give New Believers a Proper Start in Life* (London: Hodder & Stoughton, 1989), 187.

[67] Zwiep, 'Understanding', 136, original italics.

[68] Turner, *Power*, 185, 187.

Spirit' (Acts 1:4-5). Luke then guarantees 'the promise' to all who repent and are immersed (2:38-39). Therefore, all converts, not just the apostles/disciples, are to experience Spirit baptism. According to 2:33, Jesus mediates the Spirit given to him by the Father, to the apostles/disciples. Therefore, in Luke's story, the Spirit originates solely with the Father, but is mediated through the Son to believers. Jesus can therefore be said, in Lukan terms, to 'baptise in the Spirit'. That Luke's Jesus, at Pentecost, is purging and purifying national Israel need not be denied.[69] At the same time, Luke individualized the purifying experience of the Spirit. Thus, in Luke's presentation, there is a purging of the nation, one individual convert at a time, as Jesus 'baptises' converts in the Holy Spirit at their baptism.

But, the focus of this book is not upon the theological implications of Jesus giving the Spirit to purify the individual and concomitantly the community, but rather upon the mechanism of impartation/Spirit baptism. Is the baptising activity limited to Jesus? Does not Acts 8 suggest that Luke's other leading characters also baptise people in the Spirit? Heidrun Gunkel is adamant that only Jesus mediates the Spirit and therefore it cannot be that the apostles do so.[70] But, that she rightly observes from Acts 2:33 that Jesus mediates the Spirit, does not require that his followers cannot also in turn mediate, or in some way facilitate, the Spirit to others. Acts 8:17 seems to show that Jesus uses mediators as part of his act of giving the Spirit. However, Luke has Peter and John *praying* that converts will receive the Spirit. Thus, they do not act independently of God. Marguerat observes:

> The prayer preliminary to the imposition of hands is important, because it shows that Peter and John did not enjoy resident power at their disposal. Praying in the place of dependence on God's power, they seek to act, while maintaining the inviolable liberty of the Spirit.[71]

Yet, despite Marguerat's valid insight that they act in dependence upon God, his conclusion that they therefore have no resident power at their disposal does not necessarily follow. That is a false antithesis. Dependence upon God does not exclude the possibility of supernatural gifting (8:20). Luke did not depict them merely invoking the Spirit to fall out of heaven upon the initiates, or activating from a distance a new dynamic of the Spirit within the converts. Luke depicted them going from individual to individual, effecting the impartation of the Spirit through the laying on of their hands. Either the handlaying caused the Spirit to

---

[69] Cf. Perry's discussion of purification of the priests in Malachi as background for Luke, *Deliverance*, 256, 258. Cf. Turner, 'Salvation', 109.

[70] Gunkel, *Geist*, 212, 114, 135.

[71] 'La prière préliminaire à l'imposition des mains est importante, car elle montre que Pierre et Jean ne jouissent pas d'un pouvoir à demeure. Prier les place en dépendance du pouvoir de Dieu, qu'ils sollicitent d'agir, tout en maintenant l'inviolable liberté de son Esprit', Marguerat, *Actes*, 296.

fall from heaven or it transmitted the Spirit from their persons to the new believers.[72] The text does not state one or the other. However, in view of 8:20, they had a resident gift, be it for effective prayer or for actual transmission. The prayer that showed their dependence upon God occurred initially. But what followed is consonant with other Lukan stories of transmission. For example, in Luke 8:46 a woman touches Jesus and power goes out from him (Luke 8:46). Luke 9:1 has a transference of power and authority from Jesus to the Twelve. Luke 10:1 continues the theme of transference of power with its allusion to Numbers 11:17, 25, where God takes the Spirit that was upon Moses and puts it upon 70 elders.[73] Similarly, the Spirit of wisdom fills Joshua because Moses had laid his hands upon him (Deuteronomy 34:9). Clearly, in the biblical world, transmission of the Spirit does not contradict 'the inviolable liberty' of the Spirit.

Did Luke, then, fully equate the ministries of Jesus and his apostles? No, for Luke maintained a distinction between the activities of his leading characters. Luke did not apply baptising terminology to the apostles. Peter and John are not said to baptise the Samaritans in the Spirit, nor Paul the Ephesians. Luke retained the baptising concept for Jesus alone as is emphasized in the programmatic Luke 3:16 prophecy. While there are similarities between the work of Jesus and that of his followers, namely, both have received the Spirit from someone else, and both are able to pass the Spirit on to others, Luke did *not* equate the work of the ascended, exalted Christ with the work of his followers. Luke denied neither the mediatory role of Jesus' apostles, nor the uniquely mediatory position of Jesus Christ. Friedrich Büchsel said it well:

> The human being does not effect for himself the Spirit, he receives him as a gift. Also the church, respectively, the apostles, does not mediate the Spirit to him so that she effects to him the Spirit, but rather so, that the exalted Lord of the church through her gives the Spirit.[74]

Luke's Conception of the Giving of the Spirit

Was the result of the handlaying merely an impartation of gifts, or activation of spiritual manifestations, and not an impartation of the Holy Spirit in a more definitive sense, that is, in the sense in which the apostles received the Spirit at

---

[72] For the latter, cf. Elmer Harry Zuagg, *A Genetic Study of the Spirit-Phenomena in the New Testament* (private edition of Ph.D. dissertation, University of Chicago, distributed by the University of Chicago Libraries, 1917), 90.

[73] See arguments by Menzies, 'Seventy', 96-97; Susan R. Garrett, *The Demise of the Devil: Magic and the Demonic in Luke's Writings* (Minneapolis: Fortress, 1989), 47-48; Keith F. Nickle, *Preaching the Gospel of Luke: Proclaiming God's Royal Rule* (Louisville: WJKP, 2000), 114. Cf. Stronstad, *Theology*, 17.

[74] 'Der Mensch erwirkt sich den Geist nicht, er erhält ihn geschenkt. Auch die Gemeinde, bezw. die Apostel, vermitteln ihm den Geist nicht so, daß sie ihm den Geist erwirkten, sondern so, daß der erhöhte Herr der Gemeinde durch sie den Geist schenkt', Büchsel, *Geist*, 256.

Pentecost? John Chrysostom (347-407[75]) reasoned that they had received, in baptism, the Spirit, 'of remission of sins', but afterwards they received the 'Spirit of miracles'.[76] Bede, writing ca. 709-716, explained that bishops, not deacons, 'transmit the Spirit, the Paraclete, to those who are baptized'.[77] In 1524, Erasmus understood it as an impartation of the Spirit after baptism had cleansed the Samaritans of their sins.[78] Calvin (1552), however, believed that the Spirit was given in baptism and Peter and John gave spiritual gifts.[79] In 1603, Theodore Beza identified the coming of the Spirit at Pentecost as an anointing with gifts of the Spirit and he understood Samaria and Ephesus the same way.[80]

Recently, David J. Williams argued from the anarthrous πνεῦμα ἅγιον in 8:15, 17, 19, writing that it was only spiritual gifts that were imparted: 'The anarthrous ... form often seems to place greater emphasis on the Spirit's activity than on his person.'[81] However, F.F. Bruce attributed, 'no particular significance' to the anarthrous construction.[82] Dunn concludes: 'The true explanation seems to be that the variation is due to stylistic reasons and lacks any real theological significance.'[83] Moreover, the text of Acts 8 does not say gifts were imparted, but the Spirit.

J.E.L. Oulton stated that the 'inward gift of the Spirit' is received in baptism while handlaying provides a special manifestation of the Spirit.[84] Charles J. Callan asserted similarly, distinguishing between the reception of the grace of the Spirit in baptism and the 'increase of grace which comes with Confirmation'.[85] Haya-Prats argues that Acts 8, 'does not deny that in the baptism administered by Philip the Samaritans could have received the Holy Spirit in an interior, invisible, sanctifying form'.[86] In a related fashion, G.R. Beasley-Murray appealed

---

[75] Philip Schaff, *A Select Library of the Nicene and Post-Nicene Fathers of the Christian Church* (Grand Rapids: Eerdmans, n.d.), 9.5.
[76] John Chrysostom, 'A Commentary on the Acts of the Apostles', Philip Schaff (ed.), *A Select Library of the Nicene and Post-Nicene Fathers of the Christian Church* (Grand Rapids: Eerdmans, n.d.), 11.1-328; Homily XVIII, 114.
[77] The Venerable Bede, trans. Lawrence T. Martin, *Commentary on the Acts of the Apostles* (Kalamazoo: Cistercian, 1989), for date of the original work, cf. xviii.; 80; cf. 153.
[78] Erasmus, *Paraphrase*, 59.
[79] Calvin, *Acts*, 137.
[80] Beza, *Testament*, 108, 115, 128.
[81] David J. Williams, *Acts* (Peabody: Hendrickson, 1990), 156.
[82] F.F. Bruce, *The Acts of the Apostles: Greek Text with Introduction and Commentary* (Leicester: Apollos, 1990), 221.
[83] Dunn, *Baptism*, 70. Similarly, Haya-Prats, *Believers*, 12-29.
[84] J.E.L. Outlon, 'The Holy Spirit, Baptism, and Laying on of Hands in Acts', *ET* 66 (1954-1955), 236-40, 239. Preuschen sees in Acts 8:19 'die charismatische Begabung', *Apostelgeschichte*, 51.
[85] Charles J. Callan, *The Acts of the Apostles with a Practical Critical Commentary for Priests and Students* (New York: Joseph F. Wagner, 1919), 62. Similarly, Kurz, *Acts*, 142-43.
[86] Haya-Prats, *Believers*, 150.

to a giving of spiritual gifts[87] and not the Spirit to explain Acts 8 and then observed: 'It is freely to be admitted that this interpretation can only tentatively be put forward, but it does seem to make sense of an otherwise incomprehensible situation without resorting to drastic emendation of Luke's narrative.'[88]

However, Luke explicitly stated that the Holy Spirit began to be received: ἐλάμβανον πνεῦμα ἅγιον. Samkutty has argued from the word ἐπιπίπτειν that Luke used it of the Spirit, not spiritual gifts (10:44; 11:15).[89] Turner points out, 'Luke understood the gift imparted by the laying on of hands (8.17-18) in parallel to the occasion of Pentecost, and thus he understood the promise of Acts 2.38-39 to be fulfilled only after the arrival of the apostles'.[90] They were not simply experiencing manifestations of an already abiding presence. In Luke's conception, they were receiving the Holy Spirit for the first time.[91] Neither Williams', Haya-Prat's, nor Beasley-Murray's arguments can avoid the fact that Luke specifically stated they had not received the Spirit before and then contrasted this with the fact of their being 'only baptised':[92]

οὐδέπω γὰρ ἦν ἐπ' οὐδενὶ αὐτῶν ἐπιπεπτωκός,
μόνον δὲ βεβαπτισμένοι ὑπῆρχον (8:16).

Furthermore, the miracles and joy manifested among the Samaritans do not supersede Luke's direct negative statement and contrast. As Turner observes, experiencing joy at miracles was, in Luke's conception, completely possible apart from the individual in question having received the Spirit.[93] Joy is therefore not an indicator of individual Spirit-reception, but of the arrival and experience of the gospel.

Correcting the Failure

Avemarie emphasized the immediacy of the response: 'The norm has such weight, that factual deviance, as soon as established, releases immediate

---

[87] So too, N.B. Stonehouse, 'Repentance, Baptism and the Gift of the Spirit', *WTJ* 13, (November 1, 1950), 1-18; 11, 13.
[88] Beasley-Murray, *Baptism*, 119-20.
[89] Samkutty, *Mission*, 171.
[90] Turner, *Power*, 368-69.
[91] So Dunn, *Baptism*, 66. Similarly, Bovon, *Luke*, 263-64; Knowling, 'Acts', 216.
[92] So too, von Baer, *Geist*, 172; Samkutty, *Mission*, 171. Witherington, also, emphasizes 8:16 as denying any prior silent reception of the Spirit, *Acts*, 289; as does Turner, 'Renewing', 286; Cf. Axel von Dobbeler, *Der Evangelist Philippus in der Geschichte des Urchristentums: Eine prosopographische Skizze* (Tübingen: Francke Verlag, 2000), 193, 212.
[93] Turner, *Power*, 368.

measures for its rectification'.[94] Avemarie read the text correctly, for the first thing Luke showed the apostles doing when they arrive is praying for people to receive the Spirit. They pray and actively lay hands upon people who have heretofore not received the Spirit. Thus, the separation between immersion and receiving the Spirit is not something Luke's apostles allow to continue, though it may occur.

Mason observed that the word, 'only', indicates, 'that Baptism was considered incomplete without it [handlaying]'.[95] Otto Bauernfeind explained 8:16 by affirming that separation of water and Spirit is not impossible. It is an exception, though not necessarily a rare one.[96] J. Alexander Findlay reasoned, 'ver. 16 implies that the Holy Spirit did not inevitably come upon baptized believers; that is communicated by the laying on of the hands of the apostles'.[97] Kirsopp Lake and Henry J. Cadbury stated that verse 16 clearly implies the Spirit is given by the apostles' handlaying, not baptism.[98] Witherington, however, takes it as a narrative aside explaining the separation of water and Spirit: 'It suggests that Theophilus would need an explanation' because 'Theophilus might have assumed from the accounts in Acts 2-3 that water and Spirit would in the normal course of affairs come more closely together.'[99]

Turner takes a different approach to the issue of 'explanation':

> It is difficult to see how the 'explanation' in 8.16b could be anything but redundant if Luke's readers normally anticipated a gap between baptism and reception of the Spirit. The deliberate (and emphasized) 'not yet' seems rather to indicate *contra-expectation*; i.e. although they were baptized (and the reader could have been expected from the story so far to assume they had received the Spirit, as the reader would at 2.41 etc.), nevertheless the Spirit had 'not yet' (for some marked reason) come upon them.[100]

However, much depends upon how large a 'gap' is meant. Do we mean a period of days or weeks, or a gap of minutes between the act of immersion and the coming of the Spirit? The contra-expectation which Luke genuinely presented

---

[94] 'Die Norm hat solches Gewicht, dass faktische Devianz, sobald festgestellt, unverzügliche Maßnahmen zu ihrer Behebung auslöst', Avemarie, *Tauferzählungen*, 140.

[95] Arthur James Mason, *The Faith of the Gospel: A Manual of Christian Doctrine* (London: Rivingtons, 1888), 279.

[96] Otto Bauernfeind, *Kommentar und Studien zur Apostelgeschichte* (Tübingen: J.C.B. Mohr, Paul Siebeck, 1980), 126.

[97] J. Alexander Findlay, *The Acts of the Apostles: A Commentary* (London: SCM, 1934), 99-100.

[98] Kirsopp Lake and Henry J. Cadbury, *The Beginnings of Christianity,* Part I: *The Acts of the Apostles,* Volume IV, *English Translation and Commentary* (London: Macmillan, 1933), 93.

[99] Witherington, *Acts*, 286.

[100] Turner, *Power*, 360, original italics. So too, Eckhard J. Schnabel, *Early Christian Mission*, Volume 1: *Jesus and the Twelve* (Downers Grove: IVP, 2004), 680. Cf. Mason, *Confirmation*, 20.

need not be of process during the baptismal ceremony, but of breakdown of the ceremony itself. Kittel pointed out that 8:16 does not read: 'The Spirit was not fallen on them, although they were baptised'.[101] Rather, it states they were 'only' baptised: 'they found themselves only in the condition of being baptised. Thus, nothing further to them had happened'.[102] There was nothing wrong with the baptism, and, Kittel reasoned, there are no grounds for saying that it was understood that they had received the Spirit in baptism and only the outward manifestation of tongues had failed. Nowhere, he argued, including Acts 2:38, is the Spirit received in the water.[103] The 'contra-expectation' cannot be that they failed to receive the Spirit in the water, but that after baptism, they had not proceeded to receive the Spirit. Kittel does not consider the possibility (it is an impression created by the narrative, but *not* explicitly confirmed) that Jesus' prayer occurred while he was still in the water (Luke 3:21-22). For Luke to say that they were 'only immersed' could suggest to the reader that the prayer which normally accompanied immersion had not been performed. However, this is *only* a possibility, because Luke did not explicitly state that no prayer was made. All that is explicitly stated is that only immersion occurred, and that the Spirit had not come.

The statement that they were in the condition of only being immersed (μόνον δὲ βεβαπτισμένοι ὑπῆρχον – 8:16) indicates either that they were not in the condition of having had anything else done to them, or that they were not in the condition of having experienced anything else. The first option suggests that prayer or handlaying were lacking. The second suggests simply that the experience of the Spirit was lacking. Dunn reasons:

> The formulation clearly indicates that whatever had gone before had been insufficient. Whether the rationale is that the Samaritans' faith fell short of full commitment to the Lord (8.12), or that baptism even 'in the name of the Lord Jesus' was in itself not enough, Luke's point is clear: it was the reception of the Spirit ... which mattered above all else.[104]

Robert M. Price writes:

> But it is the appearance of Peter and John, *not the subsequence of the confirmation* that is the unusual point for Luke. Luke gives no sign of anything being remarkable or extraordinary in baptized persons being yet without the Spirit. In fact his wording would seem to imply just the opposite. Peter and John were on their way to impart the Spirit because the Samaritans did not already have it, simply because things had

---

[101] 'Es war der Geist nicht auf sie gefallen, obschon sie getauft waren', Kittel, 'Wirkungen', 35.
[102] 'sie befanden sich nur im Zustande des Getauftseins. Es war also an ihnen nichts weiter geschehen', *Ibid.*
[103] *Ibid.*
[104] Dunn, *Acts*, 111.

not progressed so far: 'They had only been baptized.' Luke clearly seems to imply in these words that baptism would *not* by itself impart the Spirit.[105]

The text does not give the reason for Peter and John's trip to Samaria except that it was in response to the fact Samaria had received the word.[106] Here Price is inaccurate. Yet, Price is correct to note the matter of progression, or lack thereof. Most importantly, Price argues that the 'only being baptised' comment indicates that baptism (that is, mere immersion) does not communicate the Spirit. However, someone might object that mere immersion normally does impart the Spirit (according to Acts 2:38-39) and here the exceptional factor was that they were immersed and the Spirit did not come. In other words, one can say the μόνον δὲ βεβαπτισμένοι ὑπῆρχον indicates not a procedural omission, but a failure of the expected result from a procedure properly performed.

Turner takes Acts 8 as 'a clear break with the 'norm' we might expect from Acts 2.38-39'.[107] This is surely correct for the reader will not think that water alone imparts the Spirit at Acts 2, because the reader knows from Luke 3, reinforced by Jesus' link between prayer and the Spirit in Luke 11, that the coming of the Spirit is tied to the prayer element of the baptismal ceremony. Turner is right to see a 'break from the norm' in the sense that the Spirit was expected to accompany baptism *as a ceremony* and here it did not. The 'not yet' does suggest a contra-expectation. What, then, is in the reader's presupposition pool that might be expected to occur with the water of baptism? The answer from Luke 3:21-22 and Acts 2:38-39 is Spirit-reception, but not just Spirit-reception; prayer (Luke 3) is also to be expected with immersion, and it is to prayer, not mere immersion, that Spirit-reception is already linked.

Though Luke has created the expectation that prayer accompanies immersion, and though there is no necessity for Luke to repeat this expectation every time he mentions baptism, and though Luke did *not* explicitly state that Philip and/or the Samaritans did not pray for the Spirit, there are textual signals that raise the question in the reader's mind as to whether prayer accompanied the immersions in Samaria. First, Luke stated that the apostles prayed for them to receive the Spirit. Next, Luke stated that they were only baptised. The 'only baptised' statement is made in close association with the act of prayer by the apostles, suggesting that in this context, 'only' indicates immersion without prayer for the Spirit. However, despite the textual signals for a lack of prayer, Luke did not explicitly state that Philip and/or the Samaritans did not pray. All Luke asserted explicitly is that apostles prayed for people to receive the Spirit. Luke presented a problem, not receiving the Spirit. What Luke provided was a solution – not necessarily the

---

[105] Robert M. Price, 'Confirmation and Charisma', *SLJT* 23.3 (June, 1990), original italics [accessed online, 23/02/2014, no page numbers, http://www.robertmprice.mindvendor.com/ art_confirm_charis.htm].

[106] Dunn suggests that they came because the Spirit had not been received, *Acts*, 110-11.

[107] Turner, *Power*, 360.

only solution – to the problem of not receiving the Spirit. People with the gift of God to impart the Spirit do so by means of prayer and laying on of hands.

However, Jervell states: 'It is inconceivable that the Spirit is tied to the apostolic office and therefore cannot be mediated by a non-apostle such as Philip'.[108] This book does *not* claim that Philip did not have the gift of imparting/facilitating the Spirit. Luke did not explicitly affirm nor explicitly deny that gift to Philip. But Simon, though having believed and been baptised (8:13) thought that he himself did not have the power to impart the Spirit. Peter confirmed Simon's assumption by affirming that the gift of God could not be obtained by money and stating that Simon had no part in the matter under discussion – imparting the Spirit (8:20-21). Whether or not the gift to impart the Spirit is tied to the apostolic office, the text explicitly states that one particular baptised believer did not have the gift, and the text directly states the reason: his heart was not right before God. However, that there was a gift of imparting or facilitating the Spirit to others is more than Simon's mistaken idea. Peter is the one who states that money cannot buy τὴν δωρεὰν τοῦ θεοῦ. The text leaves unanswered how many individuals possessed this gift of God. The fact that Simon thought money would help him acquire the gift suggests that the gift was not readily available, but also raises the possibility that Simon had seen other Samaritans, or perhaps Philip, obtain the gift and begin laying hands upon people. Luke did not say that none of the Samaritans were involved in facilitating reception of the Spirit. Nor did Luke say Philip was not involved. Luke only explicitly stated that Simon was not involved.

John Fleter Tipei argues that handlaying was *not* the normal means of Spirit impartation. 'The use of the verb ἐπιπίπτειν [Acts 8:16] indicates that the Spirit was expected to fall directly from heaven as the δωρεὰ τοῦ θεοῦ (cf. Acts 2.2-4; 8:39 variant; 10.44-48; 11.15).'[109] First, Tipei misreads δωρεὰ τοῦ θεοῦ in Acts 8:20. Here the referent to Peter's statement is not the Spirit, but Simon's request to buy *the ability to impart* the Spirit. Second, in reference to Tipei's argument from ἐπιπίπτειν, we note that the Spirit does not fall from heaven arbitrarily without any action on the part of initiates and/or initiators. The Spirit's coming to Jesus and to others, including the apostles at Pentecost, is linked to prayer (Luke 3:21-22; 11:13; Acts 1:14; 8:15; 9:11; 10:2, 30). However, up to this point, the reader has not seen the Spirit come to new believers, but only to longstanding members of the people of God. In those two cases (Jesus and the believers at Pentecost) the Spirit comes directly from heaven without any human mediation, so Tipei is not in error to think that a reader would have an expectation of a similar direct-from-heaven experience. Third, at Samaria, Luke made no explicit statement affirming or denying 'normality' for handlaying. An interpreter cannot, at this point in the Luke-Acts narrative, say handlaying was a part of the

---

[108] Jacob Jervell, *Luke and the People of God: A New Look at Luke-Acts* (Minneapolis: Augsburg, 1972), 126.

[109] John Fleter Tipei, *The Laying on of Hands in the New Testament: Its Significance, Techniques and Effects* (Lanham: University Press of America, 2009), 203.

standard baptismal ceremony, nor can one say it was not a standard part. Luke simply presented prayer and handlaying by gifted individuals as the solution to the lack of Spirit-reception after immersion. We carefully note that Luke did not say non-apostles could not impart the Spirit. He also did not say that all apostles can impart/facilitate the Spirit. He simply affirmed that two particular apostles can.

Luke did not state that Samaria was the only case in which the Spirit did not fall at immersion. Nor did he state it was not the only case. By telling this story, he has opened the implied reader to the possibility that mere immersion will not convey the Spirit and presented a solution to that negative situation, should it occur. But, if we accept the possibility of immersion without impartation, someone might object that this means we must picture Peter and John, or other specially gifted individuals, following up the evangelistic efforts of individuals like Philip (if one assumes that Philip did not have the gift, which this book does not claim) to confirm every new convert, or at least to confirm those who somehow fail to receive the Spirit, something considered a 'practical impossibility',[110] plus being an anachronistic reading of later historical developments back into Acts,[111] and limiting the power to impart the Spirit to the apostles. Of the latter, Johannes Munck stated: 'the Holy Spirit was too important to be a prerogative of the apostles'.[112] Perhaps most serious of all, asserting the Spirit was given through the mediation of apostles, or a special class of ministers, could bring into question the sovereign autonomy of God. How can an interpreter claim that God must neces-sarily work through humans? Can God not give the Spirit to whom he wishes, when he wishes, as he wishes?

These objections must be looked at carefully. First, strange as it may seem, it is to some degree what Luke has already presented. The apostles *did* supply what Philip's ministry had not supplied when they discovered the lack. That Peter and John caused the Spirit to be received through prayer and the laying on of their hands is explicitly stated by Luke, as the foregoing discussion of focalization has demonstrated. However, Luke did not explicitly state that Philip *himself* lacked anything, or personally failed in any way. Nor did Luke state that the Samaritans failed in anything. Nevertheless, Luke did state that though Philip's converts believed in Jesus Christ and were immersed, they did not receive the Spirit. The existence of lack cannot be denied. Luke did not, however, indicate that the absence of the Spirit was the reason why the apostles came down from Jerusalem.

---

[110] Michael Patrick Whitehouse, *Manus Impositio: The Initiatory Rite of Handlaying in the Churches of Early Western Christianity* (Notre Dame: University of Notre Dame, Ph.D. dissertation, 2008), 78; so too, Beasley-Murray, *Baptism*, 114.

[111] F. Scott Spencer, *The Portrait of Philip in Acts: A Study of Roles and Relations* (Sheffield: Sheffield Academic, 1992), 218; Beasley-Murray, *Baptism*, 114.

[112] Johannes Munck, *The Acts of the Apostles* (Garden City: Doubleday, 1967), 75. Martin Dibelius, while denying the historicity of the story, takes the opposite view, Mary Ling and Paul Schubert, trans., *The Book of Acts: Form, Style, and Theology* (Minneapolis: Fortress, 2004), 43.

Ritual Water, Ritual Spirit

Luke did not say, 'for they heard the Samaritans had not yet received the Spirit'. Nor did Luke explicitly say that they followed up Philip's further ministry. The ongoing activity of the apostles as they made their way back to Jerusalem was preaching the gospel in Samaritan villages. The preaching of the gospel and the presence of the apostles was thereby combined and the reader has reason to assume, therefore, that those converts (assuming that they did make converts) received the Spirit, either in their baptismal prayer (according to the Luke 3:21-22 pattern), or from the apostles' hands just as the converts in Samaria belatedly did.

What then of Philips' ongoing ministry? Is the reader to assume that Philip (or any other evangelist) never again had a problem with converts receiving the Spirit? Luke did not state that the problem reoccurred. Nor did he state that there was never again a similar problem. Luke did not say Samaria was unique. Nor did he say Samaria was normal. Luke simply raised the possibility of converts not receiving the Spirit at immersion. Luke also provided a solution to this problem – handlaying by individuals with the gift of God to impart/facilitate the Spirit. He has not stated that only apostles have this gift. He only explicitly stated that Simon did not have the gift.

As to the final objection to handlaying by specially gifted individuals as a means of Spirit impartation/facilitation, that in Luke-Acts, God is presented as acting sovereignly in pouring out his Spirit (witness Mary, Elizabeth, Zacharias, the day of Pentecost, etc.), one must reckon with all the data. Luke's God is sovereign. But, Luke's God also acts in response to individuals. Jesus taught his followers to pray for the Spirit. God their Father would act, but not apart from their own actions. Jesus himself was praying when the Spirit descended upon him. The believers gathered in Jerusalem awaiting the Spirit were praying. Converts at Pentecost were promised the Spirit in response to repentance and immersion – human actions. In the face of persecution, the believers prayed in Acts 4, and God poured out his Spirit again. So, while Luke's God is indeed sovereign, Luke's God gives his Spirit in response to repentance, and immersion with prayer.[113] If this point is acknowledged, then the added dimension of prayer and handlaying by gifted individuals should not be seen as compromising God's sovereignty, especially when Peter attributes his power to God, thus *affirming* God's sovereignty in the matter, not deprecating it.

The Relationship Between Prayer and Handlaying

Adler raises the question as to the exact relationship between the prayer and the handlaying. Was there one general prayer and then silent handlaying? Or does the summary statement about prayer in verse 15 find instantiation in the individual action that is detailed in verse 17? That is, did they pray every time they laid hands upon someone? One could argue that Luke gave a summary statement

---

[113] The Western text of Acts 8:38-39, with its depiction of mere immersion imparting the Spirit, will be discussed below.

(they prayed) followed by a more detailed explanation about what happened each time they prayed (they were laying on hands). Adler, however, argues that τότε in verse 17 must indicate subsequence because it does so in all its other occurrences in Acts where it starts a sentence.[114] The sequence of the action seems to support Adler. There was a general prayer followed by individual handlaying.

Whichever way the relationship between prayer and handlaying is viewed, the relationship between prayer and Spirit-reception has, up to this point in the narrative, been a direct one between the candidate's prayer and the Spirit being given by God. Now someone other than the candidate prays. There is no reason to argue that this negates what the reader has already learned about Spirit-reception. Rather, it adds to it. Here the emphasis is upon the apostles praying, not upon the candidates praying. But, understood is a willingness to receive, signified by the fact that the Samaritans allowed hands to be laid upon them. The candidate must still cooperate in the initiation. The reader thus has learned about personal prayer to God for the Spirit and adds to this receptiveness to the imposition of hands by God's representatives.

The 'Delay' of the Spirit

Was the Spirit deliberately delayed, or 'suspended' (Turner),[115] or 'withheld' (Lampe, Beasley-Murray, Carson, Stott, Schreiner, Witherington, Oden, Peterson, and Longenecker),[116] by God for some specific purpose, perhaps to teach or preserve unity,[117] reconciliation, or acceptance of the other; or reassurance of acceptance by the other;[118] or because this was a unique, extraordinary situation;[119] or because it belonged to the unfolding of salvation history?[120] Dunn has suggested that it may be better not to ask why the Spirit was not received at the moment of conversion.[121] Nevertheless, in the interest of understanding Spirit-reception and interacting with the many who do ask, we will explore the question.

---

[114] Cf. Adler, *Taufe*, 60.

[115] Turner, *Power*, 374.

[116] Lampe, *Seal*, 70, Beasley-Murray, *Baptism*, 112, Carson, *Spirit*, 145. John R.W. Stott, *The Message of Acts: To the Ends of the Earth* (Leicester: IVP, 1990), 158. Stott, *Baptism*, 33. Thomas R. Schreiner, *New Testament Theology: Magnifying God in Christ* (Nottingham: Apollos, 2008), 458. Witherington, *Acts*, 289. Thomas C. Oden, *Life in the Spirit – Systematic Theology* (New York: HarperSanFrancisco, 1992), 3.183. Peterson, *Acts*, 287. Longenecker, *Acts*, 81.

[117] Carson, *Spirit*, 145, Stott, *Message*, 157-58.

[118] Lars Hartman, *'Into the Name of the Lord Jesus': Baptism in the Early Church* (Edinburgh: T&T Clark, 1997), 137; Beasley-Murray, *Baptism*, 117. Cf. F.F. Bruce, 'The Holy Spirit in the Acts of the Apostles', *Interp.* 27.2 (1973), 166-83, 174.

[119] Lampe, *Seal*, 70; Beasley-Murray, *Baptism*, 117.

[120] Marguerat, *Actes*, 300. Unfortunately, Marguerat has only a short paragraph on baptism in the Spirit in Acts 8.

[121] Dunn, 'Response', 240.

Menzies first argues that there is no case for finding Samaria to be an exception. The text does not indicate it and distance between baptism and Spirit-reception is normal for Luke. Then Menzies writes: 'It is unlikely that the Samaritans would need any further assurance of their incorporation into the church after baptism.'[122] However, his argument that baptism alone suffices to incorporate converts into the church misses Acts 2:38, where Spirit-reception is focalized at great length and assured to all who will be baptised. Would the implied reader think Luke's crowd (understood as the characters in Luke's story, not the actual, historical crowd) at Pentecost have been satisfied with mere immersion after they had witnessed such a spectacle and received such a promise? Moreover, the implied reader, having also vicariously experienced the events of Pentecost, will also not be satisfied with mere immersion.

Menzies cites Acts 11:22-24 as an example of people incorporated into the church apart from both apostolic representatives and the gift of the Spirit.[123] Certainly, this text shows that an apostle is not required to incorporate individuals into the church. But can we say the same for Spirit-reception? This text does not mention water baptism either. Can we conclude therefore that water baptism was not administered? No, because Luke did not need to repeatedly narrate established initiatory procedures. Water baptism, as well as Spirit-reception, has already been established in the narrative as belonging to the initiation of new converts (Acts 2:38). Luke only needed to mention that people were converted. The details are understood unless Luke, as in Acts 8, indicates that something has gone awry.

The 'withholding' theory, presuming as it does the direct intervention of God preventing the standard mechanism of Spirit impartation (either faith alone, or water baptism, or some combination of the two) from functioning (Beasley-Murray called it, 'a divine and sovereign restraint in the bestowal of the Spirit'[124]), is a rather large inference without any textual signals in support. Luke did not state that God withheld the Spirit. That is an argument from silence. But, let us suppose, for the sake of discussion, that it was the case. First, it means, as Mason observed, that the Spirit refused to validate Philip's baptism.[125] One can say that the sovereign God can refuse to sanction his own ordinances when he so chooses, but one must ask whether Luke presented God as doing so. Second, we would then have to bracket off the entire time that the apostles were in Samaria and in the various villages after Samaria and conclude that as soon as they got back to Jewish territory the need for handlaying ceased because the sovereign withholding of the Spirit, associated with the Samaritans, also ceased. That strains credibility, especially seeing as Luke nowhere mentioned the ceasing of the need for handlaying and the concomitant return to 'normal' salvation historical processes.

---

[122] Menzies, *Empowered*, 206.
[123] *Ibid.*
[124] Beasley-Murray, *Baptism*, 117.
[125] Mason, *Confirmation*, 23.

Moreover, how does one account for the next story of Ananias imparting/facilitating the Spirit to Saul? Regardless of *when* Saul converted, whether on the road, or at the moment Ananias laid hands upon him, or at the moment his eyes were opened, or at his baptism, Luke's text understands his Spirit-reception as *mediated* by Ananias, for Ananias states that Jesus had sent him so that Saul would regain his sight and be filled with the Holy Spirit. This is true whether Saul received the Spirit when he was healed or, more likely, later at his baptism. The case of Saul, a Jew, shows that mediation of the Spirit was not unique to Samaritans. The fact that Paul lays his hands upon the Ephesians and the Spirit comes upon them demonstrates conclusively, as will be discussed at greater length in the book's chapter 7, that handlaying was not unique to Samaria. This is not to say that handlaying was always necessary, but only that it could be necessary in places other than Samaria.

Derek W.H. Thomas asserts, however, that, 'What took place in Samaria was unique, part of the unfolding of the plan of redemption as it made its way out of Jerusalem. It is no more repeatable than Pentecost or the incarnation.'[126] Larry W. Hurtado argues:

> It is this emphasis on the Spirit's role in the gospel's progress at these crucial, dramatic points [Pentecost, Samaria, et al.] that is the author's main concern in the passages singled out in Pentecostal teaching. The author's purpose was not to provide a basis for formulating *how* the Spirit is received, but rather it seems to have been to show *that* the Spirit prompted and accompanied the progress of the gospel at every significant juncture.[127]

Peterson, similarly, denies that the various Spirit-reception accounts have individual significance because they follow the Acts 1:8 pattern.[128]

No one doubts Luke's literary device of expanding geography found in Acts 1:8 and fleshed out in the rest of the book. However, one cannot assume that simply because Luke presented events in a particular geographical sequence the *only* communicative intent Luke had was related to geography. To claim Luke was not interested in the 'how' of initiation is an argument from silence. Neither can one assume that just because some events in Luke-Acts are presented as unrepeatable, all events in Luke-Acts are presented as unrepeatable. Luke provided no indicators that the handlaying procedure followed in Acts 8 was unique, and therefore, to claim it was unique is an argument from silence.

On the other hand, there are textual signals indicating that it was more than an exceptional occurrence. It was a human procedure functioning in combination with a supernatural gifting which the human agents possessed (τὴν δωρεὰν τοῦ

---

[126] Derek W.H. Thomas, *Acts* (Phillipsburg: P&R, 2011), 228.

[127] Larry W. Hurtado, 'Normal, But Not a Norm: "Initial Evidence" and the New Testament', Gary B. McGee (ed.), *Initial Evidence: Historical and Biblical Perspectives on the Pentecostal Doctrine of Spirit Baptism* (Peabody: Hendrickson, 1991), 189-201; 194, original italics.

[128] Peterson, *Acts*, 64.

θεοῦ Acts 8:20, Peter's words, not Simon's). It was not a purely divine action, such as the catching away of Philip, where Philip is merely the object of the Spirit and is not said to possess any ongoing gift of supernatural transportation. The handlaying procedure is established by the logic of the story as a means used in an ongoing fashion by apostles to facilitate the Spirit. It cannot be viewed as the only means of Spirit impartation, but neither can it be viewed as merely an exceptional occurrence. Thus, the argument for a unique situation and/or special 'withholding' lacks textual support, is an argument from silence, contradicts the story's own logic, and consequently must be abandoned. Adler rightly states, 'In reality, the pericope of 8:14-17 is of great importance and significance for the teaching about baptism and handlaying'.[129]

The Alternate Western Reading of the Ethiopian Eunuch Story

In the Western text's reading of the Ethiopian eunuch story (Acts 8:39), when the two ascend out of the water, the Spirit falls upon the eunuch and an angel catches away Philip.

> πνευμα αγιον επεπεσεν επι τον ευνουχον,
> αγγελος δε κυριου ηρπασεν τον Φιλιππον

If we take this alternate reading, the merits of which will be discussed below, how does that affect Luke's narrative? It indicates that Philip, whose status as being able to facilitate the Spirit was previously uncertain, is clearly able to facilitate the Spirit's coming. One might object that the text does not say Philip imparted the Spirit, but only that, when Philip had come up out of the water with the eunuch, the Spirit fell. Yet, this is precisely what had *not* been happening in Philip's previous ministry (8:16). Now the Spirit falls during a baptism ceremony conducted by a gifted minister. Luke would then be expanding the ways the Spirit can come. The Spirit can come upon an initiate without handlaying and simply by submission to water baptism administered by a gifted individual. Philip had administered water baptism before and the Spirit had not fallen. Now he administers water baptism and the Spirit falls. There is no mention of prayer, yet, the account is detailed, describing going down into the water and coming back up out of the water. The implied reader has reason to think, because of the detail, that if there had been prayer, it would have been reported. We likely have an instance of mere immersion (plus a gifted minister) imparting the Spirit.

As to the merits of the Western reading, we can say that, broadly speaking, the Alexandrian text family is recognized as having priority over other text-types. The early date of the extant Alexandrian manuscripts lends weight to arguments against the Byzantine/Majority text advocates, who place their trust in numbers rather than in the age of manuscripts. However, a minority of recognized scholars have advocated a thoroughgoing eclectic approach to text criticism. That is, they

---

[129] 'In Wirklichkeit ist die Perikope 8,14-17 von großer Wichtigkeit und Bedeutung für die Lehre von Taufe und Handauflegung', Adler, *Taufe*, 110.

would elevate internal criteria, such as a particular author's style, or the presence of Atticisms, or theological concerns, over external criteria such as the date of a manuscript, or membership in a particular text-family.

The variant reading at hand is neither Alexandrian nor Byzantine, but Western. In terms of external evidence, it is supported by A (first hand correction) 36ª 94 103 307 322 323 385 453 467 610 945 1678 1739 1765 1891 2298 2818 1 *l* 1178 it[ar, l, p, (w)] vg[mss] syr[h with] * cop[meg] arm geo slav Ephraem Jerome[1/2] Augustine.[130] Major support for the Nestle-Aland reading comes from P[45] P[74] ℵ A* B C E Ψ 33[vid] as well as the Byzantine manuscripts.[131] In terms of external, documentary evidence, the Nestle-Aland text, with the support of third century P[45] as well as Sinaiticus and Vaticanus, not to mention the Byzantine corroboration, seems the clear winner, although cop[meg] is also third century. To support the Acts 8:39 variant, one would need a willingness to follow internal criteria over external.

W.A. Strange makes such an internal argument, responding first to Bruce M. Metzger and then arguing his own case. Metzger writes, in favour of the shorter text, 1) it has better manuscript support, 2) the longer text was intended 'to make explicit that the baptism of the Ethiopian was followed by the gift of the Holy Spirit',[132] 3) the longer text was meant maintain a parallel between Philip receiving instructions by an angel, and Philip being caught away by an angel.[133] First, Strange argues that the longer text's support is sufficient for it to require consideration. Second, Strange turns Metzger's point around, arguing if the shorter text were accepted, 'this would be the only place in Acts at which baptism is not associated with the reception of the Spirit'.[134] Third, while the longer text does create a parallel, that literary nicety could be the work of the author equally as well as a scribe.[135] Strange then argues that the πνεῦμα κυρίου of the shorter reading is not Lukan style, being only used in two other places in Luke-Acts (Luke 4:18 and Acts 5:9) and those are influenced by Old Testament passages. Next, a copyist could have omitted the longer reading by accidentally skipping from πνεῦμα to κυρίου. Strange then argues that, theologically, Luke was more likely to use ἄγγελος κυρίου than πνεῦμα κυρίου because, 'The Spirit in Luke always acts through human agents, and never as a physical agent in his own right.'[136] He compares Luke 4:1 and Mark 1:12, where Jesus is led, not cast, by the Spirit, and Matthew 1:18, 20 and Luke 1:35, suggesting that Luke is not as

---

[130] Cf. Bruce M. Metzger, *A Textual Commentary on the Greek New Testament* (Stuttgart: Deutsche Bibelgesellschaft, 1994), 316; Nestle-Aland, *Novum Testamentum Graece* 27 (Stuttgart: Deutsche Bibelgesellschaft, 1993), 406; Barbara Aland, et al., *The Greek New Testament* (Stuttgart: Deutsche Bibelgesellschaft, 2012), 439.
[131] Philip W. Comfort, *New Testament Text and Translation Commentary* (Carol Stream: Tyndale, 2008), 364.
[132] Metzger, *Commentary*, 316.
[133] *Ibid.*
[134] W.A. Strange, *The Problem of the Text of Acts* (Cambridge: CUP, 1992), 66.
[135] *Ibid.*
[136] *Ibid.*, 67.

'explicit' as Matthew. Finally, he notes that ἄγγελος κυρίου is used by Luke six times and several times is used with reference to physical action (apostles are rescued, 5:19; Peter is rescued, 12:7, Herod is killed, 12:23).[137] One other argument may be added to Strange. Matthew Black, following P.H. Menoud, argues that the longer text was omitted because, 'its inclusion contradicts the narrative a few verses earlier, which implies that the Spirit came only through the hands of the apostles'.[138]

Strange's argument is intriguing. Certainly, it would make internal sense for ἄγγελος κυρίου to catch Philip away. Also, one can see how a scribe could omit the longer reading by skipping from πνεῦμα to κυρίου. However, it is hard to say that in Luke 1:35 the Spirit is not effecting an outcome in the physical world. Strange's rebuttals to Metzger's internal arguments are reasonable, but the arguments could go either way. Neither side makes a conclusive case. Black's argument is reasonable, but speculative. Strange, however, seems to downplay the issue of manuscript support. Nevertheless, if one asks what best accounts for the existence of both variants, accidental omission early in the transmission of the text effectively explains the shorter reading and its broad manuscript support. However, it would take a clever scribe to realize that by separating πνεῦμα from κυρίου one could insert an alternate version of events. To that, one could argue that the scribes were both clever and theologically compelled to supply the Spirit to the eunuch, or to associate the Spirit immediately with water baptism. In conclusion, though the external evidence sides with the shorter reading, the internal considerations are strong enough to warrant viewing both versions as equally plausible. This means that the narrative analysis must take both alternatives into account.

Menzies' View of Handlaying as Commissioning for Service

Returning to the discussion of the Samaria story, Menzies argues that, 'Acts 8.4-25 poses an insoluble problem for those who maintain that Luke establishes a necessary link between baptism/Christian initiation and the gift of the Spirit.'[139] If Christian initiation is defined strictly as immersion, or as forgiveness of sins and immersion, this is true. Acts 8 does shatter the conception that the Spirit is given solely by immersion, a conception which was never Luke's to begin with, as Luke 3:21-22 shows. Baptism for Luke is more than just immersion, it includes prayer. However, though the reader has reason to expect prayer to have accompanied the Samaritan's baptism, the fact that they did not receive the Spirit, when the reader knows that Spirit-reception is tied to prayer, raises the question as to whether they prayed. Because Luke neither explicitly affirmed nor denied

---

[137] *Ibid.*, 67-68.

[138] Matthew Black, 'The Holy Spirit in the Western Text of Acts', Eldon Jay Epp and Gordon D. Fee (eds), *New Testament Textual Criticism, Its Significance for Exegesis: Essays in Honour of Bruce M. Metzger* (Oxford: Clarendon, 1981), 159-70; 167.

[139] Menzies, *Empowered*, 211.

that the Samaritans prayed at their baptism, no conclusions can be drawn about the effectiveness of immersion *and* prayer. We do not know whether the Samaritans prayed and did not receive, or did not even pray.

However, the fact of delay in receiving the Spirit does not in itself indicate that the Spirit was not considered integral to Christian initiation, just that initiation could be viewed as a process and not as split-second event. Menzies affirms:

> The inescapable conclusion which emerges from the discussion above is that for Luke the gift of the Spirit does not constitute a Christian. On the contrary, the Spirit is a supplementary gift given to Christians, those who have already been incorporated into the community of salvation.[140]

However, this statement assumes precisely what it tries to argue, namely, that the Spirit is not part of Christian initiation. There is no statement by Luke telling us that the Samaritans were fully initiated after their baptism. Rather, Luke showed their deficit and what was done to resolve it. Menzies fails to recognize the process character of Christian initiation in Luke-Acts.

Because Menzies has rejected Christian initiation as the place and purpose of Spirit-reception, he has had to find a different place and purpose for it. He sees Spirit-reception in Acts 8 as located subsequent to initiation and for the purpose of commissioning for ministry. He argues that handlaying is linked with healing (9:12, 17; 28:8) and with 'commissioning of believers for service in the church's mission (6.6; 13.3; cf. 9.17)'.[141] He also states that handlaying is linked with Spirit-reception certainly in 8:17 and 19:6, and 'probably' in 9:17, but argues that the Spirit comes separate from handlaying and handlaying does not always impart the Spirit. He therefore concludes that imparting the Spirit is not an 'integral' function of the rite. Rather, the key functions of handlaying are healing and commissioning for service. With imparting the Spirit deemed a less important/likely function, and observing that in Acts 8 and 19 the rite is not used for healing, he determines that at Samaria and Ephesus, handlaying must indicate a 'commissioning ceremony': 'I therefore suggest that Peter and John incorporate the Samaritans, not into the church, but into the missionary enterprise of the church.'[142]

The fact that the Spirit can be given without handlaying, and that handlaying can have other purposes besides Spirit impartation/facilitation, does not detract from the fact that handlaying is used to facilitate the Spirit (without dispute at 8:17 and 19:6). Menzies wishes to make commissioning and healing more 'integral' to handlaying than facilitating the Spirit, yet handlaying can have a Spirit facilitation function. If this function is performed in Acts 8, and without doubt it is, then why the need to propose another function, commissioning? Menzies does not appeal to signals in the text to substantiate his claim. As Atkinson has argued, healing is not always done by handlaying (Luke 6:10, 19; 7:7), and handlaying

---

[140] *Ibid.*
[141] *Ibid.*, 212.
[142] *Ibid.*

does not always heal (8:17; 19:6).[143] Therefore, by Menzies' logic, healing is not integral to handlaying, but only supplementary. However, surely this is a misunderstanding of the nature of handlaying. Handlaying has no meaning in itself, but must be inserted into a rite, as a word in a sentence, to have meaning. Handlaying is an act that can be performed in several rites. The ritual context determines the meaning of the handlaying act and makes it a rite. This is especially so when we remember the Lukan emphasis upon power resident within the individual (Luke 6:19; 8:46; cf. 5:17). Luke did not present power in a ritual *per se*, but rather power in the person. Power in the person, not the rite, is more accurate to Luke's world view. Luke explicitly stated that the transfer of handkerchiefs and aprons from Paul to others to effect healing was extraordinary. Luke did not state that handlaying to transmit power was extraordinary. But the idea is that an individual has resident power, which can be transmitted to another person directly or via an object, not that a ritual act in itself has power, belongs to Luke's worldview. This helps to explain some of the variation within Luke-Acts regarding Spirit impartation/facilitation. Success does not lie in performing the ritual perfectly, success lies in having power to impart, to transfer the Spirit, or at minimum, power to facilitate the transference of the Spirit from God to the individual. Thus, the ritual has a degree of flexibility. As has already been discussed in response to Marguerat, that Peter and John prayed, showing dependence upon God, does not deny to them resident power, for Peter refers to the ability to impart/facilitate the Spirit as the gift of God.

Samaria: Simply Possible

According to Conzelmann, 'The laying on of hands must have been customary at baptism, even if Tertullian is the first to state it explicitly (*Bapt.* 8).'[144] Jervell also observes, 'Handlaying is more than a symbolic rite, because the Spirit is actually given through it.'[145] Lake accounted for the seemingly conflicting data on baptism by concluding that Acts 8 should be taken as 'the starting-point', because it is, 'the most definite of all the passages'.[146] However, Witherington objects that the fact of variety in Luke's presentation makes it impossible to claim that he had any kind of norm. He argues, 'Had Luke really been the advocate of 'early Catholicism' some have thought he was, we would expect more clarity and uniformity in the portrayal of these matters.'[147] However, that Luke identified

---

[143] Atkinson, *Baptism*, 77-78.

[144] Hans Conzelmann, *Acts of the Apostles: A Commentary on the Acts of the Apostles* (Philadelphia: Fortress, 1987), 65.

[145] 'Die Handauflegung ist mehr als ein symbolischer Ritus, denn der Geist wird tatsächlich dadurch gegeben', Jervell, *Apostelgeschichte*, 264.

[146] Lake, 'Baptism', 383; A.J. Maclean proceeds similarly, 'Baptism', James Hastings (ed.), *Dictionary of the Apostolic Church* (Edinburgh: T&T. Clark, 1915), 1.128-36; 132.

[147] Witherington, *Acts*, 289-90.

alternative procedures and possibilities does not negate the *possibility* that he also presented a norm. It is not unsurprising that a standard procedure would be augmented by alternatives.

Jean Amougou-Atangana also rejects the idea of normative Samaria:

> Of paramount importance is the fact that in the Pentecost report itself there is no discussion of Spirit-mediating handlaying. Had Luke primarily discoursed about the Spirit and his impartation through handlaying, then he would have certainly mentioned this rite, because in other passages he is certainly aware of handlaying.[148]

Amougou-Atangana does not observe the potential impact of the progressive development of the ER for baptism; Luke already linked Spirit-reception to prayer at the time of immersion. Handlaying could be read as a progressive development of the idea of prayer. The lack of mention of handlaying in Acts 2 could be explained in that there Luke described the coming of the Spirit, not the act of imparting/facilitating the Spirit. In chapter 8 he describes the power to impart/facilitate the Spirit via handlaying. Contrary to Amougou-Atangana, there is no reason that he had to have mentioned handlaying in Acts 2 when his focus was elsewhere. This is, however, only a potential outcome of the narrative. Luke, in chapter 8, did not state that Samaria is the exclusive means of Spirit impartation/facilitation, nor even the typical means. Neither did Luke state it is an exceptional means or unique to this occasion. The fact that this is the first presentation of Spirit-reception by new converts also does not require the reader to understand it as the standard means. The reader at this stage of the narrative is simply exposed to the reality of prayer and handlaying by apostles as a means of Spirit impartation/facilitation. The text constructs neither normativity nor exceptionality.

Like Witherington, Turner does not favour normativity for Samaria. Luke may have viewed the distancing of Spirit-reception from baptism as 'anomalous', but it was not 'problematic' because of the presence of the Spirit-filled Philip.[149] There is no reason to reject this view. The statement that the Samaritans were only immersed immediately follows the statement that the Spirit had not fallen, suggesting that to be 'only immersed' explains why the Spirit had not fallen. At minimum, it means that immersion does not always transmit the Spirit. But, in the narrative up to this point, Luke has led the reader to associate Spirit-reception with immersion (Acts 2:38), yet not with immersion alone, but with a unitary event composed of immersion in water and prayer (Luke 3:21-22). Here, in Acts 8, individuals are immersed, but without the Spirit. For a reader who expects

---

[148] 'Von höchster Wichtigkeit ist die Tatsache, daß im Pfingstbericht selbst von keiner geistmitteilenden Handauflegung die Rede ist. Wäre es Lukas hauptsächlich um den Geist und seine Mitteilung durch die Handauflegung gegangen, dann hätte er diesen Ritus sicherlich erwähnt, da er ja an anderer Stelle die Handauflegung kennt', Jean Amougou-Atangana, *Ein Sakrament Des Geistempfangs? Zum Verhältnis Von Taufe Und Firmung* (Freiburg: Herder, 1974), 82.

[149] Turner, *Power*, 374.

prayer to immediately follow immersion and who ties Spirit-reception to that prayer, the statement that the Samaritans had not received the Spirit but were only immersed raises the question as to whether any prayer had taken place. However, caution must be exercised, because Luke did not explicitly state that there had been no prayer. Luke's story only raises the possibility that the atypical element was the lack of prayer. Luke did not confirm that. The same applies to the handlaying of the apostles. The fact that it follows immediately after the explanation of why they had not received raises the possibility that handlaying was also something the Samaritans lacked. However, this is again only a possibility for Luke did not explicitly state that handlaying was missing, nor did Luke say that Philip had not laid hands upon the Samaritans.

How then is the implied reader expected to process the prayer and handlaying by Peter and John? How does handlaying at Samaria relate to Lukan diversity? Avemarie's struggle with this question highlights how sequentially progressive reading can contribute towards a possible resolution. With precision Avemarie laid bare the fact that handlaying is significant for Luke. He was unable, however, to resolve the apparent conundrum his data presented: does the handlaying rite belong to baptism as a standard, integral sub-element, or is it an emergency procedure to be employed only when water baptism fails to impart the Spirit? Neither case, he observed, is compatible with the Catholic position.[150] He himself could not decide which to choose. Avemarie analyzed the problem in terms of numbers: 'only two of the baptism reports speak of a handlaying'.[151] He categorized the episodes, but did not analyse them in terms of their progressive development.

Viewed according to its natural sequence, the Pentecost story focuses reader attention upon the speaking in tongues while the Samaritan story focuses upon the laying on of hands. The Pentecost story did now show converts receiving the Spirit and thus left a gap as to precisely how that happens. The reader of Acts 8 is faced with the possibility that prayer and handlaying fills in that gap. Gerhard Barth asserts, by the time of the Samaria incident, the impartation of the Spirit via handlaying during the baptismal celebration was, 'the obviously already customary liturgical usage'[152] However, this can *only* be a possibility, as it is not confirmed directly by Luke, neither in the Samaritan story nor later with the Ephesians. Nevertheless, the reader must reckon, at this point in the narrative, with that scenario. Reading sequentially and progressively thus presents to the implied reader a *possible* scenario. If Luke were to present water baptism and handlaying together in one scene, that would act to strengthen the narrative potential found in Acts 8. The rereader is certainly aware that the Ephesian Twelve

---

[150] Avemarie, *Tauferzählungen*, 167. Cf. Büchsel, who argues similarly, *Geist*, 257.

[151] 'nur zwei der Taufberichte sprechen von einer Handauflegung', Avemarie, *Tauferzählungen*, 167.

[152] 'der offenbar bereits übliche liturgische Brauch', Gerhard Barth, *Die Taufe in frühchristlicher Zeit* (Neukirchen-Vluyn: Neukirchener Verlag, 2002 [1981]), 2.61.

story presents just such a unified immersion/handlaying scene, and this book will address the impact of Acts 19 on the overall narrative. However, from the Samaria story alone, the initial reader is *not* able to conclude that prayer and handlaying is the standard initiation rite because there is the possibility that it is only an emergency procedure. Prayer and handlaying are one means of communicating the Spirit. That is all the implied reader can draw from Acts 8.

Conclusion

The ER for baptism contains immersion with prayer for the Spirit, therefore, the reader of Acts 8 has an expectation that prayer would accompany the Samaritans' immersions. The fact that the Spirit did not come to them raises the question as to whether they prayed. Luke neither affirmed nor denied that the Samaritans, or Philip, prayed. He did affirm that Peter and John prayed for them and laid hands upon them and they thereby received the Spirit. Thus, Luke did not explicitly state why the Spirit did not come. Luke simply provided a solution for the problem. The narrative focalizes handlaying and identifies it as the means, in this story, by which the coming of the Spirit was effected. The fact that Peter and John prayed shows that their handlaying was not conducted independently of God, but in dependence upon God. Luke's emphasis upon the gift of God to give the Spirit also demonstrates that though the gift is possessed by an individual, it is not possessed apart from the sovereign discretion of God.

Samaria presents a problem, the fact the immersion did not result in the Spirit's arrival, and a solution to that problem, namely prayer and handlaying by gifted individuals. By only showing apostles performing the handlaying rite, Luke created the initial impression that this is the prerogative of apostles. However, the implied reader knows that Luke did not state that only Peter and John were gifted, nor did he state that others were gifted. He only explicitly stated that Simon was not so gifted. This apostles-only impression is therefore subject to the possibility of modification. The rereader knows that it is, in fact, modified in the Ananias/Saul story. In terms of the failure of the Spirit to come, at this point in the Luke-Acts narrative, the reader does not know if there are other solutions to the problem, or if Samaria represents the sole answer. The whole ER for initiation must be allowed to develop before any conclusions about a standard initiation procedure can be drawn.

In the next chapter, with regard to the matter of Spirit-reception, Luke will deal with the question of whether only apostles can facilitate the Spirit. Then he will show people receiving the Spirit without hands being laid on them, but not without the presence of a gifted individual. Finally, he will show belief, immersion, and handlaying all together, again with laying on of hands being the aspect of initiation that facilitates the Spirit, taking place under the ministry of Paul as he had earlier shown it under the ministry of Peter.

Chapter 6

Saul's Conversion and Cornelius' House
Continuing the ER for Initiation

Section 1: Saul's Initiation by a Local Initiator

Introduction

Acts 9 expands slightly upon the now already significant ER for Spirit-reception. Saul's initiation corrects for the reader the idea that only an apostle can facilitate the Spirit and reemphasizes the idea of laying on of hands. The focus of Saul's initiation does not lie upon Spirit-reception, however. Luke centred the Acts 9 narrative around the physical loss and restoration of Saul's sight through the mediation of Ananias. The story as Luke presented it in Acts 22 and 26 will also be evaluated here. For narratological analysis of all three stories using Sternberg's categories of repetition, see the works of Witherup and Daniel Marguerat.[1]

Narrative Analysis

First Story (Acts 9:1-18)

We learn in the exposition that Saul is murderously opposed to the disciples of the Lord and that he has documentary authority from the high priest to bring such disciples as prisoners to Jerusalem. The inciting moment, the event that starts the story, occurs when a shaft of heavenly light knocks him to the ground. The action rises through dialogue with the risen Jesus. Jesus accuses him. Saul asks respectfully who it is that speaks. Jesus identifies himself and gives a command with the promise that more instructions will follow. Saul gets up from the ground blinded and must be led into Damascus. This encounter with Jesus on the road leaves several things to be resolved; namely, Saul's physical blindness and his reaction to Jesus. Is he converted or not? The reader must wait while Saul fasts.

---

[1] Witherup, 'Redundancy', 84. Daniel Marguerat, trans. Ken McKinney, Gregory J. Laughery, and Richard Bauckham, *The First Christian Historian, Writing the 'Acts of the Apostles'* (Cambridge: CUP, 2002), 179-204. Donald L. Jones only exegetes the first of the three stories and therefore does not fully address the concept of 'Lord' in Saul's conversion, 'The Title *Kyrios* in Luke-Acts', *SBL Seminar Papers* (1974), 2.85-101; 95-96.

Jesus' instructions to Ananias in a vision[2] shed light on Saul's true mental state. Jesus declares, 'For behold, he is praying' (v. 11), an ironic contrast with his previous 'breathing threat and murder' (9:1). Atkinson objects that, 'Paul's praying was no indication of prior commitment to Jesus: all Jews prayed!'[3] Gaventa is uncertain about whether the prayer indicates faith on Saul's part.[4] However, this statement was made by Jesus himself as the first basis for Ananias' going to meet him.[5] His prayer was approved by Jesus, and therefore no longer belongs to the prayer of those opposed to the Jesus community. Saul's having seen a vision with Ananias laying his hand upon him so he can receive sight provided a second basis for Ananias' journey. Jesus has identified Saul as someone 'safe' to initiate, who is already on a trajectory of entrance into the community which he once persecuted.[6] He has, at the same time, identified Ananias as someone already capable of healing and initiating Saul, as Luke did not present Ananias as receiving from Jesus either the ability to heal or 'the gift of God' to facilitate the Spirit which the apostles in Acts 8 exercised.

Now Saul has a different recommendation than he had previously from the high priest. Ananias obeys his vision of Jesus, lays his hands upon Saul, calls him 'brother'[7] and declares that the Lord Jesus sent him that he may regain his sight and receive the Holy Spirit. This is repetition with addition – Luke at first reported Jesus speaking only about healing, but Ananias says that the Lord sent him both for healing and facilitation of the Spirit. Thus, it is the Lord himself who deemed Saul a proper candidate to receive the Holy Spirit. The text states nothing about Saul making up his mind, or finally reaching a decision for Christ. The text instead describes an approved candidate for community initiation submitting to that initiation. Saul allowing Ananias, the former enemy, to pray over him, was an act of submission both to the particular believer in Jesus, and to the One who originally gave Saul the vision of that believer. Jesus' positive opinion of the candidate is confirmed by Saul's submissive behaviour. At this climactic

---

[2] Receiving a vision belongs to the 'prophetic Spirit upon God's eschatological people' ER, and, thus, does not qualify Ananias as an apostle in Luke's conception. Apostleship is not necessary to impart the Spirit. Cf. F.F. Bruce, *Acts*, 188-89.

[3] Atkinson, *Baptism*, 46.

[4] Gaventa, *Darkness*, 62.

[5] In 22:10 Saul knows it is Jesus who is speaking and asks Jesus, 'What should I do, Lord?' However, this submission of Saul to Jesus only becomes known to the reader later in the story. It is only valid when considering the chapter 9 text from a multiple readings perspective.

[6] For a ritual studies analysis of Acts 9, cf. Steven C. Muir, *Healing, Initiation and Community in Luke-Acts: A Comparative Analysis* (Ph.D. dissertation, The University of Ottawa, 1998), 1-14. For the importance of community, cf. Philip H. Kern, 'Paul's Conversion and Luke's Portrayal of Character in Acts 8-10,' *TynB* 54.2 (2003), 63-80; 72.

[7] Dunn and Turner's objection that 'brother' is unclear misses a key step in the story's development, namely that Jesus had already identified Saul as ready to be initiated. Dunn, *Acts*, 123; Turner, *Power*, 375.

point something like scales falls from Saul's eyes and he sees again, gets up, and is baptised.

Second Story (Acts 22:3-16)

This recounting of the story takes place in the context of Paul's defence before the Jewish crowd in Jerusalem. Of particular interest to the question of initiation is the sequence of Jesus identifying himself and Paul calling him Lord. Whereas in Acts 9 the reader is left in uncertainty as to Saul's response to Jesus, in Acts 22 Saul calls Jesus Lord *after* Jesus has identified himself, and then Saul specifically asks for instructions on what to do from the one he just called Lord. It becomes much more difficult to relegate Saul's response to a mere term of respect, 'sir'. At first, in verse eight, Saul does not know to whom he speaks and a rendering of, 'Who are you, sir?' is reasonable. But then Jesus identifies himself as the one being persecuted, and after that identification, Saul says, 'What should I do, κύριε?' For Saul to ask instructions from the very one whom he set out with such vigour to persecute suggests, against Dunn,[8] more than a polite, but still uncommitted 'sir'. Here 'Lord' would be more appropriate. His request shows submission to this Lord's authority.[9] The Acts 22 text makes no mention of handlaying or receiving the Spirit. Instead, there is a monologue from Ananias about Saul's privilege in seeing and hearing Jesus and Saul's missionary call.

Ananias then charges Saul to be immersed: ἀναστὰς βάπτισαι καὶ ἀπόλουσαι τὰς ἁμαρτίας σου ἐπικαλεσάμενος τὸ ὄνομα αὐτοῦ. Washing away sins is clearly attached to immersion. However, should 'calling on his name' be understood as the significance of the act of immersion, i.e., that immersion is a ritualized prayer, or that Paul was expected to pray at the time he was immersed. The only precursor to this story is Jesus' baptism, where prayer took place apparently in the waters of Jordan, but was not equated with the act of immersion. With the reader already amenable to the idea of prayer at the time of baptism, there is no reason to think that Saul's immersion itself was understood as ritual prayer. The reader expects Saul to pray *to Jesus* in addition to being immersed.

Third Story (Acts 26:9-20)

Finally, Acts 26 recounts Paul's defence before King Agrippa. Here the focus is strictly upon the vision of Jesus. No mention of Ananias, baptism or Spirit-reception is made. The point of interest for the study of initiation lies in the extent to which Jesus instructs Saul regarding his missional purpose in life, and Saul's reflection before King Agrippa that he was, 'not disobedient to the heavenly vision' (26:19). Here Luke gave the impression that the turning point for Saul was the vision and nothing else.

---

[8] Dunn, *Baptism*, 73-74.
[9] Similarly, Charles W. Hedrick, 'Paul's Conversion/Call: A Comparative Analysis of the Three Reports in Acts,' *JBL* 100.3 (September, 1981), 415-32; 424.

Theological Analysis

Turner allows the probability that Saul had faith in Jesus before Ananias arrived, but, 'his conversional *commitment* was yet to be formalized in baptism'.[10] The Acts 9 text makes the scales falling from Saul's eyes the high point of the story, while baptism in water comes anticlimactically. Luke did not narrate the receiving of the Spirit which Ananias said he had come to accomplish. For Dunn, this omission forms an impassable barrier to understanding Luke's view of Christian initiation and renders 9:17-18 unusable 'as positive evidence for the relationship either between Spirit-baptism and water-baptism, or between the gift of the Spirit and the laying on of hands'.[11] Though Eckey assumes Saul received the Spirit before his baptism, Haya-Prats writes that, 'Nothing indicates to us, however, at what point Paul received the Spirit'.[12] Robinson likewise writes that the text is 'ambiguous'.[13] Avemarie was uncertain whether it comes at the laying on of hands, or at the baptism.[14] Hur seeks to avoid the idea that the Spirit was communicated through a human and instead states that: 'The narrative suggests that Saul's reception of the Spirit is caused by the risen Lord Jesus (9:17).'[15] Similarly, Turner doubts whether laying on of hands here communicates the Spirit and assumes 'that Paul receives the Spirit either at or immediately beyond the water rite (in accordance with the paradigm set forth in 2.38)'.[16]

The narrative progression must be assessed. The Spirit-reception scene just prior to this focused much attention upon the function of laying on of hands to impart/facilitate the Spirit. Thus, the reader who has read the baptism of Jesus, the teaching on prayer, and the Pentecost sermon, and has the handlaying story of Acts 8:15-19 fresh in mind, might conclude that Saul received the Spirit when Ananias laid hands upon him and that he was baptised in water subsequent to receiving the Spirit. However, the prior narrative *also* has a clearly defined sequence of baptism and then subsequent Spirit-reception which would guide the reader to think that Spirit-reception would occur after baptism and that this initial handlaying was for healing only. Since Ananias' hands have been emphasized in the narrative, and since handlaying was heavily emphasized in the prior Samaria story, the implied reader has some expectation that they might be used again after baptism to impart/facilitate the Spirit. Luke made no explicit statement to that effect, however.

What is clearly present is Sternberg's repetition with truncation, the same device as in the Pentecost story where Peter promises that those who repent and are baptised will receive the Spirit, yet Luke did not narrate the Spirit-reception of

---

[10] Turner, *Power*, 375, original italics.
[11] Dunn, *Baptism*, 78. So too, Dunn, *Acts*, 124.
[12] Eckey, *Apostelgeschichte 1,1-15,35*, 292; Haya-Prats, *Believers*, 149.
[13] Robinson, *Hands*, 242.
[14] Avemarie, *Tauferzählungen*, 170-71.
[15] Hur, *Reading*, 243-44.
[16] Turner, *Power*, 376.

the 3000. Peter said it would happen and the reader has no textual reason to doubt it. We also see Sternberg's repetition with addition, for Jesus speaks only of healing, but Ananias speaks of both healing and imparting the Spirit.[17] Ananias said Saul would receive the Spirit, he lays hands upon Saul, an act the narrator has recently identified as imparting/facilitating the Spirit, and therefore the reader has good reason to think that Ananias has the power to impart/facilitate the Spirit in the laying on of hands. The question is whether Saul receives the Spirit before baptism at the healing, or has hands laid on him again after the baptism. However, Luke focused the story on the restoration of Saul's sight, and not on the reception of the Spirit. Without a specific statement to contravene the already well-established sequence of immersion followed by Spirit-reception, it becomes difficult to postulate Saul receiving the Spirit prior to his baptism.

The Acts 22 account buttresses the post-immersion argument, for there Paul remembers Ananias telling him to wash away his sins in baptism, calling upon the name of the Lord. Anthony A. Hoekema made a point that, given the principles of narratology, must be considered. He related Acts 2:21, καὶ ἔσται πᾶς ὃς ἂν ἐπικαλέσηται τὸ ὄνομα κυρίου σωθήσεται, with Acts 22:16, ἐπικαλεσάμενος τὸ ὄνομα αὐτοῦ. Hoekema wrote:

> Putting these two passages together, we hear Luke telling us, first, that the decisive step in being saved is to call upon the name of the Lord; and, second, that Saul had not yet taken that step when Ananias urged him to do so. We conclude that Saul's conversion was not an instantaneous happening but a three-day experience. Saul's being filled with the Spirit at the end of the three days, therefore, must not be understood as a 'Spirit-baptism' which occurred after his conversion, but as an integral aspect of his conversion.[18]

While Hoekema did not address the issue of Saul calling Jesus κύριος and asking for instructions after Jesus has identified himself, all information that the reader has and Ananias may not have, Hoekema did bring out the perspective of the Ananias character. For Ananias, regardless of the intensity of Saul's encounter with Jesus, Saul still needed to be baptised and call on the name of the Lord. Immersion and prayer go together for Ananias. Given the reader's knowledge of the submission of Saul to Jesus as Lord prior to this point, it becomes a valid question as to whether the washing away of sins was simply standard phraseology associated with water baptism since the time of John the Baptist, or whether Luke thought that Saul actually needed his sins forgiven. Turner's analysis cited above, that, 'his conversional *commitment* was yet to be formalized in baptism',[19] seems sufficient explanation for Ananias' charge. Baptism 'formalized' the submission that Saul had already demonstrated. Saul had previously asked Jesus

---

[17] Cf. Darrell L. Bock, 'here a non-apostle is mediator of the Spirit', *Acts* (Grand Rapids: Baker Academic, 2007), 362. So too, Fitzmyer, 'Saul receives through the mediation of Ananias the gift of the Spirit', *Acts*, 429.

[18] Anthony A. Hoekema, *Holy Spirit Baptism* (Exeter: Paternoster, 1972, 1972), 39.

[19] Turner, *Power*, 375, original italics.

what to do and Jesus had responded that he would be told what to do. Now, Ananias tells him to be baptised. Saul is presented as going through the ritual that every repentant sinner goes through, even though at the same time Acts 22 shows him to be submissive to the person of Jesus from the moment Jesus identifies himself. In the Cornelius story, Luke made clear that forgiveness of sins is not tied to water baptism, but to the moment of belief, for Cornelius and his friends received the Spirit precisely when Peter spoke of forgiveness of sins (10:43-44). Only afterwards were they baptised. Nevertheless, Hoekema's desire to view Saul's conversion as a 'three-day experience' fits well with the concept of the ritual process. Chapter 22 verse 10's τί ποιήσω, κύριε; makes clear that there was a moment of decision for Saul, and chapter 26's version reinforces this, but 22:16's ἀναστὰς βάπτισαι shows that this decision had to be followed by humble submission to the same initiation ritual as with every other convert.

Given the information that Acts 22 and 26 add to Acts 9, Turner's view, then, should be accepted: 'Paul receives the Spirit either at or immediately beyond the water rite (in accordance with the paradigm set forth in 2.38)'.[20] To this need only be added that the paradigm of 2:38 has been potentially supplemented by 8:17-19's depiction of the Spirit being imparted/facilitated by handlaying. Process also plays a role here. Turner observes that, 'we do not find in this narrative an instance of reception of the Spirit that is clearly subsequent to some conversion-initiation complex'.[21] The Spirit comes as an element within the ritual initiation process. Thus it is a 'complex', not a 'moment'. It is a process.

Conclusion

In summary, we have community initiation conducted by a non-apostle, but, nevertheless, one who has had a vision of Jesus; laying on of hands associated with healing and possibly with reception of the Spirit; and water baptism apparently followed by Spirit-reception. While Ananias is not one of the Twelve, as Peter and John are, he is still commissioned directly by Jesus for the task of healing and facilitating the Spirit. Additionally, Ananias represents the resolution to the logistical problem of 'gifted' individuals needed to follow up evangelistic efforts. Here is a local community that has within it a non-apostle who can impart/facilitate the Spirit. Finally, this story, when read together with the version in Acts 22, does not differ from the accumulated picture of Luke 3:21-22, Acts 2:38, and Acts 8 in viewing Spirit-reception as following immersion.

---

[20] *Ibid.*, 376. Cf. Walter Radl, '"Firmung" im Neuen Testament?' *IKaZ* (1982), 427-33; 430.
[21] Turner, *Power*, 375.

Section 2: Cornelius' Initiation (Acts 10, 11 & 15)

Introduction

Far from offering a view of initiation in conflict with what has gone before, the Cornelius episode fits nicely among the various possibilities within the Spirit-reception ER. As in Acts 8, impartation of the Spirit does not occur without the presence of an individual known within the narrative as gifted in facilitating Spirit-reception. Prayer in general, both on the part of the initiator and the initiate, plays a preparatory (though not immediate) role in Spirit-reception. The 'new' element introduced by Luke is the idea of God's ability to intervene directly during the preaching of the word before any rituals are even implemented. Because the earlier Samaritan story presented Peter as a minister specially gifted to impart/facilitate the Spirit, the implied reader has grounds for thinking that the sudden descent of the Spirit at Cornelius' house is linked to Peter's gifting. The story only raises the possibility; however, Luke did not explicitly attribute it to Peter's gifting.

Luke focalized the initiates' 'speaking with tongues and magnifying God', emphasizing this behaviour, or combination of behaviours, as the factor by which community leaders identify Spirit-reception and the common denominator between Cornelius' house and Pentecost. In a narrative aside, Luke presented the leaders evaluating new initiates' experiences by the apostolic standard of Pentecost. The phrase, 'speaking with tongues and magnifying God', contains the same elements as on the day of Pentecost, where the believers were heard speaking in various languages 'the great things of God'. The fact that tongues in Luke's narrative were already identified in Acts 2 as real languages, plus the equation of the Gentiles' Spirit experience with that of the Jews at Pentecost, indicates that Luke conceived of the Gentiles as speaking genuine languages even though he gave no list of nations who understand them.[22]

Consider the dissociative nature of the tongues speech. Cornelius and company interrupted an honoured guest with their speaking in tongues. This is not normal behaviour. It is dissociative. The group had lost touch with what Peter was saying and were caught up in the 'other' reality of Luke's storyworld – Spirit experience. The Gentiles had the same kind of dissociative language experience that the Jews encountered at Pentecost. Luke thereby clarified his presentation of Spirit experience. No one need be present who understands the language being spoken. However, just as tongues at Pentecost were intelligible languages, there must be an intelligible aspect to the initiate's experience. The text does not explain how the Jews knew the Gentiles were magnifying God. The chapter explores various possibilities such as xenolalia which was recognized by bystanders, or praise uttered in addition to the xenolalia, or recognition by some other means (facial expressions, upraised hands, etc.). Dissociative, xenolalic Spirit-

---

[22] Cf. Hovenden, *Tongues*, 71.

reception with an intelligible element was the divine *imprimatur* that confirmed the appropriateness of baptism in a contentious initiatory situation.

Analysis of the Story

Exposition and Rising Action

The trajectory of the Cornelius episode is one of initiation from the very beginning. We see Cornelius as an ideal candidate in the first verses of chapter ten. Not only is he a leader in his field, but he is pious. Luke's praise is high: Cornelius is devout, fears God, gives alms and constantly prays (10:2). Furthermore, he is able to see 'clearly' a supernatural vision. He is a worthy man indeed. Yet all this is not sufficient, for he is told that there is still something he must do, and that a particular individual, whom he must seek out, will act as his instructor and reveal the specifics to him. Cornelius obediently makes arrangements to find this teacher.

The scene shifts and we find Peter experiencing a supernatural lesson. What God cleanses he is not to label as unclean (10:15).[23] That Luke valued repetition is clear for he depicts God himself repeating the lesson three times. Ironically, while Peter initially has no idea what the sheet with all the unclean animals means (17), the reader knows what it signifies. However, the arrival of the men, and the Spirit's instructions regarding them, help Peter begin to understand. Now the reader wonders in what way Peter must 'kill and eat' for it seems that since Peter has lodged the Gentiles and accompanied them to Caesarea he knows they are not 'unclean', but where is the next step, the decisive 'killing and eating' part? Peter's first speech to Cornelius has him clearly stating what the reader knows he knows, that despite Jewish legal stipulations, he is to accept these Gentiles (10:28).

Luke brought his reader to the centre point of the whole matter. Cornelius repeats his experience and then Peter begins to speak. Peter expounds on the impartiality of God with respect to Godfearers, touches on the primacy of the 'sons of Israel' to whom the word about the Christ first came, recounts the extent of the proclamation, identifies its beginning as after the work of John the Baptist, and emphasizes the fact that Jesus of Nazareth is the one anointed by God with the Holy Spirit. Peter mentions the role he and his accompanying Jews play as witnesses to the deeds of the Anointed One, to his death, to his resurrection, and to the message about him that he is the Judge of all and that, in accordance with the Hebrew prophets, there is forgiveness of sins through his name.

---

[23] For detailed discussion of the vision, cf. John Richard Lewis Moxon, *Peter's Halakhic Nightmare: The 'Animal' Vision of Acts 10:9-16 in Jewish and Graeco-Roman Perspective* (Ph.D. dissertation, Durham University, 2011).

The Story's Climax

At this precise point about believing in Jesus and receiving forgiveness of sins, Luke recounted the Spirit falling on the ones listening to the word.[24] The reader can only conclude that Cornelius and company must certainly have believed and received forgiveness of sins.[25] According to Gustav Stählin, 'The last words of the speech ... should make it totally clear: the sending of the Spirit is answer and gift for faith'.[26] Dunn, however, insists that by locating the arrival of the Spirit at precisely this juncture, Luke *did equate* the gift of the Spirit with forgiveness. He writes,

> The natural implication is that Cornelius at that moment reached out in faith to God for *forgiveness* and received, as God's response, the *Holy Spirit* (cf.11.17; 15.9), not instead of the promised forgiveness but as the bearer of it (cf. Gal. 3.2f). The Spirit was not something additional to God's acceptance and forgiveness but constituted that acceptance and forgiveness.[27]

No one would question whether the text links forgiveness and the gift of the Spirit. However, does Dunn read the text aright when he writes that forgiveness and the Spirit are the same thing? He further asserts that, 'The obvious implication [of 11.14, 15] is that the gift of the Spirit is what effected the salvation of Cornelius.'[28] What is Dunn's logic? He continues, 'for the message, which Cornelius had been told would result in his salvation, in the event resulted in nothing other than the outpouring of the Spirit'.[29] If the mention of salvation had come in chapter 10 instead of 11, this could have been read narratologically as anticipation of salvation resolved by the surprise experience of the Spirit and could have indicated that for Luke, the experience of the Spirit is the experience of salvation, or at least integral to it. But Peter's retelling of the story and mention of salvation comes after the reader has passed the point of the arrival of the Spirit. Does this affect the meaning in any way? No, for the reader, upon encountering the specific mention of salvation (11:14) would have then reintegrated that new information into the story which had gone before, especially linking the Spirit (11:15-16) to salvation (11:14). Dunn's argument stands, if slightly modified. Luke did not

---

[24] 'The narrator repeats his artificial pattern of showing interruption of speeches only after the main points have been made', Kurz, *Reading*, 88. Similarly, Martin Dibelius, trans. Mary Ling, *Studies in the Acts of the Apostles* (London: William Clowes, 1956), 161. Cf. Joshua D. Garroway, '"Apostolic Irresistibility" and the Interrupted Speeches in Acts', *CBQ* 74.4 (October, 2012), 738-53; 751.

[25] Sternberg cites a similar situation in which a story emphasizes an action taking place at an 'exact point' in a speech, viz., Eli falling backward just when the messenger tells of the capture of the ark (*Poetics*, 421).

[26] 'Die letzten Worte der Rede ... sollen es ganz deutlich machen: die Sendung des Geistes ist Antwort und Gabe für den Glauben'. Gustav Stählin, *Die Apostelgeschichte* (Göttingen: Vandenhoeck & Ruprecht, 1966), 157.

[27] Dunn, *Baptism*, 80, original italics.

[28] *Ibid.*

[29] *Ibid.*

perfectly equate the Spirit with salvation, but made the Spirit integral to it. Salvation is forgiveness *and* the Spirit *and* belonging to the people of God.

The idea that forgiveness of sins directly equates to reception of the Spirit runs counter to the distinction already present in Luke-Acts. In Luke 3 we see that John the Baptist preached a baptism of repentance for the remission of sins without any experience of the Spirit. The baptism of the Spirit and fire (see discussion chapter 4) was the prerogative of the Coming One, distinct from the work of the Baptist. Nor is there any indication in the text that John's baptism was just preparatory for a later forgiveness that would take place under the Messiah. John preached, a baptism of repentance εἰς ἄφεσιν ἁμαρτιῶν (Luke 3:3), not for *later/future/eventual* forgiveness of sins. Luke also already distinguished between forgiveness of sins and reception of the Spirit in Acts 2:38, where repentance, water baptism, and Spirit-reception are collated but not condensed into a single moment. He did the same in chapter 8, where Dunn himself has retracted his attempt to delegitimize the initial belief of the Samaritans. Chapter 9 also has, as shown above, a temporal gap between Saul's praying, which was acknowledged by Jesus himself, and his submission to Ananias, followed then by his healing, baptism, and reception of the Spirit. With the Luke-Acts narrative up to this point making such a repeated distinction between belief/repentance/forgiveness of sins and the experience of the Spirit, one cannot argue from the Cornelius episode that forgiveness and Spirit experience would be understood to be the same, or even that the Spirit would be thought to bring forgiveness. Rather, Luke presented the Spirit as able to come as soon as forgiveness has taken place. As to the question of what effected the salvation of Cornelius, Luke presented Cornelius as totally compliant with God's instructions to him and totally ready to receive the kerygmatic message that God's servant brought. This suggests that Cornelius received forgiveness and experienced the gift of the Spirit precisely because he believed what he was told and obeyed (cf. Acts 5:32).

Dunn attempts to find in Acts 15:8-9 a confirmation of his thesis that Spirit-reception and forgiveness are identical. He states, 'God's giving of the Holy Spirit is equivalent to his cleansing of their hearts; these two are one – two ways of describing the same thing'.[30] In the next sentence he makes a slightly different assertion: 'God cleansed their hearts by giving the Spirit. God gave the Spirit to cleanse their hearts'.[31] The question becomes whether Dunn rightly interprets these two verses. Luke simply stated that faith was the means God used for cleansing. In Cornelius' case, his faith and obedience to God were already present and all he needed for salvation (cf. 11:14) was to hear the message of forgiveness through Jesus, and then he could, and did, immediately receive the Spirit (10:43-44). As Turner forcefully writes of 11:17-18: 'under no circumstances may we simply equate "the same gift (= the Spirit)" with μετάνοιαν εἰς

---

[30] *Ibid.*, 82.
[31] *Ibid.*

ζωὴν ἔδωκεν ("repentance that leads to life"): elsewhere μετάνοια is clearly the *condition* for receiving the gift of the Spirit (2.38-39) not the gift itself'.[32]

Turner emphasizes two points relating the Spirit to salvation. First, Luke's presentation of Cornelius as a Godfearer means that he was not a Christian who subsequently received the Spirit: '*once again we have returned to the 'norm' of the gift of the Spirit being immediately associated with conversional repentance and baptism*'.[33] This return is possible because of the course of the narrative; one of the two apostles noted for having the gift of imparting/facilitating the Spirit happens to be the minister preaching to Cornelius. It is no surprise that people would receive the Spirit under Peter's ministry. So part of the norm being followed here is the presence, as at Samaria, of a gifted individual who can facilitate the Spirit. Though an implied reader would think it *normal* for the Spirit to be facilitated by a gifted individual, this does *not* mean that the implied reader would think such an individual is always required for the Spirit to come. That cannot be concluded from the narrative without an explicit statement to that effect and there is no such statement. Even if the Lukan narrative were to continue to present the Spirit as mediated through humans, and it does in Acts 19, the implied reader already knows that the Spirit can be sent to believers directly from heaven (Luke 11:13; Acts 2:4). Unmediated Spirit experience is part of the ER for initiation just as mediated experience is a part of the ER.

Turner's second point is that Peter links the Gentiles' reception of the Spirit to Jesus' statement that the apostles would be baptised in the Spirit (11:16 and 1:5). Turner argues that the reason this saying applies here is, 'probably that Luke understood the logion to imply *the messiah cleanses and restores his Israel through the executive power of the Holy Spirit which he pours out*'.[34] Turner is surely correct, for the immediate context suggests that Peter recognized the quality of the Gentiles' experience as being like his own 'baptism' experience, and that experience was linked to Jesus' reference to the Baptist's saying regarding the purifying work of the Coming One.

The Mechanism of Spirit Impartation/Facilitation

Quesnel is correct that the order here is not the usual one.[35] However, this intervention does not come apart from the ministry of a qualified initiator. The significance of Peter as someone already known in the story as a minister gifted to facilitate the Spirit must be evaluated. Communication of the Spirit could thus be seen as being a natural effect of the preaching of the word by a powerful individual, or the effect of arbitrary divine intervention because of the response to the word preached. The text does not say that the Jews who came with Peter were surprised that the Spirit fell during the preaching. They were surprised that the

---

[32] Turner, *Power*, 382.
[33] Turner, *Power*, 384, original italics.
[34] *Ibid.*, 387, original italics.
[35] Quesnel, *Baptisés*, 53.

Spirit fell upon Gentiles. We cannot, therefore, rule out the possibility that Spirit impartation during preaching was not abnormal. The question then becomes whether Luke places emphasis upon the Spirit coming because of the hearers' response to the message preached, or because of the power of the preacher, or whether he attributes it purely to the sovereignty of God, or whether there is a combination of factors.

That the sovereignty of God is at play is clear from the beginning of the story when Cornelius is visited by an angel and from the continued divine intervention in the narrative. What then, of the more human factors such as ministerial giftedness and audience response? Acts 8 demonstrates that mere response to the gospel, even to the point of immersion, is not sufficient, or at least not *always* sufficient, to result in impartation of the Spirit. There Luke required the activity of ministers gifted with the power to facilitate the Spirit. But did Luke here modify his previous presentation? Peter lays hands upon no one. He does not even preach about the Spirit as a possible gift for new converts, as he did in Acts 2. Luke tied the descent of the Spirit to the moment when the audience hears about forgiveness of sins. However, we need not exclude either aspect of Spirit-reception. Peter can be recognized as a gifted minister while still factoring in the element of belief in forgiveness of sins through Jesus. To eliminate either element detracts from Luke's overall narrative. The evidence and argument for Peter functioning as a minister gifted to facilitate the Spirit in Acts 10 is found explicitly in Acts 8. A sequential/progressive analysis observes that the reader brings the information learned about Peter in Samaria forward to Caesarea.

This idea is not new. J. Duncan M. Derret observed that, 'Peter's presence alone sufficed to induce "possession"',[36] and Eric Sorensen identifies preaching (citing Acts 10:37-48) as one of the New Testament means of communicating 'divine possession'.[37] This is consonant with Luke's presentation of 'power' being simply present in the ministry of Jesus. Resident power is characteristic of John, of Jesus, of Jesus' disciples, and of Peter and Paul (Luke 1:17; 4:14; 5:17; 6:19; 8:48; 9:1; 24:49; Acts 1:8; 5:15; 19:12). So, while it is possible a reader might think that this was simply an exceptional intervention by God, it is more likely to be seen as associated with the powerful ministry of Peter, given the 'resident power' element to the Lukan ER for ministry, e.g. even Peter's shadow is thought to heal. The reader familiar with Peter's previous powerful ministry in Samaria understands that the Spirit falls because of that same ministry. Certainly God acts, but he does not act arbitrarily. He did not send the Spirit upon Cornelius apart from the preaching of the word by a minister specifically gifted in facilitating the Spirit. God acts through the kerygmatic and charismatic ministry of Peter. In this sense, then, the Spirit is mediated. Thus, in the ER for Spirit-reception

---

[36] J. Duncan M. Derrett, 'Simon Magus (Act 8 9-24)', *ZNW* 73 (1982), 52-68; 56.
[37] Eric Sorensen, *Possession and Exorcism in the New Testament and Early Christianity* (Tübingen: J.C.B. Mohr, Paul Siebeck, 2002), 146-47.

there are now four possible scenarios: a direct-from-heaven impartation in response to prayer at immersion; direct from the Father gifting in response to prayer; prayer and handlaying by initiators following immersion (and possibly prayer); spontaneous impartation (from God) in response to believing in the preaching of the word by a gifted minister.

Dissociative Xenolalia *Plus* a Praise Element as the Apostolic Standard

Kittel, critiquing the view that Cornelius' house was an exception to the norm of the Spirit being imparted in baptism, observed that the Jews were not astonished that the Spirit had been given apart from water baptism, but rather, that the Spirit was given to Gentiles.[38] How then did they know it was given? Peter's astonished assistants knew 'that also on the Gentiles the gift of the Holy Spirit has been poured out' (10:45):[39] ἤκουον γὰρ αὐτῶν λαλούντων γλώσσαις καὶ μεγαλυνόντων τὸν θεόν (Acts 10:46). With regard to the function of narrative asides Sheeley writes: 'Perhaps the most important role [of the asides is to] provide a means by which the narrators guide the readers into the correct interpretation of events.'[40] Luke explained to the reader that they knew the Gentiles had received the Spirit: 'for they were hearing them speaking with tongues and magnifying God' (10:46). Luke then showed Peter appealing to the believing community not to refuse the Gentiles water baptism based upon a commonly recognized reception of the Spirit.

In contrast to Pentecost, Luke did not give a list of nations who understood Cornelius and his friends.[41] This was a small group gathering.[42] The experience of the Gentiles is equated (10:47, 11:15, 17, 15:8) with that of the apostles at Pentecost, even though Luke did not here use the term ἑτέραις. Therefore, though Witherington, Peterson, Schneider, and Esler suggest that the speech was glossolalic,[43] even without the addition of 'other' to 'tongues', the reader understands that the Gentiles are speaking real language(s), not gibberish.

Kremer argues that here, as in Acts 19:6, λαλεῖν γλώσσαις must mean understandable languages, not unintelligible glossolalia, because the καί is to be taken epexegetically – 'speak with tongues, even praise God'. He writes, 'The expression, well-known from the tradition, "speaking in tongues," ... is more closely

---

[38] Kittel, 'Wirkungen', 33-34.
[39] Cf. Ulrich Wilckens, *Die Misssionsreden der Apostelgeschichte: Form – und Traditionsgeschichteliche Untersuchungen* (Neukirchen-Vluyn: Neukirchener Verlag des Erziehungsvereins GMBH, 1963), 2.67.
[40] Sheeley fails to comment on glossolalia and narrative asides. Sheeley, *Asides*, 175, cf. 13, 176.
[41] Turner observes that in 10:46 and 19:6, 'there are no "outsiders" present to hear the spontaneous outbursts of prophetic praise', *Power*, 272.
[42] Bruce sees a link back to Acts 2:11, *Acts*, 264.
[43] Witherington, *Acts*, 360; Peterson, *Acts*, 340; Gerhard Schneider, *Apostelgeschichte 9,1-28,31* (Freiburg: Herder, 2002 [1982]), 80; Philip F. Esler, 'Glossolalia and the Admission of Gentiles into the Early Christian Community', *BTB* 22 (1992), 136.

defined through the following, "and glorifying God."[44] For Kremer, 10:46 and 19:6 represent, 'Spirit-worked and obviously understandable praise of God'.[45] While this is an attractive suggestion and grammatically possible, it does not necessarily fit the story logic, for the experience of the Gentiles is repeatedly equated with the Jews' Pentecost experience. The Pentecost tongues, while certainly understandable, were viewed as something supernatural. So too, the Jews at Cornelius' house were not astounded that Gentiles should praise God, nor even that they should be moved by the Spirit to praise God. The Jews were amazed that Gentiles, by the Spirit, should do what the Jews had done at Pentecost – speak in languages they could not otherwise have spoken in.

There are four basic possibilities for understanding how it was known that they were magnifying God. First, the καί could be coordinating. The Gentiles supernaturally spoke languages recognized by the Jews (e.g., fluent Aramaic) *and* the Gentiles naturally spoke words of praise in a common language (Greek). Second, the καί could be coordinating. The Gentiles supernaturally spoke languages *not* recognized by the Jews (e.g., Tibetan and English) *and* spoke words of praise in a common language (Greek). That the xenolalia was unrecognized is suggested by the fact that Luke did not provide a list of the languages, though he clearly wants to compare Cornelius' house with Pentecost. However, the lack of a language list does not conclusively demonstrate that the languages were not recognized because Luke gave no explicit statement to that effect. On the other hand, it is an argument from silence to say that the languages were recognized. Luke did not say that either. We cannot know whether the languages were recognized.

Third, one could take the καί as epexegetical and read that, 'they spoke in languages, even magnified God *in the content of their speaking*', and assume that the content was understood because it was a language known to Jews and not (at least not fluently) to Gentiles (viz., Aramaic, Hebrew – though Roman soldiers who were Gentile Godfearers likely spoke some Hebrew and Aramaic, it is not likely that their speech was accent free; such would qualify as supernatural speech). If this argument were accepted, then it would mean that the common denominator between Jerusalem and Caesarea was xenolalia alone. Fourth, one could take the καί as epexegetical and read that the xenolalia was not understood linguistically, but, perhaps because of its ecstatic nature,[46] tone of voice, facial expressions, raising of the hands, etc., was understood to be uttered in praise of God. Again, this is an argument from silence. If this were the case, then the common denominator between Jerusalem and Caesarea is, again, strictly xenolalia. If one understood the speaking in tongues and magnifying God as a hendiadys with the idea of tongues blended with the idea of praise, one would still have to

---

[44] 'Der aus der Tradition bekannte Terminus ‚in Sprachen reden' ... wird durch den folgenden ‚und Gott lobpreisen' näher bestimmt', Kremer, *Pfingstbericht*, 194.
[45] 'geistgewirkte und offenkundig verständliche Gotteslob', *Ibid.*
[46] Witherington, *Acts*, 360.

Ritual Water, Ritual Spirit

decide between the four options for how the hearers knew that the content of the languages was praise.

To find the common denominator as solely xenolalia (recognized or unrecognized) means that the Jewish leadership understood xenolalia as an aspect of their experience of the Spirit which could be employed evidentially. That is, they knew the Gentiles had experienced the Spirit because they supernaturally spoke in languages they had not learned. It does not exclude the possibility that other phenomena could serve as evidence, it only affirms that xenolalia can serve as evidence and that this was the evidence used by early church leadership at an important juncture in Luke's story. It does not logically make tongues the *sine qua non* of Spirit experience. However, if xenolalia (supernatural utterance, whether recognized or unrecognized) *plus* natural language (e.g. Greek, Latin) praise is what took place, then the common denominator is not supernatural language *simpliciter*, but a combination of supernatural utterance and intelligible praise. Luke did not narrate how the Jews knew that the Gentiles magnified God and therefore we cannot confidently affirm any of the four options listed above. All that can be affirmed is that the early church leadership employed, on one significant occasion, 'speaking in tongues and magnifying God' as evidence that converts had received the Holy Spirit.

But, one might object, could not the 'them' of 'they heard them' be viewed as a group? The group as a whole spoke with tongues and magnified God. Individuals did one thing or the other, or perhaps neither. There is then no rigid requirement for all individuals to speak in tongues. If some members of a group speak in tongues that should suffice to evidence that the group in question has experienced the Spirit. Praise instead of tongues would also suffice as evidence of Spirit-reception. While seemingly attractive, these proposals have several flaws. First, as Keener observes, 'By itself, conventional praise would not have persuaded Peter's colleagues that the Spirit had been poured out, since this activity occurred regularly in the temple and perhaps in many synagogues.'[47] Keener's objection is historical. From a narrative point of view, from what the implied reader knows of the Jewish characters in Luke's story, would they have accepted mere praise as evidence that Gentiles had received the Spirit? Luke's Jews needed convincing and it took Peter's recounting of a genuine miracle among the Gentiles equal to the miracle they themselves had experienced (which, at least for the initial group, was more than natural praise) to finally persuade.

Second, the text does not add 'some' to the sentence. It does not state, 'some spoke in tongues, some magnified God'. One is moving beyond the explicit text to suggest that. It is an argument from silence. However, one could respond that the idea of a group is ambiguous by nature and cannot, except by a woodenly literal rendering, be forced to mean *every* member of the group. One could propose the following example sentence: 'they ate fish and chicken'. Without knowing the context it is impossible to assert that each in the group at *both* fish and

---

[47] Keener, *Acts*, 2.1814.

chicken. If the context is a restaurant, the chances are that some ordered fish and some chicken. A reader has a conceptual frame for restaurants and uses that frame to understand the example sentence. If the context is a backyard grill party, the chances are greater that each ate some of both. Again, the reader uses a different conceptual frame. But still one could not say for certain.

In the case of Acts, it is the implied reader's conceptual frame for initiation which we do not have *a priori* and are trying to recover. The only conceptual frame for initiation that we do have is the one developed over the course of Luke's narrative, the ER for initiation. The Pentecost story has created a programmatic expectation that initiates will speak in tongues, but the reader knows that Luke has not explicitly excluded other phenomena from manifesting Spirit-reception. Luke has also modified the Acts 2:38 expectation of the sequence of repentance, baptism, and Spirit-reception (Cornelius received the Spirit *before* being baptised). So the question is whether Luke modified his expectation of tongues for every initiate, or whether that expectation compels the reader to understand that every member of the group spoke in tongues.

Luke did not here focus upon individual Gentiles as he had focused upon individual Jews at Pentecost where tongues of fire sat ἐφ' ἕνα ἕκαστον αὐτῶν (Acts 2:3) and where it states that all πάντες were filled with the Holy Spirit and began to speak in other tongues (2:4). However, Peter does equate the experience of the Gentiles as a group with the experience of the Jews as a group. Peter asks who is able to refuse water to the Gentiles οἵτινες τὸ πνεῦμα τὸ ἅγιον ἔλαβον ὡς καὶ ἡμεῖς. One could argue that ὡς here is not indicating a comparison of *how* the Spirit was received but simply of the *fact* that the Spirit was received.[48] BDAG's first two definitions render ὡς '1. a comparative particle, marking the manner in which someth. proceeds', and '2. a conjunction marking a point of comparison'.[49] One could select option two and decide that the point of comparison was simply the fact of the Spirit's arrival, not the manifestation of that arrival.

However, when Peter repeats the comparison a second time the aspect of comparison of manner becomes stronger: ἐπέπεσεν τὸ πνεῦμα τὸ ἅγιον ἐπ' αὐτοὺς ὥσπερ καὶ ἐφ' ἡμᾶς ἐν ἀρχῇ (Acts 11:15). Here Peter compares the falling on the Gentiles to the falling upon the Jews 'at beginning'. Peter continues in verse 16 to reference Jesus' statement about being baptised in the Holy Spirit, again, an indication not merely of the fact of the Spirit's coming, but the manner of the coming. Finally, in verse 17, Peter states: εἰ οὖν τὴν ἴσην δωρεὰν ἔδωκεν αὐτοῖς ὁ θεὸς ὡς καὶ ἡμῖν (11:17a). God gave the equal (ἴσην) gift to the Gentiles as he gave to the Jews. Luke demonstrated comparison between the two groups, not just of the fact of receiving the Spirit, but of the manner.

The question arises whether Luke compared the Gentiles' experience to just the initial group of Jews or to both the initial group and the 3,000 converts. This is significant because Luke affirmed that, at Pentecost, *all* the initial group of

---

[48] Similarly, Witherington, *Acts*, 360.
[49] Bauer, *Lexicon*, 1103-1106.

Jews were filled with the Spirit and spoke in tongues. But, the assertion that all 3,000 spoke in tongues, while implied, is not made explicitly. The tempting proposal that because Peter makes no differentiation between the initial Jews and the 3,000 converts, therefore in his (or Luke's) understanding, there was none, is, unfortunately, an argument from silence. Even Peter's (11:15) statement, that the Spirit fell on the Gentiles ὥσπερ καὶ ἐφ' ἡμᾶς ἐν ἀρχῇ, does not clarify the matter because ἐν ἀρχῇ could be *all* the day of Pentecost, not just the first descent of the Spirit, and the ἡμᾶς could be all the Jews, not just the apostles. However, Luke did not narrate the falling of the Spirit upon the 3,000. Within the confines of Luke's story, the only 'beginning' that the implied reader has access to is the initial experience of the apostles and disciples. On this narrative basis it can be argued that ἐν ἀρχῇ refers to the initial falling of the Spirit described by Luke. The Gentile group, then, is equated with the initial Jewish group. Therefore, because all the members of the initial Jewish group uttered xenolalia, all the members of the Gentile group uttered xenolalia.

What can be conservatively affirmed is that if a group of converts can be said to 'speak in tongues and magnify God', that group has experienced the Spirit in an equivalent way to what was understood by the Jews in Luke's narrative to be an authoritative manifestation of the Spirit with which other manifestations could be compared. In other words, the experience of 'the beginning' was the standard experience against which the Jews compared the experience of the Gentiles. The only 'beginning' described by Luke is that of the initial '120'. However, the wind and fire of the beginning are not used by Luke for comparative purposes. The only narrated phenomenon of the beginning is supernaturally spoken languages the content of which was τὰ μεγαλεῖα τοῦ θεοῦ (Acts 2:11). The explicitly stated common denominator between Pentecost and Cornelius' house is λαλούντων γλώσσαις καὶ μεγαλυνόντων τὸν θεόν (10:46). For Luke, if Spirit-reception is to be like Pentecost, there must be supernatural speaking in languages and there must be magnification of God.

Cornelius' House as Programmatic

If the common denominator is the xenolalia/magnification of God, then how does this function in the narrative? Luke narrated in an aside to his reader how speaking with tongues and magnifying God was the means, on this occasion, of identifying Spirit-reception and then reinforced that narration with one of his primary narrative spokespersons, an apostle, appealing to the phenomenon as the thing which established the Gentiles' experience as equal to the experience of the Jewish believers/apostles at Pentecost (10:47). This convergence of informational axes creates the implied suggestion that the reader is to identify Spirit-reception in the same way as the Jewish leaders – by comparing the S/spirit experience in question with the day of Pentecost. Luke did not state that this is the *only* way that Spirit-reception can be identified, but he made it clear that this is how the leadership of the early church did it on this important occasion. Reading sequentially, the expectation of xenolalia derived from the Pentecost narrative is reinforced by the story of Cornelius' house. Xenolalia/magnification of God can thus be seen as programmatic for Luke.

But again, Luke did not explicitly deny that other manifestations could not equally attest Spirit-reception. He did not say, 'xenolalia and only xenolalia'. He positively affirmed one reality but did not negatively exclude other possibly realities. How then is the implied reader to understand Luke's affirmations? The reader knows what the apostolic leadership did and taught. The rulings of the apostolic council cannot be viewed as lacking precedential power for Luke's implied reader.

Don Jackson raises an objection to making Cornelius' house normative:

> If this pattern were normative, then such a statement [Peter's 11:15 reference to Pentecost] would have made no sense. Peter would only have said that they were converted just as the Jews in Jerusalem and Judea, or the Samaritans in Samaria, or anyone else had been since the day of Pentecost. But the fact is that the experience of Cornelius and his household had only one other parallel: Pentecost.[50]

Jackson, however, overlooks the fact that, in Luke's story, Peter must defend his actions at Cornelius' house. He cannot do so with some minor example that could easily be dismissed; rather, he uses a highly significant event personally known to the individuals he is seeking to persuade – Pentecost. Moreover, it is Pentecost, not Samaria or any other scene, upon which Luke expended his energy describing what Spirit experience looks like. Thus, Pentecost figures in Luke's narrative strategy as the archetypal Spirit experience to which the implied reader compares all other Spirit experiences.[51]

The 'Spirit Baptism' Metaphor

What then is to be made of the concept of 'being baptised in the Spirit'? Schneider rightly observes: 'One cannot, therefore, also later at every Spirit-event speak of a 'new Pentecost', rather only of a *renewed Pentecost*'.[52] When Peter refers to the concept of 'being baptized in the Holy Spirit',[53] Schneider notes that this is the same terminology as at Pentecost and therefore: 'One also may not call later Spirit-events "baptism in Holy Spirit" in the sense of special occurrences which

---

[50] Jackson, 'Theology', 335-43; 340.
[51] If this was the case, one might speculatively inquire how tongues died out as the archetypal Spirit experience. This question goes beyond the strictly intra-textual focus of the dissertation. However, one may *speculate* that as the church grew, the need to integrate large numbers of converts overtaxed the ability of the church to integrate them all with an experiential Spirit baptism. Gradually, non-experiential initiation replaced experiential initiation.
[52] 'Man kann daher auch später nicht bei jedem Geistereignis von einem «neuen Pfingsten» sprechen, sondern nur von einem *erneuerten Pfingsten*', Schneider, *Geist*, 45.
[53] The noun form, 'Spirit baptism' or 'baptism in the Holy Spirit' is not Luke's terminology.

go beyond the "normal coming-to-faith".'[54] Rather, Schneider recommends that we think of this in terms of experiences that 'incorporate us' and 'let us participate' in the events recorded in Acts.[55] From this perspective it would be permissible, then, to speak of 'being baptized in the Holy Spirit' as an experience which a believer has which unites her/him with the experience of the church of Acts. Thus, 'being Spirit baptised' should be viewed as normal, not extraordinary.

Turner argues the opposite:

> the very nature of the metaphor, its restricted use and the way it is handled, suggest he does not think that all Christians in this age (or even many) have sufficiently intense experiences of the Spirit as to warrant the application of the metaphor in their case. We should probably follow him and reserve use of the phrase for particularly spectacular corporate occasions of receiving the Spirit, if we use it at all.[56]

Turner observes that, historically, the metaphor of being baptised with the Spirit was not in use in the time between Pentecost and Cornelius' house.[57] But we must ask whether Luke instituted it as a metaphor for his reader or perhaps related an etiological story of how the metaphor came to be. The implied reader hears Peter, at this important juncture, use the baptism metaphor to describe a reception of the Spirit that is Pentecost-like in its interruptive, dissociative nature, in its tongues-speaking and magnifying of God, and then s/he hears Peter anchor that description in a saying of Jesus. It would seem, then, that the implied reader is expected to come away from the story with a new metaphor in hand to use to describe similar situations.

So the question becomes whether Luke expected all initiates to have the same overwhelming Pentecost-like experience when they receive the Spirit. A positive answer is not new. Leipoldt, citing Acts 10 and 19, wrote, 'The persuasion that one receives the Spirit at baptism partly hinges on the ecstatic element: the baptisand begins, in the presence of the church, to speak with tongues.'[58] However, Luke presented not simply a quiet prayer language as the apostolic standard, but a dissociative experience. To the degree that the implied reader is expected to follow the teachings of the early church leaders, the reader is expected to compare the experience of initiates with that of the apostles at Pentecost. Luke expected initiates to have a sufficiently 'intense experience' of the Spirit. It must be a 'baptism'[59] because that is what the apostles had.

---

[54] 'Man darf daher auch nicht spätere Geistereignisse «Taufe im Heiligen Geist» nennen im Sinne von besonderen Ereignissen, die über das «normale Gläubigwerden» hinausgehen', *Ibid.*

[55] Schneider, *Geist*, 45-46.

[56] Turner, 'Endowment', 52.

[57] *Ibid.*

[58] 'Die Überzeugung, daß man bei der Taufe den Geist empfange, hängt teilwiese mit dem ekstatischen Elemente zusammen: der Täufling beginnt, in Gegenwart der Gemeinde, mit Zungen zu reden', Leipoldt, *Taufe*, 35.

[59] Contrary to James M. Hamilton, Jr., 'Rushing Wind and Organ Music: Toward Luke's Theology of the Spirit in Acts', *RFT* 65:1 (April, 2006), 15-33; 22.

Thus, Turner rightly critiques the idea of applying baptism phraseology to mild Spirit experiences. However, Luke set the bar high, and for him only a baptism in line with Pentecost would suffice. Just as Jesus (Acts 1:5) promised his followers that they would be 'baptised in the Holy Spirit', and this promise was fulfilled for the apostles, the corporate experience of the apostles (minus the wind and fire) was promised to all the individuals who would repent and be baptised in water.[60] Luke thereby distributed the Spirit-baptism experience to all. The same intense, even dissociative, Spirit experience was expected by Luke for every individual at initiation. He did not discuss the possibility that individuals might have a gradual, growing experience of the Spirit. One might object that if this was the case, why is there no record of it in other New Testament writings? First, one biblical record is all that is needed. Second, the epistles are circumstantial. They do not discuss every church-related situation.

Conclusion

The reader now has four ways the Spirit may come: direct from heaven during baptismal prayer, direct from heaven in response to prayer alone, by laying on of hands, or through powerful apostolic preaching. The Western Text also depicts immersion without accompanying prayer imparting the Spirit. Acts 2:38 promises the Spirit upon repentance and immersion. However, the reader of Luke's gospel has reason to think that immersion is not conducted without prayer. Therefore, apart from the Western text, it is not possible to conclude with certainty from Acts 2:38 that Luke thought immersion without accompanying prayer would impart the Spirit. Contrary to Bock, who states regarding the outpouring of the Spirit, 'There is no apostolic intermediary on earth who helps with the distribution',[61] Luke did not show Cornelius receiving the Spirit on his own, apart from the already established community, but rather through the ministry of a powerful individual already known in the story as one possessing the gift of facilitating the Spirit. In this sense, the Spirit continues to be facilitated by the believing community. Luke also clarified the relationship between Spirit-reception and immersion. Both are elements in proper community initiation. The supernatural *imprimatur* is paired with the natural human act of immersion. While Dunn errs in directly equating the Spirit with forgiveness, he is not mistaken in closely associating reception of the Spirit with salvation. The Spirit is part of a salvation concept that includes forgiveness of sins and acceptance into the people of God. However, Cornelius' makes clear that there must be an intelligible element to the supernatural language utterances. That is, if no one is able to recognize the languages being spoken, there must be some identification of Godward praise. Luke did not state how. Finally, Luke presented the expectation of replicating Pentecost not merely in terms of xenolalia/magnifying God as the apostolic standard

---

[60] Cf. Bruce D. Chilton, 'One God, the Same God', Jacob Neusner, et al., *Do Jews, Christians, and Muslims Worship the Same God?* (n.pl.: Abingdon, 2012), 55-83; 72.

[61] Bock, *Acts*, 401.

for initiates, but replicating Pentecost in terms of an intense, even dissociative experience to which the metaphor of baptism is suited.

Chapter 7

The Culmination of the ER for Initiation – Paul, Apollos, and the Ephesians (Acts 18:24-28; 19:1-7)

Introduction

This has not been seen as an easy passage. Von Baer believed we could not, 'out of this dark passage, draw any implications at all'.[1] Käsemann wrote, 'Taken as an isolated passage, Acts 19:1-7 is the despair of the exegete.'[2] A sequential approach avoids such isolation of the passage and does not find it quite as dark as von Baer did. By cautiously evaluating it, observant of possible objections, in the light of Luke's distinctive use of John's baptism as a demarcation line between Jesus and John, some of the passage's exegetical difficulties can be addressed. Despite significant scholarship advocating a Christian connection between Apollos and the Ephesians, the chapter concludes that the Ephesians are strictly disciples of John, members of the people of God, but not yet followers of Jesus. Apollos is likely presented as having a Spirit experience, but, without knowing the baptism of Jesus, it is unlikely, though not impossible, for him to have known the particular Pentecostal Spirit experience associated with the baptism of Jesus. Luke affirmed with Paul, his narrative spokesman, the Acts 2:38 unity which had seemingly been broken in the Samaria episode. Luke reiterated for Paul, as for Peter, that reception of the Spirit, when not coming some other way, is facilitated by handlaying.

The Linguistic Argument for Christian 'Disciples'

The status of the Ephesian disciples remains a hotly contested matter. Dunn insists that they could not have been Christian because they did not possess the Spirit.[3] Witherington agrees with him.[4] One can identify three possible sub-categories to this line of reasoning. One may exclusively address Lukan material and argue that in Acts Spirit possession always characterizes being a Christian, as does Witherington. Or one may appeal, as does Marshall, to the broader New

---

[1] 'aus dieser dunklen Stelle überhaupt irgendwelche Konsequenzen ziehen', Von Baer, *Geist*, 178.
[2] Ernst Käsemann, 'The Disciples of John the Baptist in Ephesus', *Essays on New Testament Themes* (London: SCM, 1964), 136-48; 136.
[3] Dunn, *Baptism*, 86.
[4] Witherington, *Acts*, 570.

Testament context and claim that there being a Christian requires possession of the Spirit[5] and therefore here in Acts the individuals in question could not have been Christians. Or one may, as Dunn, combine the two approaches and argue the point from both the broader material and Acts.[6]

Menzies, however, argues they were disciples of Jesus:

> It is not improbable that there existed, predominantly in Galilee, groups of former disciples of the Baptist who had come to believe in Jesus as the Coming One without receiving Christian baptism (i.e. in the name of Jesus) or instruction concerning the nature and availability of the Pentecostal gift. ... Apollos was converted by a member of such a group; and the twelve Ephesians were probably converted by Apollos.[7]

Knut Backhaus proposes a similar hypothesis: they were originally disciples of John who encountered the Jesus movement, and then lost contact with it before Easter and Pentecost.[8] Guthrie was unclear in his assessment, stating that they, 'had not yet reached the stage of Christian belief',[9] but then also saying, 'We must conclude that these "disciples" were not in the main stream of Christianity'.[10] Avemarie, as Menzies, argued that Luke allowed them to be Christian without possession of the Spirit – a fundamental difference from Dunn.[11] He concluded that the Ephesian disciples were already Christians when Paul met them, and that he simply added a proper baptism and the Spirit to their faith.[12] Avemarie made two arguments. First, Acts usage of πιστεύω and μαθητής requires these words in chapter 19 to mean that the Ephesian disciples were Christians.[13] Second, the Ephesian story is dependent on the Apollos account which identifies Apollos as a Christian in 18:25 – for Avemarie the *Schlüsselvers*. Avemarie is not alone. Backhaus argues the passages are

> bound together with one another through contextual sequence, redactional linkage (cf. Acts 19:1), the location of the event (cf. Acts 18:24; 19:1), the foundational motif of conversion and the single motif of Johannine baptism (cf. Acts 18:25; 19:3) as well as Spirit possession (cf. Acts 18:25; 19:2).[14]

---

[5] I. Howard Marshall, *The Acts of the Apostles, An Introduction and Commentary* (Leicester: IVP, 1980), 305.
[6] Dunn, *Baptism*, 86.
[7] Menzies, *Empowered*, 220.
[8] Knut Backhaus, *Die 'Jüngerkreise' des Täufers Johannes: Eine Studie zu den religionsgeschichtlichen Ursprüngen des Christentums* (Paderborn: Ferdinand Schöningh, 1991), 211.
[9] Guthrie, *Theology*, 547.
[10] *Ibid.*
[11] Dunn, *Baptism*, 228.
[12] Avemarie, *Tauferzählungen*, 73.
[13] *Ibid.*, 70. Regarding 'disciples', so too Shelton, *Mighty*, 134.
[14] 'durch kontextuelle Sequenz, redaktionelle Verknüpfung (vgl. Apg 19,1), den Ort des Geschehens (vgl. Apg 18,24; 19,1), das Grundmotiv der Bekehrung und die

Witherington writes Luke coupled the two passages, 'intending a comparison'.[15] William and Robert Menzies also link the passages and affirm that the Ephesians were Christians.[16] Bock argues that since Apollos does not need to repent and is not baptised, he does not undergo Lukan conversion.[17] Jervell, too, concludes from 18:25 that Luke viewed Apollos as a Christian, as do Marshall, Käsemann, Fitzmyer, Witherington, Eckey, and Peterson.[18] Conzelmann argued from v. 25 that Apollos knew the gospel story up to Luke 24.[19] Barrett recognizes that v. 25 naturally suggests that Apollos was a Christian, but is not satisfied with any explanation of why he had not undergone Christian baptism.[20] Pesch and Käsemann argued that Luke modified the historical reality that Apollos really did know Christian baptism in order to denigrate Apollos.[21] Their arguments will not be engaged here, as the discussion is of the Lukan story, not an attempt to recreate the actual history. Schneider, on the other hand, stated that Apollos was not a Christian: 'Apollos was to a certain extent a Jewish 'Jesus adherent', but not yet Christian.'[22]

Avemarie said that in the eighteen occurrences in Acts outside chapter 19 of πιστεύω without an object, it never refers to anything which could be construed as other than the belief of the early church.[23] In ten more locations,[24] πιστεύω has an object that refers to God or Jesus Christ. In its other eight occurrences,[25] the word references various things but never any non-Christian religion. Therefore he concluded that when Paul asks the Ephesian disciples if they had received the Holy Spirit when they believed, the word πιστεύω can only be a reference to Christian belief in Jesus. Moreover, since πιστεύω occurs in Paul's statement,

---

Einzelmotive der Johannestaufe (vgl. Apg 18,25; 19,3) wie des Geistbesitzes (vgl. Apg 18,25; 19,2) miteinander verbunden', Backhaus, *'Jüngerkreise'*, 190.

[15] Witherington, *Acts*, 569.
[16] Menzies and Menzies, *Spirit*, 74.
[17] Bock, *Acts*, 592.
[18] Jervell, *Apostelgeschichte*, 470; Marshall, Acts, 303-304; Käsemann, 'Disciples', 137; Fitzmyer, *Acts*, 639; Witherington, *Acts*, 564-66; Wilfried Eckey, *Die Apostelgeschichte: Der Weg des Evangeliums von Jerusalem nach Rom, Teilband II 15,36-28,31* (Neukirchen-Vluyn: Neukirchener Verlagsgesellschaft mbH, 2011), 2.527; Peterson, *Acts*, 526.
[19] Conzelmann, *Acts*, 158.
[20] C.K. Barrett, *A Critical and Exegetical Commentary on the Acts of the Apostles* (London: T&T Clark, 1998), 2.887-89.
[21] Rudolf Pesch, *Die Apostelgeschichte: 2. Teilband, Apg 13-28* (Köln: Benziger Verlag; Neukirchen-Vluyn: Neukirchener Verlag des Erziehungsvereins mbH, 1986), 161. Käsemann, 'Disciples', 144-47.
[22] 'Apollos war also gewissermaßen jüdischer 'Jesusanhänger', aber noch nicht Christ'. Schneider, *Apostelgeschichte 9,1-28,31*, 261.
[23] Cf. Avemarie, *Tauferzählungen*, 70. Acts 2:44; 4:4, 32; 8:13; 11:21; 13:12, 39, 48; 14:1; 15:5, 7; 17:12, 34; 18:8, 27; 19:18; 21:20, 25.
[24] Acts 5:14; 9:42; 10:43; 11:17; 14:23; 16:31, 34; 18:8; 19:4; 22,19, *Ibid*.
[25] Acts 8:12; 9:26; 13:41; 15:11; 24:14; 26:27; 27:25, *Ibid*.

and Luke did not correct that statement by some counter-indication, then it must be from Luke's point of view.

Similarly, Avemarie observed that μαθητάς is dependent upon εὑρεῖν. Luke himself narrated the comment that Paul found disciples. In every one of the 27 other places μαθητής occurs in Acts, it exclusively refers to Jesus' followers. Moreover, he notes that the word appears without the word 'Christian' or any other such obvious adjective, except for 9:1 μαθητὰς τοῦ κυρίου, so that the simple noun in 19:1 with only the adjective τινας, 'some/certain disciples', is the expected designation for 'Christian disciples'. To this concept, Dunn objects that the anarthrous character of the noun in 19:1 sets it apart from the otherwise universal arthrous Acts usage, οἱ μαθηταί. Moreover, Dunn observes that quite often the city where the disciples are accompanies the noun.[26] Avemarie responded that in Acts 9:10 with Ananias there is no article. It reads: τις μαθητής. Therefore, Avemarie concluded that Luke definitely did not intend to designate the Ephesians as anything but Christian.[27] Furthermore, he noted that Luke regularly distinguished between Jesus' disciples and John's. In two of the three places where he mentioned John's disciples, he took over the differentiation from his sources (Luke 5:33 from Mk 2:18 and Luke 7:18 from Q – cf. Matt. 11:2, plus possibly Luke 11:1), indicating that this was a fixed idiom for Luke. Thus, the reader can expect that since he makes no such differentiation here, he intends none, and the disciples in question are Jesus' followers.[28] Similarly, Scott Shauf argues that they could not have been John's disciples because μαθητής and πιστεύσαντες are used absolutely and because, 'when μαθηταί are disciples of John, the relationship is made explicit in the text'.[29]

The Argument for Christian 'Disciples' from the Relationship to Apollos

Robert P. Menzies and Friedrich Avemarie – Apollos and the Ephesians Were Christian

Menzies argues that the disciples had actually been evangelized by Apollos.[30] Avemarie makes the connection because of textual/narrative proximity,[31] as the Ephesian disciples' story directly follows the Apollos account which definitively showed, in 18:25, that Luke could consider a person a Christian who had only received John's baptism. Either way, both Menzies and Avemarie assume that

---

[26] Dunn, *Baptism*, 84.
[27] Avemarie, *Tauferzählungen*, 70. Ervin adds Tabitha (9:36) and Timothy (16:1), *Conversion-Initiation*, 59. Eckey does not argue from grammar, but simply from Luke's frequent use of 'disciple', *Apostelgeschichte 15,36-28,31*, 532.
[28] Avemarie, *Tauferzählungen*, 71.
[29] Scott Shauf, *Theology as History, History as Theology: Paul in Ephesus in Acts 19* (Berlin: Walter de Gruyter, 2005), 147-48.
[30] Menzies, *Empowered*, 220.
[31] So too, Michael Wolter, 'Apollos und die ephesinischen Johannesjünger (Act 18 24 – 9 7)', *ZNW* 78 (1987), 49-73; 68.

he was a Christian before Aquila and Priscilla met him. Menzies argues this because: (1) Paul, in his epistles, does not reference any conversion of Apollos by Priscilla and Aquila; (2) τὴν ὁδὸν τοῦ κυρίου was Luke's style; (3) Luke employed ἡ ὁδός to speak of things Christian;[32] (4) ζέων τῷ πνεύματι finds a parallel in Romans 12:11, indicating it was Christian.[33]

Avemarie reasoned that with the above description of having a Holy Spirit experience[34] and teaching Jesus (18:25), though Apollos knew only the baptism of John, he must have been a Christian in Luke's eyes. With ζέων τῷ πνεύματι, Avemarie understood 'Holy Spirit' rather than Apollos' 'spirit'.[35] He observed that where Luke used πνεῦμα without an attributive, such as 'holy', he rarely meant a human spirit and usually meant either God's Spirit or demons.[36] Furthermore, he argued that the reference to heat points to the Holy Spirit. He thoroughly reviewed the literature on this debate, recognizing that the dative mostly describes the human spirit but noting that it can also be used for the divine Spirit, or his sphere of influence, citing the classic cases of Galatians 3:3, 5:16 and 1 Peter 3:18 and arguing that the simple fact of the dative case does not allow for a definite decision.[37]

Avemarie pointed out the close narrative connection between the Apollos and the Ephesian-disciples pericopae: mention of John's baptism last occurred in Acts 13:24 and does not occur again; the city of Ephesus provides scenic continuity. He concluded that despite obvious differences – such as Apollos' preaching and Spirit endowment versus the Ephesians' ignorance, correction versus rebaptism and bestowal of the Spirit – the reader has every reason to understand that the Ephesian disciples were Christians.[38] Avemarie concluded that John's baptism does not necessarily indicate one is John's disciple.[39] Atkinson, however, reads the differences as eliminating the Apollos/Ephesians link,[40] as does Turner, who argues the Ephesians could not have been Christians, because Paul

---

[32] Similarly, Pesch, *Apg 13-28*, 161; Schneider, *Apostelgeschichte 9,1-28,31*, 260.
[33] Menzies, *Empowered*, 220. Pesch suggests both human excitement and Holy Spirit, *Apg 13-28*, 161. Loisy argues from Romans 12:11 that it must have been Apollos' spirit, not the Holy Spirit, *Actes*, 712.
[34] Avemarie, *Tauferzählungen*, 71.
[35] *Ibid.*, 71. So too Turner, 'Endowment', 45; Turner, *Power*, 389; Dibelius, *Überlieferung*, 188; Keener, email correspondence 12/05/14.
[36] Avemarie gives the following breakdown: Holy Spirit: Luke 2:27; 4:1, 14; Acts 6:10; 8:29; 10:19; 11:12, and – here Avemarie expresses some ambiguity about the shorter text of NTG[27] – Acts 6:3; 8:18. Demons: Luke 9:39; 10:20; 24:37, 39; Acts 16:18; 23:8, 9. Human spirit: Luke 1:80 (but Avemarie is not certain), Acts 19:21; 20:22, Avemarie, *Tauferzählungen*, 71.
[37] *Ibid*. Beasley-Murray points out that Acts 17:16 cites Paul's spirit as being provoked: παρωξύνετο τὸ πνεῦμα αὐτοῦ but concludes Acts 18:25 refers to the Holy Spirit (*Baptism*, 110).
[38] *Ibid.*, 72.
[39] *Ibid.*, 71.
[40] Atkinson, *Baptism*, 55.

had to explain Jesus to them and baptise them in Jesus' name.[41] Nevertheless, it is clear that any discussion of Acts 19:1-7 must engage with the discussion at 18:24-28.

Conrad Gempf – Apollos Alone Was Christian

Conrad Gempf, while not arguing that the Ephesians were Christians, employs a narratively sensitive argument to make the case that Apollos was a Christian, though deficient in doctrine and social acceptance by the Christian community.[42] His argument could be used to bolster the Apollos/Ephesians connection and so will be considered here. Gempf reasons that the story must be analysed as one would a healing story in terms of 'before' and 'after'. He explains that if one did not know the meaning of 'withered arm' in the first part of a healing story, one could derive the meaning from the second part, the 'after', in which the arm functioned normally.[43] So too, one can derive information about the debated initial state of Apollos from the information given about his state after being corrected.

Gempf finds five aspects of Apollos' post-correction condition that shed light on his pre-correction situation. First, the Christian community had confidence in Apollos and recommended him. Second, Apollos helped the Christian community. These two aspects show contrast between the 'before' and the 'after' situation of Apollos. The third point, that Apollos powerfully refuted the Jews, remains in continuity with his previous life. Fourth, he used the scriptures. This Gempf also sees in continuity with the early Apollos' facility with scripture. Fifth, Apollos demonstrated Jesus was the Christ. This point Gempf finds problematic, since while Apollos was said to teach accurately about Jesus in the 'before' section, demonstrating that Jesus is Christ is a part of the 'after' section and therefore represents the result of the 'correction'.

Gempf sees several possible conclusions from this before/after pattern. First, Apollos could have anachronistically spoken accurately about Jesus, with his teaching 'fitting' Jesus, but without Apollos actually knowing it was the specific individual named Jesus who fulfilled the accurate teaching. Gempf rejects this possibility on two grounds: (1) why did Luke not use the word 'Christ' instead of the specific word 'Jesus'? (2) 'the way of the Lord' which Apollos was instructed in indicates post-John faith, since this term is used in Acts of believers in Jesus. Second, Gempf sees the possible conclusion that Apollos knew about Jesus to an extent, but not fully. Perhaps he saw Jesus only as an Elisha succeeding the Elijah, John the Baptist, or had some knowledge, like Felix, but not full

---

[41] Turner, *Power*, 389.
[42] Conrad Gempf, 'Apollos and the Ephesian Disciples: Befores and Afters (Acts 18:24-19:7)', I. Howard Marshall, Volker Rabens, and Cornelis Bennema (eds), *The Spirit and Christ in the New Testament and Christian Theology* (Grand Rapids: Eerdmans, 2012), 119-37; 136-37.
[43] *Ibid.*, 121.

knowledge. Gempf rejects this too, writing, 'Apollos appears not to need rebaptism or to receive the Spirit; he is adjusted rather than converted.'[44] Ultimately, Gempf sees Apollos as a Spirit-possessing Christian who needed correction in his Christology and social acceptance by the Christian community.[45]

Response to the Argument from Apollos – John's Baptism as a Demarcation Line[46]

Spirit Experience Belongs to the People of God

Gempf's before/after approach to the Apollos story must be integrated into a narrative analysis. The only question is whether Gempf has utilized all the before/after data contained within the story. Avemarie's point also is well taken. The case for 'Holy Spirit' in Acts 18:25 cannot be disallowed from the grammar. Turner writes, 'Had Apollos not received the Spirit, Priscilla and Aquila would have had more to give him than additional precision on an unspecified theological issue.'[47] However, this argument overlooks that within Luke's narrative, it is possible to have believed in Jesus and been baptised in this name, but still be without the Spirit.

Yet, Luke's presentation of John as filled with the Spirit from his mother's womb forms an important aspect of the Apollos story that has been left out of the foregoing analyses. Though we must recognize, as Turner and Atkinson point out, that Luke sometimes avoided direct reference to the Spirit prior to Pentecost,[48] Luke did not always do so. Within Luke's storyworld, powerful Holy Spirit experience was entirely possible before Pentecost. Witness the unborn John, leaping in the womb as his mother is filled with the Spirit (Luke 1:41). Consider Zacharias, Simeon, and the prophetically gifted Anna. In Luke's pre-Pentecost narrative, Jesus also taught his followers to pray to receive the Spirit without any indication from Luke that this teaching was only meant for the post-Pentecost community. For Luke, Holy Spirit experience belongs to the *people of God*.

The Demarcating Function of John's Baptism

The narrative impact of the early Acts chapters describing believers receiving the Holy Spirit within the context of the Jesus community would not go unfelt by the reader of chapters 18 and 19. Indeed, after the triangulating repetition of Acts 2:16, 33, and 38, Spirit-reception has been definitely linked by the narrative to kerygmatic acceptance of Jesus as the resurrected, ascended, exalted Christ of

---

[44] *Ibid.*, 135.
[45] *Ibid.*, 136-37; cf. the similar conclusion of Mark Lee, 'Evangelical Dialogue on Luke, Salvation, and Spirit Baptism', *Pn.* 26.1 (Spring, 2004), 81-98, 95.
[46] Käsemann also uses the concept of 'line of demarcation', but in regards to Spirit possession as differentiating John's baptism from Jesus' (cf. 'Disciples', 144).
[47] Turner, *Power*, 389.
[48] Atkinson, *Baptism*, 82, Turner, *Power*, 336.

prophecy and this link is only reinforced in subsequent scenes, even if the work of Christ is seen as sometimes mediated through gifted representatives of the Church.[49] Without an explicit directive from the narrator to the contrary, the reader must assume that a Holy Spirit experience belongs to the type of experience inaugurated at Pentecost and bestowed by the exalted Christ. Menzies, Avemarie, and Gempf are not wrong in their assumption at this point.

However, it has gone virtually unnoticed[50] that Luke *did* in fact make such an explicit corrective of the norm. Luke specifically cited John's baptism in the text as the delimitation of Apollos' knowledge – ἐπιστάμενος μόνον τὸ βάπτισμα Ἰωάννου. The apostles, by contrast, knew both the baptism of John and the baptism of Jesus; not because they knew Jesus' baptism in the sense of having undergone it, but because they were aware of it and even administered it. This statement redirects the reader's thinking to the time in the Lukan storyworld before Christ, when Spirit experience could be had apart from personal knowledge of the man Jesus, but not apart from membership in the people of God. Thus, if one reads Apollos as having a genuine Holy Spirit experience, and there is no need to deny this, it does not place him post-Pentecost; it merely places him within the people of God. He would still need to experience the nexus of Spirit activities that became available at Pentecost and was associated with the baptism of Jesus (Acts 2:38). To know only the baptism of John excludes knowledge of the day of Pentecost, for from that day the baptism of Jesus was preached and the Pentecostal gift of the Spirit was promised.

One might object that the Spirit could have fallen upon Apollos in the Pentecostal nexus without his knowing the baptism of Jesus. However, as Gempf has pointed out, Apollos was corrected in his understanding of Jesus as Christ. The Pentecostal gift of the Spirit was tied to the exaltation of Jesus as the Christ at God's right hand. For Luke, the Spirit was the proof of Jesus' exaltation. Therefore, within Luke's story, to have a deficient understanding of Jesus as Christ makes it probable that there was an accompanying deficiency in understanding of the Spirit given by the Christ.

Luke's references to John's baptism provide a framework within which the reader can place that delimiting statement of 'knowing only the baptism of John'. What Avemarie, Gempf, Menzies and others have not done is to analyse these Lukan usages of references to John's baptism with respect to their narrative function in defining Apollos and the Ephesian disciples. These usages show that Luke consistently and structurally employed the baptism of John as a demarcation line between Jesus' ministry and John's. It is not that Avemarie was unaware of the five references to John's baptism, but rather that he has not analysed them in

---

[49] Cf. Acts 2:32-33; 5:30-32.
[50] Lee comments on it, 'Dialogue', 95. Loisy addresses it. To know only John's baptism is to not know the baptism of Christ which is to not know the Spirit. Apollos is paralleled with the Ephesian Twelve. This is, however, not the historical reality of Apollos, but only a redactor's denigration of Apollos who was actually an apostle in his own right (*Actes*, 712-13). Similarly, Käsemann, 'Disciples', 144-47.

terms of their narrative function relative to Apollos and Acts 18:25. Instead, he reacted to Backhaus' appeal to these Baptistic references and consequent claim that the Ephesian disciples must have been baptised by John himself.[51] For Avemarie, a baptism according to the Johannine rite was all that the text supports. The references using John's baptism to demarcate the work of John from Jesus are familiar passages: Luke 3:16, Acts 1:5, Acts 1:21,22, Acts 10:36, 37, 38a, Acts 11:15-16, Acts 13:23,24. Acts 2:38 supplies a further relevant passage.

Six points summarize the demarcation structure. First, Luke distinguished the two ministries by two qualitatively different kinds of baptisms, water and Spirit. Second, John's baptism marked both the beginning point, in the opinion of the apostles, of their association together in Jesus' ministry, and the chronological counterpoint to his ascension. Third, God's preaching of peace through Jesus Christ to Israel began from Galilee, μετὰ τὸ βάπτισμα, *after* the baptism which John preached. Fourth, in an expansion of the first point, and contrast to the second, Pentecost marked 'the beginning'.[52] Fifth, John's preaching of a baptism of repentance took place *before* the entrance, πρὸ προσώπου τῆς εἰσόδου (13:24), of Israel's promised Saviour. In terms of 'before' and 'after', John's baptism came before Jesus, and Jesus ministered after John's baptism.

It may be objected that Jesus' own disciples knew only the baptism of John, for Luke nowhere said that they were baptised in Jesus' name. That is true in terms of having physically undergone only the baptism of John. However, Luke himself never said of the apostles that they 'knew only the baptism of John'. They had not been physically baptised in Jesus' name, but in terms of awareness, they knew much more than the baptism of John. They knew enough about baptism in Jesus' name to preach it and administer it.

Thus, contrary to Gempf, when Acts 18:25 says that Apollos, 'was speaking and teaching accurately the things concerning Jesus, knowing only the baptism of John', Luke used the phrase τὰ περὶ τοῦ Ἰησοῦ at least to some degree anachronistically. By the time a reader reaches Acts 18, s/he knows a considerable amount about 'the things concerning Jesus'. Mention of such 'things', at this late stage in the narrative, should recall the full kerygma. However, Luke's statement, ἐπιστάμενος μόνον τὸ βάπτισμα Ἰωάννου, *counteracts the initial impression* and places Apollos before what Luke already delimited as the time of God's preaching of peace to Israel through Jesus, that is, before the ministry of Jesus. Even if one argues that 'knowing only the baptism of John' does not exclude the time of Jesus' ministry, *it must exclude the day of Pentecost*. The baptism of Jesus began

---

[51] Avemarie, *Tauferzählungen*, 73-74; cf. Backhaus, *'Jüngerkreise'*, 204-205.

[52] David P. Moessner comments on this apparent contradiction: 'the prologues to Luke and Acts create an "intratext," characterized by a primary and a secondary beginning (Luke 3; Acts 2)', David P. Moessner, 'The Appeal and Power of Poetics (Luke 1:1-4): Luke's Superior Credentials (παρηκολουθηκότι), Narrative Sequence (καθεξῆς), and Firmness of Understanding (ἡ ἀσφάλεια) for the Reader', *Jesus and the Heritage of Israel: Luke's Narrative Claim upon Israel's Legacy* (Harrisburg: Trinity, 1999), 84-123; 105.

to be preached at Pentecost (no attempt to integrate John 3:22-26; 4:1-2 will be made, the focus here is upon Luke's story) and therefore, to not be aware of the Jesus baptism is to not be aware of Pentecost where Jesus was proclaimed the exalted Christ.

The full force of Gempf's analysis only comes when all the data are brought to bear. 'Before/after' analysis suggests that since Apollos taught Jesus as the Christ *after* being corrected, he likely had not done that before. Including the structural data from the broader narrative regarding the demarcating function of John's baptism confirms this and makes it difficult to view Apollos as needing only 'a doctrinal change or adjustment concerning his Christology'.[53] The paraphrase of 18:25 which Gempf considers but then rejects, 'his teaching about the coming one fitted Jesus accurately, even though his knowledge went no further than the baptism of John',[54] should be given greater consideration. However, even if he did know of Jesus, his knowledge had to have been of Jesus before Pentecost, when the baptism of Jesus began to be preached. This means his Pneumatology needed correcting as well as his Christology. If Pentecost at all represents a new nexus of activities of the same Spirit that had previously been experienced by God's people, and Acts 1:4-5 indicates that it does, then Apollos, fervent in the Spirit though he may have been, still lacked the Pentecostal experience. The narrative suggests he lacked what Joel spoke of – the promise of the Father.

The Argument from Authorial Intent for the Ephesians as Christians

What is to be made of Luke's concept of 'disciple'? Does Luke intend his reader to understand the Ephesians as genuine μαθηταί? If he does, then surely we must accept that they were Christians? First, we agree with Avemarie that Luke genuinely viewed the Ephesians as 'disciples'. Avemarie's clear and grammatical argumentation that Luke did not use the indicative of things not considered to be true (against Haacker and Marshall, who maintain that Luke presented things from the perspective of Paul,[55] and contrary to Parratt, who held that they had not even received a proper Johannine baptism, but only 'a proselyte lustration'[56]), finds confirmation in a basic principle of poetics – narrative authority. That is, Luke never indicated to his reader that he should do anything but implicitly trust everything he said. A narrator has the ability to do just the opposite, presenting himself to the reader as fallible, or even tricky and deceptive, challenging the

---

[53] Gempf, 'Apollos', 137.
[54] *Ibid.*, 135.
[55] Avemarie, *Tauferzählungen*, 72. K. Haacker, 'Einige Fälle von "Erlebter Rede" im Neuen Testament', *NT* 12 (1970), 70-77; 75. Marshall, *Luke*, 306.
[56] J.K. Parratt, 'The Rebaptism of the Ephesian Disciples', *ET* 79 (1968), 182-83; 182.

reader to decide what to believe and what to disbelieve.[57] Luke, however, perceived his narrative statements to be authoritative for his reader, as is clear from his introductory remarks to Theophilus. The authority of Luke's narrative presentation is never in the least brought into question in either of his two volumes. Here in chapter 19, Luke stated simply that Paul found τινες μαθηταί at Ephesus. He did this from his own, and not his character's perspective, as would occur in a phrase such as 'Paul, seeing what he took to be disciples' or 'Paul, thinking that he had found disciples', and as does occur on various occasions in Acts (27:13, 16:13, 27). Considering that Luke employed the convention of indicating character perspective with some added word such as 'supposing', some indication of the character's perspective would be required to read the text as presenting the perspective of Paul. Nor does Luke indicate any deficiency in their Johannine baptism, as Parratt assumed. We may therefore, on the basis of poetics, conclude with Avemarie that Luke unequivocally held the Ephesians for disciples.

Response to the Argument from Authorial Intent – Luke's 'People of God' Concept

Does acknowledging that Luke intended his reader to understand the Ephesians as genuine disciples mean that Luke considered them Christians? It certainly means that being a μαθητής was a distinctive thing. Paul recognized them as such. But the people of God has been a distinctive group in Luke's thought since the beginning of Luke-Acts. The nativity stories are filled with righteous, blameless, devout, Spirit-influenced individuals. These righteous are contrasted with the brood of vipers to whom John preaches who cannot consider Abraham as their father without genuine repentance (Luke 3:8). For Luke, membership in the covenant of Abraham (Luke 1:72-73), was a matter of moral standing, not just physical birth, and beginning with John, it was marked by ritual immersion. Though the disciples of John are presented as a group distinct both from the ordinary Israelite and from Jesus' disciples (Luke 7:18-24), they are not like the unbaptised Pharisees and lawyers (7:29-30). They are not outside the people of God. Luke simply indicated progression along the way of the Lord, because the least in the kingdom of God is greater than John (7:27-28).

Thus, Luke's statement that Paul found τινες μαθηταί can be understood within the narrative context of the evolving people of God and does not require Paul to have found 'Christians'. Since Luke qualified the assertion that they were μαθηταί with the information that they did not know about the Holy Spirit[58] and that they were baptised with John's baptism,[59] the weight of evidence shifts from their being Christians toward their being strictly disciples of John. They were

---

[57] Wayne C. Booth, *The Rhetoric of Fiction* (Chicago: University of Chicago Press, 1983), 158-59. Peter J. Rabinowitz, 'Truth in Fiction: A Reexamination of Audiences', *CI* 4.1 (Autumn, 1977), 121-41; 133-34.
[58] Similarly, Pesch, *Apg 13-28*, 165; Marshall, *Acts*, 305.
[59] *Ibid.*

members of the people of God, but not yet Christians. Thus, against J.C.O'Neill,[60] Paul's question whether they had received the Holy Spirit 'having believed', does not reflect a misjudgement on the apostle's part. Nor, as Marshall suggests, did they only seem to Paul to be disciples, while Paul nevertheless entertained doubts about their status.[61] Luke did not contravene Paul's initial assumption that they really had believed – they believed the gospel John preached (Luke 3:18). Against Shauf, Luke made the relationship between μαθηταί and the disciples of John explicit by referencing John's baptism as the extent of the knowledge of these disciples.[62]

The Ephesian Disciples and Luke's Initiation Ritual

Paul's Questions About the Spirit and Luke's Focalization of Baptism

Having found 'certain disciples,' Paul asked them, Εἰ πνεῦμα ἅγιον ἐλάβετε πιστεύσαντες? Interestingly, they respond with more than just a yes or no answer. Their comment that they had not heard of the Spirit, if taken literally as Avemarie took it,[63] excludes them from being followers of the later John and of Jesus; for in Luke's storyworld, John the Baptist began, at some unknown point in his ministry, to proclaim Jesus as the baptiser in the Holy Spirit, and Jesus himself taught on the Spirit.

Schneider, however, suggests that the Ephesian Twelve probably did have the Spirit, similarly to Apollos, but just were not consciously aware that they had the Spirit: 'One can also have the Spirit through faith in Jesus, without it being that one knows that one has him.'[64] For Schneider, this case is like that of the Samaritans. It was only Paul's post-baptismal handlaying that brought them to the awareness of what they already possessed, either through some unknown means, such as with Apollos, or through the baptism which Paul asked them to undertake. But this strains Luke's text. Luke did not say the Twelve had the Spirit but were unaware of what they had. Luke did not say that the Spirit was given in the water and Paul merely imparted 'salvation-historical awareness and an integration in the collective Christendom'.[65] The Ephesian disciples, like the Samaritans with Peter and John before them, did not come into possession of the Spirit until Paul laid his hands upon them. Their response to Paul's next question about their baptism identifies them simply as followers of the early Baptist, not of Jesus. They were truly without the Spirit.

---

[60] J.C. O'Neill, 'The Connection Between Baptism and the Gift of the Spirit in Acts', *JSNT* 63 (1996) 87-103; 97.
[61] Marshall, *Acts*, 306.
[62] Shauf, *Paul*, 147-48.
[63] Avemarie, *Tauferzälungen*, 74-76.
[64] 'Man kann auch den Geist haben durch den Glauben an Jesus, ohne daß man *weiß*, daß man ihn hat', Schneider, *Geist*, 49.
[65] 'heilsgeschichtlichen Erkenntnis und einer Einbindung in die Gesamtchristenheit', *Ibid*.

But Paul's question itself is significant. Coppens pointed out that Paul initially took the group for believers in Jesus, and only after questioning finds out that they had merely believed John's message.[66] Coppens was surely correct, for no signal in the context suggests that Paul would have been asking about belief other than in Christ. This indicates that belief in Christ and Spirit-reception do not necessarily go hand in hand. Separation between belief and receiving the Spirit was possible in Luke's presentation of Paul's thought. Paul's perspective is that of a normative character and is not contravened by the authoritative narrator and thus represents the view of Luke himself. As Atkinson writes: 'The record of Paul's question coincided with Luke's thought: belief was possible without reception of the Spirit.'[67]

But the Ephesus story is not to be read alone. Cho has rightly associated Samaria with Ephesus,[68] for when this story is read, the previous story of Samaria is in the reader's ER for initiation. This reinforces the idea that not only was belief possible without Spirit-reception, but that it was not an unusual circumstance – this is now the second time in the narrative it has happened. Luke presented a person with the gift of God to impart/facilitate the Spirit making an inquiry to discern whether anyone needed the exercise of his gift. Initiation on the mission field is shown to be less than air-tight. People did fail to get fully initiated, and this problem Luke specifically addressed.

Kittel pointed out Paul's response to their answer cannot be construed as merely a reaction to their not having the Holy Spirit.[69] They told him more than that. Paul responds to their not being aware of the Spirit.[70] Kittel rightly stated that Christian baptism without the Spirit was possible, but not Christian baptism without *hearing* about the Spirit. Kittel further remarked that Paul asked whether they received the Spirit when they believed, not when they were baptised.[71]

Paul then asks, 'Into what, then, were you baptised?' He did not ask whether or not they had been baptised. He assumes that. He asks what they were baptised into. On what basis then could he have assumed baptism? He knows that they were disciples and had believed. A reader can reasonably conclude that Paul assumes they have been baptised because baptism was associated with believing the good news (cf. Luke 3:18) and becoming a disciple (of either John or Jesus). The fact that they had not heard about the Spirit prompts Paul to ask about the nature of their baptism. This means that at minimum, information about the Spirit was normally presented at Christian baptism. Paul wants to know what kind of baptism they had had where there was no mention of the Spirit.

---

[66] Coppens, *L'Imposition*, 191.
[67] Atkinson, *Baptism*, 65. Cf. David A. Handy, 'Acts 8:14-25', *Interp.* 47.3 (July, 1993), 289-94; 291.
[68] Cho, *Spirit*, 156.
[69] Kittel, 'Wirkungen', 36.
[70] Atkinson, *Baptism*, 44. Bruce compares the idiom of John 7:39, *Acts* 406.
[71] Kittel, 'Wirkungen', 36.

They respond to Paul's second question by saying it was into John's baptism, and Paul rehearses that John baptised with a baptism of repentance and preached that people should believe in the one coming after him, Jesus. But how could they be John's disciples and yet not know of the Spirit? Leisegang provided a historical critical answer that fits within Luke's narrative. Originally, John did not speak about the Coming One's baptism.[72] Luke's narrative indicates that John began, at the point in his ministry when the people had reached a point of expectancy and discussion about whether he might be the Christ, to preach about this coming baptism (Luke 3:15-16). Thus, they accept Paul's teaching and he baptises them in Jesus' name. However, they do not receive the Spirit in the act of immersion. Paul lays his hands upon them, and then the Holy Spirit comes upon them and they speak in tongues and prophesy. As Kittel observed, the baptism was completed when the Spirit-facilitating handlaying took place. While recognizing that at that time, handlaying and immersion occurred close together, Kittel nevertheless insisted that the function of handlaying to impart/facilitate the Spirit not be imposed upon baptism (in the sense of immersion).[73] However, Kittel must be taken with a certain caution, for there remains the possibility that Paul noticed that even after immersion the Spirit did not come and *therefore* he did the extra ritual of handlaying. In other words, Luke did not explicitly state that immersion plus handlaying was the standard ceremony. Handlaying could have been a supplementary ritual.

What, then, is the meaning of the focalization of immersion, when the Spirit is received after the immersion and through the laying on of hands? In answer to this question we observe first that the initial question was not about immersion, but about Spirit-reception and belief. Immersion was assumed to have taken place at belief. Failure receive the Spirit does not explain what prompted Paul's question about immersion because Luke has already depicted believers being immersed in Jesus' name yet without receiving the Spirit. However, the Ephesians' further statement that they lacked knowledge of the Spirit presents itself as a possible trigger for Paul's question. The focalization on immersion thus arises out of the necessity of clarifying the distinction between John's immersion and Christian immersion. At Christian immersion, initiates can be expected to have at least heard of the Spirit, even if they are not expected to always have received the Spirit. We can conclude that while the Spirit is not given in the water, the gift of the Spirit is most certainly associated with the Christian immersion ceremony which included, at minimum, information about the Holy Spirit.[74]

---

[72] Leisegang, *Pneuma*, 73.
[73] Kittel, 'Wirkungen', 36.
[74] Cf. Canon J. Giblet, 'Baptism in the Spirit in the Acts of the Apostles', *OiC* 10 (1974), 162-71; 169.

Timing of Belief and Spirit-Reception

Dunn references Romans 8:9 and then asserts that the Paul of Acts is no different from the Paul of Romans because Paul's second question, 'Into what then were you baptised?' demonstrates that Paul definitively linked commitment to Jesus expressed in baptism with Spirit-reception.[75] One can agree with Dunn, in contrast to Menzies,[76] that the second question indicates Spirit-reception was linked to baptism.

However, since Spirit-reception is linked by Luke to both belief and water baptism, and since Luke spoke of only one Spirit-reception, not two, must that mean that belief occurred simultaneously with water baptism? Dunn reasons as follows:

> In the case of the Ephesians the sequence of Paul's questions indicates that πιστεῦσαι and βαπτισθῆναι are interchangeable ways of describing the act of faith: baptism was the necessary expression of commitment, without which they could not be said to have truly 'believed'.[77]

However, the 'sequence of Paul's questions' indicates no more than that belief and immersion were both part of initiation and both associated with receiving the Spirit, not that they were simultaneous. Moreover, one cannot conclude that just because an aorist verb (πιστεύσαντες) is coincident, its coincidence must be split-second simultaneous. One could easily use a coincident aorist to express general coincidence. For example, Luke 4:29:

> καὶ ἀναστάντες ἐξέβαλον αὐτὸν ἔξω τῆς πόλεως καὶ ἤγαγον αὐτὸν ἕως ὀφρύος τοῦ ὄρους ἐφ' οὗ ἡ πόλις ᾠκοδόμητο αὐτῶν ὥστε κατακρημνίσαι αὐτόν·

They did not cast him out of their city the split-second they arose. Dunn states the ambiguity of the aorist participle but then claims that here with Paul's question it must be coincident aorist.[78] However, the story of Samaria demonstrates that in Luke's mind, belief and Spirit-reception were not always coincident. The rest of the Ephesian story confirms this, for the Ephesians were immersed in Jesus' name before Paul laid hands on them to receive the Spirit. One could view the Ephesians' case as coincident only in a general sense.

Baptism and Laying on of Hands

Drawing upon both Acts 8 and 19, Kremer writes, 'The reception of the Holy Spirit is ... indeed closely tied to baptism, however, not indissolubly so.'[79] Sim-

---

[75] Dunn, *Baptism*, 86. So too, Fitzmyer, *Acts*, 643.
[76] Menzies, *Empowered*, 221.
[77] Dunn, *Baptism*, 96.
[78] *Ibid.*, 87.
[79] 'Der Empfang des heiligen Geistes ist ... zwar eng mit der Taufe verknüpft, aber nicht unlöslich damit verbunden', Kremer, *Pfingstbericht*, 200.

ilarly, Udo Schnelle asserts that in Acts, handlaying, baptism, and Spirit-reception belong close together, but do not always coincide.[80] George Dion Dragas sees the coming of the Spirit as a 'necessary sequel' to baptism.[81] Stott, however, did not 'think the order is very significant'.[82] The various elements of the Ephesian's initiation, 'belonged together and cannot be separated'.[83] Dunn argues similarly: baptism and laying on of hands are one ceremony,[84] the climax of which is the handlaying. However, he then goes on to say that 'The laying on of hands is almost parenthetical; the sequence of events is "baptism (resulting in) ... Spirit".'[85] He likens Paul's handlaying to the giving of the right hand of fellowship.[86] Turner likewise reasons:

> No separation of receiving the Spirit from their Christian baptism is necessarily to be deduced from the statement that the Spirit was conferred in the laying on of hands (v. 5), for the latter may well have been part of Paul's baptismal procedure.
>
> Luke certainly does not encourage the view that laying on of hands is a necessary condition of receiving the Spirit.[87]

Witherington, however, appeals to the sequence of verses 5 and 6 to affirm that the Spirit did not come in the immersion, but in Paul's handlaying. Though, Witherington denies that this was a normal procedure.[88] Avemarie stated that, based on the sequence of the report and the presence of the genitive absolute, that Luke (in this instance) connected the impartation of the Spirit primarily to handlaying.[89] The fact that a genitive absolute, 'is unconnected with the rest of the sentence (i.e., its subject – the genitive noun or pronoun – is different from the subject of the main clause)',[90] cannot be taken to mean that the genitive ab-solute is parenthetical in the sense of irrelevant. Wallace states that in a genitive absolute construction, 'the participle is normally (about 90%

---

[80] Udo Schnelle, 'Taufe II, Neues Testament' (Berlin: Water de Gruyter, 2001), 663-74; 671.
[81] George Dion Dragas, 'The Seal of the Gift of the Spirit: the Sacrament of Chrismation', *GOTR* 56.1-4 (Spring-Winter, 2011), 143-59, 152.
[82] Stott, *Baptism*, 36.
[83] *Ibid.*
[84] Similarly, New, 'Note XI', 136.
[85] Dunn, *Baptism*, 87.
[86] *Ibid.*
[87] Turner, *Power*, 391.
[88] Witherington, *Acts*, 571-72.
[89] Avemarie, *Tauferzählungen*, 165. Similarly, Heckel, *Segen*, 329; Backhaus, '*Jüngerkreise*', 227; Windisch, *Taufe*, 92. Hartman, *Name*, 139. Cf. F.M. Rendtorff, who was certain about the general link between handlaying and Spirit-reception, *Die Taufe im Urchristentum im Lichte der Neueren Forschungen, ein Kritischer Bericht* (Leipzig: J.C. Hinrichs'sche Buchhandlung, 1905), 52. For Howard Clark Kee, Paul's handlaying 'symbolizes and effects the transfer of divine power', *To Every Nation under Heaven: The Acts of the Apostles* (Harrisburg: Trinity, 1997), 228.
[90] Wallace, *Grammar*, 655.

of the time) *tem-poral*, though it can on occasion express any of the adverbial ideas'.[91] Thus, the Spirit came 'when' Paul laid his hands upon the Ephesians. This is by no means irrelevant to understanding the story, for it links the act of handlaying to the gift of the Spirit on this occasion. No matter how much Dunn seeks to link the Spirit directly to faith actualized in water, Luke narrated a second act of handlaying which communicated the Spirit. Neither faith nor the water itself communicated the Spirit. Turner's acknowledgement that Paul's handlaying may have been part of his standard baptismal procedure must be taken seriously.[92]

Avemarie went a step beyond Turner and Dunn in emphasizing the particular function of handlaying (in this instance, though not normally[93]) as the primary means of communicating the Spirit, without separating handlaying from the baptismal ceremony. Dunn and Turner are correct in seeing Paul as performing one unitary initiation ceremony and not two. However, in this particular story about Paul initiating a group of new believers, the ritual act with which the coming of the Spirit was associated was not immersion, but handlaying.

The Ephesian Story and the ER for Initiation

From Acts 8 and 19, Schulz provocatively concludes:

> With Luke, the Spirit no longer blows where he wills (as in John 3:8), and he is also no longer without further action conferred through the sacrament of baptism, but rather is bound to the twelve original apostles and their successors who stand in apostolic succession, the church office-bearers.[94]

Does a narrative analysis lead inexorably to the conclusion that the Spirit is no longer free, but 'regulated and controlled' by apostles and their successors?[95] Not entirely, because sequential reading does not evaluate Acts 8 and 19 alone. While recognizing the narrative power of these passages, sequential analysis considers the Spirit-reception stories previous to Acts 8 and 19. Acts 19 cannot be snipped off from the series and assumed to contain all data on Spirit-reception. The previous scenes lend meaning to the elements in the final scene.

---

[91] *Ibid.*
[92] Cf. more generally, Karl-Heinrich Bieritz, *Liturgik* (Berlin: Walter de Gruyter, 2004), 571; Jesaja Langenbacher, *Firmung als Initiation in Gemeinschaft: Theologie von Firmlingen – eine Herausforderung und Bereicherung für die Lebens – und Glaubenskommunikation in der Kirche* (Berlin: Lit Verlag, W. Hopf, 2010), 365; Alfred Wikenhauser, *Die Apostelgeschichte* (Regensburg: Verlag Friedrich Pustet, 1951), 79.
[93] Acts 2:38 is the normal model, Avemarie, *Tauferzählungen*, 139.
[94] 'Der Geist weht bei Lukas nicht mehr, wo er will (so Joh. 3,8), und er wird auch nicht mehr ohne weiteres durch das Taufsakrament verliehen, sondern ist an die zwölf Urapostel und ihre in apostolischer Sukzession stehenden Nachfolger, die kirchlichen Amtsträger, gebunden', Schulz, *Mitte*, 140.
[95] *Ibid.*

So, John's baptism of the crowds introduces baptism of repentance. Jesus' baptism introduces the element of Spirit empowerment and associates it with prayer at the time of immersion. Jesus' teaching on prayer reinforces this link between prayer and Spirit experience. The Pentecost story focalizes dissociative xenolalia, identifies it as both prophecy and doxological speech, motifs which will be highlighted in later stories, and identifies it with the nexus of Spirit activity prophesied by Joel and spoken of by Jesus. It creates a programmatic expectation, though one still open to the possibility of modification, that new initiates are to receive this nexus upon repentance and immersion in Jesus' name. Samaria shows, for the first time in the narrative, new converts receiving the Spirit. In that depiction, Luke focalized handlaying by specially gifted individuals and identified it as the mechanism of Spirit facilitation on that occasion. Luke also clarified any impression from Acts 2:38 that immersion alone would always impart the Spirit – it does not always do so. The Ethiopian Eunuch story, Western text, shows the Spirit coming at immersion and apart from handlaying. Where Philip's ministry had previously not facilitated the Spirit, now it did. Saul's conversion reiterates that a non-apostle can be gifted to facilitate the Spirit. Cornelius' house contributes the concept of Spirit-reception occurring spontaneously in response to acceptance of the kerygma preached by a gifted minister (cf. the concept of resident power, Luke 5:17; 6:19; 8:46; Acts 5:15). It highlights the doxological aspect of tongues from Acts 2 and explains that the early leadership identified Spirit-reception, not by tongues alone, but by tongues and magnifying God. An element of intelligibility is needed. Finally, the Ephesian story shows Paul, the protagonist, conducting an initiation consisting of immersion in Jesus' name, handlaying, and charismatic Spirit-reception. It highlights the prophetic aspect of tongues, again combining tongues with intelligible utterances, and gives the last instantiation of the ER for initiation. Being last does *not* mean that Luke included every aspect of the ER for initiation in the Ephesian story. Prayer, both on the part of the initiates and the initiator, is conspicuously absent. However, the book is not claiming that Ephesus is the full exemplar containing every detail of the baptism ceremony. Ephesus is one instantiation of the baptism ER. The full ER is constructed cumulatively. It need not be completely described in any particular story to exist as the accumulation of knowledge from all the stories.

Is Schulz, then, correct? The Spirit, in this particular story, is not given in immersion but through handlaying by a notable minister of whom, just a few verses later, Luke will state that he did extraordinary miracles (Δυνάμεις τε οὐ τὰς τυχούσας Acts 19:11). The question becomes how typical Ephesus is for Lukan initiation. Was Paul's handlaying simply an emergency procedure employed because he saw that the Spirit had not come upon the Ephesians? That is possible, but an argument from silence. Luke made no such indication. Neither did Luke state that immersion followed by handlaying was the typical procedure. That is simply what Luke showed the reader in this particular instance. What should be clear after the repetition of handlaying at Samaria and Ephesus is that if a convert does not receive the Spirit without human assistance, human assistance is to be rendered.

What then, are the ways the Spirit can come? He comes in prayer at the time of immersion (Luke 3:21-22). He comes simply in response to prayer (Luke 11:13). Acts 2:38 assures the gift of the Spirit upon repentance and immersion, but the reader, based upon Luke 3, expects not merely immersion, but also prayer to accompany that immersion. It is therefore not possible to state conclusively that Luke presented the Spirit as attached to immersion alone. But if immersion (and/or prayer, it is not clear whether prayer was present at Philip's baptisms) does not effect the Spirit, then prayer and handlaying by gifted ministers can (Acts 8). The Spirit, in the Western text, can come after immersion apart from any prayer or ritual. The Spirit can also come simply in response to faith, apart from any ritual (the presence of a gifted minister *may* also contribute to the coming of the Spirit in the Cornelius situation). Finally, the Spirit can come through handlaying after immersion.

What then, is the implied reader to draw from Luke's presentation? There is variety in the Spirit's modes of coming, yet there is consistency in that when the Spirit does not come, handlaying is presented as a means of facilitating the Spirit's arrival. Luke never stated handlaying is the only ritual to be practiced if the Spirit fails to come, but it is the only such ritual which he presents. In this limited sense then, Schulz has an element of truth, but even the gifted are not gifted apart from the sovereignty of God.[96] However, the descent of the Spirit at Pentecost, unmediated by any except for the exalted Christ, remains in the ER for Spirit-reception, as does Jesus' teaching on prayer for the Spirit. The reader knows the Spirit can come from the Father, through Christ, in response to prayer. This means the apostles and their successors (if one wishes, as Schulz, to consider Ananias and Paul in this sense)[97] do not have an absolute monopoly on the Spirit.

Conclusion

This chapter has addressed a notoriously difficult passage by appealing to narrative structure to resolve the status of Apollos and the Ephesian disciples. Some have argued for the Ephesians to be Christians from linguistic considerations which seem to suggest that πιστεύω and μαθητής are distinctly Christian in their connotations. To this is added the argument that, based upon the Acts 18:25 description of Apollos as 'seething in the Spirit' and teaching accurately about Jesus, he must have been a Christian before he met Priscilla and Aquila. Gempf also argues with the 'before' and 'after' approach that Apollos was a Christian. Apollos and the Ephesians are linked by some commentators and so the argument

---

[96] Though Peter and John pray, and thus demonstrate dependence upon God, Luke did not depict Paul praying. Perhaps Paul is presented as greater, or, more likely, the reader is expected to fill in the gap with prayer based upon the prayer-filled ER.

[97] *Ibid.*, 139-40.

runs that if Apollos was a Christian, then the Ephesians must have been as well. However, the chapter has shown that Luke consistently used John's baptism as a demarcation line between the ministries of John and Jesus. Therefore, when Luke qualified what otherwise looks like 'Christian' terminology with reference to the baptism of John, he redirected attention to the time before Jesus when the people of God had Spirit experiences, the 'way of the Lord' was being prepared, and the gospel was being preached by John and believed by multitudes. However, if one sees this as too hard and fast a break between the ministries of John and Jesus, the latest possible date for Apollos' knowledge of Jesus is just prior to Pentecost, for it is from that point that the baptism of Jesus began to be preached. Apollos thus needed correction not just in his Christology, but probably also in his Pneumatology, for though he had a Spirit experience, if he was unaware of Pentecost, and unaware that Jesus had been exalted to the right hand of God, the implied reader would expect him to also have been unaware of the nexus of Spirit activities that proceeded from the exalted Christ.

Paul's initial questioning of the Ephesians reveals that Luke could separate belief from Spirit-reception. When this is read against the background of separation of belief and Spirit-reception in Acts 8 and 9, this suggests that Paul's question was not extraordinary. The implied reader would think it not unusual for believers, like those at Samaria, to have not received the Spirit. Paul's second question, 'Into what, then, were you immersed?' indicates that Paul assumes that they were immersed when they believed. This implies that Paul, when he asked his *first* question, thought one could believe and be immersed without having received the Spirit. It is their reply that they had *not heard* about the Spirit that prompts his inquiry into what baptism they had received. While Paul's first question precludes one from saying that Spirit-reception was automatic at immersion, his second question indicates that information about the Spirit *was* expected to be given at Christian immersion. The evident focalization of immersion thus arises out of the necessity of clarifying the distinction between John's immersion and Christian immersion.

The chapter addressed Dunn's argument that there is no process in Christian initiation: 'to believe' and 'to be baptised' both mean the 'act of faith'. First, Dunn presses the grammatical category of coincidence too far: it does not necessitate split-second coincidence. 'When' can mean 'around the time' one believed without meaning 'at the split-second' one believed. Moreover, stories previous to this point (Acts 2:37-38, Acts 8, Acts 9) separate belief and Spirit-reception so the reader has no reason to assume that they must be absolutely coincident here. Dunn, Turner, and Avemarie were then compared in terms of their view of handlaying and reception of the Spirit. Dunn and Turner see the Spirit coming in response to the immersion ceremony, which they recognize as including (at least in this instance) handlaying. Avemarie, in the case of the Ephesians, specifically identified handlaying as the means, within the immersion ceremony, of imparting the Spirit. The chapter argued that the initiation ceremony can be analysed in terms of its elements. Luke identified handlaying as the mechanism for Spirit facilitation which Paul used, just as Peter and John before him.[98] Finally, the chapter placed Acts 19:1-7 in context of the accumulated ER for Spirit-reception. Most of the elements are together: baptism in Jesus' name, handlaying (which was associated with prayer in Acts 8), and Spirit-reception manifesting with tongues plus an intelligible utterance, in this case, prophecy. The elements do not occur simultaneously, but neither is there any subsequence from the ceremony of initiation. However, the chapter has *not* claimed that Acts 19:1-7 represents a typical initiation. Yet, Luke included the scene in his work to Theophilus and so its potential for instructive value cannot be lightly dismissed. Luke presented a variety of ways the Spirit can come. However, he also presented handlaying as a way in which, if the Spirit does not come in some other fashion, the Spirit can be facilitated to come. Handlaying is, at minimum, a supplementary procedure. The fact that it occurs in two expanded initiation scenes (Acts 8 and 19; possibly also Acts 9) means it was not insignificant for Luke and suggests, but does not require, that it played a more regular role in initiation than simply the odd emergency.

---

[98] Cf. chapter 6 section 3 for why Ananias is not listed here.

Conclusion

The book has found that Luke created a programmatic expectation of dissociative xenolalia/magnifying God as the experience of the Spirit which takes place when the Spirit comes during Christian initiation. Luke did not explicitly exclude the possibility that other phenomena might equally attest to the Spirit's arrival. However, neither did he present any other phenomena as being used by the early church leadership to verify the Spirit's arrival. The ways the Spirit comes, however, are various, though not random. Luke associates the Spirit's descent with prayer at the time of immersion, and also with prayer alone. If one adopts the Western text in 8:39, then immersion alone can facilitate the Spirit. If immersion and prayer do not bring the Spirit, then handlaying by individuals gifted in facilitating the Spirit is employed. The Spirit may also come in response to belief in the message preached without handlaying or prayer. Luke does not exclude the possibility that the Spirit could be facilitated by other means.

The book has made an original contribution in its analysis of focalization in Acts 2. There it was shown that the story excludes wind and fire from the narrative discussion and, through focalization, identifies dissociative xenolalia (with God magnifying content) as the referent for Peter's discourse about the Spirit. Therefore, when Peter promises the Spirit to all future converts upon repentance and immersion, the implied reader expects all converts to experience dissociative xenolalia. The book has argued that this programmatic expectation can and should be acknowledged *without* concluding straightaway that xenolalia is the *sine qua non* experience of Spirit-reception because Luke does not explicitly negate other Spirit experiences. Luke does not state, 'xenolalia and only xenolalia'. Therefore, the implied reader must finish the whole Lukan narrative before arriving at a definitive conclusion regarding manifestation of Spirit-reception.

The book has also contributed by pointing out that in Jesus' Jordan experience, the close association of immersion with prayer, and the attachment of the descent of the Spirit to the prayer aspect of the overall experience, leads the implied reader, reading sequentially through the narrative, to arrive at Acts 2 and expect prayer to accompany immersion and not to expect mere immersion to impart the Spirit. So too, Saul's calling upon the name of the Lord should be understood as a prayer accompanying his immersion.

The book's study of focalization in Acts 8 shows that handlaying, following prayer, was the mechanism, on that particular occasion, of facilitating the coming of the Spirit to new converts. It was not simply Simon's mistaken idea. The book has also pointed out that the very popular argument that the delay of the Spirit to the Samaritans was due to a deliberate withholding on the part of God is merely an argument from silence. Luke did not explicitly state why the Spirit did not come. Luke simply provided a solution to the problem – prayer and handlaying by gifted individuals. Luke did not state how many believers are so gifted. It could be that all believers whose hearts are right with God can equally facilitate the coming of the Spirit. However, the fact that Philip, for whatever unknown reason, did not facilitate the Spirit to his converts before the arrival of Peter and John, speaks against this. However, Philip likely acquired the ability to facilitate the Spirit after the arrival of the apostles, for the Western text in 8:39 depicts Philip's convert as receiving the Spirit. Samaria cannot be claimed as standard procedure, nor as an exceptional case, for Luke did not state either way. Samaria is simply a possible solution to a possible problem.

Cornelius' house is significant because it shows church leaders looking to Pentecost as the standard Spirit experience against which other Spirit experiences are compared. This increases the possibility of *sine qua non* character for xenolalia, though, as cautioned above, the entire narrative is not yet complete and, without an explicit 'xenolalia and only xenolalia' statement, Luke has, until his last sentence, the ability to modify or alter the impressions, strong though they may be, that he has earlier presented.

At Cornelius' house Luke does make a clarification to his previously emphasized expectation of xenolalia. He presents not simply xenolalia, which may or may not be recognized and understood, but xenolalia/magnifying God, as evidence that the Spirit has come. This does not indicate that Luke thought tongues were non-language, for he identified tongues at Pentecost as xenolalia. There is no reason to think that Luke ceased viewing tongues as genuine language. However, at Pentecost, people were present who understood the languages, but at Cornelius' house no list of recognized languages is provided. Nevertheless, Luke maintains the intelligible aspect of charismatic behaviour by noting that they both spoke in tongues and magnified God. He does not state whether the magnification was in addition to the tongues or the content of the tongues, nor does he state how the utterance and/or behaviour was identified as magnifying God. Any suggestion is argument from silence. He also does not say that some spoke in tongues and some magnified God. That too would be an argument from silence. Rather, he equates the Gentiles' experience with that of the Jews at Pentecost, who, in the narrated portion of the story, all spoke in tongues. Luke also presents the experience of the Spirit as having a dissociative element. He expects initiates' experiences to be comparable to being 'baptised in the Spirit'.

Finally, the story of the Ephesians repeats the idea of handlaying as a means of facilitating the coming of the Spirit. Luke did not state that this is the standard ritual initiation, nor did he state that it is an exceptional occurrence. He simply presented it as what was done, on a particular occasion, by an early Christian leader. Inasmuch as the implied reader looks to the early Christian leadership as worthy of emulation (Acts 2:42 'they were devoting themselves to the teaching of the apostles' indicates a positive answer to the question), Ephesus provides a model. This marks a second occasion when the Spirit explicitly did not come in the water of immersion, but in the handlaying rite. Luke did not explicitly state how much time elapsed between immersion and handlaying, but he did not narrate any other events in between these two, suggesting that the time gap was inconsequential to the story. He also did not state whether the handlaying was a supplementary procedure because the Spirit failed to come earlier. But, handlaying, if the Spirit has not already come, is clearly a procedure followed by apostolic leadership.

Does Luke, then, have a standard ritual procedure? The book concludes that Luke presented a standard framework within which there is a limited amount of variety. Luke 3:21-22 and Acts 2:37-39 function programmatically, presenting immersion plus prayer as the standard ritual ceremony. Handlaying may be added to the ceremony if the Spirit does not come through the other elements or immediately upon belief. For success, handlaying requires giftedness in facilitating the Spirit; however, Luke did not explicitly delimit who has this gifting except to exclude those whose heart is not right with God. The order of the elements may, by sovereign intervention of God, be reversed, but otherwise the apostolic teaching of Peter in Acts 2:38 stands as programmatic.

What, then, of xenolalia and Spirit-reception? Luke again narrated not mere xenolalia, but xenolalia plus prophecy. Again, he did not state that some spoke in tongues and some prophesied. That is, he did not explicitly contradict the programmatic expectation of xenolalia; but neither did he present xenolalia without clearly intelligible utterance. The book recognizes several features of Luke's presentation. First, there is a programmatic expectation of xenolalia upon Spirit-reception, first presented at Pentecost and later reinforced at Cornelius' house. Second, Luke presented church leaders employing as a standard of comparison, not mere xenolalia, but xenolalia/magnifying God. That is, there was an intelligible aspect to the initiates' utterances. This intelligible aspect is reinforced in the Ephesus story with prophecy. Third, though Luke never explicitly excluded the possibility that Spirit-reception could be signalled by another phenomenon, or by no manifestation, neither did he affirm such a possibility. That is, he concluded his last Spirit-reception scene without undermining his initial programmatic expectation of xenolalia. Thus, the book has shown that Luke prioritized xenolalia to an extent far greater than generally recognized.

What then is the way forward in research? The question now is to ask how Luke's attention to initiation relates to the works of John and Paul. Sociologically, Luke's understanding of receiving the Spirit needs to be examined in terms of what is known about 'spirit' possession in other cultures of the world. Finally, Luke's concept of initiation needs to be addressed from the standpoint of ritual studies. Does Luke have a concept of liminality? Of communitas?

Bibliography

Adler, Nikolaus. *Das erste christliche Pfingstfest: Sinn und Bedeutung des Pfingstberichtes Apg 2, 1-13*, NTA 18/1. Münster: Aschendorffsche Verlagsbuchhandlung, 1938.

——. *Taufe und Handauflegung: Eine Exegetisch-Theologische Untersuchung von Apg 8, 14-17.* Münster: Aschendorffsche Verlagsbuchhandlung, 1951.

Aker, Benny C. 'Acts 2 as a Paradigmatic Narrative for Luke's Theology of the Spirit'. A paper presented at an Evangelical Theological Society session on Luke-Acts, no date [posted to web 10/30/2001].

Aland, Barbara, et al. *The Greek New Testament* 4th Revised Edition. Stuttgart: Deutsche Bibelgesellschaft, 2012.

Alexander, Loveday. *Acts in its Ancient Literary Context: A Classicist Looks at the Acts of the Apostles.* London: T&T Clark, 2005.

——. *The Preface to Luke's Gospel: Literary Convention and Social Context in Luke 1.1-4 and Acts1.1.* SNTS.MS 78. Cambridge: CUP, 1993.

Alter, Robert. 'Biblical Type-Scenes and the Uses of Convention'. *CI* 5.2 (Winter 1978), 355-368.

——. *The Art of Biblical Narrative.* N.pl.: Basic Books, 1981.

Amit, Yairah, trans. Yael Lotan. *Reading Biblical Narratives: Literary Criticism and the Hebrew Bible.* Minneapolis: Fortress, 2001.

Amougou-Atangana, Jean. *Ein Sakrament Des Geistempfangs? Zum Verhältnis Von Taufe Und Firmung.* Freiburg: Herder, 1974.

Anderson, R. Dean, Jr. *Ancient Rhetorical Theory and Paul*, Rev. Ed. Leuven: Peeters, 1999.

Anderson, Janice Capel. 'Double and Triple Stories, the Implied Reader, and Redundancy in Matthew'. *Se.* 31, 1985, 71-89.

Arend, Walter. *Die Typischen Scene bei Homer.* PFKP 7. Berlin: Weidmannsche Buchhandlung, 1933.

Atkinson, William P. *Baptism in the Spirit: Luke-Acts and the Dunn Debate.* Eugene, OR: Pickwick, 2011.

Austin, Gerard. *The Rite of Confirmation: Anointing with the Spirit.* Collegeville, MN: Liturgical, 2004.

Avemarie, Friedrich. *Die Tauferzählungen der Apostelgeschichte: Theologie und Geschichte.* WUNT 139. Tübingen: Mohr Siebeck, 2002.

Backhaus, Knut. *Die 'Jüngerkreise' des Täufers Johannes: Eine Studie zu den religionsgeschichtlichen Ursprüngen des Christentums.* PaThSt 19. Paderborn: Ferdinand Schöningh, 1991.

Baer, Heinrich von. *Der Heilige Geist in den Lukasschriften.* BWANT 39. Stuttgart: Verlag W. Kohlhammer, 1926.

Bal, Mieke. *Narratology: Introduction to the Theory of Narrative*, 3rd Ed. Toronto: University of Toronto Press, 2009.

Barth, Gerhard. *Die Taufe in frühchristlicher Zeit.* 2., verbesserte Auflage. Neukirchen-Vluyn: Neukirchener Verlag, 2002 [1981].

Barrett, C.K. *A Critical and Exegetical Commentary on the Acts of the Apostles*, Vol. I. London: T&T Clark, 1994.

—. *A Critical and Exegetical Commentary on the Acts of the Apostles*, Vol. II. London: T&T Clark, 1998.

—. 'Light on the Holy Spirit From Simon Magus (Acts 8,4-25)'. J. Kremer, ed., *Les Actes des Apôtres: Traditions, rédaction, théologie.* Leuven: Leuven University Press, 1979, 281-295.

Bauer, Walter, rev. and ed. Frederick William Danker, et al. *A Greek-English Lexicon of the New Testament and other Early Christian Literature.* 3rd Ed. (BDAG). Chicago: University of Chicago Press, 2000.

Bauernfeind, Otto. *Kommentar und Studien zur Apostelgeschichte.* WUNT 22. Tübingen: J.C.B. Mohr, Paul Siebeck, 1980.

Beale, G.K. *The Temple and the Church's Mission: A Biblical Theology of the Dwelling Place of God.* NSBT. Downers Grove, IL: IVP, 2004; Leicester: Apollos, 2004.

Beasley-Murray, G.R. *Baptism in the New Testament.* London: Macmillan; New York: St Martin's, 1962.

Bede, The Venerable, trans. Lawrence T. Martin. *Commentary on the Acts of the Apostles.* CistSS 117. Kalamazoo, MI: Cistercian, 1989.

Berger, Klaus. 'Propaganda und Gegenpropaganda im Frühen Christentum: Simon Magus als Gestalt des Samaritanischen Christentums'. Lukas Bormann, Kelly Del Tredici and Angela Standhartinger, eds. *Religious Propaganda & Missionary Competition in the New Testament World, Essays Honoring Dieter Georgi.* Leiden: E.J. Brill, 1994, 313-317.

Berlin, Adele. *Poetics and Interpretation of Biblical Narrative.* Sheffield: Almond, 1983.

Beza, Theodore, trans. L. Tomson. *The New Testament of our Lord Jesus Christ, translated out of Greeke by Theod. Beza.* Dort: Isaac Canin, 1603.

Bieritz, Karl-Heinrich. *Liturgik.* DGL. Berlin: Walter de Gruyter, 2004.

Bird, Michael F. 'The Unity of Luke-Acts in Recent Discussion'. *JSNT* 29.4 (2007), 425-448.

Black, Matthew. 'The Holy Spirit in the Western Text of Acts'. Eldon Jay Epp and Gordon D. Fee, eds. *New Testament Textual Criticism, Its Significance for Exegesis: Essays in Honour of Bruce M. Metzger.* Oxford: Clarendon, 1981, 159-170.

Blanc, Douglas A. *A Theological Construction of Spirit Baptism: Seeking a Consensus Between Baptists and Pentecostals in the USA.* Ph.D. dissertation, University of Wales: Trinity St. David, 2012.

Blass, F. and A. Debrunner, trans. Robert W. Funk. *A Greek Grammar of the New Testament and other Early Christian Literature.* Chicago: The University of Chicago Press, 1961.

Blomberg, Craig L. *From Pentecost to Patmos: An Introduction to Acts through Revelation*. Nashville: B&H, 2006.
— and Jennifer Foutz Markley. *A Handbook of New Testament Exegesis*. Grand Rapids: Baker Academic, 2010.
Böhlemann, Peter. *Jesus und der Täufer: Schlüssel zur Theologie und Ethik des Lukas*. SNTS.MS 99. Cambridge: CUP, 1997.
Böhm, Martina. *Samarien und die Samaritai bei Lukas*. WUNT2 111. Tübingen: J.C.B. Mohr, Paul Siebeck, 1999.
Bock, Darrell L. *Acts*. BECNT. Grand Rapids: Baker Academic, 2007.
Booth, Wayne C. *The Rhetoric of Fiction*. 2nd Ed. Chicago: University of Chicago Press, 1983.
Bornhäuser, D. Karl. *Studien zur Apostelgeschichte*. Gütersloh: Verlag C. Bertelsmann, 1934.
Bovon, Francois. *Luke the Theologian: Fifty-five Years of Research (1950-2005)* 2nd Rev. Ed. Waco, TX: Baylor University Press, 2006.
Bozung, Douglas C. 'The Pentecostal Doctrine of Initial Evidence: A Study in Hermeneutical Method'. *JMT* (Spring, 2004), 89-107.
Brawley, Robert L. *Centering on God: Method and Message in Luke-Acts*. Louisville, KY: Westminster/John Knox, 1990.
Brewer, William F. 'The Nature of Narrative Suspense and the Problem of Rereading'. Peter Vorderer, Hans Jürgen Wulff, Mike Friedrichsen, eds. *Suspense: Conceptualizations, Theoretical Analyses, and Empirical Explorations.* Mahwah, NJ: Lawrence Erlbaum, 1996, 107-128.
Britt, Brian. 'Prophetic Concealment in a Biblical Type Scene'. *CBQ* 64.1 (2002), 37-58.
Brown, Gillian and George Yule, *Discourse Analysis*. Cambridge: CUP, 1983.
Brown, Jeannine K. *The Disciples in Narrative Perspective: The Portrayal and Function of the Matthean Disciples*. ABib 9. Leiden: Brill, 2002.
Brown, Schuyler. '"Water-Baptism" and "Spirit-Baptism" in Luke-Acts'. *AThR* 59.2 (April 1977), 135-151.
Bruce, F.F. 'Luke's Presentation of the Spirit in Acts', *CrThR* 5.1, 1990, 15-29.
—. *The Acts of the Apostles: Greek Text with Introduction and Commentary*. 3rd Rev. and Enl. Ed. Leicester: Apollos; Grand Rapids: Eerdmans, 1990.
—. 'The Holy Spirit in the Acts of the Apostles'. *Interp.* 27.2 (1973), 166-183.
Bruner, Frederick Dale. *A Theology of the Holy Spirit: The Pentecostal Experience and the New Testament Witness*. London: Hodder and Stoughton; n.p.: Eerdmans, 1970.
Büchsel, Friedrich. *Der Geist Gottes im Neuen Testament*. Gütersloh: T. Bertelsmann, 1926.
Burnside, W. F. *The Acts of the Apostles: The Greek Text Edited with Introduction and Notes for the Use of Schools*. Cambridge: CUP, 1916.
Burridge, Richard A. 'The Gospels and Acts'. Stanley E. Porter, ed. *Handbook of Classical Rhetoric in the Hellenistic Period 330 B.C. – A.D. 400*. Leiden: Brill, 1997, 507-532.

Cadbury, Henry J. *The Style and Literary Method of Luke*. HThS VI. New York: Kraus, 1969 [OUP, 1920].

Caldwell, Mark Darrel. *Interpreting Spirit-Baptism in Acts: 2:37-39 as a Paradigm*. Ph.D. dissertation, Southwestern Baptist Theological Seminary, 2007.

Callan, Charles J. *The Acts of the Apostles with a Practical Critical Commentary for Priests and Students*. New York: Joseph F. Wagner, 1919.

Calvin, John. *Acts*. CCC. Wheaton, IL: Crossway, 1995 [Vol. 1, 1552; Vol. 2, 1554].

Camp, Ashby L. 'Re-examining the Rule of Concord in Acts 2:38'. *RestQ* 39.1 (1997), 37-42.

Caneday, A.B. 'Baptized in the Holy Spirit: Epochal Theology in Luke-Acts'. Paper presented to the annual Upper Midwest region meeting of the Society for Biblical Literature, April 8-9, 1994 [https://www.academia.edu/1916368/Baptized_in_the_Holy_Spirit_electronic_resource_epochal_theology_in_Luke-Acts_by_AB_Caneday; accessed on 04/07/14].

Caragounis, Chrys C. *The Development of Greek and the New Testament: Morphology, Syntax, Phonology, and Textual Transmission*. WUNT 167. Tübingen: Mohr Siebeck, 2004.

Carson, D.A. *Showing the Spirit: A Theological Exposition of 1 Corinthians 12-14*. BTCL. Carlisle: Paternoster, 1995; Grand Rapids: Baker, 1987.

Chase, Frederic Henry. *Confirmation in the Apostolic Age*. London: Macmillan, 1909.

Chatman, Seymour. *Story and Discourse: Narrative Structure in Fiction and Film*. Ithaca, NY: Cornell University Press, 1978.

Chilton, Bruce D. 'One God, the Same God'. Jacob Neusner, et al., *Do Jews, Christians, and Muslims Worship the Same God?* N.pl.: Abingdon, 2012, 55-83.

Chinn, Christopher M. 'Before Your Very Eyes: Pliny *Epistulae* 5.6 and the Ancient Theory of Ekphrasis'. *CP* 102.3 (July, 2007), 265-280.

Cho, Youngmo. *Spirit and Kingdom in the Writings of Luke and Paul: An Attempt to Reconcile these Concepts*. PBM. Milton Keynes: Paternoster, 2005.

Chrysostom, John. 'A Commentary on the Acts of the Apostles'. Philip Schaff, ed. *A Select Library of the Nicene and Post-Nicene Fathers of the Christian Church* 1st Series, Vol. XI. Grand Rapids: Eerdmans, n.d., 1-328.

Clark, Matthew. 'Formulas, metre and type-scenes'. Robert Fowler, ed. *The Cambridge Companion to Homer*. Cambridge: CUP, 2004, 117-138.

Cohn, Robert L. 'The Literary Logic of 1 Kings 17-19'. *JBL* 101.3 (1982), 333-350.

Cole, Graham A. *He Who Gives Life: The Doctrine of the Holy Spirit*. Wheaton: Crossway, 2007.

Comfort, Philip W. *New Testament Text and Translation Commentary*. Carol Stream, IL: Tyndale House, 2008.

Bibliography

Cooper, Guy L., after K.W. Krüger. *Attic Greek Pose Syntax*. Volume 1. Ann Arbor, MI: University of Michigan Press, 1998.

Compton, R. Bruce. 'Water Baptism and the Forgiveness of Sins in Acts 2:38'. *DBSJ* 4 (Fall, 1999), 3-32.

Conzelmann, Hans. *Acts of the Apostles: A Commentary on the Acts of the Apostles*. Philadelphia: Fortress, 1987.

—. *Die Mitte der Zeit: Studien zur Theologie des Lukas*. 4. Auflage. BHTh 17. Tübingen: J.C.B. Mohr, Paul Siebeck, 1962 [1954].

Cook, Guy. *The Discourse of Advertising*. 2nd Ed. London and New York: Routledge, 2001.

Coppens, Joseph. *L'Imposition des Mains et Les Rites Connexes dans le Nouveau Testament et dans L'Église Ancienne: Étude de Théologie Positive*. Paris: J. Gabalda, Éditeur, 1925.

Cornils, Anja. 'La métalepse dans les *Actes des Apôtres*: un signe de narration fictionnelle?' John Pier and Jean-Marie Schaeffer, eds. *Métalepses: Entorses au pacte de la représentation*. Paris: Éditions de l'EHESS, 2007, 95-107.

—. *Vom Geist Gottes erzählen: Analyzen zur Apostelgeschichte*. TANZ 44. Tübingen: Francke Verlag, 2006.

Cotterell, Peter and Max Turner. *Linguistics and Biblical Interpretation*. Downers Grove, IL: IVP, 1989.

Culpepper, R. Alan. *Anatomy of the Fourth Gospel: A Study in Literary Design*. Philadelphia: Fortress, 1983.

Cutten, George Barton. *Speaking with Tongues Historically and Psychologically Considered*. New Haven: Yale University Press, 1927.

Danker, Frederick W. *Jesus and the New Age: A Commentary on St. Luke's Gospel*. Philadelphia: Fortress, 1988.

Danvers, H. *A Treatise of Laying on of Hands. With the History Thereof, Both from the Scripture and Antiquity*. London: Fran. Smith, 1674.

Das, A. Andrew. 'Acts 8: Water, Baptism, and the Spirit'. *ConJ* 19.2 (April, 1993), 108-134.

Davis, J.C. 'Another Look at the Relationship Between Baptism and Forgiveness of Sins in Acts 2:38'. *RestQ* 24.2 (1981), 80-88.

De Jong, Irene. *A Narratological Commentary on the Odyssey*. Cambridge: CUP, 2001.

—. *Narrators and Focalizers: The Presentation of the Story in the Iliad*. 2nd Ed. London/New York: Bristol Classical Press, Bloomsbury Academic, 2004.

Denova, Rebecca. *The Things Accomplished Among Us: Prophetic Tradition in the Structural Pattern of Luke-Acts*. JSNT.S 141. Sheffield: Sheffield Academic, 1997.

Derrett, J. Duncan M. 'Simon Magus (Act 8 9-24)'. *ZNW* 73 (1982), 52-68.

DesCamp, Mary Therese. *Metaphor and Ideology: Liber Antiquitatum Biblicarum and Literary Methods Through a Cognitive Lens*. Leiden: Brill, 2007.

Dibelius, Martin. *Die urchristliche Überlieferung von Johannes dem Täufer.* FRLANT 15. Göttingen: Vandenhoeck & Ruprecht, 1911.

—. trans. Mary Ling. *Studies in the Acts of the Apostles.* London: William Clowes, 1956.

—, trans. Mary Ling and Paul Schubert. *The Book of Acts: Form, Style, and Theology.* FCBS. Minneapolis: Fortress, 2004 [London: SCM, 1956].

Dickerson, Patrick L. 'The Sources of the Account of the Mission to Samaria in Acts 8:5-25'. *NT* 39.3 (July, 1997), 210-234.

Dijk, Teun A. van. *Text and Context: Explorations in the Semantics and Pragmatics of Discourse.* New York: Longman, 1977.

Dix, Dom Gregory. *The Theology of Confirmation in Relation to Baptism: A Public Lecture in the University of Oxford Delivered on January 22nd 1946.* Westminster: Dacre, 1946.

Dobbeler, Axel, von. *Der Evangelist Philippus in der Geschichte des Urchristentums: Eine prosopographische Skizze.* TANZ 30. Tübingen: Francke Verlag, 2000.

Dockery, David S. 'The Theology of Acts'. *CTRev* 5.1 (1990), 43-55.

Dragas, George Dion. 'The Seal of the Gift of the Spirit: the Sacrament of Chrismation'. *GOTR* 56.1-4 (Spring-Winter, 2011), 143-159.

Dunn, James D.G. *Baptism in the Holy Spirit: A Re-examination of the New Testament Teaching on the Gift of the Spirit in Relation to Pentecostalism Today.* London: SCM, 1970. Reprint, Philadelphia: Westminster, n.d.

—. 'Baptism in the Holy Spirit... yet once more'. *JEPTA* 18 (1998), 3-25.

—. 'Baptism in the Spirit: A Response to Pentecostal Scholarship on Luke-Acts'. *The Christ and the Spirit:* Volume 2, *Pneumatology.* Edinburgh: T&T Clark, 1998.

—. *Christology in the Making: An Inquiry into the Origins of the Doctrine of the Incarnation.* 2nd Ed. London: SCM, 1989 [1980].

—. 'Rediscovering the Spirit (1)'. *The Christ and the Spirit:* Volume 2, *Pneumatology.* Edinburgh: T&T Clark, 1998, 43-61.

—. *The Acts of the Apostles.* Peterborough: Epworth, 1996.

—. 'The Birth of a Metaphor – Baptized in the Spirit'. *The Christ and the Spirit:* Volume 2, *Pneumatology.* Edinburgh: T&T Clark, 1998, 103-117.

—. 'They Believed Philip Preaching (Acts 8:12)'. *The Christ and the Spirit:* Volume 2, *Pneumatology.* Edinburgh: T&T Clark, 1998, 216-221.

—. *Jesus and the Spirit: A Study of the Religious and Charismatic Experience of Jesus and the First Christians as Reflected in the New Testament.* London: SCM, 1975.

—. '"The Lord, the Giver of Life": The Gift of the Spirit as Both Life-giving and Empowering'. I. Howard Marshall, Volker Rabens, and Cornelis Bennema, ed., *The Spirit and Christ in the New Testament and Christian Theology: Essays in Honor of Max Turner.* Grand Rapids: Eerdmans, 2012.

Bibliography

Eckey, Wilfried. *Die Apostelgeschichte: Der Weg des Evangeliums von Jerusalem nach Rom, Teilband I 1,1-15,35*. 2. Auflage. Neukirchen-Vluyn: Neukirchener Verlagsgesellschaft mbH, 2011.

—. *Die Apostelgeschichte: Der Weg des Evangeliums von Jerusalem nach Rom, Teilband II 15,36-28,31*, 2. Auflage. Neukirchen-Vluyn: Neukirchener Verlagsgesellschaft mbH, 2011.

Edwards, Mark W. 'Homer and Oral Tradition: The Type-Scene'. *OT* 7.2 (1992), 284-330.

—. *Homer: Poet of the Iliad*. Baltimore: Johns Hopkins University Press, 1987.

Edwards, Otis Carl, Jr. 'Exegesis of Acts 8:4-25 and Its Implications for Confirmation and Glossolalia: A Review Article on Haenchen's Acts Commentary'. *AThR.SS* 2 (September, 1973), 100-112.

Edwards, Richard. 'Uncertain Faith: Matthew's Portrait of the Disciples'. Fernando F. Segovia, ed. *Discipleship in the New Testament*. Philadelphia: Fortress, 1985, 47-61.

Eisen, Ute E. *Die Poetik der Apostelgeschichte: Eine Narratologische Studie*. NTOA 58. Fribourg: Academic, 2006; Göttingen: Vandenhoeck & Ruprecht, 2006.

Elbert, Paul. 'Acts 2:38 in Light of the Syntax of Imperative-Future Passive and Imperative-Present Participle Combinations'. *CBQ* 75.1 (January, 2013), 94-107.

Ellis, E. Earle. *The Old Testament in Early Christianity: Canon and Interpretation in the Light of Modern Research*. WUNT 54. Tübingen: J.C.B. Mohr, Paul Siebeck, 1991.

Emmott, Catherine. *Narrative Comprehension: A Discourse Perspective*. Oxford: OUP, 1999.

Erasmus, Desiderius, trans. Robert D. Sider. *Paraphrase on the Acts of the Apostles*. CWE 50. Toronto: University of Toronto Press, 1995 [1524].

Ervin, Howard M. *Conversion-Initiation and the Baptism in the Holy Spirit: A Critique of James D.G. Dunn, Baptism in the Holy Spirit*. Peabody, MA: Hendrickson, 1984.

—. *Spirit Baptism: A Biblical Investigation*. Peabody, MA: Hendrickson, 1987.

—. *These Are Not Drunken as Ye Suppose*. Plainfield, NJ: Logos, 1968.

Esler, Philip F. 'Glossolalia and the Admission of Gentiles into the Early Christian Community'. *BTB* 22 (Spring, 1992), 136-142.

Estrada, Nelson P. *From Followers to Leaders: The Apostles in the Ritual of Status Transformation in Acts 1-2*. London: T&T Clark, 2004.

Everts, Jenny. 'Tongues or Languages? Contextual Consistency in the Translation of Acts 2'. *JPT* 4 (1994), 71-80.

Fabien, Patrick. 'La conversion de Simon le magicien (Ac 8,4-25)'. *Bib.* 91.2 (2010), 210-240.

Fahnestock, Jeanne. *Rhetorical Style: The Uses of Language in Persuasion*. Oxford: OUP, 2011.

Fee, Gordon D. *Gospel and Spirit: Issues in New Testament Hermeneutics*. Grand Rapids: Baker Academic.

Ferguson, Everett. *Baptism in the Early Church: History, Theology, and Liturgy in the First Five Centuries*. Grand Rapids/Cambridge: Eerdmans, 2009.

Fitzmyer, Joseph A. *The Acts of the Apostles: A New Translation with Introduction and Commentary*. New York: Doubleday, 1998.

Findlay, J. Alexander. *The Acts of the Apostles: A Commentary*. London: SCM, 1934.

Finnern, Sönke. *Narratologie und biblische Exegese: Eine integrative Methode der Erzählanalyze und ihr Ertrag am Beispiel von Matthäus 28*. WUNT 285. Tübingen: Mohr Siebeck, 2010.

Fisher, J.D.C. *Confirmation: Then and Now*. London: Alcuin /SPCK, 1978.

Flemington, W.F. *The New Testament Doctrine of Baptism*. London: SPCK, 1964.

Fludernik, Monika, trans. Patricia Häusler-Greenfield and Monika Fludernik. *An Introduction to Narratology*. London: Routledge, 2009 [German, 2006].

Forbes, Christopher. *Prophecy and Inspired Speech in Early Christianity and its Hellenistic Environment*. WUNT2 75. Tübingen: J.C.B. Mohr, Paul Siebeck, 1995.

Forbes, G.H. *The Panoply*. Vol. III. Burntisland: Pitsligo, 1863-1869.

Fowler, Robert M. 'Who is "The Reader" in Reader Response Criticism?' *Se.* 31 (1985), 3-30.

Funk, Robert W. *The Poetics of Biblical Narrative*. Sonoma, CA: Polebridge, 1988.

García Landa, José Angel. 'Rereading (,) Narrative (,) Identity (,) and Interaction', *Interculturalism: Between Identity and Diversity*. Beatriz Penas Ibáñez and Mª Carmen López Sáenz, eds. Bern: Peter Lang, 2006.

Garrett, Susan R. *The Demise of the Devil: Magic and the Demonic in Luke's Writings*. Minneapolis: Fortress, 1989.

Garroway, Joshua D. '"Apostolic Irresistibility" and the Interrupted Speeches in Acts'. *CBQ* 74.4 (October, 2012), 738-753.

Gaventa, Beverly Roberts. *From Darkness to Light: Aspects of Conversion in the New Testament*. Philadelphia: Fortress, 1986.

—. 'Toward a Theology of Acts: Reading and Rereading'. *Interp.* 42.2 (April 1988), 146-157.

Gelpi, Donald L. 'Breath-Baptism in the Synoptics'. *Charismatic Experiences in History*. Peabody, MA: Hendrickson, 1985, 15-43.

Gempf, Conrad. 'Apollos and the Ephesian Disciples: Befores and Afters (Acts 18:24-19:7)'. I. Howard Marshall, Volker Rabens, and Cornelis Bennema, eds. *The Spirit and Christ in the New Testament and Christian Theology: Essays in Honor of Max Turner*. Grand Rapids: Eerdmans, 2012, 119-137.

Gerrig, Richard J. 'Re-experiencing Fiction and Non-Fiction'. *JAAC* 47.3 (Summer, 1989), 277-280.

Bibliography

Giblet, Canon J. 'Baptism in the Spirit in the Acts of the Apostles'. *OiC* 10 (1974), 162-171.

Glombitza, Otto. 'Der Schluss der Petrusrede Acta 2:36-40: Ein Beitrag zum Problem der Predigten in Acta'. *ZNW* 52.1-2 (January 1, 1961), 115-118.

Godet, F., trans. E.W. Shalders. *A Commentary on the Gospel of St. Luke: Volume First*. Edinburgh: T&T Clark, n.d.

Goguel, Maurice, trans. H.C. Snape. *The Birth of Christianity*. London: George Allen & Unwin, 1953 [*La Naissancce du Christianisme*. Paris: Payot, 1946].

—, trans. H.C. Snape. *The Primitive Church*. London: George Allen & Unwin, 1964 [French edition, 1947].

Gonzalez, Justo L. *Acts: The Gospel of the Spirit*. Maryknoll, NY: Orbis, 2001.

Goppelt, L. *Theologie des Neuen Testaments*. 3. Auflage. GTL. Göttingen: Vandenhoeck & Ruprecht, 1980 [1976].

Grafton, Thomas E. 'Just As It Was Spoken: Annunciation Type-Scenes and Faithful Response in Luke's Birth Narrative'. *CBibW* 31 (2011), 143-161.

Green, Joel B. 'From 'John's Baptism' to 'Baptism in the Name of the Lord Jesus': The Significance of Baptism in Luke-Acts'. *Baptism, the New Testament and the Church: Historical and Contemporary Studies in Honour of R.E.O. White*. JSNT.S 171. Sheffield: Sheffield Academic, 1999, 157-172.

—. 'Internal repetition in Luke-Acts: contemporary narratology and Lucan historiography'. Ben Witherington, ed. *History Literature and Society in the Book of Acts*. Cambridge: CUP, 1996, 283-299.

Gregory, Andrew. 'The Reception of Luke and Acts and the Unity of Luke-Acts'. *JSNT* 29.4 (June, 2007), 459-472.

—. *The Reception of Luke and Acts in the Period Before Irenaeus*. WUNT2 169. Tübingen: Mohr Siebeck, 2003.

Grethlein, Jonas and Antonios Rengakos. *Narratology and Interpretation: The Content of Narrative Form in Ancient Literature*. Berlin: Walter de Gruyter, 2009.

Grundmann, Walter. *Das Evangelium Nach Lukas*. 2. Auflage. ThHK 3. Berlin: Evangelische Verlagsanstalt Berlin, n.d.

—. 'Der Pfingstbericht der Apostelgeschichte in seinem theologischen Sinn'. *Studia Evangelica* Volume II: *Papers Presented to the Second International Congress on New Testament Studies, Part I: The New Testament Scriptures*. Berlin: Akademie-Verlag, 1964, 584-594.

Gunkel, Hermann. *Die Wirkungen des Heiligen Geistes: Nach der Populären Anschauung der Apostolischen Zeit und nach der Lehre des Apostels Paulus: Eine Biblisch-Theologische Studie*. 2. unveränderte Auflage. Göttingen: Vandenhoeck & Ruprecht, 1899 [1888].

Gunkel, Heidrun. *Der Heilige Geist bei Lukas: Theologisches Profil, Grund und Intention der lukanischen Pneumatologie* WUNT 2 389. Tübingen: Mohr Siebeck, 2015.

Guthrie, Donald. *New Testament Theology*. Leicester: IVP, 1981.

Haacker, K. 'Einige Fälle von "Erlebter Rede" im Neuen Testament'. *NT* 12 (1970), 70-77.

Haenchen, Ernst. *The Acts of the Apostles: A Commentary*. Oxford: Basil Blackwell, 1971.

Hamilton, James M., Jr. *God's Indwelling Presence: The Holy Spirit in the Old and New Testaments*. NACS. N.p.: B&H, 2006.

—. 'Rushing Wind and Organ Music: Toward Luke's Theology of the Spirit in Acts'. *RFT* 65.1 (April 2006), 15-33.

Handy, David A. 'Acts 8:14-25'. *Interp.* 47.3 (July, 1993), 289-294.

Harm, Frederick R. 'Structural Elements Related to the Gift of the Holy Spirit in Acts'. *ConJ* 14.1 (January, 1988), 28-41.

Harrison, Randall. *L'Esprit dans le Récit de Luc: Une Recherche de Cohérence dans la Pneumatologie de L'Auteur Implicite de Luc-Actes*. Self-published Ph.D. dissertation, La Faculté Libre de Théologie Évangélique Vaux-sur-Seine, 2007.

Hartman, Lars. *'Into the Name of the Lord Jesus': Baptism in the Early Church*. Edinburgh: T&T Clark, 1997.

Haufe, Günter. 'Taufe und Heiliger Geist im Urchristentum'. *ThLZ* 8 (August, 1976), 561-566.

Haya-Prats, Gonzalo, trans. Scott A. Ellington, ed. Paul Elbert. *Empowered Believers: The Holy Spirit in the Book of Acts*. Eugene, OR: Cascade, 2011.

—, trans. José J. Romero and Hubert Faes. *L'Esprit, Force de l'Église: Sa nature et son activité d'après les Actes des Apôtres*. LeDiv 81. Paris: Cerf, 1975.

Heath, Malcolm. 'Invention'. Stanley E. Porter, ed. *Handbook of Classical Rhetoric in the Hellenistic Period 330 B.C. – A.D. 400*. Leiden: Brill, 1997, 89-119.

Heckel, Ulrich. *Der Segen im Neuen Testament*. WUNT 150. Tübingen: Mohr Siebeck, 2002.

Hedlun, Randall J. *The Social Function of Glossolalia in Acts with Special Attention to the Ephesian Disciples Pericope (Acts 18:24-19:7)*. Ph.D. dissertation, University of South Africa, 2009.

Hedrick, Charles W. 'Paul's Conversion/Call: A Comparative Analysis of the Three Reports in Acts'. *JBL* 100.3 (September, 1981), 415-432.

Hoekema, Anthony A. *Tongues and Spirit-Baptism: A Biblical and Theological Evaluation*. Grand Rapids: Baker, 1972.

—. *Holy Spirit Baptism*. Exeter: Paternoster, 1972; Eerdmans, 1972.

Hoennicke, Gustav. *Die Apostelgeschichte*. ETBKNT. Leipzig: Verlag von Quelle & Meyer, 1913.

Hoffmann, Jella and Andreas Fahr, 'Reexperiencing Suspense and Surprise: Processes of Repeated Exposure to Narrative Fiction'. Lecture at the 'Panel Exploring the Cognitive and Affective Effects of Narrative'. 57th Annual Conference of the International Communication Association, 2007, San Francisco, USA.

Holladay, Carl R. 'Baptism in the New Testament and Its Cultural Milieu: A Response to Everett Ferguson, *Baptism in the Early Church*'. *JECS* 20.3 (Fall, 2012), 343-369.

Hooker, Morna D. 'John's Baptism: A Prophetic Sign'. Graham N. Stanton, Bruce W. Longenecker, Stephen C. Barton, eds. *The Holy Spirit and Christian Origins: Essays in Honor of James D.G. Dunn*. Grand Rapids: Eerdmans, 2004.

Hornik, Heidi J., and Mikeal C. Parsons. 'Philological and Performative Perspectives on Pentecost'. Steve Walton, et al. ed. *Reading Acts Today: Essays in Honour of Loveday C.A. Alexander*. LNTS. London: T&T Clark, 2011.

Hovenden, Gerald. *Speaking in Tongues: The New Testament Evidence in Context*. London: Sheffield Academic, 2002.

Hühn, Peter, Wolf Schmid, Jörg Schönert, ed. *Point of View, Perspective, and Focalization: Modeling Mediation in Narrative*. Nar. 17. Berlin/New York: Walter de Gruyter, 2009.

Hui, Archie Wang Do. *The Concept of the Holy Spirit in Ephesians and its Relation to the Pneumatologies of Luke and Paul*. Ph.D. dissertation, University of Aberdeen, 1992.

Hull, J.H.E. *The Holy Spirit in the Acts of the Apostles*. London: Lutterworth, 1967.

Hur, Ju. *A Dynamic Reading of the Holy Spirit in Luke-Acts*. London: T&T Clark, 2004; Sheffield: Sheffield Academic, JSNT.S 211, 2001.

Hurtado, Larry W. 'Normal, But Not a Norm: "Initial Evidence" and the New Testament'. Gary B. McGee, ed. *Initial Evidence: Historical and Biblical Perspectives on the Pentecostal Doctrine of Spirit Baptism*. Peabody, MA: Hendrickson, 1991, 189-201.

Iser, Wolfgang. 'Interaction Between Text and Reader'. Susan R. Suleiman and Inge Crosman, eds. *The Reader in the Text: Essays on Audience and Interpretation*. Princeton: Princeton University Press, 1980.

—. *The Act of Reading: A Theory of Aesthetic Response*. Baltimore: Johns Hopkins University Press, 1978.

—. *The Implied Reader: Patterns of Communication in Prose Fiction from Bunyan to Beckett*. Baltimore: Johns Hopkins University Press, 1974.

Jackson, Don. 'Luke and Paul: A Theology of One Spirit from Two Perspectives'. *JETS* 32.3 (September, 1989), 335-343.

Jeremias, Jörg. 'Die Anfänge der Schriftprophetie'. *ZThK* 93.4 (December 1996), 481-499.

Jervell, Jacob. 'Das Volk des Geistes'. Jacob Jervell and Wayne A. Meeks, eds. *God's Christ and His People: Studies in Honour of Nils Alstrup Dahl*. Oslo: Universitetsforlaget, 1977, 87-106.

—. *Die Apostelgeschichte: Übersetzt und erklärt*. Göttingen: Vandenhoeck & Ruprecht, 1998.

—. *Luke and the People of God: A New Look at Luke-Acts*. Minneapolis: Augsburg, 1972.

—. 'Sons of the Prophets: The Holy Spirit in the Acts of the Apostles'. *The Unknown Paul: Essays on Luke-Acts and Early Christian History*. Minneapolis: Augsburg, 1984, 96-121.

Johnson, Benjamin J.M. 'What Type of Son is Samson? Reading Judges 13 as a Biblical Type-Scene'. *JETS* 53.2 (June, 2010), 269-286.

Johnson, Luke Timothy. *Scripture and Discernment: Decision Making in the Church*. Nashville: Abingdon, 1996.

—. *The Acts of the Apostles*. Collegeville, MN: Michael Glazier, Liturgical, 1992.

—. *The Literary Function of Possessions in Luke-Acts*. SBL.DS 39. N.pl., USA: Scholars, 1977.

—. 'Literary Criticism of Luke-Acts: Is Reception History Pertinent?' Andrew F. Gregory and C. Kavin Rowe, eds., *Rethinking the Unity and Reception of Luke and Acts*. Columbia, SC: University of South Carolina Press, 2010.

Jones, Donald L. 'The Title *Kyrios* in Luke-Acts'. *SBL Seminar Papers* 2 (1974), 85-101.

Käsemann, Ernst. 'The Disciples of John the Baptist in Ephesus'. *Essays on New Testament Themes*. London: SCM, 1964, 136-148.

Kee, Howard Clark. *To Every Nation under Heaven: The Acts of the Apostles*. NTesC. Harrisburg, PA: Trinity, 1997.

Kee, Min Suc. 'The Heavenly Council and its Type-scene'. *JSOT* 31.3 (March, 2007), 259-273.

Keener, Craig S. *Acts, An Exegetical Commentary* Volume 1. Grand Rapids: Baker Academic, 2012.

—. *Acts, An Exegetical Commentary* Volume 2. Grand Rapids: Baker Academic, 2013.

—. *The Spirit in the Gospels and Acts: Divine Purity and Power*. Peabody, MA: Hendrickson, 1997.

—. 'Why does Luke use Tongues as a Sign of the Spirit's Empowerment?' *JPT* 15.2, 177-184.

Kennedy, George A. *New Testament Interpretation Through Rhetorical Criticism*. Chapel Hill: University of North Carolina Press, 1984.

Kern, Philip H. 'Paul's Conversion and Luke's Portrayal of Character in Acts 8-10'. *TynB* 54.2 (2003), 63-80.

Kilpatrick, G. D. 'The Spirit, God, and Jesus in Acts'. *JTS* 15 (1964), 63.

Kim, Hee-Seong. *Die Geisttaufe des Messias: Eine kompositionsgeschichtliche Untersuchung zu einem Leitmotiv des lukanischen Doppelwerks*. Frankfurt am Main: Peter Lang, 1993.

Kittel, G. 'Die Wirkungen der christlichen Wassertaufe nach dem Neuen Testament'. *ThStKr* 87 (1914), 25-53.

Bibliography

Klauck, Hans-Josef, trans. Brian McNeil. *Magic and Paganism in Early Christianity: The World of the Acts of the Apostles*. Edinburgh: T&T Clark, 2000.

Klein, William W., Craig L. Blomberg, Robert L. Hubbard. *Introduction to Biblical Interpretation*. Rev. and Exp. Nashville: Thomas Nelson, 1993.

Knowling, R.J. 'The Acts of the Apostles'. W. Robertson Nicoll, ed. *The Expositor's Greek Testament*. Vol. II. London: Hodder and Stoughton, 1900.

Koch, Dietrich-Alex. 'Geistbesitz, Geistverleihung und Wundermacht Erwägungen zur Tradition und zur lukanischen Redaktion in Act 8 5-25'. *ZNW* 77 (1986), 64-82.

Koet, Bart J. *Dreams and Scripture in Luke-Acts: Collected Essays*. CBET 42. Leuven: Peeters, 2006.

Kosnetter, Johann. *Die Taufe Jesu: Exegetische und religionsgeschichtliche Studien*. ThSLG 35. Wien: Verlag Mayer, 1936.

Kress, Gunther and Theo van Leeuwen. *Reading Images: The Grammar of Visual Design*. 2nd Ed. London and New York: Routledge, 2006.

Kremer, Jacob. *Pfingstbericht und Pfingstgeschehen: Eine exegetische Untersuchung zu Apg 2, 1-13*. SBS 63/64. Stuttgart: Verlag Katholisches Bibelwerk GmbH, 1973.

—. 'Was Geschah Pfingsten? Zur Historizität des Apg 2, 1-13 berichteten Pfingstereignisses'. *WuW* 3 (1973), 195-207.

Krodel, Gerhard. 'The Functions of the Spirit in the Old Testament, the Synoptic Tradition, and the Book of Acts'. Paul D. Opsahl, ed. *The Holy Spirit in the Life of the Church From Biblical Times to the Present*. Minneapolis: Augsburg, 1978, 10-46.

Kruschwitz, Jonathan. 'The Type-Scene Connection between Genesis 38 and the Joseph Story'. *JSOT* 36.4 (2012), 383-410.

Kuecker, Aaron J. 'The Spirit and the 'Other': Social Identity, Ethnicity and Intergroup Reconciliation in Luke-Acts'. Ph.D. dissertation, University of St. Andrews, 2008.

Kurz, William S. *Acts of the Apostles*. Grand Rapids: Baker Academic, 2013.

—. 'Images of Judaism in Luke-Acts'. *JAAR* 61.2 (Summer, 1993), 388-390.

—. *Reading Luke-Acts: Dynamics of Biblical Narrative*. Louisville, KY: Westminster John Knox, 1993.

Kürzinger, Josef. *The Acts of the Apostles*. NTSR 5. London: Sheed and Ward, 1969.

Lake, Kirsopp. 'Baptism (Early Christian)'. James Hastings, et al. ed. *Encyclopaedia of Religion and Ethics*. Vol. II. New York: Charles Scribner's, n.d., 379-390.

—. 'The Theology of the Acts of the Apostles'. *AJT* 19.4 (October, 1915), 489-508.

Lake, Kirsopp, and Henry J. Cadbury. *The Beginnings of Christianity, Part I: The Acts of the Apostles,* Volume IV, *English Translation and Commentary*. London: Macmillan, 1933.

Lampe, G.W.H. *God as Spirit: The Bampton Lectures 1976*. London: SCM, 1983 [Oxford: OUP, 1977].

—. 'The Holy Spirit in the Writings of St. Luke'. D.E. Nineham, ed. *Studies in the Gospels: Essays in Memory of R.H. Lightfoot*. Oxford: Basil Blackwell, 1957, 159-200.

—. *The Seal of the Spirit, A Study in the Doctrine of Baptism and Confirmation in the New Testament and the Fathers*. Eugene, Oregon: Wipf and Stock, 2004 [SPCK, 1951].

Langenbacher, Jesaja. *Firmung als Initiation in Gemeinschaft: Theologie von Firmlingen – eine Herausforderung und Bereicherung für die Lebens – und Glaubenskommunikation in der Kirche*. KTI. Berlin: Lit Verlag, W. Hopf, 2010.

Lee, Mark. 'An Evangelical Dialogue on Luke, Salvation, and Spirit Baptism'. *Pn.* 26.1 (Spring, 2004), 81-98.

Leeuwen, Theo van, and Carey Jewitt. *The Handbook of Visual Analysis*. London: SAGE, 2001.

Leipoldt, Johannes. *Die urchristliche Taufe im Lichte der Religionsgeschichte*. Leipzig: Verlag von Dörssling & Franke, 1928.

Leisegang, Hans. *Pneuma Hagion: Der Ursprung des Geistbegriffs der synoptischen Evangelien aus der griechischen Mystik*. VFVRG 4. Leipzig: J. C. Hinrichs'sche Buchhandlung, 1922.

Leitch, Thomas M. 'For (Against) a Theory of Rereading'. *MFSt* 33.3 (Fall, 1987), 491-508.

Lentzen-Deis, Fritzleo. *Die Taufe Jesu nach den Synoptikern: Literarkritische und gattungsgeschichtliche Untersuchungen*. Frankfurt am Main: Josef Knecht, 1970.

Levison, John R. *Filled with the Spirit*. Grand Rapids: Eerdmans, 2009.

Lincoln, A.T. 'Theology and History in the Interpretation of Luke's Pentecost'. *ET* 96 (1984-1985), 204-209.

Loder, Thomas A. 'An Examination Of The Classical Pentecostal Doctrine Of The Baptism In The Holy Spirit: In Light Of The Pentecostal Position On The Sources Of Theology'. M.A. thesis, Providence Theological Seminary, 2000.

Lohse, Eduard. *Die Einheit des Neuen Testaments: Exegetische Studien zur Theologie des Neuen Testaments*. Göttingen: Vandenhoeck & Ruprecht, 1973.

Loisy, Alfred. *L'Évangile Selon Luc*. Paris: Émile Nourry, 1924.

—. *Les Actes des Apôtres*. Paris: Émile Nourry, 1920.

Longacre, Robert E. *The Grammar of Discourse*. 2nd Ed. New York: Plenum, 1996.

Longenecker, Richard N. *Acts*. EBC. Grand Rapids: Zondervan, 1995.

—. *Biblical Exegesis in the Apostolic Period*. N.pl.: Eerdmans, 1975.

Longinus, trans. H.L. Havell. *On the Sublime*. London: Macmillan, 1890.

Bibliography

Lyon, Robert W. 'Baptism and Spirit Baptism in the New Testament'. *WTJ* 14.1 (Spring, 1979), 14-26.
MacArthur, John F., Jr. *Charismatic Chaos*. Grand Rapids: Zondervan, 1992.
Maclean, A.J. 'Baptism'. James Hastings, ed. *Dictionary of the Apostolic Church*. Vol. I. Edinburgh: T.&T. Clark, 1915, 128-136.
Maddox, Robert. *The Purpose of Luke-Acts*. Edinburgh: T&T Clark, 1982.
Mainville, Odette. *L'Esprit dans l'oeuvre de Luc*. HP 45. N.pl.: Fides, 1991.
Mallen, Peter. *The Reading and Transformation of Isaiah in Luke-Acts*. LNTS 367. London: T&T Clark, 2008.
Marguerat, Daniel. *Les Actes des Apôtres (1-12)*. CNTDS. Genève: Labor et Fides, 2007.
—, trans. Ken McKinney, Gregory J. Laughery, and Richard Bauckham. *The First Christian Historian, Writing the 'Acts of the Apostles'*. SNTS.MS 121. Cambridge: CUP, 2002.
Marshall, I. Howard. *Luke – Historian and Theologian*. 3rd Ed.: Paternoster, 1988.
—. *The Acts of the Apostles, An Introduction and Commentary*. TNTC. Leicester: IVP; Grand Rapids, Michigan: Eerdmans, 1980.
—. *The Gospel of Luke: A Commentary on the Greek Text*. Exeter: Paternoster, 1978.
—. 'The Significance of Pentecost'. *SJTh* 30 (1997), 347-369.
Martin, Ralph P. 'Salvation and Discipleship in Luke's Gospel'. *Interp.* 30 (1976), 366-380.
Mason, Arthur James. *The Faith of the Gospel: A Manuel of Christian Doctrine*. London: Rivingtons, 1888.
—. *The Relation of Confirmation to Baptism as Taught in Holy Scripture and the Fathers*. London: Longmans, Green, 1891.
McComiskey, Douglas S. *Lukan Theology in the Light of the Gospel's Literary Structure*. Milton Keynes: Paternoster, 2004.
McDonnell, Kilian and George T. Montague. *Christian Initiation and Baptism in the Holy Spirit, Evidence from the First Eight Centuries*. 2nd Rev. Ed. Collegeville, Minnesota: Liturgical, Michael Glazier, 1994.
McIntyre, Luther B., Jr. 'Baptism and Forgiveness in Acts 2:38'. *BS* 153 (January-March, 1996), 53-62.
McNamara, Patrick. *Spirit Possession and Exorcism: History, Psychology and Neurobiology,* Volume 1, *Mental States and the Phenomenon of Possession*. Santa Barbara, CA: Praeger, 2011.
Mendez-Moratalla, Fernando. *The Paradigm of Conversion in Luke*. London: T&T Clark, 2004.
Menzies, Robert P. *Empowered for Witness: The Spirit in Luke-Acts*. London/New York: T&T Clark, 2004 [1991].
—. *The Language of the Spirit: Interpreting and Translating Charismatic Terms*. Cleaveland, TN: CPT, 2010.

—. 'Luke's Understanding of Baptism in the Holy Spirit: A Pentecostal Dialogues with the Reformed Tradition'. *JPT* 16.2 (April, 2008), 86-101.
—. *The Development of Early Christian Pneumatology with Special Reference to Luke-Acts*. JSNT.S 54. Sheffield: Sheffield Academic, 1991.
—. 'The Role of Glossolalia in Luke-Acts'. *AJPS* 15:1 (2012), 47-72.
—. 'The Sending of the Seventy and Luke's Purpose'. Paul Alexander, Jordan Daniel May, and Robert G. Reid, eds. *Trajectories in the Book of Acts, Essays in Honor of John Wesley Wyckoff*. Eugene, OR: Wipf and Stock, 2010, 87-113.
Menzies, William W. and Robert P. Menzies. *Spirit and Power, Foundations of Pentecostal Experience*. Grand Rapids: Zondervan, 2000.
Merenlahti, Petri. *Poetics for the Gospels? Rethinking Narrative Criticism*. London: T&T Clark, 2002.
Metzger, Bruce M. *A Textual Commentary on the Greek New Testament*. 2nd Ed. Stuttgart: Deutsche Bibelgesellschaft, 1994.
Metzger, James A. *Consumption and Wealth in Luke's Travel Narrative*. Leiden: Brill, 2007.
Mills, Watson E. *A Theological/Exegetical Approach to Glossolalia*. New York: University Press of America, 1985.
Mittelstadt, Martin William. *The Spirit and Suffering in Luke-Acts: Implications for a Pentecostal Pneumatology*. London: T&T Clark, 2004.
Mirguet, Francoise. 'The Francophone Appropriation and Continuation of Narrative Criticism Applied to the Bible: The Example of Point of View'. *PoeT* 30.2 (Summer, 2009), 353-362.
Moessner, David P. 'The Appeal and Power of Poetics (Luke 1:1-4): Luke's Superior Credentials (παρηκολουθηκότι), Narrative Sequence (καθεξῆς), and Firmness of Understanding (ἡ ἀσφάλεια) for the Reader'. *Jesus and the Heritage of Israel: Luke's Narrative Claim upon Israel's Legacy*. Harrisburg, PA: Trinity, 1999, 84-123.
Montague, George T. *Holy Spirit: Growth of a Biblical Tradition*. Peabody, MA: Hendrickson, 1976.
Moreton, M.J. 'A Reconsideration of the Origins of a Christian Initiation Rite in the Age of the New Testament'. *Studia Biblica 1978:* III. *Papers on Paul and Other New Testament Authors*. JSNT.S 3. Sheffield: JSOT, 1980, 265-275.
Morlan, David S. *Conversion in Luke and Paul: Some Exegetical and Theological Explorations*. PhD Durham University, 2010.
Moxon, John Richard Lewis. *Peter's Halakhic Nightmare: The 'Animal' Vision of Acts 10:9-16 in Jewish and Graeco-Roman Perspective*. Ph.D. dissertation, Durham University, 2011.
Muhlack, Gudrun. *Die Parallelen von Lukas-Evangelium und Apostelgeschichte*. Frankfurt am Main: Peter Lang, 1979.
Muir, Steven C. *Healing, Initiation and Community in Luke-Acts: A Comparative Analysis*. Ph.D. dissertation, University of Ottawa, 1998.

Bibliography

Munck, Johannes. *The Acts of the Apostles*. Garden City, NY: Doubleday, 1967.

Nazianzen, Gregory. 'Oration XLI On Pentecost'. Philip Schaff and Henry Wace, ed. *A Select Library of Nicene and Post-Nicene Fathers of the Christian Church*. 2nd Series, Vol. 7. Grand Rapids: Eerdmans, n.d., 378-385.

Nestle-Aland. *Novum Testamentum Graece 27*. Stuttgart: Deutsche Bibelgesellschaft, 1993.

New, Silva. 'Note XI. The Name, Baptism, and the Laying on of Hands'. F.J. Foakes Jackson and Kirsopp Lake, eds. *The Beginnings of Christianity, Part I: The Acts of the Apostles*. Kirsopp Lake and Henry J. Cadbury, ed. Volume V, *Additional Notes to the Commentary*. London: Macmillan, 1933, 121-140.

Nickle, Keith F. *Preaching the Gospel of Luke: Proclaiming God's Royal Rule*. Louisville, KY: Westminster John Knox, 2000.

Niederhoff, Burkhard. 'Focalization'. Peter Hühn, et al. ed. *The Living Handbook of Narratology*. Hamburg: Hamburg University Press. URL = hup.sub.uni-hamburg.de/lhn/index.php?title=Focalization&oldid=1561 [view date: 19 June, 2012].

Niehaus, Jeffrey J. *God at Sinai: Covenant and Theophany in the Bible and Ancient Near East*. SOTBT. Grand Rapids: Zondervan, 1995.

Nohrnberg, James. *Like unto Moses: The Constituting of an Interruption*. ISBL. Bloomington: Indiana University Press, 1995.

Oberlinner, Lorenz. 'Das Wirken des Geistes und das Handeln der Menschen: Der Weg der Mission in der Apostelgeschichte'. Philipp Müller, ed. *Seelsorge in der Kraft des Heiligen Geistes: Festschrift für Weihbischof Paul Wehrle*. Freiburg: Herder, 2005, 161-177.

O'Connell, Robert H. 'Proverbs VII 16-17: A Case of Fatal Deception in a "Woman and the Window" Type-Scene'. *VT* 41.2 (April, 1991), 235-241.

Oden, Thomas C. *Life in the Spirit – Systematic Theology: Volume 3*. New York: HarperSanFrancisco, 1992.

O'Neill, J.C. 'The Connection Between Baptism and the Gift of the Spirit in Acts'. *JSNT* 63 (1996), 87-103.

Osborn, Grant R. *The Hermeneutical Spiral: A Comprehensive Introduction to Biblical Interpretation*. Rev. and Exp. Downers Grove, IL: IVP, 2006.

Oulton, J.E.L. 'The Holy Spirit, Baptism, and Laying on of Hands in Acts'. *ET* 66 (1954-1955), 236-240.

Panagopoulos, Johannes. 'Zur Theologie der Apostelgeschichte'. *NT* 14.2 (April, 1972), 137-159.

Pao, David W. *Acts and the Isaianic New Exodus*. Grand Rapids: Baker Academic, 2002; Mohr Siebeck, 2000.

Parratt, J.K. 'The Holy Spirit and Baptism, Part I: The Gospels and the Acts of the Apostles'. *ET* 82 (1970-1971), 231-235.

—. 'The Rebaptism of the Ephesian Disciples'. *ET* 79 (1968), 182-183.

Parsons, Mikeal C. *Acts*. PCNT. Grand Rapids: Baker Academic, 2008.
Pawson, David. *The Normal Christian Birth: How to Give New Believers a Proper Start in Life*. London: Hodder & Stoughton, 1989.
Penney, John Michael. *The Missionary Emphasis of Lukan Pneumatology*. Sheffield: Sheffield Academic, 1997.
Perry, Andrew. *Eschatological Deliverance: The Spirit in Luke-Acts*. Ph.D. dissertation, University of Durham, 2008.
Perry, Menakhem. 'Literary Dynamics: How the Order of a Text Creates its Meanings [With an Analysis of Faulkner's "A Rose For Emily"]'. *PoeT* 1.1/2 (Autumn, 1979), 35-64 + 311-361.
Pervo, Richard I. *Acts*. Hermeneia. Minneapolis, MN: Fortress, 2009.
Pesch, Rudolf. *Die Apostelgeschichte: 1. Teilband, Apg 1-12*. EKK V. Köln: Benziger Verlag; Neukirchen-Vluyn: Neukirchener Verlag des Erziehungsvereins GmbH, 1986.
—. *Die Apostelgeschichte: 2. Teilband, Apg 13-28*. EKK V. Köln: Benziger Verlag; Neukirchen-Vluyn: Neukirchener Verlag des Erziehungsvereins GmbH, 1986.
Peterson, David G. *The Acts of the Apostles*. PiNTC. Grand Rapids: Eerdmans; Nottingham: Apollos, 2009.
Peterson, David L. *Zechariah 9-14 & Malachi: A Commentary*. London: SCM, 1995.
Petts, David. *Baptism in the Holy Spirit in Relation to Christian Initiation*. M.Th. dissertation, University of Nottingham, 1987.
—. *The Holy Spirit: An Introduction*. Mattersey: Mattersey Hall, 1998.
Pfleiderer, Otto. *Der Paulinismus: Ein Beitrag zur Geschichte der Urchristlichen Theologie*. Leipzig: Fues's Verlag, R. Reisland, 1873.
Phillips, Barbara J. and Edward F. McQuarrie, 'Beyond Visual Metaphor: A New Typology of Visual Rhetoric in Advertising'. *MarT* 4 (June, 2004), 113-136.
Phillips, Peter M. *The Prologue of the Fourth Gospel: A Sequential Reading*. London: T&T Clark, 2006.
Philo, trans. Charles Duke Yonge. *The Works of Philo Judaeus: The Contemporary of Josephus, Translated from the Greek*. London: H.G. Bohn, 1854-1890.
Pier, John. 'Metalepsis'. Peter Hühn, et al. ed. *The Living Handbook of Narratology*. Hamburg: Hamburg University Press. URL = hup.sub.uni-hamburg.de/lhn/index.php?title=Metalepsis&oldid=1509 [view date: 11 October, 2012].
Pokorný, Petr. *Theologie der lukanischen Schriften*. FRLANT 174. Göttingen: Vandenhoeck & Ruprecht, 1998.
Polzin, Robert. '"The Ancestress of Israel" in Danger'. *Se*. 3 (1975), 81-98.
Popper, K.R. *Conjectures and Refutations: The Growth of Scientific Knowledge*. London: Routledge & Kegan Paul, 1963.

Porter, Stanley E. 'Literary Approaches to the New Testament: From Formalism to Deconstruction and Back'. Stanley E Porter and David Tombs, eds. *Approaches to New Testament Study*. JSNT.S 120. Sheffield: Sheffield Academic, 1995, 77-128.

Powell, Mark Allan. *What is Narrative Criticism?* Minneapolis: Fortress, 1990.

Preuschen, D. Erwin. *Die Apostelgeschichte*. HNT 4. Tübingen: Verlag von J. C.B. Mohr, Paul Siebeck, 1912.

Price, Robert M. 'Confirmation and Charisma'. *SLJT* 23.3 (June, 1990) [accessed online, 02/23/2014, no page numbers, http://www.robertmprice.mindvendor. com/art_art_confirm_charis.htm].

Quesnel, Michel. *Baptisés dans L'Esprit: Baptême et Esprit Saint dans les Actes des Apôtres*. LeDiv 120. Paris: Les Éditions du Cerf, 1985.

Quintillian, trans. H.E. Butler. *The Institutio Oratoria of Quintilian*. Cambridge, MA: Harvard University Press; London: William Heinemann, 1921.

Rabinowitz, Peter J. 'Truth in Fiction: A Reexamination of Audiences'. *CI* 4.1 (Autumn, 1977), 121-141.

Reicke, Bo. *Glaube und Leben der Urgemeinde: Bemerkungen zu Apg. 1-7*. AThANT 32. Zürich: Zwingli-Verlag, 1957.

Reinmuth, Eckart. *Hermeneutik des Neuen Testaments: Eine Einführung in die Lektüre des Neuen Testaments*. Göttingen: Vandenhoeck und Ruprecht, 2002.

Reitzenstein, R. *Die Vorgeschichte der christlichen Taufe*. Leipzig: B.G. Teubner, 1929.

Rendtorff, F.M. *Die Taufe im Urchristentum im Lichte der Neueren Forschungen, ein Kritischer Bericht*. Leipzig: J.C. Hinrichs'sche Buchhandlung, 1905.

Richardson, Brian. 'Singular Text, Multiple Implied Readers'. *Sty*. 41.3 (Fall, 2007), 259-274.

Ridderbos, H.N. *The Speeches of Peter in the Acts of the Apostles*. Leicester: Tyndale, 1962.

Radl, Walter. "'Firmung' im Neuen Testament?' *IKaZ* (1982), 427-433.

Robertson, A.T. *A Grammar of the Greek New Testament in the Light of Historical Research*. Nashville: Broadman, 1934.

Robinson, Clayton David. *The Laying on of Hands: With Special Reference to the Reception of the Holy Spirit in the New Testament*. Ann Arbor: ProQuest LLC, 2008.

Robinson, H. Wheeler. 'Hand'. James Hastings, ed. *Dictionary of the Apostolic Church* Vol. I. Edinburgh: T.&T. Clark, 1915.

Rordorf, Willy. 'The Lord's Prayer in the Light of its Liturgical Use in the Early Church'. *StLi* 14.1 (1981-81), 1-19.

Roth, S. John. *The Blind, the Lame and the Poor: Character Types in Luke-Acts*. JSNT.S 144. Sheffield: Sheffield Academic, 1997.

Rothschild, Clare K. *Luke-Acts and the Rhetoric of History: An Investigation of Early Christian Historiography.* WUNT2 175. Tübingen: Mohr Siebeck, 2004.

Rowe, C. Kavin. 'History, Hermeneutics, and the Unity of Luke-Acts'. Andrew F. Gregory and C. Kavin Rowe, eds. *Rethinking the Unity and Reception of Luke and Acts.* Columbia, SC: University of South Carolina Press, 2010, 43-65.

Ruthven, Jon. "This Is My Covenant with Them': Isaiah 59.19-21 as the Programmatic Prophecy of the New Covenant in the Acts of the Apostles (Part I)'. *JPT* 17 (2008) 32-47; 36-38.

Ryken, Leland. *How to Read the Bible as Literature and Get More Out of It.* Grand Rapids: Zondervan, 1984.

—. *Words of Delight: A Literary Introduction to the Bible.* 2nd Ed. Grand Rapids: Baker, 1992.

Samkutty, V.J. *The Samaritan Mission in Acts.* London: T&T Clark, 2006.

Sanford, Anthony J. and Catherine Emmott. *Mind, Brain and Narrative.* Cambridge: CUP, 2012.

Savran, George. 'Theophany as Type Scene'. *PTX*, 23.2 (Spring, 2003), 119-149.

Schaff, Philip. *A Select Library of the Nicene and Post-Nicene Fathers of the Christian Church.* 1st Series. Vol. IX. Grand Rapids: Eerdmans, n.d.

— and Henry Wace, ed. *A Select Library of Nicene and Post-Nicene Fathers of the Christian Church.* 2nd Series. Vol. 7. Grand Rapids: Eerdmans, n.d.

Schlatter, Adolf. 'Holy Spirit'. James Hastings, ed. *Dictionary of the Apostolic Church.* Vol. I. Edinburgh: T&T Clark, 1915, 573-581.

Schmid, Wolf. 'Implied Reader'. Peter Hühn, et al. ed. *The Living Handbook of Narratology.* Hamburg: Hamburg University Press. URL = hup.sub.uni-hamburg.de/lhn/index.php?title=Implied Reader&oldid=2015 [view date: 20 March, 2013].

—. *Narratology: An Introduction.* Berlin/New York: Walter de Gruyter, 2010.

Schmidt, Daryl D. 'Anti-Judaism and the Gospel of Luke'. William R. Farmer, ed. *Anti-Judaism and the Gospels.* Harrisburg, PA: Trinity, 1999.

Schnabel, Eckhard J. *Early Christian Mission,* Volume 1: *Jesus and the Twelve.* Downers Grove, IL: IVP, 2004.

Schneider, Dieter. *Der Geist, der Geschichte macht: Geisterfahrung bei Lukas.* Neukirchen-Vluyn: Aussaat Verlag, 1992.

Schneider, Gerhard. *Apostelgeschichte 1,1-8,40.* HThK. Freiburg: Herder, 2002 [1980].

—. *Apostelgeschichte 9,1-28,31.* HThK. Freiburg: Herder, 2002 [1982].

Schreiner, Thomas R. *New Testament Theology: Magnifying God in Christ.* Nottingham: Apollos, 2008.

Schnelle, Udo. 'Taufe II, Neues Testament'. *TRE* 32. Berlin: Water de Gruyter, 2001, 663-674.

Bibliography

Schröter, Jens. 'Die Taufe in der Apostelgeschichte'. David Hellholm, et al. ed. *Ablution, Initiation and Baptism: Late Antiquity, Early Judaism and Early Christianity*. Berlin: Walter de Gruyter, 2011, 557-586.

Schulz, Siegfried. *Die Mitte der Schrift: Der Fühkatholizismus im Neuen Testament als Herausforderung an den Protestantismus*. Stuttgart: Kreuz Verlag, 1976.

Schürmann, Heinz. *Das Lukasevangelium, Erster Teil: Kommentar zu Kap. 1,1-9,50*. Freiburg: Herder, 1969.

Schweizer, Eduard. 'πνεῦμα'. *ThWNT*. Band VI. Stuttgart: W. Kohlhammer GmbH, 1959, 387-453.

—. trans. Reginald H. and Ilse Fuller, *The Holy Spirit*. Philadelphia: Fortress, 1980 [German 1978].

Schwertner, Siegfried M. *Internationales Abkürzungsverzeichnis für Theologie und Grenzgebiete*. 2. Auflage. Berlin: Walter de Gruyter, 1992.

Seidl, Theodor. 'Mose und Elija am Gottesberg. Überlieferungen zu Krise und Konversion der Propheten'. *BZ* 37.1, (1993), 1-25.

Sellner, Hans Jörg. *Das Heil Gottes: Studien zur Soteriologie des lukanischen Doppelwerks*. BZNW 152. Berlin: Walter de Gruyter, 2007.

Shauf, Scott. *Theology as History, History as Theology: Paul in Ephesus in Acts 19*. BZNW 133. Berlin: Walter de Gruyter, 2005.

Sheeley, Steven M. *Narrative Asides in Luke-Acts*. JSNT.S 72. Sheffield: JSOT, 1992.

Shellberg, Pamela. *From Cleansed Leapers to Cleansed Hearts: The Developing Meaning of* Katharizo *in Luke-Acts*. Ph.D. dissertation, Marquette University, 2012.

Shelton, James B. *Mighty in Word and Deed: The Role of the Holy Spirit in Luke-Acts*. Peabody, MA: Hendrickson, 1991.

Shepherd, William H., Jr. *The Narrative Function of the Holy Spirit as a Character in Luke-Acts*. SBL.DS 147. Atlanta: Scholars, 1994.

Shiell, William David. *Reading Acts: The Lector and the Early Christian Audience*. BibIS 70. Leiden: Brill, 2004.

Smidt, Udo. *Die Apostelgeschichte Übersezt und ausgelegt*. Kassel: J.G. Onken, 1951.

Smith, Mitzi J. *The Literary Construction of the Other in the Acts of the Apostles: Charismatics, the Jews, and Women*. Cambridge: James Clarke, 2011.

Smuts, Aaron. 'The Desire-Frustration Theory of Suspense'. *JAAC* Vol. 66.3 (Summer, 2008), 281-290.

—. 'The Paradox of Suspense'. *SEP* (Fall, 2009), 1-15.

Sorensen, Eric. *Possession and Exorcism in the New Testament and Early Christianity*. WUNT2 157. Tübingen: J.C.B. Mohr, Paul Siebeck, 2002.

Spencer, F. Scott. *Acts*. Sheffield: Sheffield Academic, 1997.

—. *The Portrait of Philip in Acts: A Study of Roles and Relations*. JSNT.S 67. Sheffield: Sheffield Academic, 1992.

Stamps, Dennis L. 'Rhetorical and Narratological Criticism'. Stanley E. Porter, ed. *Handbook to Exegesis of the New Testament*. Leiden: Brill, 1997, 219-239.

Sternberg, Meir. *The Poetics of Biblical Narrative: Ideological Literature and the Drama of Reading*. Bloomington: Indiana University Press, 1987.

Stevens, Gerald L. 'Luke's Perspective on Pentecost in Acts 1–12'. AAR/SBL Southwest Regional Meeting, March 17-18, 2001, Dallas, TX.

Stewart-Sykes, Alistair, ed. *Tertullian, Cyprian and Origen on the Lord's Prayer*. St Vladimir's Seminary Press, 2004.

Stonehouse, N.B. 'Repentance, Baptism and the Gift of the Spirit'. *WTJ* 13 (November 1, 1950), 1-18.

Stott, John R.W. *Baptism and Fullness: The Work of the Holy Spirit Today*. Leicester: IVP, 1975.

—. *The Message of Acts: To the Ends of the Earth*. Leicester: IVP, 1990.

Stählin, Gustav. *Die Apostelgeschichte*. NTD 5. Göttingen: Vandenhoeck & Ruprecht, 1966.

Strange, W. A. *The Problem of the Text of Acts*. Cambridge: CUP, 1992.

Stromberg, A. von. *Studien zur Theorie und Praxis der Taufe in der christlichen Kirche der ersten zwei Jahrhunderte*. Aalen: Scientia Verlag Aalen, 1973 [1913].

Stronstad, Roger. 'Forty Years On: An Appreciation and Assessment of Baptism in the Holy Spirit by James D.G. Dunn'. *JPT* 19.1 (April, 2010), 3-11.

—. *The Charismatic Theology of St. Luke*. Peabody, MA: Hendrickson, 1984.

—. *The Prophethood of All Believers: A Study in Luke's Charismatic Theology*. Cleveland, TN: CPT, 2010 [1999].

Suleiman, Susan Rubin. 'Redundancy and the "Readable" Text'. *PoeT* 1.3 (1980), 119-142.

Swete, Henry Barclay. *The Holy Spirit in the New Testament: A Study of Primitive Christian Teaching*. London: Macmillan, 1931.

Syreeni, Kari. 'Peter as Character and Symbol in the Gospel of Matthew'. David Rhoads and Kari Syreeni, eds. *Characterization in the Gospels: Reconceiving Narrative Criticism*. JSNT.S 184. Sheffield: Sheffield Academic, 1999, 106-152.

Talbert, Charles H. *Literary Patterns, Theological Themes, and the Genre of Luke-Acts*. Missoula, MT: Scholars and SBL, 1974.

—. *Reading Acts: A Literary and Theological Commentary on the Acts of the Apostles* Rev. Ed. Macon, GA: Smyth & Helwys, 2005.

Tannehill, Robert C. *The Narrative Unity of Luke-Acts: A Literary Interpretation*, Volume 1: *The Gospel According to Luke*. Philadelphia: Fortress, 1986.

—. *The Narrative Unity of Luke-Acts: A Literary Interpretation*, Volume 2: *The Acts of the Apostles*. Minneapolis: Augsburg Fortress, 1990.

Bibliography

Tannen, Deborah. 'What's in a Frame?' Deborah Tannen, ed. *Framing in Discourse*. Oxford: OUP, 1993, 14-56.

Taylor, Jeremy. *Antiquitates Christianae: Or, The History of the Life and Death of the Holy Jesus: As also the Lives, Acts and Martyrdoms of His Apostles*. London R. Royston, 1675.

—. *ΧΡΣΙΣ ΤΕΛΕΙΩΤΙΚΗ A Discourse of Confirmation*. London: Richard Royston, 1664.

Taylor, Joan. *John the Baptist Within Second Temple Judaism: A Historical Study*. London: SPCK, 1997.

Thiselton, Anthony C. *The Hermeneutics of Doctrine*. Grand Rapids: Eerdmans, 2007.

—. *The Holy Spirit: In Biblical Teaching, Through the Centuries, and Today*. London: SPCK, 2013.

Thomas, Derek W. H. *Acts*. Phillipsburg, NJ: P&R, 2011.

Thompson, Alan J. *The Acts of the Risen Lord Jesus: Luke's Account of God's Unfolding Plan*. NSBT 27. Nottingham: Apollos; Downers Grove: IVP, 2011.

Thompson, Richard P. *Keeping the Church in Its Place: The Church as Narrative Character in Acts*. New York: T&T Clark, 2006.

Thornton, L.S. *Confirmation: Its Place in the Baptismal Mystery*. Westminster: Dacre, 1954.

Tipei, John Fleter. *The Laying on of Hands in the New Testament: Its Significance, Techniques and Effects*. Lanham, MD: University Press of America, 2009.

Toolan, Michael. *Narrative: A Critical Linguistic Introduction*. 2nd Ed. London/New York: Routledge, 2001.

Toussaint, Stanley D. 'Acts'. John F. Walvoord and Roy B. Zuck, ed. *The Bible Knowledge Commentary: An Exposition of the Scriptures*, Volume 1. Colorado Springs: David C. Cook, 1983.

Trobisch, David. 'The Book of Acts as a Narrative Commentary on the Letters of the New Testament: A Programmatic Essay'. Andrew F. Gregory and C. Kavin Rowe, ed. *Rethinking the Unity and Reception of Luke and Acts*. Columbia, SC: University of South Carolina Press, 2010, 119-127.

Troftgruben, Troy M. *A Conclusion Unhindered: A Study of the Ending of the Acts Within Its Literary Environment*. WUNT2 280. Tübingen: Mohr Siebeck, 2010.

Trompf, G.W. *The Idea of Historical Recurrence in Western Thought: From Antiquity to the Reformation*. Berkeley: University of California Press, 1979.

Turner, Cuthbert Hamilton. *Studies in Early Church History: Collected Papers*. Oxford: Clarendon, 1912.

Turner, Max. '"Empowerment for Mission"? The Pneumatology of Luke-Acts: An Appreciation and Critique of James B. Shelton's *Mighty in Word and Deed*'. *VoxEv* 24 (1994), 103-122.

—. 'Interpreting the Samaritans of Acts 8: The Waterloo of Pentecostal Soteriology and Pneumatology?' *Pn.* 23.2 (Fall, 2001), 265-286.

—. 'Jesus and the Spirit in Lucan Perspective'. *TynB* 32 (1981), 3-42

—. 'Luke and the Spirit: Renewing Theological Interpretation of Biblical Pneumatology'. Craig G. Bartholomew, Joel B. Green, Anthony C. Thiselton, eds. *Reading Luke: Interpretation, Reflection, Formation.* SHS 6. Milton Keynes: Paternoster, 2005; Grand Rapids: Zondervan, 2005, 267-293.

—. *Power from on High: The Spirit in Israel's Restoration and Witness in Luke-Acts.* JPT.S 9. Sheffield: Sheffield Academic, 2000 [1996].

—. 'Spirit Endowment in Luke/Acts: Some Linguistic Considerations'. *VoxEv* 12 (1981): 45-63.

—. 'The Spirit and Salvation in Luke-Acts'. Graham N. Stanton, Bruce W. Longenecker, and Stephen C. Barton, eds. *The Holy Spirit and Christian Origins.* Grand Rapids: Eerdmans, 2004, 103-116.

—. 'The Spirit of Christ and "Divine" Christology'. Joel B. Green, Max Turner eds. *Jesus of Nazareth, Lord and Christ: Essays on the Historical Jesus and New Testament Christology.* Grand Rapids: Eerdmans; Carlisle: Paternoster, 1994.

Twelftree, Graham H. *People of the Spirit: Exploring Luke's View of the Church.* London: SPCK, 2009; Grand Rapids: Baker Academic, 2009.

Tyson, Joseph B. *Images of Judaism in Luke-Acts.* Columbia, SC: University of South Carolina Press, 1992.

Uidhir, Christy Mag. 'The Paradox of Suspense Realism'. *JAAC* 69.2 (Spring, 2011), 161-171.

Uspensky, Boris. *A Poetics of Composition: The Structure of the Artistic Text and Typology of a Compositional Form.* Berkeley: University of California Press, 1973.

Vennemann, Theo. 'Topics, sentence accent, and ellipsis: a proposal for their formal treatment'. Edward L. Keenan, ed. *Formal Semantics of Natural Language: Papers from a colloquium sponsored by the King's College Research Centre, Cambridge.* Cambridge: CUP, 1975, 313-328.

Volz, Paul. *Der Geist Gottes und die verwandten Erscheinungen im Alten Testament und im anschließenden Judentum.* Tübingen: J.C.B. Mohr, Paul Siebeck, 1910.

Voss, Gerhard. *Die Christologie der Lukanischen Schriften in Grundzügen.* SN 2. Paris: Desclee de Brouwer, 1965.

Wall, Robert W. '"Purity and Power" According to the Acts of the Apostles'. *WTJ* 34.1 (Spring, 1999), 64-82.

Wallace, Daniel B. *Greek Grammar Beyond the Basics: An Exegetical Syntax of the New Testament.* Grand Rapids: Zondervan, 1996.

Walston, Rick. *The Speaking in Tongues Controversy: The Initial, Physical Evidence of the Baptism in the Holy Spirit Debate.* USA, n.p.: Xulon, 2003.

Warrington, Keith. *Discovering the Holy Spirit in the New Testament*. Peabody, MA: Hendrickson, 2005.
Webb, Ruth. *Ekphrasis, Imagination and Persuasion in Ancient Rhetorical Theory and Practice*. Farnham: Ashgate, 2009.
Wenk, Matthias. *Community Forming Power: The Socio-Ethical Role of the Spirit in Luke-Acts*. JPTS 19. Sheffield: Sheffield Academic, 2000.
Whitehouse, Michael Patrick. *Manus Impositio: The Initiatory Rite of Handlaying in the Churches of Early Western Christianity*. Notre Dame, IN: University of Notre Dame, Ph.D. dissertation, 2008.
Wifstrand, Albert. *Epochs and Styles*. WUNT 179. Tübingen: Mohr Siebeck, 2005; Sweden: Mailice Wifstrand, 2005.
Wilckens, Ulrich. *Die Misssionsreden der Apostelgeschichte: Form – und Traditionsgeschichteliche Untersuchungen*. 2. Auflage. WMANT. Neukirchen-Vluyn: Neukirchener Verlag des Erziehungsvereins GMBH, 1963.
Wilkens, W. 'Wassertaufe und Geistempfang bei Lukas'. *TZ* 23 (1967), 26-47.
Williams, David J. *Acts*. Peabody, MA: Hendrickson, 1990.
Williams, James G. 'The Beautiful and the Barren: Conventions in Biblical Type-Scenes'. *JSOT* 17 (1980), 107-119.
Williams, Joel F. *Other Followers of Jesus: Minor Characters as Major Figures in Mark's Gospel*. Sheffield: Sheffield Academic, 1994.
Windisch, Hans. 'Jesus und der Geist nach Synoptischer Überlieferung'. Shirley Jackson Case, ed. *Studies in Early Christianity*. New York: Century, 1928, 209-236.
—. *Taufe und Sünde im ältesten Christentum bis auf Origenes: Ein Beitrag zur altchristlichen Dogmengeschichte*. Tübingen: J.C.B. Mohr, Paul Siebeck, 1908.
Witherington, Ben. *New Testament Rhetoric: An Introductory Guide to the Art of Persuasion in and of the New Testament*. Eugene, OR: Cascade, 2009.
—. *The Acts of the Apostles: A Socio-Rhetorical Commentary*. Grand Rapids: Eerdmans; Carlisle: Paternoster, 1998.
—. *The Problem with Evangelical Theology: Testing the Exegetical Foundations of Calvinism, Dispensationalism and Wesleyanism*. Waco, TX: Baylor University Press, 2005.
Witherup, Ronald D. 'Cornelius Over and Over Again: "Functional Redundancy" in the Acts of the Apostles'. *JSNT* 49 (1993), 45-66.
—. 'Functional Redundancy in the Acts of the Apostles: A Case Study'. *JSNT* 48 (1992), 67-86.
Wikenhauser, Alfred. *Die Apostelgeschichte*. RNT 5. Regensburg: Verlag Friedrich Pustet, 1951.
Wolter, Michael. 'Apollos und die ephesinischen Johannesjünger (Act 18 24 – 9 7)'. *ZNW* 78 (1987), 49-73.
Woods, Edward J. *The 'Finger of God' and Pneumatology in Luke-Acts*. JSNTS 205. Sheffield: Sheffield Academic, 2001.

Wucherpfennig, Ansgar. 'Acta Spiritus Sancti: Die Bedeutung der vier Sendungen des Geistes für die Apostelgeschichte, *In memoriam* Fredrich Avemarie'. *ThPh* 88 (2013), 194-210.

Yanal, Robert J. *Paradoxes of Emotion and Fiction*. University Park, PA: Pennsylvania State University, 1999.

Zehnle, Richard F. *Peter's Pentecost Discourse: Tradition and Lukan Reinterpretation in Peter's Speeches of Acts 2 and 3*. SBL.MS 15. New York: Abingdon, 1971.

Zuagg, Elmer Harry. *A Genetic Study of the Spirit-Phenomena in the New Testament*. Private edition of Ph.D. dissertation, University of Chicago, 1917.

Zwiep, Arie W. *Christ, the Spirit and the Community of God: Essays on the Acts of the Apostles*. WUNT 293. Tübingen: Mohr Siebeck, 2010.

—. 'Luke's Understanding of Baptism in the Holy Spirit: An Evangelical Perspective'. *PeSt* 6.2 (2007), 127–149.

Author index

Adler, N., 11-13, 41, 133-134, 139, 146, 160, 164
Aker, B.C., 97, 127
Alexander, L., 49, 54
Alter, R., 43, 68, 69, 110, 143
Amit, Y., 43
Amougou-Atangana, J., 168-169
Anderson, J.C., 65
Anderson, R.D. Jr., 72
Arend, W., 67, 69
Atkinson, W.P., 39-40, 41, 100, 116, 167, 173, 197, 199, 205
Auerbach, E., 43
Austin, G., 1
Avemarie, F., 2, 32-35, 41, 75, 76, 100, 101, 105, 106, 123, 126, 127, 138, 142, 149, 154, 170, 175, 194, 195, 196, 197, 199, 200, 201, 202, 203, 204, 208, 209, 212

Backhaus, K., 194, 201, 208
Baer, H. von, 8-10, 16, 28, 41, 60, 86, 89, 90, 100, 102, 109, 139, 140, 141, 147, 148, 154, 193
Bal, M., 63
Barrett, C.K., 130, 133, 137, 140, 195
Barth, G., 170
Bartlett, F., 60
Bauernfeind, O., 155
Baur, W., 107, 187
Beale, G.K., 106-107
Beasley-Murray, G.R., 83, 93, 153, 154, 159, 161, 162, 197
Bede, 153
Berger, K., 142
Berlin, A., 43, 143
Beza, T., 111, 153
Bieritz, K.-J., 209
Bird, M.F., 53, 54, 55

Black, M., 165, 166
Blanc, D.A., 74
Blass, F., 133
Blomberg, C.L., 74, 75, 76, 128
Bock, D.L., 176, 191, 195
Böhlemann, P., 89
Böhm, M., 139
Booth, W.C., 203
Bornhäuser, D.K., 97
Bovon, F., 90, 141, 154
Bozung, D.C., 121, 122
Brawley, R., 144
Brewer, W.F., 52
Britt, B., 68, 107
Brown, G., 57, 58
Brown, J.K., 52-53
Brown, S., 122, 123
Bruce, F.F., 94, 153, 161, 173, 184, 205
Bruner, F.D., 9, 16-18, 20, 41, 138, 149
Büchsel, F., 10-11, 41, 152, 170
Burnside, W.F., 109
Burridge, R., 72
Butler, H.E., 72

Cadbury, H.J., 90, 155
Caldwell, M.D., 2
Callan, C.J., 153
Calvin, J., 111, 153
Camp, A.L., 129
Caneday, A.B., 144, 150
Caragounis, C.C., 132
Carson, D.A., 1, 110, 122, 138, 149, 161
Chase, F.H., 150
Chatman, S., 44, 144
Chilton, B.D., 191
Chinn, C.M., 83
Cho, Y., 35-36, 41, 125, 127, 205
Chrysostom, J., 153

Clark, M., 67
Cohn, R.L., 56
Cole, G.A., 2, 75, 76
Confort, P.W., 165
Compton, R.B., 128
Conzelmann, H., 15, 41, 168, 195
Cook, G., 77
Cooper, G.L., 90, 91
Coppens, J., 146, 205
Cornils, A., 3, 64, 127, 146, 147
Cotterell, P., 3
Culpepper, R.A., 48
Cutten, G.B., 111

Danker, F.W., 89
Das, A., 122
Davis, J.C., 128
Debrunner, A., 133
Derret, J.D.M., 183
Devova, R., 117
DesCamp, M.T., 69
Dibelius, M., 88, 159, 180, 197
Dickerson, P.L., 145
Dijk, T.A. van, 57
Dix, D.G., 88
Dobbeler, A. von, 154
Dockery, D.S., 74, 76
Dragas, G.D., 208
Dunn, J.D.G., 19-21, 28, 29, 30, 32, 33, 34, 36, 39-40, 41, 81, 82, 83, 89, 90, 100, 103, 116, 117, 118, 119, 120, 128, 129, 130, 131, 132, 138, 139, 153, 154, 156, 157, 161, 173, 174, 175, 180, 181, 191, 193, 194, 196, 207, 208, 209, 212

Ecerts, J., 111
Eckey, W., 108, 149, 175, 195, 196
Eco, U., 56
Edwards, M.W., 67, 68
Edwards, O.C., 145

Edwards, R., 56
Eisen, U., 3, 44, 141, 142
Elbert, P., 133
Ellis, E.E., 113
Emmott, C., 3, 52, 56, 62
Erasmus, D., 153
Ervin, H.M., 123, 124, 138, 196
Esler, P.F., 184
Estrada, N.P., 108

Fabien, P., 142
Fahnstock, J., 72
Fahr, A., 52
Fee, G., 74, 75
Ferguson, E., 90
Findlay, J.A., 155
Finnern, S., 43
Fitzmyer, J.A., 142, 176, 195, 207
Flemington, W.F., 88
Fludernik, M., 64
Forbes, C., 112
Fowler, R.M., 51
Funk, R.W., 109

Garrett, S.R., 152
Garroway, J.D., 180
Gaventa, B.R., 61, 173
Gelpi, D.L., 90
Gempf, C., 198, 200, 202, 211
Gennette, G., 63
Gerrig, R.J., 51
Giblet, J., 206
Glomika, O., 127
Godet, F., 89
Goguel, M., 1, 139
Gonzalez, J.L., 140
Goppelt, L., 127
Grafton, T.E., 68
Green, J.B., 3, 44, 57, 58, 60-61, 62, 63, 79, 124, 140
Gregory, A.F., 53
Gregory of Nazianzen, 111
Greimas, A.J., 31

Author Index

Grethlein, J., 44
Grundmann, W., 89, 105
Gunkel, H., 5, 41, 109
Gunkel, Feidrun, 151
Guthrie, D., 108, 123, 194

Haacker, K., 202
Haenchen, E., 122, 142
Hamilton, J.M., 123, 190
Handy, D.A., 205
Harm, F.R., 122
Harrison, R.A., 2, 3, 36-37, 41, 44
Hartman, L., 161
Havell, H.L., 72
Haya-Prats, G., 21-22, 41, 118, 119, 120, 153, 154, 175
Heath, M., 71-72, 73
Heckel, U., 142, 208
Hedlun, R.J., 38-39, 42
Hedrick, C.W., 174
Hoekema, A.A., 111, 176, 177
Hoennicke, G., 111
Hoffmann, J., 52
Holloday, C.R., 87
Hooker, M.D., 102
Hornick, H.J., 83
Hovenden, G., 109, 112, 178
Hubbard, R.L., 74, 75, 76
Hui, A.W.D., 117
Hull, J.H.E., 124, 126, 142
Hur, J., 1, 30-32, 44, 90, 139, 141, 142, 175
Hurtado, L.W., 163

Iser, W., 46, 52, 55

Jackson, D., 142, 189
Jeremias, 49, 107
Jervell, J., 54, 116, 157, 168, 195
Jewett, C., 77
Johnson, B.J. Jr., 68

Johnson, L.T., 53, 54, 56, 63, 76-77, 141
Jones, D.L., 172
Jong, I. de, 44, 63

Käsemann, E., 193, 195, 199, 200
Kee, H.C., 208
Kee, M.S., 68
Keener, C.S., 1, 75, 76, 109, 111, 112, 120, 186, 197
Kennedy, G.A., 45, 72
Kern, P.H., 173
Kilpatrick, G.D., 74
Kim, H.-S., 89
Kittel, G., 155, 156, 184, 205, 206
Klauck, H-J., 2
Klein, W.W., 74, 75, 76
Knowling, R.J., 150, 154
Koch, D.-A., 141
Koet, B.J., 89
Kosnetter, J., 87
Kremer, J., 91, 102, 107, 108, 111, 118, 120, 184, 185, 207
Kress, G., 77
Krodel, G., 132
Krüger, K.W., 91
Kuecker, A.J., 1
Kurz, W., 44, 48-49, 99, 114, 148, 153, 180
Kürzinger, J., 1

Lake, K., 1, 134, 155, 168
Lampe, G.W.H., 1, 2, 13-15, 41, 88, 161
Landa, G., 51
Landa, J.A.G., 47
Lee, M., 199
Leeuwen, T. van, 77
Leipoldt, J., 145, 190
Leisegang, H., 6-8, 102, 206
Leitch, T.M., 47, 51
Lentzen-Deis, F., 87
Levison, J.R., 90

245

Lincoln, A.T., 100
Loder, A.T., 75
Lohse, E., 108
Loisy, A., 87, 121, 147, 197, 200
Longacre, R.E., 66-67, 80, 113
Longnecker, R., 113, 126, 161
Lyon, R.W., 124

MacArthur, J.F. Jr., 32
Maclean, A.J., 168
Maddox, R., 49, 50
Mainville, O., 86, 100
Mallen, P., 100
Marguerat, D., 127, 151, 161, 167, 172
Markley, J.F., 128
Marshall, I.H., 1, 74, 90, 108, 112, 114, 193, 195, 202, 203, 204
Martin, R.P., 106
Mason, A.J., 6, 150, 155, 162
McComiskey, D.S., 46
McDonnell, K., 1
McIntyre, L.B. Jr., 128-129, 131, 132
McNamara, P., 92
McQuarrie, E.F., 78
Mendez-Moratalla, F., 4
Menoud, P.H., 165
Merenlahti, P., 78
Metzger, B.M., 165, 166
Metzger, J.A., 3, 44
Menzies, R.P., 5, 9, 23-25, 27, 31, 33, 39, 40, 42, 49, 74, 75, 82, 92, 94-95, 105-106, 107, 111, 112, 116, 125, 126, 152, 161, 162, 166-168, 194, 195, 196, 197, 200, 207
Menzies, W.W., 74, 75, 195
Michie, D., 43
Mills, W.E., 112
Mirguet, F., 43
Mittelstadt, M.W., 3, 44

Moessner, D.P., 201
Montague, G.T., 1, 138
Moreton, M.J., 1
Morlan, D.S., 109, 129
Moxon, J.R.L., 179
Muhlack, G., 46
Muilenburg, J., 43
Muir, S.C., 173
Munck, J., 159

New, S., 1, 2
Nickle, K.F., 152
Niehaus, J., 106
Nohrnberg, J., 107

Oberlinner, L., 125
O'Connell, R.H., 68
Oden, T.C., 161
O'Neill, J.C., 204
Osborn, G., 74
Oulton, J.E.L., 153

Panagopoulos, J., 67
Pao, D., 100, 101
Parratt, J.K., 6, 202, 203
Parsons, M.C., 2, 83
Pawson, D., 150
Penney, J.M., 89, 121
Perro, R.I., 140
Perry, A., 101, 103, 105, 106, 151
Perry, M., 47, 55, 79
Pesch, R., 108, 132, 145, 195, 197, 203
Peterson, D.G., 74, 75, 76
Peterson, D.L., 103, 109, 161, 163, 184, 195
Petts, D., 22-23, 39, 41, 42
Pfleiderer, O., 8
Phillips, B.J., 78, 79
Phillips, P.M., 55, 56, 63
Pier, J., 64
Pokorný, P., 2
Polzin, R., 56

Author Index

Popper, K.R., 57
Porter, S.E., 43
Powell, M.A., 43
Preuschen, D.E., 111, 153
Price, R.M., 156, 157

Quesnel, M., 132, 182

Rabinowitz, P.J., 203
Radl, W., 177
Reicke, B., 117
Reinmuth, E., 65
Reitzenstein, R., 138
Rendtorff, F.M., 208
Rengakos, A., 44
Rhoads, D., 43
Richardson, B., 50-51
Ridderbos, H.N., 73
Robertson, A.T., 90, 128, 150
Robinson, C.D., 37-38, 41, 175
Rordorf, W., 93
Ross, R.N., 60
Roth, J.S., 44, 56, 63
Rothschild, C.K., 46
Rowe, C.K., 53, 54
Ruthven, J., 104-105, 106, 109
Ryken, L., 68

Sanford, A.J., 52
Samkutty, V.J., 142, 154
Savron, G., 70
Schlatter, A., 139
Schmid, W., 52, 63-64
Schmidt, D.D., 62
Schneider, D., 108, 142, 145
Schneider, G., 102, 184, 189-190, 195, 197, 204
Schnelle, U., 208
Schreiner, T.R., 161
Schröter, J., 121
Schulz, S., 139, 209, 210, 211
Schürmann, H., 90
Schweizer, E., 1, 15-16, 27, 41, 120

Seidl, T., 107
Sellner, H.J., 121
Shauf, S., 196, 204
Sheeley, S.M., 44, 65, 184
Shellberg, P., 56
Shelton, J.B., 82, 126, 194
Shiell, W.D., 46, 50
Shepherd, W.H., 1, 44, 123
Smidt, U., 138
Smith, M.J., 142
Smuts, A., 51
Sorensen, E., 183
Spencer, F.S., 135, 159
Stählin, G., 180
Stamps, D.L., 43
Sternberg, M., 43, 65, 66, 110, 172, 176, 180
Stevens, G.L., 127
Stewart-Sykes, A., 93
Stomberg, A. von, 9
Stonehouse, N.B., 154
Stott, J.R.W., 2, 125, 132, 161, 208
Strange, W.A., 165-166
Stronstad, R., 74, 82, 104, 114, 125, 152
Suleiman, S., 65
Swete, H.B., 150
Syreeni, K., 56

Talbert, C.H., 1, 46
Tannehill, R.C., 44, 58, 69, 70, 90, 100, 101, 141, 142
Tannen, D., 60
Taylor, J., 90
Thiselton, A.C., 74
Thomas, D.W.H., 163
Thompson, A.J., 138
Thompson, R.P., 73
Tipei, J.F., 158
Toolan, M., 3, 63, 64
Toussaint, S.D., 128
Trobisch, D., 76
Troftgruben, T.M., 47

247

Trompf, G.W., 46
Turner, C.H., 139
Turner, M.M.B., 3, 5, 20, 23, 26-30, 32, 33, 36, 37, 39, 40, 41, 44, 81, 82, 84, 87, 89, 90, 92, 94, 100, 101, 102, 103, 104, 105, 107, 116, 117, 124, 125, 138, 140, 150, 151, 154, 155, 157, 161, 169, 173, 175, 176, 177, 181, 182, 184, 190-191, 197, 198, 199, 208, 209, 212
Twelftree, G., 148-149
Tyson, J.B., 48

Uidhir, C.M., 52
Uspensky, B., 141

Vennemann, T., 3, 58, 59, 63
Volz, P., 139
Voss, G., 90

Wall, R.W., 116
Wallace, D.B., 150, 208
Walston, R., 75, 76, 79
Warrington, K., 140
Webb, R., 83
Wenk, M., 5, 100, 105, 106

Wheeler Robinson, H., 139
Whitehouse, M.P., 142, 159
Wifstrand, A., 91
Wikenhauser, A., 209
Wilckens, U., 184
Wilkins, W., 130, 131-132
Williams, D.J., 153, 154
Williams, J.F., 69-70
Williams, J.G., 71
Windisch, H., 83, 120, 124
Witherington, B., 2, 72, 73, 75, 76, 77, 80, 140, 154, 155, 161, 168, 169, 184, 185, 187, 193, 195, 208
Witherup, R.D., 4465, 66, 76, 143, 144, 172
Wolter, M., 196
Woods, E.J., 92
Wucherpfennig, A., 116

Yanal, R.J., 52
Yonge, C.D., 107
Yule, G., 57, 58

Zehnle, R.F., 127
Zuagg, E.H., 152
Zwiep, A.W., 74, 115, 149, 150

Scripture index

Genesis
7:17-24   66
9:1-17   66

Exodus
7:3   106
11:9-10   106

Numbers
11   94
11:16-30   86, 92
11:17   152
11:25   152
12:6   85, 114

Deuteronomy
4:34   106
6:22   106
7:19   106
34:9   152

2 Kings
2:9   92

2 Chronicles
5:12   107
7:1   107
7:3   107

Psalms
2:7   85
69:19   105

Isaiah
6   105
8:18   106
9:14   113
32:15   100
40:2   102
40:3-5   100, 102
58   101

59:19   104, 105, 106
59:20   104
61   101
61:1-2   27

Jeremiah
31:33   19

Ezekiel
5:5   113
36   27
36:27   19

Daniel
2:28   113
4:24   113
5:25   113

Joel
2:28-32   113
3   27

Zechariah
1:10   113
1:19   113
5:3   113
5:6   113

Malachi
1:6-2:9   103
3:1   103
3:2-3   103
4:1   102, 103
4:6   102

Matthew
1:18   165
1:20   165
3   102
3:10   102
3:11   102

3:12   102
3:16   88
5:22   102
7:19   102
10   102
10:20   8
11:2   196
12   102
12:43-45   92
13:40   102
13:42   102
13:50   102
18:8   102
24:15   54
25:41   102

Mark
1:10   18, 89
1:12   165
2:18   196
9:43-49   102
13:11   8
13:14   54

Luke
1-2   27
1:2   48
1:3-4   50
1:4   48, 49
1:9   60
1:10   86
1:17   102, 183
1:35   27, 83, 85, 165, 166
1:41   199
1:42   112
1:46   112
1:67-79   117
1:68   112
1:72-73   203
1:76   103
1:80   197n.36

249

Ritual Water, Ritual Spirit

2:15   113
2:27   197n.36
2:49   12
3   62, 63, 82, 86, 95, 102, 130, 181, 211
3:1-20   62
3:2   102
3:3   133, 181
3:4-6   100, 102
3:7   130
3:8   203
3:15-16   206
3:16   101, 102, 104, 150, 152, 201
3:17   102
3:18   204, 205
3:21   70, 101
3:21-22   36, 62, 83, 86, 89, 90, 95, 136, 137, 155, 157, 158, 160, 166, 169, 177, 211, 216
3:22   101
4   101
4:1   7, 82, 165, 197n.36
4:14   7, 183, 197n.36
4:18   33, 165
4:29   207
4:40   140
5:17   168, 183, 210
5:33   196
6:10   167
6:12   78
6:19   167, 168, 183, 210
6:35   133
7:7   167
7:18   196
7:18-24   203
7:21   28
7:22   28
7:27   103
7:27-28   203
7:29-30   61, 93, 203
8:9-10   49
8:9-15   49
8:46   168, 210
8:48   183
8:53   12
9   102
9:1   86, 152, 183
9:1-2   101
9:28   78
9:28-36   49
9:30   106
9:31   106
9:39   197n.36
9:54   102
10   7, 92
10:1   86, 101, 152
10:9   94, 101
10:17   94
10:19   101
10:19-20   92
10:20   197n.36
11   17, 24, 92, 95, 126
11:1   196
11:2   95
11:3   95
11:5-8   49
11:5-13   92
11:10   95
11:11-13   92
11:13   81, 85, 86, 94, 96, 100, 140, 158, 182, 211
11:14-26   92
11:20   28
11:21-26   92
11:23   93
12:1-12   49
12:12   8
12:35-48   49
12:41   49, 50
12:49-50   103
13:13   140
16:1-9   49
17   102
17:7-10   49
17:29   102
19:17   133
19:19   117
20:31   133
21   48
21:36   133
22:19-20   48
22:29-32   48
22:35-37   48
23:34   60
23:44-45   115
24   37, 195
24:37   197n.36
24:39   197n.36
24:47   130
24:49   97, 100, 183

John
2:19   132
3:5   18, 83, 83n.11
3:8   209
3:22-26   202
4:1-2   202
7:39   205n.70
7:53   129
15:6   102

Acts
1   60
1:1   28, 54
1:4-5   100, 150, 151, 202
1:5   97, 101, 104, 182, 191

Scripture Index

1:5-8 150
1:8 9, 16, 39, 100, 101, 163, 183
1:12-26 100
1:13-14 108
1:14 13, 158
1:15 108
1:20 114
1:21 201
1:22 201
2 13, 25, 31, 39, 73, 82, 105, 106, 116, 123, 126, 130, 135, 137, 148, 149, 157, 169, 178, 183
2-3 155, 187
2:1 108, 140
2:2 104, 111
2:3 108, 111
2:2-4 70, 106, 158
2:4 29, 107, 108, 111, 112, 118, 182, 187
2:6 109, 110, 112
2:6-13 109n.59
2:7 110
2:8 110, 112
2:11 110, 112, 188
2:12 110
2:13 110, 149
2:16 113, 114, 117, 121, 122, 149, 199
2:17 35, 70, 85, 119
2:18 35, 116, 126
2:19 106
2:20 214
2:21 176
2:22 106, 115
2:25 114

2:30 12
2:32-33 200n.49
2:33 21, 105, 117, 118, 119, 121, 122, 149, 150, 151, 199
2:37-38 212
2:37-39 95, 127, 216
2:38 3, 4, 5, 6, 9, 11, 12, 20, 22, 24, 29, 35, 37, 61, 62, 81, 96, 120, 121, 122, 124, 126, 127, 128, 129, 130, 132, 133, 134, 135, 136, 141, 147, 149, 161, 162, 169, 175, 177, 181, 187, 191, 193, 199, 200, 201, 209n.93, 210, 211, 216
2:38-39 29, 31, 32, 35, 36, 86, 87, 122, 125, 148, 151, 154, 157, 182
2:38-40 17
2:39 35, 120, 121, 122
2:41 17, 79, 122, 123, 124, 125, 131, 155
2:42 215
2:43 106
2:44 195n.23
2:47 123
3 157
3:17 12
3:22 106, 114
3:26 129

4 76, 160
4:4 3, 4, 123, 195n.23
4:11 113
4:31 9, 13, 89, 121, 123, 124, 140
4:32 195n.23
5:9 165
195n.24
5:15 183, 210
5:19 165
5:30-32 200n.49
5:31-32 25
5:32 181
6 60
6:3 197n.36
6:6 140, 167
6:10 197n.36
8 13, 21, 22, 25, 31, 32, 34, 35, 36, 59, 70, 81, 123, 136, 137, 145, 147, 148, 151, 153, 154, 157, 162, 163, 167, 168, 169, 170, 171, 173, 177, 178, 181, 183, 207, 209, 212, 213, 214
8:4-25 138-139, 142n.38, 166
8:5 138, 208
8:6 208
8:12 138, 156, 195n.25
8:13 158, 195n.23
8:14-16 144
8:14-17 142n.38, 164
8:15 153, 158, 160
8:15-17 70

251

8:15-19   173
8:15-25   141
8:16   50, 125, 155, 156, 158, 164
8:17   12, 144, 147, 149, 151, 153, 160, 167
8:17-18   118, 154
8:17-19   177
8:18   12, 141, 142, 144, 197n.36
8:18-19   142n.38
8:19   12, 141, 144, 145, 153
8:20   140, 142, 151, 152, 158, 163
8:20-21   158
8:29   197n.36
8:38-39   160n.113
8:39   119, 158, 164, 165, 214, 215
8:46   152
9   17, 25, 29, 81, 140, 172, 174, 175, 177, 181, 207, 212, 213
9:1   173, 196
9:1-18   172-174
9:10   196
9:11   158, 173
9:12   167
9:17   167, 175
9:17-18   175
9:17-19   36, 73
9:26   195n.25 196n.27
9:42   195n.24
10   17, 25, 32, 35, 81, 123, 133, 143, 178, 190
10:2   70, 158, 179
10:9   70, 78

10:15   179
10:17   179
10:19   197n.36
10:28   179
10:30   70, 158
10:36   201
10:37   201
10:37-48   183
10:38   28, 33, 201
10:43   195n.24
10:43-44   177, 181
10:44   118, 140, 154
10:44-48   36, 158
10:45   184
10:45-47   78
10:46   65, 70, 184, 184n.41, 185, 188
10:47   39, 184, 188
10:47-48   122
10-11   31
11   17, 143, 157, 178
11:12   197n.36
11:14   180, 181
11:15   154, 158, 180, 184, 187, 188, 189
11:15-16   180, 201
11:15-18   150
11:16   182, 187
11:17   18, 116, 141, 180, 184, 187, 195n.24
11:17-18   181
11:21   195n.23
11:22-24   162
12:7   165
12:23   165
13:2   119

13:3   140, 167
13:12   195n.23
13:23   201
13:24   197, 201
13:39   195n.23
13:41   195n.25
13:43   79
13:48   195n.23
14:1   195n.23
14:23   195n.24
15   145, 178
15:5   195n.23
15:7   195n.23
15:8   184
15:8-9   20, 25, 29, 31, 33, 181
15:9   180
15:11   195n.25
15:28   119
16:1   196n.27
16:6   119
16:13   143, 203
16:18   197n.36
16:27   143, 203
16:31   195n.24
16:34   195n.24
17:12   195n.23
17:16   197n.37
17:24   144
17:34   195n.23
18   199, 201
18:8   195n.23, 195n.24
18:24   194
18:24-28   193, 198
18:24-19:7   39
18:25   194, 195, 196, 197, 197n.37, 199, 201, 202, 211
18:27   195n.23
19   7, 13, 25, 31, 32, 63, 70, 73,

Scripture Index

123, 167, 170,
182, 190, 194,
195, 199, 203,
209, 213
19:1 194, 196
19:1-7 36, 88,
193, 198, 213
19:2 194
19:3 194
19:4 195n.24
19:6 70, 118, 184,
184n.41, 185
19:11 210
19:12 183
19:18 195n.23
19:19 195n.24
19:21 197n.36
19:22 195n.24
19:25 144
20 25
20:22 197n.36
21:20 195n.23
21:25 195n.23
22 172, 174, 176,
177
22:3-16 174
22:10 173n.5, 177
22:16 18, 73, 176,
177
20:29-30 48
23:8 197n.36
23:9 197n.36
24:14 195n.25
26 172, 174
26:19 174
16:27 195n.25
27:13 143, 203
27:25 195n.25
28:8 140, 167

Romans
8:9 207
8:15 83, 83n.11
12:11 197,
197n.33

1 Corinthians
6:11 18
14 111

Galatians
3:2 180
3:3 197
4:6 83, 83n.11
5:16 197

Ephesians
4:8 105
4:26 132
5:18 149

Titus
3:5 83, 83n.11
3:5-6 18

James
4:7 133

1 Peter
3:18 197

Revelation
20:13 129

Subject index

Aaron, 85
Abner, 143
Abraham, 203
Agrippa, 174
amplification, 71-72
Ananias, 13, 17, 34, 35, 36, 37, 66, 162, 171, 172-177, 181, 196, 211, 213n.98
angels, 58
Anna, 199
Annas, 102
Apollos, 14, 18, 20, 25, 29, 32, 193, 194, 195, 196-198, 199, 200-201, 202, 204, 211, 212
apostles, the, 11, 18, 19, 26, 29, 34, 37-38, 61, 101, 113, 116, 123, 124, 138, 141, 148, 152, 154, 157, 159, 160, 161, 163, 165, 182, 184, 188, 190, 201, 209
Aquila, 197, 199, 211
Asahel, 143
audience response, 61
aurality, 46
authority, 148

baptism, 1, 2, 3, 5, 6, 12, 13, 14, 15, 18, 20, 21, 24, 25, 26, 29, 30, 32, 34, 36, 37, 40, 50, 58, 60, 61, 62, 70, 79, 81, 118, 122, 123, 126, 126n.147, 127-131, 131-135, 146, 147, 155, 156, 157, 161, 164, 166, 166, 167, 175, 178, 181, 182, 184, 187, 195, 196, 197, 199, 200, 204, 205, 206, 207-209, 208, 210, 212
Beelzebub, 92, 93
belief, 3, 63, 159, 195, 205

Caiaphas, 102

Cato, 73
charismata (gifts), 5, 29, 31
communitas, 216
community, 16, 30, 62, 94, 104, 108, 115, 116, 123, 125, 126, 134, 139, 150, 167, 173, 198
confirmation, 6, 13
conversion, 1, 15, 20-21, 22, 25, 26, 29, 32, 35, 36, 37, 40, 61, 161, 176
Cornelius (Cornelius' household), 5, 9, 12, 18, 20, 23, 29, 33, 37, 66, 125, 129, 131, 134, 143, 178, 179, 180, 181, 182, 183, 184, 185, 187, 188-189, 190, 191, 210, 211, 215
covenants, 105

Damascus, 14, 36
Demetrius, 144
Dionysius, 7
discourse analysis, 3, 45, 57, 57, 79

ekphrasis, 83
Eli, 180n.25
Elijah, 92, 97, 102, 106, 107, 198
Elisha, 92
Elizabeth, 70, 160
ellipsis, 66
Ephesus (Ephesians), 6, 14, 18, 20, 21, 25, 29, 32, 33, 34, 36, 38, 39, 70, 125, 130, 152, 153, 163, 167, 170, 193, 194, 195, 196, 197, 198, 200, 200n.50, 201, 202, 203, 204, 205, 206, 207, 208, 209, 209-212, 215, 216
equipping of the saints, 8
Erasmus, 139
eschatology, 26, 31, 104, 173n.2

Subject Index

evil spirits,   92
exodus, the,   92, 97, 106
exorcism,   93, 94, 95, 101, 117
experience,   5, 8, 10, 15, 19, 21, 26, 28, 29, 30, 33, 51, 60, 70, 71, 75, 81, 82, 83, 85, 94, 95, 96, 98, 103, 109-112, 109n.59, 110, 112, 114, 115, 117, 118, 119-120, 124, 150, 150-152, 154, 178, 179, 180, 182, 185, 186-187, 189n.51, 193, 197, 199, 200, 210, 212, 214, 215
Ethiopian eunuch, the,   14, 164-165, 166, 210

faith,   5, 16, 19, 20, 21, 22, 25, 29, 30, 36, 41, 116, 129, 130, 131, 173, 181, 190, 198, 207, 209
Felix,   198
focalization,   3, 63-64, 67, 77, 79, 80, 97-98, 109, 110, 111, 113, 117, 119, 120, 122, 127, 137, 139-145, 178, 206, 210, 214
forgiveness of sins,   11, 12, 15, 17, 20, 23, 25, 29, 33, 117, 121, 127-131, 166, 179, 180, 181, 183, 191
'frame',   60-61, 69
functional redundancy,   65-66

Gabriel,   58
God as Helper,   31; as Sender,   31
grace,   17, 33, 130

handlaying,   1, 2, 5, 6, 9, 11, 12, 13, 14, 17, 18, 23, 25, 29, 31, 34, 35, 37-38, 41, 60, 62n.94, 63, 66, 79, 118, 137-171, 150, 152, 153, 154, 155, 156, 157, 158, 159, 160, 160-161, 163, 164, 166-168, 170, 171, 173, 184, 193, 204, 206, 207-209, 208-209, 210-211, 213, 215, 216
healing,   173, 176, 181
Hellenism,   6
Herod,   165
Holy Spirit, the,   1, 2, 5, 6, 7, 12, 13, 15, 21, 22, 23-24, 59, 60, 70, 78, 91, 92-93, 109, 146, 178, 186, 195, 201, 203, 205, 206, 214; and prophecy,   23, 27, 30, 31, 32, 39, 113; as Object,   31; baptism in,   22-23, 26, 32, 50, 82, 83, 97, 100, 102, 120, 122, 124, 132, 146, 147, 150, 151, 175, 189-191, 189n.53, 215; bestowal,   108; delay of,   161-164; fire, and,   102-105, 110, 150, 181, 187; freedom of,   16; fullness of (filling with),   7, 60, 101, 108, 118, 123, 124, 146, 162; gift, as,   82, 94, 99, 116, 117n.102, 118, 123, 125, 127, 129, 132, 139, 141, 150, 152, 162, 166, 167, 168, 171, 175, 180, 182, 182, 200, 205; gifts of,   13, 25, 26, 93; identity-marker, as,   115-116; impartation of,   11, 145, 148, 156, 157, 158, 160, 164, 166-168, 169, 176, 182-184; led by,   7; liberty of,   151, 152; life of,   150; outpouring, and,   115, 118, 160; of prophecy,   16, 94, 116, 173n.2; prayer for,   24; promise, as,   99, 100, 191; reception of,   1, 2, 5, 8, 9, 10, 11, 12, 14, 16, 17, 18, 20, 22, 24, 25, 29, 30, 31, 32, 33, 34, 35, 37, 39, 40, 45, 58, 63, 65, 73, 76, 78, 79, 81, 86, 95, 96, 99-100, 102, 109, 115, 116, 120, 122, 123, 124, 125, 126, 131-135, 138, 140, 145, 147, 150,

154, 155, 156, 157, 159, 161, 162, 166, 169, 171, 173, 175, 177, 178, 181, 184, 186-188, 199, 205, 207, 208, 209, 210, 211, 212, 214, 216; sin against, 7; transmission of, 14; wisdom, of, 152
Homer, 68-70

identification, 113-127
implied impact, 52
implied reader, 47-48, 49, 50, 84, 86, 94, 115, 124, 137, 148, 159, 162, 182, 187, 190
initiation, 1, 2, 4, 6, 23, 24, 26, 30, 31, 38, 40, 41, 61, 62, 63, 79, 81, 83, 95, 122, 126, 166, 167, 179, 189n.51, 205, 208-209, 212, 213, 216
intertestamental period, 23
Israel, 100, 101, 151, 201

Jacob, 71
James, 143
Jesus Christ, 2, 6, 7, 9, 11, 18, 26, 33, 66, 70, 71, 91, 99, 101, 105, 142, 148, 151, 152, 160, 172, 177, 179, 193, 198, 205, 210; ascended, the, 199; ascension, 76; authority, 174; baptism of, 6, 7, 8, 15, 17, 19, 35, 71, 81-91, 93, 126, 135, 148; Coming One, the, 150, 206; conception of, 7; death, 179; exalted, the, 199, 200, 202, 211, 212; incarnation, 163; Lord of the church, 152, 176; Messiah (Christ), 62, 126, 131, 198, 200; name of, 32, 138; prayer of, 7, 13, 17, 101, 156; resurrected, the, 199; resurrection, 179; return of, 48; risen, 172, 175; Saviour, as, 201; sonship of, 19, 85; temptation of, 28; unique, 85
Joel, 210
John, 6, 18, 25, 31, 40, 140, 145, 147, 148, 151, 151n.71, 152, 153, 156, 157, 159, 167, 168, 170, 171, 177, 204, 205, 211n.96, 213, 216
John the Baptist, 7, 23, 32, 36, 70-71, 94, 101, 103, 130, 134, 150, 176, 179, 181, 182, 193, 198, 199, 200, 201, 203, 204, 210
Judas, 100, 114
Jubilee, 101
Jubilees, 105
judgment, 23, 102, 103, 104

kingdom of God, 24, 29, 35-36, 93, 94, 101, 203

law, the, 15, 19, 24
legal stipulations, 179
liminality, 216
literary theory, 3
Lord's Supper, the, 11
Lord's Prayer, the, 49, 92, 93
Luke, 1, 4, 25-26, 31, 40, 58, 77, 163, 186-188

Mary, 7, 160
Messianic calling, 9
metalepsis, 64-65, 80
miracles, 16, 24, 30, 34, 94, 112, 115, 154, 210
Miriam, 85
mission, 16, 24, 26, 27, 31, 33, 40, 41, 123
missionary call, 174
Moses, 85, 92, 97, 106, 107, 152
Moses' servant, 71
mount of transfiguration, 106

Subject Index

narrative, 2
narrative asides, 64-65
narrative criticism, 43
narratology, 64
narrator, 48
new age, 103
new covenant, 83
new Exodus, 28, 29, 93, 100-101, 101
normality, 57, 58, 79, 158

On the Sublime, 72

paganism, 6
Paul (Saul), 5, 6, 13, 17, 18, 20, 23, 25, 26, 29, 31, 32, 34, 35, 36, 37, 39, 40, 59, 66, 73, 76, 130, 143, 144, 152, 162-163, 171, 172-192, 193, 194, 195, 196, 202, 203, 204, 205, 206, 207, 208, 209, 210, 211, 211n.96, 212, 214, 216
peaks, 66-67, 113
   action peaks, 66-67, 78, 79
   didactic peaks, 66-67, 78, 79, 80, 113
Pentecost, 7, 8, 9, 12, 14, 16, 17, 18, 19, 21, 24, 26, 28, 31, 37, 38, 66, 67, 71, 82, 83, 84, 86, 92, 96, 102, 103, 104, 106, 108, 114, 115, 116, 123, 131, 134, 149, 150, 154, 158, 160, 163, 168, 170, 178, 184-185, 187, 188, 190, 194, 199, 200, 201, 202, 210, 216
people of God as Receiver, 31
Peter, 6, 12, 18, 31, 35, 36, 39, 49, 50, 58, 65, 78, 79, 87, 98, 99, 113, 114, 116, 117, 119, 120, 122, 123-124, 125, 129, 133, 134, 140, 142, 143, 145, 147, 148, 151, 151n.71, 152, 153, 156, 157, 158, 159, 160, 163, 165, 167, 168, 170, 171, 175-176, 177, 178, 179, 180, 182, 183, 184, 186-188, 193, 204, 211n.96, 213, 214, 216
persecution, 7, 48, 59, 174
Pharisees, 94
Philip, 14, 22, 29, 34, 37, 59, 145, 147, 148, 157, 158, 159, 160, 162, 163, 164-165, 166, 169, 170, 210, 211, 215
Philo, 7, 105, 107
Plutarch, 7
pools/entity representation (ER), 3, 45, 62-63, 79, 80, 81, 82, 85, 86-87, 88, 95, 99, 105, 106, 126, 137, 149, 169, 171, 172, 178, 182, 183, 187, 205, 209-211
possessions, 3, 44
power, 8, 13, 23, 27, 32, 35, 62, 82, 94, 100, 101, 118, 151, 158, 159, 160, 168, 183
praise, 186, 191
prayer, 8, 12, 16, 31, 34, 62n.94, 63, 70, 78, 91, 92-95, 135, 137-171, 141, 142, 143, 148, 151-152, 155, 156, 157, 159, 160-161, 164, 170, 173, 174, 178, 184, 210, 211, 214, 215
preaching, 5, 11, 17, 24, 25, 178, 182-183, 184, 197, 201, 202, 206
presuppositions, 58-59, 60-63, 79-80, 157
Priscilla, 197, 199, 211
prophecy, 107-108, 109, 114, 115, 152
prophets, 10
Psuedo-Jonathan, 105
purification, 103, 104, 104n.30, 151

Quintilian, 72

redaction criticism, 75
remission of sins, 2, 134, 153

repentance, 3, 15, 17, 19, 24, 25, 29, 30, 35, 36, 40, 62, 63, 79, 103, 123, 126, 128, 129, 130, 145, 151, 175, 181, 187, 201
repetition, 65-66
repossession, 92-95
rhetorical criticism, 71-73

salvation, 27, 30, 33-34, 36, 82, 117, 180, 182
Samaria (Samaritans), 6, 12, 13, 14, 17, 18, 20, 23, 24, 29, 33, 34, 37, 39, 66, 89, 137-138, 148, 149, 152, 153, 154, 156, 157, 158, 159, 160, 161, 162-163, 166, 167, 168-170, 171, 181, 182, 183, 189, 193, 204, 205, 210-211, 212, 215
'script', 60
sequential reading, 3, 45, 57, 61, 62, 73
service, 166-168
Simeon, 199
Simon, 17, 34, 138, 139, 140, 141, 142, 144, 150, 158, 163, 214
speaking in tongues, 8, 9, 10, 11, 17, 21-22, 26, 29, 30, 31, 32, 33, 36, 38-39, 40, 42, 65, 75, 77, 79, 97, 98, 107, 108, 109-110, 112, 118, 124, 149, 156, 178, 184-185, 186-188, 189n.51, 190, 215
spirituality, 11
suffering, 2, 44
suspense, 51-52

Tabitha, 196n.27
Tertullian, 168
Theodotian, 113
Theophilus, 48, 49, 50, 54n.57, 155, 203
Timarchus, 7, 8
Timothy, 196n.27
type scenes, 3, 45, 67-71, 80, 85, 86, 96

Virgil, 69
vision(s), 87-88, 119

wealth, 2, 44
witness, 28, 29, 34, 101, 119
woman at the well, the, 70
woman who touches Jesus, the, 152

Zacchaeus, 117

www.ingramcontent.com/pod-product-compliance
Lightning Source LLC
Chambersburg PA
CBHW061437300426
44114CB00014B/1723